YORKS
(West Riding)

CHESHIRE

R. Ribble

R. Mersey

SCALE 1 0 1 2 3 4 5 6 7 8 9 10 MILES

THE HISTORY OF

Lancashire
County Council

1889 to 1974

THE HISTORY OF
Lancashire County Council

1889 to 1974

edited by
J. D. MARSHALL

with the assistance of
MARION E. McCLINTOCK

Martin Robertson

First published in 1977 by Martin Robertson & Co. Ltd, 17 Quick Street, London N1 8HL

ISBN 0 85520 215 7

Contents

Preface

I trust that we, representing the largest population of any county in England and next largest to the metropolis, realise that, along with the great honour which has been conferred upon us, we have undertaken great responsibilities. I trust that not only when we meet as a provisional Council but when we assemble as a County Council proper we shall bring to bear in our communications those habits of courtesy, fairness and gentlemanly dealing which will tend to place this first County Council of the County Palatine of Lancaster in the very first rank of such administrative bodies. I wish God speed to this first County Council of the County of Lancashire in the great work that it has undertaken.

WITH these words Sir John Hibbert, the first chairman of the first Lancashire County Council, concluded his opening address at its first meeting in Preston in January 1889.

Joseph Chamberlain, who could not inappropriately be called the Father of County Councils, once said that there was no more rewarding work to which a man or woman could devote his or her time than local government. This is certainly true of the men and women who, down the years, whether as members, officers, or employees, have applied themselves to the work of the Lancashire County Council. This book is the record of their achievements. The mention of Joseph Chamberlain reminds me of a function that I attended in Birmingham Town Hall some years ago when the Lord Mayor of the day said that both sides on the City Council claimed with equal enthusiasm to be the spiritual descendants of Joseph Chamberlain. As far as I know, this has never been said of any member of the Lancashire County Council, and it is, on the whole, unlikely that it ever will be. But there have been some very remarkable men among both its members and officers, and Dr Marshall has referred to a number of them and has incorporated

vii

a wealth of extremely interesting information about them. One of the most remarkable was the first chairman.

John Talbot Hibbert was born in Oldham in the year 1824. His father had helped to found and had been a partner in the firm of Hibbert and Platt, textile machinists. This business prospered and the Hibbert family became wealthy as a result. After being educated first at a preparatory school at Silloth, then at Shrewsbury and finally at St John's College, Cambridge, Hibbert was called to the Bar in 1849. But he never practised. With a substantial private income, he had no need to earn his living. After an unsuccessful contest in 1859 he was elected as Member of Parliament for Oldham in May 1862 in the Liberal interest. He soon made his mark in the House of Commons, his first-hand knowledge of the Poor Law being a particular advantage. This had been acquired by his work on the local Board of Guardians. He was at all times a perfervid admirer and most loyal supporter of his leader. 'Gladstone was a good man', he once said, and tears came into his eyes when he said it; he remained his devoted and loyal supporter throughout. When the Liberal Party was split by Joseph Chamberlain on the issue of Irish Home Rule, Hibbert adhered to Gladstone. His ability and loyalty were rewarded and in due course he was taken into the government. In 1872 he became secretary to the Local Government Board. Two years later his party lost the general election and went into opposition, but when they returned to power in 1880 he was again given office, returning to the Local Government Board. He held office in each of Gladstone's subsequent governments, being appointed secretary to the Admiralty in 1885 and to the Treasury in 1892. He remained a Member of Parliament until July 1895 when he was defeated in that election and did not stand again. Thus, for the first six years of his chairmanship of the Lancashire County Council he was a Member of Parliament and for three of these years a member of the Government.

Meanwhile Hibbert had married and had two children. He had also bought some farms near Lindale, in the Furness district of Lancashire, and here in due course he built himself a house which was designed to become his home. He decided to call it Hampsfield. It was a delightful place with beautiful views over Morecambe Bay and the Lake District fells. He moved in very early in 1885 and one of his first visitors was Gladstone, who came over from Holker where he had been staying. This was shortly after the murder of General Gordon, and a day or two later, while standing on the platform at Carnforth Station waiting for the train that would take him back to London, Gladstone received the famous telegram *en clair* from Queen Victoria: 'These news from Khartoum are frightful and to think that all this might have been prevented and many lives saved by earlier action is too fearful.' To which Gladstone replied: 'Mr Gladstone has had the honour this day to receive your Majesty's telegram *en clair* – Mr Gladstone does not presume to estimate the means of judgment possessed by your Majesty but as far as his information goes he is not altogether able to follow the conclusion which your Majesty has been pleased thus to announce to him.'

As soon as County Councils were established, Hibbert decided to stand for the district in which Hampsfield was situated. He was duly elected and became the first chairman. He was also chosen to be the first president of the newly created County Councils' Association. One of the first things that the new County Council did was to elect thirty aldermen. Hibbert himself of course was one of these, and another who merits special mention was William Joseph Fitzherbert-Brockholes of Claughton Hall near Garstang, a landowner and a member of a very old Roman Catholic family that had lived in the district for generations. What entitles him to special mention is the fact that he was to be succeeded on the County Council by his son and grandson, and this is the only case there has been of three generations on the Council.

Another distinguished chairman (1931–7) was Sir J. Travis-Clegg, whose career is also dealt with in the introductory chapter. In addition to what Dr Marshall says about him, it may be mentioned that Travis-Clegg was a member of the Selection Committee that originally chose Churchill as the Conservative candidate for Oldham, and was its chairman when Churchill crossed the floor of the House and became a Liberal; and it was to Travis-Clegg that Churchill wrote announcing his decision to do so and giving his reasons, which did not commend themselves to Travis-Clegg at all. He was already an influential member of the County Council when, in 1915, Churchill became chancellor of the Duchy of Lancaster; but in that capacity, unlike many chancellors, he never visited County Hall, thereby sparing Travis-Clegg an encounter that might have caused some embarrassment.

Dr Marshall also makes some significant comments on some of the early chief officers and particularly on their rate of remuneration in real terms relative to that of some of their modern successors. To what is said in the introduction about Sir Harcourt Clare it may be added that his total remuneration for all his clerkships was between £12,000 and £15,000 per annum. When it is remembered that, before 1914, taxation even on the highest part of that income was never more than 1s 2d in the pound, and that its purchasing power was at least fifteen times what it is today, it will be appreciated that he was in a position to enjoy a far higher standard of living than any modern chief officer.

It is sometimes said that the early County Councils were completely dominated by the landed gentry. In some counties this may have been so, but as Dr Marshall quite rightly points out, Lancashire was not one of them. There were not more than ten members of the original Lancashire County Council, out of a total of nearly one hundred, who were landed gentry in the strict sense.* The majority were drawn from a very wide cross-section of the middle class – manufacturers, businessmen and professional men, with a fair sprinkling of people who had retired. The rise of the Labour Party had not yet taken place. Indeed, for its first few years the Lancashire County Council's affairs were not conducted on party lines at all.

The activities of the first County Councils were insignificant compared with those of today. In 1889 those activities were confined to the matters formerly under the control of the magistrates at Quarter Sessions. These included highways, licensing and control of intoxicating liquors, county lunatic asylums, the control of the movement of cattle and an authority shared with the magistrates over the police. Education was still dealt with by the old school boards and continued to be so until 1902, when the Education Act of that year abolished them and transferred their powers to the education committees of the County Councils. Of the matters that came under the jurisdiction of the County Council immediately it was created, highways were the most important. Here the position that it inherited was chaotic. In county districts, the roads had been largely the responsibility of the magistrates who operated through local overseers, constables and 'surveyors', often farmers who tended to be prejudiced in favour of their own and their relations' farms. But 'through roads', i.e. those leading from one part of the county to another or between large towns, had generally been created and continued to be run by turnpike trusts, which had statutory power to levy tolls. In Lancashire there were ninety-two of these. Then, in urban areas there were highway boards, whose jurisdiction frequently overlapped that of the magistrates. How the County Council took over all this muddle and by degrees replaced it with the splendid system of roads, including trunk roads and motorways, that we now enjoy is very thoroughly and ably explained in Chapters 7 and 15.

An extremely interesting part of this book is the chapter dealing with public health and the administration of the sanitary law (Chapter 6). Apart from the magistrates, the chief repositories of power in this field were the Poor Law Guardians. They dealt with health and the Poor Law, though the County Council had power to appoint a health officer. Like highways, public health was in a state of confusion. Side by side with the Guardians, there existed sanitary boards and health boards set up

* I.e. included in *Burke's Landed Gentry*.

under the Public Health Acts, and the jurisdiction of these latter frequently overlapped that of the Guardians, particularly in urban areas.
The Guardians have since been abolished and their powers were at first
transferred to the County Council, the administration of what was
originally the Poor Law being vested in the Public Assistance Committee.
Later, the County Council itself was deprived of this power, the whole
matter of Poor Law Relief being vested in the central government.
During the short time that it was in the hands of the County Council,
the issue of the adminstration of the Poor Laws gave rise to some of the
most acrimonious debates in its history, the public assistance committees
being the scene of bitter inter-party feuds. There were occasions when the
entrance to County Hall was blocked by angry demonstrators from east
Lancashire protesting against the limited scales of relief.

A flood of statutes passed since 1888 conferred ever-increasing powers
on the County Council, and new fields of activity were constantly
brought within its purview, all of which are dealt with most adequately
in this book. All these additional responsibilities, combined with inflation,
led to an enormous increase in the annual budget, as is pointed out both
in the introductory chapter and in those on finance (Chapters 3 and 11).
There was, of course, also a great increase in rateable value, and in this
connection too the chapters on finance are of considerable interest.

This book is the result of a great deal of hard work, scholarship and
painstaking research. It is the record of the selfless devotion of a very
large number of members, officers and employees of the former Lancashire
County Council, many of whom have been and still are, I am proud to
say, my friends. I most confidently and cordially commend it.

Chairman, Library and Leisure   *D. H. Elletson*
Committee of the Lancashire County Council

Acknowledgements

MANY hands helped to bring this volume to its completion. A research team had to find common ground and some parallel interests; and the former Lancashire County Council provided assistance in many ways, through the advice and help of past members and officers. It was understood from the commencement that the academic contributors were to have the normal privilege of expressing their own views and conclusions throughout, and so our numerous guides and advisers are absolved from responsibility for the ultimate use of the information they have so willingly made available. On the Council's side, the following county aldermen and councillors took an active interest in the preparatory work throughout: D. H. Elletson (who chaired the Editorial Committee); J. G. Barber-Lomax CBE, TD, DL (whose financial and other knowledge helped us greatly); J. Foulkes, OBE, JP; R. C. Quick, JP; E. Roscoe, OBE, JP; Ellis Wood, OBE, JP; and T. Jackson, OBE; the late T. Hourigan, CBE, JP, DL; and, very patiently, the Council's last chairman, Sir Henry Lumby, CBE, JP, DL. We have had much help from former officers and staff members at County Hall and in the field, and our chief regret is that straitened space has often made it difficult to do justice to the ample information and insights we have received from them. We wish especially to acknowledge the help of Mr A. Longworth, the County Librarian; Mr R. Sharpe France, MBE, County Archivist until 1976; Mr Keith Bishop, his successor; and of course their respective staffs. Virtually all the main departments of the old Council encouraged us to use their records, or gave guidance, and we would like to thank, as regards the broader work of the Council, Sir Robert Adcock, CBE; Sir Patrick McCall, MBE, TD, DL; Mr Thomas Barton; Mr P. D. Inman, CBE, the present clerk; Sir James Drake, CBE and Mr H. L. Yeadon for their guidance on the working of the road construction and surveying services; Mr J. S. B. Boyce, TD; Mr Conrad Rainbow; Mr

W. D. Eade and, in particular, Mr William Whalley for their help regarding the education service; Mr J. Conway and staff for their advice and assistance regarding the County's finances; and Dr S. C. Gawne, Mr Harold Counsell and Messrs Worden, Sowerbutts, Robinson and Hoggarth for providing insights into the health services. Mr Jeffrey Rowbotham and his staff enabled us to include a survey of the authority's planning work, just as Miss Marion Jay and Miss Ruth White, both experienced former field officers, helped us to understand something of the day-to-day work of the Children's Department. Mr Frank Young, CBE, gave us important information on the Council's diplomatic work with regard to other local authorities.

Inevitably, much of our information has come from minute books and reports, some of them of a highly intractable nature, and it would be ungracious not to acknowledge the great help of our main research assistant, Mr Terence Karran, who laboured both intelligently and prodigiously at a vast and varied mountain of material. Elsewhere, at shorter periods, we had valued help from Mr Michael Williams and Miss G. Erike. Also on the University's side, two further helpers call for especial acknowledgement; Mrs Marion McClintock, whose organising skills in preparing meetings and manuscripts have proved to be beyond praise, and whose background work at the Centre for North-West Regional Studies kept our discussions steadily in progress, and Professor P. A. Reynolds, senior pro-vice-chancellor, whose sage advice helped our navigation in crucial ways. Meanwhile, Dr A. F. Davie, the sole contributor to the published volume who was not on the staff of the University of Lancaster, travelled long distances, without complaint, to take part in our discussions and to give us the benefit of his detailed knowledge of county administrative history.

County Councils have not in the past been seen as political animals of any great forcefulness. Yet we discovered that Lancashire's had a most interesting record, and the following political party officials were both kind and helpful in their guidance: Mrs H. Keane, and Messrs E. C. Bradbury, D. T. Laws, R. C. Wallis, and L. Dole.

Finally, this research project was assisted by a grant from the old Lancashire County Council. Although the resulting work was administered through the Centre for North-West Regional Studies, the Centre wishes to thank the University's administrators, and the departments of Politics and Economics, which gave every facility to our research assistants.

J. D. Marshall

University of Lancaster
August 1977

PART I

Introduction

CHAPTER 1

The Government of Lancashire from 1889: Its Roots and Characteristics

I

THE Lancashire governmental system of 1889 was in fact deeply rooted in the past. Over many generations before that date, the administration of the county had been the responsibility of the magistracy alone, social leaders who were also nominees of the Duchy of Lancaster. The Local Government Act (or County Councils Act) of 1888 brought the elective principle to great areas of rural England. Naturally there was some excitement. The Lancastrian citizen, studying his newspaper and feeling appropriately impressed at the achievement of Lord Salisbury's ministry in bringing this about, might well have failed to understand how little his life was to be affected, and how little the administrative machinery of the county was, at first, to be altered.

The new Lancashire County Council (January 1889) took over the fuctions of the Court of Annual General Sessions, which had administered the county since 1798, and which in the course of time was responsible for the police, bridges, asylums, finance, main roads, prevention of cattle disease, control of food and drugs, and reformatories and industrial schools in the geographical county outside certain Quarter Sessions boroughs.[1] This administrative institution, formed in pursuance of the Lancashire Sessions Act (1798), was unlike any other in England in that it was legally empowered to secure a court of magistrates to conduct county administrative business. It carried on its business after 1850 through appropriate standing committees, and it was remarkably like the Council that succeeded it, except that its members were not elected by rate-payers.[2] It appointed officers, including a Clerk of the Peace and a Treasurer; and so the Council of 1889 inherited an already operative administrative machine. Its geographical centre was in the town of

3

Preston, where the Annual General Sessions met, and the new County Council gathered in the same town. Nevertheless, the earlier body represented a regime inappropriate to a progressively more democratic age, and both Conservatives and Liberals found common ground in desiring to end such a state of affairs.[3]

By the late summer of 1888, then, the Lancashire political reading public, a very considerable one, was following the progress of C. T. Ritchie's 'Bill to amend the Laws relating to Local Government in England and Wales' as it ground through its ultimate total of 126 clauses, thereby occupying a lion's share of parliamentary time between March and August. Inevitably, such a protracted affair had the effect of arousing expectations, even though the informed Lancastrian could have been forgiven for not having traced its immediate political origins in a group of Gladstonian MPs and Liberal radicals, notably Sir Charles Dilke. Dilke, as chairman of the Local Government Board in 1883, had led a committee which drafted a Local Government Bill far more radical than the one that eventually received the Royal Assent; the former had provided for elected county councils that controlled the Poor Law, public health and education, thereby anticipating actual events in a remarkable fashion.[4] It was left to Lord Salisbury's Conservatives to further a less radical measure, which originally kept the control of the police out of the hands of elected representatives, at the same time leaving the Poor Law and education on one side.

Yet, as we have seen, a great deal was expected of the new Bill. The *Lancaster Observer* expressed a fairly typical viewpoint in its encomium of 23 March 1888:

> The thoroughness of the new principle of County Government expounded by Mr Ritchie amazed even the radicals, while the old-fashioned Conservatives were simply staggered by the number of clauses.... It is, indeed, a measure for all sorts of persons, and is practically a revolution for the counties. The magistrates, who have administered the chief part of the county business, are by the Bill, relieved of all their functions but one – that of jurisdiction.

The *Lancaster Observer* then listed the functions of the proposed new County Council; and, although it omitted to point out the plain truth of the matter, these were in few important details different from the functions of the Annual General Sessions and its related committees and staff ('rates, roads, bridges, lunatic asylums, reformatories, industrial schools, electoral registration, public health, cattle disease...'). It went on:

> Each county will be a little republic doing its utmost to develop its

resources, to improve its communications and conveniences, and to make the lives of its inhabitants as happy and comfortable as possible, and at the lowest possible cost.... Mr Ritchie ... has made his bill democratic; at the same time he has dealt justly by the magistracy; and no country gentleman, who now serves the county, will be excluded from the Council, and from influencing it on behalf of his class.

Some six years later, the *Lancaster Guardian* (22 December 1894) was to comment that: 'Throughout the county the best of the magistrates have offered their services as elected representatives, and many of them have been elected, and by so acting have secured for themselves more influence than they previously possessed.'

If, then, the advance of democracy had brought only the strengthened rule of the magistracy, and if the new county authority was doing much the same things as the old, it is clear that the formation of the County Council was a resounding anticlimax. Fortunately for all who study history, however, events are rarely as simple, or as simply characterised, as this. There was little or no reason why a county electorate, which had previously become accustomed to doing without a franchise, should suddenly rush into paroxysms of republican and radical activity at the behest of Lord Salisbury and Mr Ritchie, or even of Sir Charles Dilke. What is impressive, meanwhile, is the seriousness with which the new measure was regarded, and the eagerness with which the election of county representatives was anticipated. When the election duly took place, in January 1889, there was a general upsurge of interest that was not to be repeated in kind until the middle of the following century.

How did Lancashire fare in the election of its county councillors? First of all, the county was one of those that experienced a vigorous contest on party lines. There were Liberal victories in Cumberland and the West Riding, to take examples from neighbouring areas; but Lancashire, with Cheshire, Northamptonshire and Wiltshire, produced a body of councillors that was fairly evenly balanced politically.[5] As Mr Hands and Mr Denver show, there were initially forty divisions (out of 105) in which contests took place, and two main groups of councillors emerged: a mainly rural group composed of gentry, farmers and landowners, and a larger one made up of industrialists and factory-owners. The involvement of any wider sections of the public was quite plainly incidental and superficial, and in the next election, in 1892, only fourteen seats were contested in the entire county.[6] Thereafter the low level of public interest was a continual feature of county politics, and the Council established itself as an institution in which a given type, or group of types, of social leader could become committed and involved, very often in the course of an extension of activity from district politics.

The chairmanship of Lancashire County Council, meanwhile, belonged to a distinguished Liberal who believed sincerely in grass-roots government. Sir John Hibbert was from the political *milieu* shared by Dilke and Gladstone, and he had been secretary to the Poor Law Board in 1880–3. Accordingly, he was exceptionally well versed in the problems of local government, although it is noteworthy that he approached the latter from the position of a dedicated administrator with little interest in party differences. Nevertheless, Sir John was a keen supporter of democratic government at the local and parish level, and he saw the development of second-tier authorities in 1894 as an opportunity for the flowering of political democracy.[7] There was, indeed, a somewhat smaller wave of excitement in that year when radicals and democrats toured the north Lancashire countryside promulgating what they saw as 'Hodge's Charter' – the Parish Councils Act – and campaigning for 'the village for the villagers'.[8] As is well known, the same Local Government Act of 1894 also produced the urban and rural district councils which lasted until 1974. By a mild irony, however, the County Council itself was defining and fathering the new district councils, acting as a boundary commissioner by delegated authority from the central government, while the urban and rural district councils were in general made up of groups of parishes. The determination of boundaries was a complex task, because the earlier rural sanitary authorities were based on and shaped by the older Poor Law Unions, which often overlapped county boundaries and divisions, and the Parliamentary Committee of the County Council, under Councillor V. K. Armitage, was engrossed in much exhausting labour during May and June 1894.[9] Thus the Council gave shape to the new two-tier system but did not breathe life into it; for Lancashire local patriotism ran easily into the mould thus fashioned, and Hibbert's vision was by no means dashed. Lancashire's county rulers nevertheless strengthened an already existing moral ascendancy.

The preoccupations of 1894 seemed also to define and characterise the work of Council as something tedious and often apparently detached from the immediate interests of local communities. This impression did not of course gain credence from the events of 1894 alone, for the supervision of main roads and policemen simply did not stir even the more educated groups in society; and there were at this period few county services that seemed patently concerned with the personal welfare, as distinct from the coercion, of members of the public. The county authority was not as yet far removed from the image and functions of the Court of Annual General Sessions, while at the same time the work load of the administrative mechanism had, in the general opinion of the

Clerks of the Peace, increased by about one-half.[10] The augmented burden was unquestionably and mainly attributable to the recurrent problems of boundary adjustment (and to a far lesser degree to the establishment of new services such as technical education and public health), and in a large county like Lancashire this was especially so. Fifteen county boroughs simply followed each other in claiming boundary extensions; within a few months of the Council's formation, Burnley and Manchester sought extensions totalling some 100,000 acres, and by 1895 St Helens and Liverpool were claiming an even greater total.[11] Such incursions involved a fall of nearly £2 million in rateable values on the county's side.

The Parliamentary Commission created by the 1888 Local Government Act was still worrying its way through anomalies of this kind in 1892, when the Attorney-General described Lancashire's case as one of 'a very peculiar nature', in that the fifteen 'holes in the carpet' – the county boroughs – took away a great deal of the county's share of the moneys from Goschen's brain-child, the Exchequer Equalisation Account.[12] The Commissioners helped to bring about an ultimate settlement, and the Council's Financial Adjustments Committee made agreements with the county boroughs. But the problem of legal border warfare remained an intractable one, principally because the lifetime of the County Council coincided with massive pressures of suburbanisation around the great towns; and time brought another and complicating problem – that of large-scale population shifts within broader areas of the county. The immediate effect, in this earlier period of the nineties, was to give work, responsibility and status to the Clerk's Department, much of it of a kind that could not benefit the rate-paying public in any serious manner. This was a tragedy in more ways than one, because the first Clerk to the Council, Frederick Campbell Hulton, almost certainly wore himself out and died prematurely after a succession of eighteen-hour days.[13] Sir John Hibbert had good reason to appreciate Hulton's 'ability and zeal',[14] manifested despite the inadequate staffing of most of the new county departments,[15] and there is little doubt that he was the principal architect of the new county administration. But an officer with an appetite for work can also gain disproportionate influence when he is surrounded by gentleman amateurs of politics and government; and following Hulton's untimely death Lancashire acquired a succession of unusually powerful and influential clerks and senior officers; so much so that this can be seen as a characteristic of the Council's history.

A mere local lawyer, however able, would in theory be more than counterbalanced by a man of the eminence of Sir John Hibbert. Nevertheless, the latter could regard the chairmanship of the Council as a strictly part-time occupation, to be carried on additionally to his service to central government; in 1892–5 he was financial secretary to the Treasury, and when he retired in 1895 he was enabled to retain the Council chairmanship until 14 March 1908 – this after a life of intense political and administrative activity. It is fair to add that Sir John had extremely able vice-chairmen in, successively, Sir W. H. Houldsworth (1892–1906) and (Sir) William Scott Barrett (1906–08); but the distinguished statesman was nevertheless to hold office to the age of eighty-four. Very long chairmanships by leading county gentry or aristocracy were of course quite common in county councils at this period; but the Lancashire post was rather more than a matter of formalities, and its first holder was clearly enabled to continue to such an advanced age with the assistance of two factors; (i) the existence of a group of increasingly experienced senior aldermen, men from business and the professions as well as gentry, to whom key committees could safely be trusted, and (ii) a growing tendency on the part of the administrative machinery to run itself and to become more formalised. This in turn was accentuated by two negative influences; the lack of interest in council proceedings on the part of public opinion, and the corresponding lack of debate in the council chamber.

Some evidence bearing on these marked tendencies is supplied by Mr Hands and Mr Denver in Chapter 4 below.[16] That they could be manifested in many a smaller county need not surprise us; that these negative influences could also be powerful in a great industrial county is of considerably more interest. Their existence does not, of course, necessarily detract from the importance of the work of individuals, of individual services or of the general administration of Lancashire. On the contrary; the work of personalities tends to be thrown into relief, as does the emergence of a stable inner group of senior members of the Council (this despite a very considerable turnover of membership of that body, brought about by a steady flow of new volunteers from uncontested divisions, i.e. before 1914). Roughly one-quarter of the Council membership was replaced after each triennial election. Attendance, however, was also rather poor, being less than sixty per cent in one period, 1904–07, and it is clear that a substantial proportion of councillors did not maintain enthusiasm or seek to turn county administration into a career of social leadership. This not surprising discovery serves to draw attention to the minority of council veterans who played a major part in virtually all its committees and activities, a group that tended to grow larger before the 1930s. Despite the considerable strength of the manu-facturing and mill-owning element on the Council, the 'veteran' group had, again not unsurprisingly, a somewhat disproportionately large element of gentry and landowners, although it must also be said that the out-standing council leaders, almost without exception, had a background in trade or industry. But they also had one advantage in common with the established members of the gentry – that of leisure as well as education – and the members of this veteran group, from whom the leaders generally came, were in fact men who were willing and able to devote so much time to county work that they were professionals in a true sense, professional county politicians who had already made their mark in district or borough organisations or on the Bench or Board of Guardians.

That established county gentry could still play an important part in Lancashire government tells us something of the pressures and advantages that led to their continued dominance in less workaday counties. The old Lancashire gentry families of Starkie of Huntroyde, Assheton of Downham, Hulton of Hulton, Egerton of Worsley, de Trafford and Fitzherbert-Brockholes all contributed representatives to the Council of 1889. W. J. Fitzherbert-Brockholes, of Claughton Hall near Garstang, a considerable landowner,[17] was the first representative on the Council of a family that produced three generations of councillors; and his career exemplifies the types of interest and involvement that created service opportunities for county gentlemen – attendance at the meetings of the Diseases of Animals Committee and on the respective Smallholdings and Allotments Committees, leading ultimately to the chairmanship of the Lancashire Agricultural Committee (1920), with parallel interests in the Standing Joint Committee (that *sine qua non* for a senior country magistrate) and, very notably, in the Education Committee. The field of education offered local commitments, as did other committees, and Fitzherbert-Brockholes was until 1924 the chairman of his Area Elementary Education Committee,[18] one of the several dimensions of his thirty-five years of council service. R. C. Assheton of Downham became the senior veteran of the first generation of councillors, and served from 1892 to 1949, while W. W. B. Hulton was chairman of Main Roads and Bridges Committee from 1889 to 1907 and Le Gendre N. Starkie was chairman of the Standing Joint Committee from 1894 to 1899. It is true to say, therefore, that the 'old' gentry made a contribution out of all proportion to the size of their social group on the Council.

The motivations of country gentlemen may be fairly discernible, according to viewpoint – *noblesse oblige*, loyalty to the ideals of their own social group or desire to keep law and order in the interest of their own notion of a properly run society. The great majority of the councillors, however, consisted of men whose social identities were broadly in the occupations listed by returning officers – cotton-spinners, professional people, members of the business community generally. Nevertheless, a significant pattern of social gradations appears in this larger group of Council members, and relates to the comparative nearness of the social situation of individuals to the ideal of the gentleman's life-style. The essential ingredient of this life-style was *leisure*, whether for public service, amusement or culture, and an ability to allow others to look after sources of income. As we shall see, a dedicated council leader had to be willing to devote great tracts of time, of an extent quite unavailable to the common citizen, to committee work, to local politics and to public activities. Indeed, it is almost certainly true that leadership tended to pass to those who had not only the strongest inclination to quasi-professional council work, but who had also the most leisure. Local standing could be immensely important, but this was nurtured in the arena of district politics or office, a necessary training area for aspirant leaders.

As regards the social gradations themselves, it is useful to distinguish, first of all, the members of the older industrial families of nineteenth-century Lancashire who were at the same time leisured and cultured and politically experienced enough to form what was in effect a 'new' gentry. These were second- or third-generation representatives of established industrial families like those of Deacon and Muspratt (famous names in industrial chemistry), Armitage of Swinton, Greg of Lunesdale, Jacson of Preston and Barton or, as an example of such a family whose members had become country landowners, Garnett of Quernmore.[19] Yet it should at the same time be stressed that social status, or even influence, did not necessarily lead to predominance in council affairs – hard work, education and simple ability also entered into the story, and this meant that the Council's élite groups were always likely to be recruited from what may be termed working industrialist or professional members, who in turn made up the majority of the Council's membership. Many of these 'working' representatives, senior partners or (as happened increasingly) directors of their own firms were already justices of the peace and established leaders of their local communities, for instance George Walmsley, cotton-spinner of Church and one of the pioneer aldermen, Alfred Barnes of Farnworth with a similar background and position, and William Garnett of the famous cotton firm at Low Moor, Clitheroe.[20]

Very occasionally a professional man with outstanding expertise would rise rapidly to a position of eminence; Edwin Guthrie, the Council's first chairman of the Finance Committee, who was appropriately a professional accountant, is one such example, while (Sir) George A. Pilkington, surgeon of Southport and a pioneer chairman of the Public Health Committee, was another.[21] Indeed, mention of this committee and of its associated activities brings into sharp focus the degree to which specialist knowledge could, on its own, contribute to council work. The doctor members of the Council naturally tended to be interested in public health, but subsequently found a direct outlet for their professional judgement in the Midwives Act Committee (newly formed in 1902) on which they served *en bloc*. Specialised professional knowledge of this kind, however, ceased to be an advantage if other administrative or political skills were less in evidence; and only two of the doctors (out of seven who served up to 1913) reached peripheral membership of the inner élite of this period: Richard Sephton (chairman of Public Health and Housing Committee from 1901 to 1916) and John Chadwick of Milnrow, who contributed with distinction to the work of the Public Health and Housing Committee and the Midwives Act, Lunatic Asylums and Tuberculosis Committees during twenty-eight years of membership of the Council (1898–1925).

Surprisingly few councillors seem to have brought such specialised training to bear on their work, even though a substantial majority of them had much general knowledge of business affairs and administration, and even though there was an immense absorption in the details of committee and departmental working, an absorption that was disturbed by few political storms for at least a generation. The ideal was common devotion to public service (the 'consensus model' of political behaviour characterised by Mr Hands and Mr Denver below); and those who were thus devoted did not necessarily move into their positions through political pressure or conspiracy. Nevertheless, we are justified in asking what other factors, besides ability and leisure, caused the most prominent leaders to emerge; and it would appear that the answers lie in a mixture of accumulated expertise in administrative detail, sometimes assisted by legal knowledge, and above all in *style* as a committee chairman.

A leader-figure had to represent and symbolise virtues that appealed to fellow members of the Council and to its most experienced veterans. Sir John Hibbert's great standing as a public figure tends to set him apart from criteria of this kind, and his successor, Scott Barrett, more fairly represents the ethos of his age. The latter was chairman of the Council during a period of steady administrative growth pressure (1908–21), broken only by war, and characterised in turn by a countervailing concern with economy. Barrett, on his retirement from the chair, expressed his conviction that 'public expenditure was being watched very carefully, and that the motto of the County Council was "Efficiency is true economy" '.[22] In Scott Barrett's case, the diligent businessman and colliery owner, the public servant and the old-fashioned Liberal, suspicious of central control and expenditure, were combined in one. Henry Wade Deacon, chairman from 1927 to 1931, also displayed qualities that his colleagues valued, 'impartiality and courtesy' combined with the 'conspicuous ability of his long charge of the finances of the Council'.[23] Wade Deacon, it may be noted, not only was a competent financial administrator but also had some early legal training, and he was one of those whose great leisure (he retired from all business activities at the age of thirty-nine) was given almost entirely to council work. Legal training, enjoyed by Sir John Hibbert as well as Wade Deacon, was in general absent from the Council, only five members of which had such training in 1898, and only four in 1928,[24] although, of course, the most prominent leaders acquired great working knowledge of statute law.

This discussion of chairmen and leaders should tell the reader a little about the types and manner of men who led Lancashire through its highest organ of local government, the County Council. Although it was customary for the Council chairmen and county officers to receive knighthoods, it is true to say that the great burden of their work was undertaken outside the public view, and that it had few of the advantages of temporary lionisation that might have been enjoyed in, for example, a local mayoralty. As has been made clear, the Council was rarely newsworthy in the eyes of the regional press, and it accordingly attracted the kind of political personality that really did have a deep sense of responsibility and dedication. It would of course be very difficult to show, in the absence of a detailed social analysis of Lancashire leaders of all kinds, how representative the Council's leaders were in the light of such a wider view. The Council chairmen of what may be called the 'middle' or interwar period of its history tended to become less directly associated with industry and, to an even greater degree, more the leisured leader-type than those who had preceded them. (Sir) James Travis-Clegg, who succeeded (Sir) Henry Wade Deacon in 1931, was an old Etonian, although – such are the curiosities of social classification – it is very doubtful whether he would have been accepted as a member of the established county gentry. Nevertheless, he had a life-style and background that qualified him for quasi-professional council activity, and we learn that 'he took up public work after leaving school';[25] early in his council career he was described in electoral lists as 'Gentleman'. His successor, Sir William Hodgson (1937–45), had a career history that was surprisingly similar; like Travis-Clegg, he had a background in purely local politics and administration, was described as 'Gentleman', and had a presence and style that was admired. Hodgson had a good administrative memory and sense of observation, while Travis-Clegg was deeply interested in educational provision. Sir James was described (by a Labour member) as 'one of God's Englishmen',[26] and Sir William (by a colleague) as 'a real English gentleman'.[27] Up to this point, it is safe to say that Lancashire's senior council leaders were *not* representative of the industrial middle class that was so closely identified with cotton, coal, chemicals and engineering, but that they represented either a social evolution from it, or an incarnation of qualities to which that class aspired or which it admired.

Whatever the case, nearly all those leaders had an important characteristic in common; they had roots in local politics which gave them authority in the diplomacy demanded by the county's mass of second-tier authorities. Three of the chairmen of the early and middle periods of the Council's history had also aimed for higher political honours, and had attempted to reach Parliament – Sir James Aitken, Sir Henry Hibbert and Travis-Clegg – but only Henry Hibbert, like his more famous namesake Sir John, actually reached the Commons, and his stay there was brief (1913–18). Far more important was the fact that Aitken, a solicitor from the small community of Barrowford, made his name in nearby Nelson before entering the County Council, while Sir Henry Hibbert (chairman from 1921 to 1927) was a greatly esteemed leader in Chorley Conservative politics, with a record of long service in the town itself; and Travis-Clegg had important political and personal connections in the Crompton–Oldham area. Of the middle period chairmen, Sir William Hodgson had equal standing in his own home district, the northern Fylde. Such men, as experience showed, were better equipped to deal with local loyalties and urban patriotisms, so typical of the county, than the older-style gentry or aristocracy who dominated other and more rural county councils.

On the Council itself, the most effective leaders inevitably became specialists in the subject matter of key committees. Although Finance was the most important of these, and was in effect a basic co-ordinator of policy, the massive county enterprise of Education, following 1903, absorbed the attentions of Henry Hibbert (the first chairman of the latter), Travis-Clegg and Aitken, thereby providing a complex and humane training ground for leaders. The structure and status of committees is dealt with elsewhere (Chapter 3), and all that need be said here is that the most prominent council members could sometimes achieve records of committee service, in breadth as well as depth, that were scarcely less than awe-inspiring. Sir William Hodgson's achievement in this respect most emphatically falls in that category, covering twelve main committees between 1901 and 1945,[28] and of course several times that number of sub-committees.

II

This book is in effect divided into two main parts, one concerned with the Council before 1929 and the other with its history after the fateful Local Government Act of that year. The more detailed story may with profit be subdivided. There was a formative period of the Council, stretching from its foundation in 1889 to the Education Act of 1902, which in turn led to the greatest single administrative upheaval before 1929; then there was a period of steady but unspectacular growth, broken by the war, and marked by some still quite striking expansion in educational provision, and by some noteworthy experiments in the health field. There was then a phase, which we take arbitrarily as lasting from 1929 to 1944, which can be described as the 'middle period', wherein continuing and newer trends were mixed, and wherein the old sometimes came into conflict with the new; and there was a final period of massive administrative upheaval and economic growth between 1944 and 1974. In this, the story of the greatest provincial local authority, is mirrored much in the history of modern English local government.

However, the book itself is not meant to be an illustrative primer in this sense; nor is it purely a record of achievement, administrative or personal. It is meant, as far as is reasonable and possible, to show how, under uniquely local social, political and economic pressures, a distinctively Lancashire-flavoured form of organisation developed as groups of individuals, representing wider social segments, reacted to those pressures. In undertaking this daunting task the team of contributors was well aware of certain dangers; there is a shortage of certain kinds of evidence relative to important events, especially in the more distant past, as letter books and written personal reminiscences have proved to be unobtainable, and as data relating to the interaction of the local and the central governmental authority are sometimes shown to be prohibitively difficult to work through. The inner story of certain departments would in each case require a separate monograph, and would even then be only a partial record of decision-making processes. Nevertheless, the example set by Professor Lee, Mr Wood and their helpers in *The Scope of Local Initiative* (1974) shows how careful if sometimes impressionistic enquiry (in Cheshire) can reveal the distinctive flavour and style of a county government body reacting to given sets of circumstances. In face of a much greater time span – the entire lifetime of the 'old' Lancashire Council – the present contributors decided to concentrate on those structural and political trends that lent themselves to sustained analysis. Inevitably, these general movements suggest innumerable questions, some of which should stimulate further research, and some of which are of their nature impossible of solution, including a number of very large questions indeed – what, for example, was the overall quality of Lancashire administration? Or of committee control, or of efficiency, compared with other counties?

In a number of cases we have provided pieces of evidence that suggest that a certain service could exhibit some apparent economies of scale when provided in a great county. But these indicators, however relevant, should be the starting point for research in the areas concerned in what is, after all, a sadly under-researched field. In the matter of the behaviour and style of administrators and representatives, or of local initiatives or of *types* of economic growth, we have rather more to say; Mr MacGregor-Reid (Chapter 11), in a highly technical study which repays careful reading, indicates that the capital expenditure pattern of a great authority seems to have proceeded according to its own momentum and almost irrespective of central controls and *dicta*; and this, in so far as the discovery has wider applications, leads to considerations that are both momentous and worrying in the light of our present concerns. Much of the book (Chapters 9–16) relates to comparatively recent Lancashire history, for antiquarianism is certainly not our preoccupation, and the earlier part of the story is of value principally for the light it throws on regional development. Mention of this subject must necessarily bring in allusion to Professor J. M. Lee's *Social Leaders and Public Persons*, which must remain a model study of its kind in its characterisation of changing Cheshire élites. We leave students to decide how far the transition from one (the dominant county gentry with a 'natural leader' role) to the other (the public person or professional representative not strictly related to social caste) applies in the Lancashire case. Our own impression is that the model, or pattern, of social evolution is not markedly profitable in the case of a great industrial county, in that it is likely to sacrifice far too many social nuances – although it is quite clear that the 'public person' became dominant in due course, as did the administrator in a field outside politics. Mr Hands and Mr Denver have given this field of study some important pioneering cultivation, in dealing primarily with political models. Here, the work and political record of Lancashire's county leaders is subjected to dispassionate examination, and their social composition is analysed in some detail.

Perhaps the most startling feature of Lancashire county government is its sheer scale and complexity, and this fact emerges even in the early or formative years of the Council. Dr Davie's thorough account of the authority's early committee structure and development has to be seen in relation to the more general history of county councils. The County Council *Yearbook* for 1891 indicates this complexity very effectively, by permitting comparison with all other county councils of that time. Although other counties, like Nottinghamshire or Cheshire, proliferated committees (Cheshire even had a 'Committee for Proposed Bridge over River Mersey Between Runcorn and Widnes'), Lancashire had more standing committees, sub-committees and joint committees, taken together, than any other county – and, of course, more council members to operate them. More than this, however, its sheer size and rateable value gave it room for manoeuvre, and it is perhaps no accident that, together with the West Riding, it was a pioneer county in appointing a medical officer of health,[29] when other, more backward, county bodies were apt to behave as though sanitation was of little moment. A great urban industrialised county naturally produced members with experience of local sanitary organisation, and with some opinions as to its desirability. Many in the Lancashire Council were not in favour of the appointment of a medical officer, however. Other elements of the committee structure of counties were, of course, more or less standardised, like the Standing Joint Committees (for control of the police), Finance Committees, Main Roads and Bridges and Executive Cattle Plague Committees. In one important educational sphere, that of technical education, the counties tended to rush into action, principally by virtue of the bait of beer and spirit excise money ('whisky money')[30] provided in support, with the additional qualification that the associated agricultural education interested the most bucolic councillors, and engaged the support of the most suspicious backwoodsmen.

Just as Lancashire was quickly off the mark by forming committees to deal with river pollution and environmental health problems, so its comparatively large-scale commitment to technical education helped to pave the way for the more massive educational organisation of post-1902. The effect of educational expansion on county councils and their members must be seen as significant and profound, in that it represented the first of the great personal service movements in modern local government; and, in so far as it involved the supervision of schools and education at the local level, it brought with it innumerable creative grass-roots contacts that were very far from merely bureaucratic.

The implementation of the 1902 Act accompanied the rise to influence of a far greater force in Lancashire county than the then Director of Education, Dr Lloyd Snape. This was Harcourt Everard Clare, the new Clerk of the Council, who had succeeded F. C. Hulton in 1899, and who came from the clerkship to the Liverpool Corporation, thus creating a precedent for a regular succession of appointments to this high office from Liverpool or Manchester. The first ten years of the Council's existence had done little to allay the hostility felt by some non-county boroughs and other district countils to the new county authority, and the County Council's tutelage function was by no means universally accepted. The new education authority had the task of securing the co-operation of local councillors and others in the working of district elementary education committees – in what was in effect a vast pioneering scheme of partial delegation – and of persuading district councillors to act as partners with the county authority in fostering secondary schools under the terms of the new Act. Harcourt Clare early stated that one of his aims was 'to bring a more cordial feeling and more co-operation in(to) Lancashire's local government',[31] and in so doing he helped to formulate a diplomatic approach which was also an important ingredient in the county's style of administration during the next half-century – in this instance by assisting the smooth working of district secondary education committees. This deep consciousness of district attitudes and needs continued, then, to pervade county policy, and was reflected in the work of the next clerk, George Hammond Etherton, and, after him, R. H. Adcock. It should not however be thought that their diplomacy was necessarily always effective, and on the retirement of Sir Harcourt Clare a local newspaper remarked that district councils would 'always have their grievances against central authority of an unmanageably large area like Lancashire'.[32]

The size and generally unwieldy shape of Lancashire did indeed create many problems, especially in an age when few members of administrative staffs had motor transport, and when a police message could, even after the installation of telephone switchboards, take two-and-a-half hours to travel from one end of the county to the other. Yet the fact remains that, however extraordinarily, and after recurrent discussion of the possibility of dividing the county into Ridings, this vast local government machine nevertheless contrived to work. It is possible that, had not Preston been such a well situated railway centre (and, later, a road one) the day-to-day functioning of the Lancashire County Council would have been impossible from the standpoint of senior officers alone. Such officials were obliged to spend much of their working time in railway carriages, and as diplomatic and other visits to districts became more necessary, so more responsibility for the immediate tasks of office administration fell upon less qualified or more junior members of staff. In time, of course, local government officers became professionalised and well organised, but the staff of this early period were often without any kind of paper qualification, and were trained on the job. Hence, Dr Sergeant, the medical officer to the county, left much of his paper work to Mr Gee, his chief clerk, in the course of his travels about Lancashire, and these two men effectively provided the environmental health service on the part of the Edwardian county authority. It is a piquant thought that, among other even more obvious factors, a mixture of geographical accident, diplomatic need, communication timing and technology, and plain parsimony (the 'economy' praised by Scott Barrett) helped to bring about the testing, training and professionalisation of the middle staff grades.

Not all departments were as sparsely staffed as Public Health, and the first generation of the Council's existence saw a striking growth in administrative staff, handsomely augmented by the Education Department.[33] County Hall* was, by the accession of George V, a populous place in which the ungainly typewriters of the age rattled before their long-skirted clerical assistants (although, it might be noted, eventually seasoned male officers, as in the Public Health Office, rose from the ranks after many years of doing their own typing).[34] Meanwhile, the most senior officers, paid more in salary from the beginning than any chief officials outside the metropolis,[35] inevitably became something of a superior caste as more and more incidental duties were showered upon the Council in dozens of government enactments, and as an increasing premium was placed upon skilled advice to chairmen and committees. It is true to say that the position of Clerk to the Council, always dignified by its joint tenure of the Clerkship of the Peace, became a steadily more influential office during (Sir) Harcourt Clare's period of service.

The clerkship was, as we have seen, complicated by the large number of joint committees including representatives of other authorities and interests (to supervise asylums, river cleanliness, sea fisheries and assize courts), and Clare was generally believed to have turned this to his own advantage by obtaining salaries for his clerkship of the Lancashire asylums and other boards, over and above his salary as Clerk of the Council.[36] Taking real values into account, therefore, he was probably the most highly paid clerk in his own or any period, and it was not for nothing that Lady Clare was regarded as the best-dressed woman in the more polite society of the county. It would be wrong, however, to imply that her husband was somehow a *parvenu*; he was, on the contrary, an old Reptonian with considerably more background and presence than many of the highly placed persons with whom he dealt, and his achievement (which some may envy) in securing rewards for his numerous commitments would not have been possible in a later age, or in a more contentious and observant one. It should be borne in mind that Clare's mandarin flamboyance belonged to an age of quiescence in council politics, and his frequently produced bottles of port matched the tastes of visiting chairmen and of plenipotentiaries from Lancashire districts. This was one side of his character; a man of immense animal energy (he would occasionally walk nine or ten miles from County Hall to his home at Bank Hall near Bretherton); he had a great appetite for work; and it may be said

---

* The original County Hall (1882) on Fishergate, Preston, was an adjunct to the police offices (1878), which were taken over for general administration after the 1902 Education Act. The great block on Pitt Street, with its main entrance facing the railway lines, was built in 1930–4. Further extension has since taken place behind this block.

that, after his partially successful attempts to placate county districts, he played a major part in bringing doctors in Lancashire (who were in many cases opposed to the conditions set out by the National Insurance Act of 1911) into a tactfully formulated scheme which ensured a measure of co-operation from the profession: 'on the Appointed Day a complete medical panel was set up in Lancashire and the Act successfully implemented'.[37] This consolidated Clare's reputation with central government, and he became 'a valued consultant' on bills affecting local administration. Here we touch on another important topic of much wider application; a great county authority like Lancashire necessarily interacted powerfully with the senior officialdom of ministries, and was by no means the passive recipient of instructions from above. All of the Lancashire clerks and senior officers – and especially chief education officers – stood in a special position as advisers and consultants, and at least one such officer, Sir George Gater, afterwards became an outstandingly distinguished civil servant.

Nor was the interaction merely on the advisory plane; irrespective of its relative or *per capita* wealth, a county with such huge absolute resources and such a large staff could initiate administrative and technological experiments of an important kind, whether in tuberculosis treatment, midwifery services, police patrol systems, motorway building (Lancashire's experiments in this direction really started before 1930, with the building of the East Lancashire Road) or in the planning of new urban satellites to take population overspill. The Ministries of Health, Housing, Education, Transport and the Home Office all had good reason to encourage and to study Lancashire experiments and to learn from them; and official policies of a more general application grew from these local experiences. There is such a vast and rewarding field in these areas of local–central interaction that it is amazing to find it largely ignored by students of government; and a general historical survey cannot, unhappily, take adequate account of it.

The senior officers of Lancashire, then, were apt to carry much national weight; but it should not be forgotten that the leading elected representatives also made their mark in such bodies as the County Councils' Association (of which Sir John Hibbert was the first president) and the Association of Education Committees (in which Sir James Aitken had a similar office). Lancashire's pace-setting propensities or special authority could find expression in gatherings of this kind; yet, not altogether paradoxically, it was in its relations with the other associations of local government bodies – the Rural District Councils Association, the Urban District Councils Association and the Association of Municipal Corporations – that the county made a special and memorable contribution. More than any county in England, it found itself obliged to enter into discussion with the national and regional representatives of these bodies; and, as a later expression of the same approach to local democracy and, often, delegatory functions, it took a lead in forming the National Association of Divisional Executives in Education. It should be borne in mind that, throughout much of the 'old' Council's history, a substantial proportion of its members were also district councillors, and that, therefore, a unique pattern of county–district relationships developed. It can very properly be argued that such a complex pattern of diplomatic lines of approach may have made for a workable two-tier system of government, but may also have made for much expenditure of time in discussion. The allaying of suspicions may not, after all, remove the causes of those suspicions. On the other hand, councillors and local officials were given a voice, and the worst effects of centralised bureaucracy were often countered in an increasingly technological and complex age. What is still more important for the theory and practice of local government, Lancashire experience recognised that the neighbourhood or district loyalty is the most powerful of all loyalties – a fact cautiously revealed in the one really serious piece of research included in the corpus of the Redcliffe–Maud Commission enquiries.[38] The conclusions of this research, which the Commission found to be of an intractable and not easily usable kind, were long before recognised in day-to-day Lancashire experience.

The later chapters in this volume are essentially thematic, and they contain, set out in pursuit of their themes, numerous case studies. Although no major county service or department has been flagrantly ignored, the strongest stress is on important fields like education, planning (covered in its economic and organisational aspects by Mr Daniels), finance (by Mr MacGregor-Reid) and the health services (by the present writer). Mr Daniels also contributes an important section on motorways, in which, as we have seen, Lancashire was a pioneer. Indeed, the post-1944 period brought such a rich and complex pattern of administrative events and technological experiment that it is all too easy to become immersed within that pattern to the exclusion of all else. Mr Hands and Mr Denver deal with the political and social realities that appear either as a superstructure on the vast administrative machine or as a genuine struggle for control of that machine. The last generation of the Council's history was not only one of great departments and powerful officers, but one of strong contention between the Labour and Conservative Parties.

The circumstances of this period brought increased vitality into council debates, closer party control of aldermanic appointments, relatively high polling figures at elections and fewer uncontested seats than at any time in the century. Interestingly, the new, apparently divisive, political ethos was ultimately absorbed and seemingly accepted by senior officers, and especially by the clerks, because it was supposed to lead to co-ordination of policies across departments, and to what passed for 'ministerial' government with party direction of chairmen – a plausible theory which involves consideration of how deep, and in what detail, the direction went. Administration became vastly more complex; and, inevitably, more power came into the hands of those who directed both the central and the divisional machinery. Power, professionalisation and specialisation in this later age may be contrasted, in retrospect, with the ostensibly much clearer situation of the early and middle periods, with their 'professional mandarins' of chairmen, mainly consensus politics and a merely embryonic professionalism on the part of most staff members.

Lancashire tended to nurture its own administrative leaders in the geographical or dynastic senses; that is to say, where its clerks did not come across the borders from Liverpool or Manchester, they were (as after the 1940s) trained in the same department before succeeding their seniors, and such general factors were effective also in the cases of the medical officers, who in a succession of cases served for long periods in the county before taking the highest office. Chief education officers came from elsewhere, and then stayed on their respective pinnacles until retirement, with the exception of (Sir) George Gater, who left (in 1924) to take over education for the London County Council; where else, after all, could a Lancashire chief officer go?[39] The use of home-grown products is sometimes thought to indicate an innate conservatism, but this presumption may be misleading; the final determinants are surely the character of man, the nature of the period in which he operates and the opportunities with which he is presented – and, further, the nature of his own profession or technology. In this sense, Dr George Lissant Cox, Lancashire's fine tuberculosis officer, or Sir James Drake, its eminent postwar road-builder, were emphatically not conservative, whereas other senior officers were far more so. The age of the mandarins encouraged the more conservative approaches, even where an officer such as Lissant Cox, presented with social needs and opportunities, could transcend this conservatism (e.g. during the interwar years). The postwar years brought upheaval, change and experimentation, and officers had to keep up with the demands of the age. Meanwhile, the social composition of the Council changed drastically too, with managerial, trade union and female members playing a far greater role.

Leaving aside the more subtle processes of change, the reader should remember one thing. The near-marvellous aspect of the Lancashire County Council and its administrative machine may be summed up in a few words – this great agglomeration of sometimes disparate services, in a supremely sprawling and capriciously shaped geographical area, actually worked. Moreover, during some crucial periods it worked with some semblance of democracy, or at least it brought a large number of public representatives, from more than a hundred districts as well as from the County Council, into some kind of formal contact with parts of the machinery described. The same cannot be said of the statutory bodies that now provide some key regional services. Here we shall follow Mr Jeffrey Stanyer's advice[40] and avoid moralising, for efficiency may be more important than democracy. The reader can in any case draw his own conclusions.

Although acknowledgements are given elsewhere, one falls naturally into place in this final few words of introduction. In 1937 the County Council received a petition from the Central Lancashire Branch of the Historical Association asking for the establishment of a county 'muniment room'. The threat of wartime destruction of documents led to the formation of a Record Office in March 1940, and in this way one of the most famous county record offices in England (which commenced life with Mr R. Sharpe France, county archivist until 1976, as its sole staff member) began to evolve into the widely popular institution that now exists, with its staff of qualified assistant archivists and its county archaeologist.

This volume was commissioned when the old Lancashire County Council was moving towards its demise during the period 1972–4. The Lancashire County Record Office, which was taking over many tons of documents from the old Council for storage and cataloguing, immediately offered its help, and all those who have contributed to the volume have made use of its facilities. The Council's main departments, it need scarcely be added, were no less helpful, and the University of Lancaster research team played some part in the identification and salving of useful documents. All that need be added is that great tracts of fascinating material await their investigators. This book should be the beginning of research, and will certainly not be its conclusion.

PART II
The Old Order
1889-1929

CHAPTER 2

The Growth and Range of County Services

As has been shown, county government had deep roots in the past, and the Lancashire County Council of 1889 was partially built on existing institutions: a committee system previously designed to serve the Annual General Sessions, a police organisation and an Office of the Clerk of the Peace, as well as an administration serving justice, gaols and lunatic asylums. In fundamentals, county government in Lancashire did not differ from that in other counties. A glance at the constitution of Lancashire County Council soon after its formation shows that it shared features in common with (say) Northumberland, Cheshire and Shropshire.[1] Each had a Finance Committee, and a Standing Joint Committee to deal with the police and a Roads and Bridges Committee, plus a committee to control cattle disease (known in Lancashire as the Executive Cattle Plague Committee). Northumberland and Cheshire had committees to deal with local asylum administration, but it is at this point that Lancashire's uniqueness begins to emerge. The sheer size of the county and its requirements meant that several of the main committees had sub-committees which were sub-regional, so that the Finance Committee had sub-committees (as Dr Davie shows, below[2]) for each Quarter Sessions district in Lancashire, and so did the Executive Cattle Plague Committee. The Northumberland Roads and Bridges Committee had no sub-committee, while Lancashire's had three by 1891.[3] Cheshire, like Lancashire, had a Parliamentary Committee by 1891 (i.e. a body charged with attention to parliamentary bills and the legal protection of the county's boundaries and interests), but other counties often did not, just as many of them were slow to acquire Public Health Committees.

Lancashire's Lunatic Asylum Committee was a massive affair with, as well as twenty-seven nominated county councillors on it, three rep-

TABLE 2.1

Committees and the Membership Numbers in Lancashire County Council*

	1891	1909	1929
Standing committees			
Finance	29 – (4)	29 – (4)	29 – (4)
Main Roads and Bridges	36 – (3)	36 – (2)	36 – (2)
Parliamentary	20	20	20
Public Health	20	20	27 (and Housing)
Technical Instruction	27	54 – (10) Education	54 – (1)
Executive Cattle Plague	18 – (5)	38 – (2) Diseases of Animals	20 – (12)
Smallholdings and Allotments / Agricultural		36	— (merged with Agricultural)
Financial Adjustment	9		
Railway and Canal Rates	10		
Midwives Act		15	15
Local Pensions		(n.s.)	18
Tuberculosis			(n.s.)
Committee of Chairmen			(n.s.)
Standing Joint (Police)	18	18	18
Joint committees (county members only)			
(Joint) County Rate	12	12	12
Lunatic Asylum	27 – (4)	38 – (4)	16
Manchester Assize Courts	6	4	4
Mersey & Irwell Joint Boards	8	8	8
Ribble Fishery Board	9	9	9
Lune, Wyre etc. Fishery	12+	12+	
Kent, Bela etc. Fishery	12+	12+	
Lancashire Sea Fisheries (and Western)	12	8	8
Lancashire Inebriates Act	18	18 – (3)	

*Lancashire County Council members only counted in the case of joint bodies; numbers of sub-committees are given in parentheses. Sub-committees include district or special area committees, except in the case of education.

resentatives from each of sixteen county boroughs. The joint bodies proliferated more than in the case of any other county, although Cheshire had more committees (twenty-two in 1892) but fewer sub-committees. If we count all the Lancashire sub-committees on which a councillor could possibly have served, there were at least seventeen before the First World War, in addition to a further eighteen standing committees or joint bodies and innumerable local school governorships or managerships (i.e. after 1902). The disparate yet far-reaching interests of county government are portrayed in Table 2.1, which omits a few ephemeral or special committees (like an early one on *The Printed Proceedings of Sub-Committees!*). As can be seen, the committee pattern tended to become more varied as time went on, although there were also some simplifications, in that several interests (including allotments, animal diseases, land drainage) were combined in the Lancashire Agricultural Committee in 1920. Education added a string of sub-committees by 1913, and of all the services provided by county authorities, this experienced the most momentous developments, especially after the Act of 1902. The Education Department, too, established District Committees for Higher and Elementary Education; it was the first authority in England to organise itself in such a manner (see Chapter 5). The ensuing development of a school health service led the County Council straight into the field of social welfare as well as preventive medicine; so, indeed, did the National Insurance Act of 1911, which empowered county councils to form tuberculosis committees.

The Council's activities, then, as is indicated by Table 2.1, fell into six main areas: the traditional concern with justice and the police, and a similar one with lunatic asylums, followed by roads, agriculture and fisheries, education and incidental matters relative to the environment such as sanitation and control of pollution. Lancashire made rapid strides in technical education in the nineties, although the cut-price evening class system, so far behind lavish continental provisions of technical instruction, was a modest enough thing in itself; and the successor body, the county Education Committee (1903), simply became the controller of a vast organisation inheriting numerous sub-standard voluntary and church schools. Meanwhile, the Education (Administrative Provisions) Act of 1907 in effect inaugurated school health services, which meant that the personal service aspect of the Council's activities was much augmented.

County administration, then, was therefore a collector of tasks from central government; the operator of a variety of functions bestowed with little thought of interrelation and integration of groups of services, except in so far as one occasionally grew out of another, as in the instance given in the previous sentence. It has been estimated that some 227 Acts of Parliament affected county government between 1889 and 1929,[4] although only a few of these, including the examples already given, had considerable repercussions. The County Council itself introduced a number of parliamentary enactments, including the Lancashire Inebriates Acts Board Act of 1900, which diverted the attention of some councillors temporarily from the mentally ill to the problems of alcoholics. Otherwise, the recognised county role of collector of functions was to have ultimately serious effects, especially in a great county like Lancashire, which had the necessary means of stimuli, as well as the obligation, to develop great departments, with their own insularities and professional preoccupations.

Although, unhappily, we have few accurate statistics relating to administrative staff at County Hall before 1914, we do have indicative items in the Council's published accounts for its early years. The Clerk of the Peace, F. C. Hulton, received a salary of £4500, out of which he had to pay his two deputies; the quite substantial residue, vastly augmented in the time of Hulton's successor, Sir Harcourt Clare, may be compared with the salary offered to the clerk in the smaller county of Hertfordshire, £950 in 1890.[5] The Lancashire treasurer (1897) was paid £1884 for his own salary and that of a number of clerks, whereas his Hertfordshire opposite number received £250.[6] Lancashire's chief constable received £1000 per annum, whereas the Hertfordshire officer had only £540 in 1890.[7] On the side of clerical labour, however, the Lancashire authority expected much for very little money, and the continual references to 'economy and efficiency' on the part of council leaders may be taken to mean that they expected chief officers to drive the lesser mortals they employed: only £1453 was allotted for the payment of clerks in the Clerk of the Peace's office in 1897,[8] a figure suggesting that not more than fifteen clerks were employed there. The volume of work exacted from even the more senior staff may be gauged from the case of Mr J. E. Gee, chief clerk to the medical officer of health, who received a mere £91 in 1897, although Mr Gee was in fact in charge of the small department in his chief officer's absence.[9]

Despite such concern over economy, the steady increase of legal and administrative obligations placed upon the Council led to a steady growth in staffing[10] which was perceptible even in the economically rather lean Edwardian years; that is to say, the marked development of such services as education, school health, road maintenance and improvement, and the strengthening of the police force in what was still an area of growing population, all led to more council expenditure in those departments. The Lancashire cotton industry was, of course, in the final stages of its maturity and enjoying a resounding success in overseas markets; but real wages were falling in these prewar years, and Lancashire life had many grim and evil corners. Yet the evidence of an uneven and sporadic growth of social welfare is there, and the latter was to surge forth remarkably after the First World War, in intention and also in execution, as far as the health and welfare services were concerned. The growth of services, implicit in the data given in Table 2.2, shows quite impressively that even the local government of pre-1929 was a developing area. The largest growth in the entire period covered was in personal services (education, health, welfare), and it may be that these particulars express much more clearly the character and emphasis of the authority's work at successive stages, in that the personnel listed were the people who made decisions, carried out instructions, dealt with public problems and shaped the day-to-day work of the Lancashire Council. The list does not include teachers and policemen, nor does it count the accredited midwives under the general direction of the Midwives Act Committee and medical officer. A large part of the labour incidentally employed by the Council – for instance, that of roadmen – is also not included, but the picture is clear enough. The Council was by degrees concerning itself with people far more, and with institutions rather less.

Although central control was strong, and the County Hall staff (as is implicit in Table 2.2) was growing considerably, there were also more workers out in the field as time went on. As some oral evidence shows, central control did not, up to an undetermined critical point, mean depersonalised relations between the central administration and the fieldworker (school nurse, health visitor or other staff member). Individual departmental staffs were still small enough to know their most distant outdoor members well.[11] The county had long been divided for specific administrative purposes, and the county road surveyors of 1889, with their northern, eastern and southern districts, represented the original divisional 'outdoor' officers.[12] By 1930 there were no fewer than 203 outdoor officials who, during the year ending in the March, had made 41,405 journeys for which expenses were paid – roughly four journeys a week. About one-third of the Council's staff was so engaged, and about half of the outdoor staff used motorcars or motorcycles.[13] The age of the motor vehicle was beginning to affect county government by influencing concepts of viable administrative regions, divisions or districts. At this period, however (i.e. in 1930), only district surveyors and peripatetic instructors in agriculture were provided with cars by the Council.[14]

TABLE 2.2
Manpower Growth in Lancashire County Council Employees 1913–30

General areas and departments	1913–14 Officials	Total salaries	1921–2 Officials	Total salaries	1929–30 Officials	Total salaries
		£		£		£
Common service						
Clerk of Council	28	8,546	31	19,273	34	20,030
Treasurer	36	8,160	65	23,624	91	22,808
Architect	24	5,528	45	22,616	65	21,056
Totals	88	22,234	141	65,513	190	63,894
Education						
Higher Education	12	2,208	22	8,767	24	7,825
Elementary Education	25	4,290	36	16,029	35	12,653
Education, Agricultural	15	2,564	20	6,059	21	6,017
Education, Library	—	—	—	—	6	1,382
Education Accounts	10	1,460	11	4,328	11	3,489
Totals	62	10,512	89	24,183	98	31,366
Health/Welfare						
School medical staff	9	1,625	12	6,009	22	7,028
School medical officers	10	2,825	17	15,850	18	17,200
Dental surgeons	—	—	3	1,350	14	8,025
School nurses	19	1,503	54	13,816	61	13,829
Orthopaedic nurses	—	—	—	—	3	860
Tuberculosis (central)	8	1,207	21	7,584	24	7,551
Tuberculosis (medical officers)	7	2,240	17	16,590	18	15,010
Tuberculosis (health visitors)	—	—	30	7,446	33	7,328
Tuberculosis (dispensary clerks)	—	—	10	2,107	12	2,353
Totals	52	9,300	164	70,752	205	79,184
Environmental health						
Public health	10	2,071	16	7,207	20	6,807
Sanitary inspectors	4	850	4	2,354	4	2,050
Analyst	7	1,789	8	3,924	8	3,321
Totals	21	4,710	28	13,485	32	12,178
Highways and Bridges	25	5,255	30	14,912	59	23,324
Other						
Local taxation	11	1,014	9	3,224	7	2,328
Lancashire agricultural	3	354	9	3,100	11	3,519
Global totals	264	53,489	470	206,169	601	215,793
Clerical staff, all departments	151		251		305	

The motorcar and 'waggon' were beginning to have an effect on county roads as early as 1902.[15] As Dr Davie makes clear below,[16] the heavier traffic and vehicles of the age were damaging county bridges regularly after 1905, and there was a considerable dust nuisance affecting drivers, pedestrians and cyclists. This, too, was the age of the electric tramway, which displaced the horse tram and which, by about 1912, made it possible to travel up to thirty miles across the south-east Lancashire conurbation by continuous use of tram transport. The horses and drays of the still-thriving pre-1914 Lancashire cotton industry hammered at granite setts, and increases in road expenditure were regular and marked. After the intermission of the First World War, the motor vehicle multiplied in numbers and made even greater demands on road engineers: the trams, meanwhile, lasted until the end of this period, but were themselves displaced by trackless motor vehicles after 1930, leaving more problems in the form of useless tram rails.

The postwar organisation of the Highways and Bridges Department was much strengthened, and its technical staff of engineers, surveyors and draughtsmen was increased from eleven in 1914 to thirty-six in 1929.[17] The relatively massive expenditure of the Department, however, is not explained by facts like these, but by the great number of road-workers engaged by the surveyors – as many as 2480 at one time by 1931.[18] The labour costs of road improvement are reflected in these growth figures: from a total expenditure of £174,846 in 1903–04[19] to £262,706 in 1913-14, and well over the million mark by the later twenties.

The police, affected as they were by environmental factors like roads and road traffic, naturally became more communications-conscious in the course of time. But, although they had telephones at their disposal before the First World War, the adoption of motor transport gave only limited advantages to officers, when a journey from Preston to a distant police station in Lancashire could still, in interwar road conditions, occupy two-and-a-half hours.[20] It is probably fair to say that the police were, before and during this period, the most traditionally minded of county servants, and that their organisation (described in Chapter 8) changed comparatively little.

Lancashire's most significant achievement, in the two decades or so before 1929, was the building of a tuberculosis service. This advance, a bold and humane response to a major scourge of the industrial society of the time, is outlined in the following chapter. The scope of the service is indicated in Table 2.2; the gross expenditure on it, only £2395 for 1913-14, had risen to £154,450 during 1921-2. Its value is to be measured not only in the lives it saved or repaired; it was a model for the rest of the country to follow.[21]

The growth of the remaining health services, while considerable, was somewhat less spectacular. There was some marked achievement on the school front; where there had been one school clinic in the administrative county in 1914, there were over thirty by 1929, and arrangements had been made 'with 22 Hospitals for the treatment of tonsils and adenoids and eye defects'.[22] Nor should we forget that the social welfare of the period was tested in economic and social conditions that were often sad and ugly; the great growth of county health and welfare services, inadequate as it may have been when seen in terms of need, was in part a response to the dire requirements of the time, as seen through the eyes of the newly formed Ministry of Health (1919), as well as those of the local councillors. It is a sad reminder of the period that up to £20,000 a year could be spent by the Council on the feeding of necessitous schoolchildren. Yet the idea that the children of the nation were also its capital had already struck roots, and following the Maternity and Child Welfare Act of 1918, a Child Welfare Sub-Committee of the Council, under the guidance of the medical officer, worked in co-operation with the School Medical Sub-Committee of the Education Committee, with the result that child welfare centres and school clinics were often one unit. The areas that these served were also made into administrative districts for the supervision of midwives (in 1920) by the assistant county medical officer of health. As the standard of midwifery rose, so the incidence of deaths at birth declined steadily.

The post-1918 surge of welfare and other services is an interesting phenomenon, which in part anticipated the greater and more significant wave of welfare legislation following 1944. In each case the Council merely followed national policy, only in a few sectors showing initiatives or originality on its own account. Its activities were widely diffused, if greater in scale than any other non-metropolitan authority, and its problems were also those of scale and administration. The Local Government Act of 1929 was instrumental in bringing about a greater upheaval in county welfare and other services than any that had preceded it, save perhaps the Education Act of 1902.

A sense of the administrative and financial involvement of the Council, and of the social and political backgrounds of those responsible for its work, is conveyed in the following two chapters. The meticulous scholarship of Dr A. F. Davie spells out the organisational and legal implications of the committee system before 1929, and Mr Hands and Mr Denver look at the councillors themselves.

CHAPTER 3

Administration and Finance

THE Local Government Act of 1888 established county councils for every administrative county in England and Wales, and transferred to them, from 1 April 1889, the administrative business hitherto carried on by the county justices of the peace in Quarter Sessions assembled. In Lancashire this administrative business had been transacted at a special court – the Court of Annual General Sessions – established for that purpose under the Lancashire Sessions Act of 1798. To the new county councils was transferred the making and levying of all county rates, their application and expenditure, the preparation and revision of a standard for the county rates, the borrowing of money and the passing of accounts, as well as the appointment and removal of all county officers,[1] whose salaries were paid out of county rates, and all county property, including assizes courts and police stations. County councils became responsible for the provision, maintenance and repair of all main roads, of county and Hundred bridges and of county asylums and for the establishment and maintenance of, or contributions towards, reformatory and industrial schools. County councils also became the local authority under various acts relating to contagious diseases of animals, wild birds, destructive insects, weights and measures and gas meters. A register of parliamentary voters had to be compiled for county constituencies and these had to be divided into polling districts. Lastly, coroners, hitherto elected by the freeholders of the county, were now appointed by the county councils.

As has been shown, Lancashire County Council was fortunate in that the Court of Annual General Sessions, which for some ninety years had administered the county, had developed a quite comprehensive system of administration involving a committee system. It was, therefore, a question of deciding which committees to retain and what new committees were required. As will be clear, not all committees generated or required a large

administrative staff, but some idea of the staffing behind the main committees, like Finance, can be gleaned from Table 2.2 above.

The main committees of the County Council were termed 'standing',
i.e. permanent, but they were elected annually. The Council decided not
to form a General Purposes Committee, which under the justices had never
performed any important function. The most prominent committee
formed, therefore, was the statutorily required Finance Committee. Orders
for the payment of sums from the county fund could not be made, and
any debt or liability could not be incurred, except if under fifty pounds,
unless authorised by a resolution of the Council upon the recommendation
of the Finance Committee. At the beginning of each financial year
the Finance Committee had to present to the Council an estimate of
expenditure for each six months of that year, and also had to
present yearly in March the county accounts for the current financial
year.

In Lancashire, the Finance Committee was afforded the power of
ordering the county treasurer to make all payments as they fell due. To
the committee, too, was entrusted the superintendence of all county
buildings, including courthouses, and all matters in connection with
weights and measures and reformatory and industrial schools were referred
to it.[2] The securities to be given by all county officers entrusted with
money, previously a function of the General Purposes Committee of the
Annual General Sessions, were now to be determined by the Finance
Committee. As the County Council was responsible for the salaries and
expenses of the county coroners, the examination of their accounts was
undertaken by the Finance Committee. Where a coroner's district included
a county borough, a new appointment was made by a joint committee,
but otherwise all matters in connection with a new appointment made by
the Council itself were referred to the Finance Committee.

Under the 1888 Act, all towns with a population of 50,000 and over
became county boroughs and were excluded from the control of the
Council, which body administered the rest of the county termed the
'administrative county'. Provision was therefore made under the Act for
the adjustment of financial arrangements between the County Council and
these county boroughs. In Lancashire, an Adjustment Committee of
nine members was formed to carry on negotiations with the Lancashire
county boroughs and, failing settlements, to present cases to the Commissioners set up under the Act. This committee functioned until 1906,
by which time most of the adjustments had been determined, and then
its functions were transferred to the Finance Committee.[3] This committee
was entrusted, from time to time, with matters that did not appear to
come within the terms of reference of any other committee, and was there-

fore in effect (at least until the end of the First World War) also a general purposes committee.

The membership of the committee was settled at twenty-nine members.[4] The District Finance Committees, composed of members of the committee resident in the Quarter Sessions areas, established by the Annual General Sessions, were retained as sub-committees with a supervising function within their areas. The Finance Committee met monthly and transacted a considerable volume of business. It was fortunate to have in its early years an experienced county treasurer, Henry Alison,[5] who had been since 1860 county treasurer under the justices; and it became, under pressure of events, the key committee of the Council.

Under the 1888 Act a county council was authorised to oppose Bills in Parliament by way of petition but not itself to promote Bills. Lancashire County Council, however, being the successor to the Annual General Sessions, which had exercised that power, claimed and in fact exercised the power of promoting Bills and securing Acts of Parliament. The position was regularised by the County Councils (Bills in Parliament) Act of 1903, which empowered all county councils to promote Bills in Parliament.

In 1889 Lancashire County Council formed a Parliamentary Committee which was required to watch all Bills introduced into Parliament that might affect the interests of the Council, especially in the case of Lancashire local Bills, and to direct the attention of the Council to parliamentary committees of enquiry and royal commissions. Much central government legislation over the extensions of Lancashire county boroughs and in connection with water boards, railways, canals, tramways, gas undertakings and electric lighting affected county interests. The Parliamentary Committee's function was to see that county interests in connection with county roads, and financial adjustments in the case of county borough extensions, were safeguarded either by the insertion of appropriate clauses in the Bill in question or by the withdrawal of objectionable clauses. Often this was done by agreement, but if not, on the Committee's recommendation, the Council would resolve to present a petition against the relevant Bill to Parliament and the steps to secure this were undertaken by the Parliamentary Committee.

The Local Government Act of 1894, as we have seen, laid upon the county councils the duty of creating a new system of 'local' government[6] – in Lancashire out of the former system of local boards, improvement commissioners, sanitary districts, highway boards and highway parishes. The financial and sanitary sections of the Act were referred to the Finance and Public Health Committees respectively, but the rest of the powers and duties of the county council under the Act were delegated to the Parliamentary Committee. This entailed much work in connection with local councils, their wards and their boundaries. The Local Government (Elections) Act of 1896 authorised county councils to resolve or remove any difficulties in the holding of district council and parish council elections and the elections of Boards of Guardians and to make regulations in connection with them. In 1896 the powers and duties of the council under these two headings were delegated to the Parliamentary Committee, which was also responsible for dealing with county council elections and electoral areas. Yearly, therefore, the Committee was involved in settling dates of elections, making arrangements for elections if necessary, and ordering fresh elections on the death of a candidate or if any irregularity had occurred. On all these matters the Committee made recommendations to the County Council. Further powers were delegated to the Parliamentary Committee under the Small Dwellings Acquisition Act of 1899, the Advertisements Regulation Acts and the Ancient Monuments Protection Acts, but the powers under these Acts were little used.

The Parliamentary Committee, a main standing committee of the County Council, because of the volume of business transacted often met twenty times a year. It had no staff and no permanent sub-committees. Special committees of two or more members were appointed to deal with enquiries under the Acts or to examine into any matter requiring detailed investigation. On presenting a report to the main committee, these special committees lapsed.[7]

Lancashire County Council continued the Executive Cattle Plague Committee set up by the justices to carry out duties in connection with the Contagious Diseases (Animals) Acts and retained their Quarter Sessions area committees as sub-committees. In 1904 the Committee was renamed the Diseases of Animals Acts Committee[8] and the County Council's duties under the Wild Bird's Protection Acts were also, by that time, delegated to it. The area sub-committees were abolished and replaced by one sub-committee of eight members – the Finance and Acting Sub-Committee – to deal with the finance and implementation of the Committee's instructions. The main duties of the Committee were to make applications to the Home Secretary for orders in connection with wild birds and to the Board of Agriculture[9] over cattle diseases; to administer these and other orders of the ministeries within the administrative county; and to keep statistics and make returns of these to the ministeries. J. F. Hutchinson, veterinary surgeon of Chorley, was appointed to investigate cattle diseases, especially anthrax, but his appointment was terminated in 1912 and thereafter recourse was had to the bacteriological laboratories at the Universities of Manchester and Liverpool. An inspector was appointed to enforce the regulations over potato diseases.

Further duties accrued to the Committee on the passing of the
and Feeding Stuffs Act of 1893, the Dogs Act of 1906, the Destructive
Insects and Pests Act of 1907 and the Poisons and Pharmacy Act of 1908.
Under the first-named act, the Committee appointed the county analyst[10]
as its agricultural analyst, to be remunerated by fees for analysing
samples,[11] and police inspectors were appointed as official samplers.

As required under the Allotments Act of 1890, the County Council
established an Allotments Committee and, under the Small Holdings Act
of 1892, a Small Holdings Committee. These committees had the same
personnel under different chairmen. In 1907, however, the Small Holdings
and Allotments Act of that year laid upon the county councils the duty
of carrying into effect schemes for smallholdings, while allotments were
left to the parishes, the County Council acting only in the case of their
default. These two committees were amalgamated into one, entitled the
Small Holdings and Allotments Committee.[12] This new committee established sub-committees for each Hundred of the county, which included
representatives of the committee, local authorities in the Hundred and not
more than four co-opted members to conduct enquiries within their
Hundred. The Board of Agriculture and Fisheries appointed commissioners to enquire into the demand for smallholdings and how far the Act
was being implemented. Thereupon the Lancashire committee set themselves quite vigorously to the task of purchasing or leasing land for
smallholding estates. These had so increased by 1912 that a land agent[13]
was appointed, and he replaced the sub-committees, which were abolished.
The County Council also made loans to farmers to enable them to purchase their farms. By 1918 the Council had fifteen estates scattered over
the county from Heysham to Huyton aggregating 2612 acres, of which
2045 had been purchased and the rest leased. These had been converted
into 126 smallholdings, and the experience thus gained was to be of some
importance in settling ex-servicemen on the land.

During the First World War the Board of Agriculture and Fisheries
established for Lancashire a War Agricultural Committee and an Executive
Committee to deal with wartime agriculture in Lancashire. In 1919 these
were combined into one committee, the Agricultural Executive Committee.
In the same year, under the Land Drainage Act of 1918, the County
Council formed a Land Drainage Committee;[14] and at the same time
the membership of the Small Holdings and Allotments Committee and
the Diseases of Animals Acts Committee was in each case reduced. Thus
four separate committees dealt with the allied subjects of agriculture,
smallholdings, drainage and diseases of animals. On considering these facts
the County Council in 1920 merged the four committees into one – the
Lancashire Agricultural Committee – according to a scheme approved by

the Board. All the powers and duties of the County Council that had been delegated to the four superseded committees were now delegated to the Lancashire Agricultural Committee. To deal with such an extensive range of activities four main sub-committees were formed – an Accounts Sub-Committee, Small Holdings and Allotments, Diseases of Animals and Land Drainage – although there were others for specific purposes. A county Land Department was established under the county land agent. Agricultural education, however, remained with Lancashire Education Committee. The Lancashire Agricultural Committee had no authority to contract for the purchase or leasing of land, and it required the consent of the Finance Committee before increasing or reducing rents of smallholdings.

After the war the Government wished to settle ex-servicemen on the land and favoured the establishment of colonies on co-operative lines, these ideas having been embodied in two Acts passed in 1916 and 1918.[15] It was intended that county councils in this matter should act as agents of the Ministry of Agriculture and Fisheries. The idea was not favourably regarded in Lancashire. Instead, the Lancashire Agricultural Committee acted under the Land Settlement (Facilities) Act of 1919, under which the Government undertook to recompense local authorities for losses on smallholding schemes for each of the years 1919–20 to 1925–6, and county councils were authorised to make loans to smallholding tenants for the purchase of stock, seeds, fertilizers and implements. Another government idea authorised by the Act, and of which the Committee approved, was the provision of cottage holdings of an acre or less for the keeping of poultry and the cultivation of vegetables, which would be suitable for disabled ex-servicemen. In order to stimulate the provision of these holdings the Ministry made a grant of seventy-five per cent of any loss in providing them.

Several estates had been acquired by the Small Holdings and Allotments Committee in 1919. These were now sub-divided into smallholdings and a vigorous policy was pursued of building farmhouses, farm buildings and cottages: existing farmhouses were modernised including the installation of bathrooms; additional outbuildings, including dutch barns, were built; and sanitation and drainage were improved or provided on existing holdings. By 1929 the Committee had 4416 acres of land divided into 417 holdings of which 121 were cottage holdings.[16]

Lancashire County Council, in order to supersede the Acts that had established the drainage commissioners (whose powers had been transferred to them) and to secure additional powers, especially compulsory powers to compel landowners to clear watercourses, secured an Act of Parliament – the Lancashire County Council Drainage Act of 1921. Pursuant to this act the Drainage Sub-Committee established sub-committees for each drainage area, each consisting of equal numbers of members of the Drainage Sub-Committee and the area's rate-payers. A programme of drainage improvements to combat flooding was embarked upon – the deepening of rivers, the digging of new cuts and the strengthening of embankments – as schemes for unemployment relief. At first these schemes were left to the Clerk of the Works on each site, but in 1924 a drainage officer[17] was appointed and in 1926 an engineering assistant. The work was carried out by direct labour, suitable men being supplied from the nearest labour exchange. To deal with persistent flooding of the River Alt and the Primrose Brook, near Bootle, a resident engineer was appointed to work under the direction of the River Alt Sub-Committee. This programme of public works was followed by the even more important one of the East Lancashire Road.

After the war, the chief problem facing the Diseases of Animals Acts Committee concerned the great increase of rats and mice during the war; furthermore, the Rats and Mice Destruction Act of 1919 required county councils to enforce the Rats Order of 1918. By 1924, the Committee had appointed thirty-three veterinary inspectors, one or two for each police division, to deal with diseases of animals. Police officers continued to carry out duties in connection with Diseases of Animals Acts and as samplers under the Fertilizers and Feeding Stuffs Acts.

Under the 1888 Act, public health became a function of the County Council and a Public Health Committee was formed in Lancashire to enforce its powers under the Public Health Act, the Sale of Food and Drugs Acts and the Shops Acts. Until after the First World War it did not form any sub-committees, small special sub-committees being appointed as required for specific enquiries. The Council's powers and duties in connection with sanitary matters under the Local Government Act of 1894 were referred to the Committee. When in 1909 the Council delegated its powers under the Housing and Town Planning Act of 1909 to the Committee, it was renamed the Public Health and Housing Committee.[18] This committee was involved in much detailed work over applications for opening and closing hours and late nights under the Shops Acts and with local authorities over sewage treatment and disposal, water supplies and the oversight of new housing, and it authorised all appointments of medical officers of health and inspectors of nuisances for county districts.[19] Much of the work of administration was left to the Committee's officers – a county medical officer of health, a county analyst, a county sanitary inspector and a county shops inspector.

The formation of a Ministry of Health in 1919 to replace the Local Government Board gave a new impetus to the provision of health services for the nation, and a series of Acts placed new responsibilities on the county councils. The Maternity and Child Welfare Act of 1918 required county councils to appoint committees to carry out its provisions, but Lancashire County Council appointed the Public Health and Housing Committee to do this work. The Council also amalgamated the school medical and child welfare medical staffs, putting them under the control of the county medical officer of health, although these services continued to be administered separately by the respective committees. The Public Health and Housing Committee formed a Child Welfare Sub-Committee to which were appointed two co-opted women members. This sub-committee worked in close co-operation with the School Medical Sub-Committee of the Lancashire Education Committee, and occasionally these two sub-committees formed a joint sub-committee to deal with specific matters, especially appointments. By 1929 a county day nursery had been established at Leyland and fifty-seven child welfare centres had been set up. Many of these centres were joint school clinics and child welfare centres, and all were staffed by school medical officers and nurses who were both school nurses and health visitors.

Lancashire County Council also designated the Public Health and Housing Committee as its committee under the Blind Persons Act of 1920. A Sub-Committee for the Blind was formed, but it was decided to deal with the administrative county's blind through voluntary societies and other local authorities.[20] Accordingly use was made of seventeen voluntary societies for the care of the blind centred on Lancashire boroughs, and annual grants were made to them. Agreements were made with nine work-shops for the blind in Lancashire towns to train and employ county blind workers. Lastly, a scheme for the maintenance of unemployable blind persons was put into force. The responsibility for the education and training of blind children, however, remained with Lancashire Education Committee.

A wartime regulation, the Public Health (Venereal Diseases) Regulation of 1916, placed on county councils and county borough councils the responsibility for the treatment of venereal diseases. As a health matter this duty was delegated to the Public Health and Housing Committee. After the war a sub-committee was formed to initiate and conduct a drive to combat these diseases and prevent their spreading, and propaganda by lectures and leaflets was carried on in all county districts. Medical officers who were willing to act were designated by the County Council for their treatment, and unqualified persons so doing were prosecuted at the instance of the sub-committee.

The Milk (Special Designations) Order of 1923 placed on the Committee the duty of issuing milk licences in the administrative county to sellers and producers of Grade A milk, and the Milk and Dairies Order of 1926 the duty of keeping a register of cow keepers and particulars of their premises. Additional work, too, was placed upon the county analyst and his staff when the Milk and Dairies Consolidation Act of 1915 came into operation in 1925, in that it involved the examination of all dairy cattle and the taking and testing of samples for bovine tuberculosis. After the war, too, the Committee, whose sanitation staff now consisted of a chief sanitary inspector and three inspectors, vigorously pursued their duty of the sanitary inspection of county districts. This considerable increase of functions greatly increased the postwar importance of the Public Health and Housing Committee.

The National Insurance Act of 1911 imposed on the County Council duties in connection with the treatment and eradication of tuberculosis. After the First World War, the areas were reorganised into five larger areas with two small areas centred on the High Carley and Elswick sanatoria respectively.[21] By 1929 each of these areas had a central dispensary and branch dispensaries, to a total of twenty-four, and each area was staffed by a consultant tuberculosis officer, two assistant tuberculosis officers and from four to seven tuberculosis health visitors. The Council had now built eight sanatoria[22] with 431 beds and rented a further 481 beds in sanatoria or hospitals of other local authorities. The county register of tuberculosis patients held over eight thousand names, most being in their own homes and attending at dispensaries. The Committee provided on loan to these home-based patients bedsteads, bedding, mattresses, air cushions, bedrests and bedpans. Voluntary bodies supplemented the work of the Committee. As encouraged to do so by the Public Health (Tuberculosis) Act of 1921, after-care committees had been formed in nineteen county districts and they supplied these out-patients with milk, groceries, clothing and other necessities. The Council made grants to these voluntary bodies – at first 25 per cent and then $33\frac{1}{3}$ per cent of the amount of actual assistance distributed by them. In addition, several Relief Funds for Consumptives were operated and the money raised was used to give financial help to necessitous cases and provide additional equipment for dispensaries.[23]

The history of the County Education Committee and its work is outlined in the following chapter. As is there emphasised, its establishment following 1902 in place of the Technical Instruction Committee was one of the most momentous occurrences in the Council's existence, not only in terms of the sheer scale of operation, but also in terms of involvement in local educational activity, whether in the form of council school management and area administration, or of technical and adult education. Furthermore, the work of tending for necessitous, unhealthy or verminous schoolchildren brought county involvement in social welfare, and symbolised very appropriately the new spirit of the twentieth century. The work of the County Library, an offshoot of the Education Committee, is also dealt with elsewhere (see Chapter 10).

In 1920 a Committee of Chairmen was formed,[24] consisting of the chairman and vice-chairman of the County Council and the chairmen of all its standing committees, and this became a standing committee in 1927. Its function was to consider the numbers and salaries of the staffs of the various committees, new scales of salaries proposed and any changes in existing scales and to make recommendations thereon. Any proposal to create a new post had to be referred to this committee and, if approved, passed to the Finance Committee which, if it concurred, made a recommendation for county council approval. The control of the County Architect's Department was transferred from the Finance Committee to the new committee. The Committee was dissolved in 1931 and replaced by a Co-ordination Committee.

Besides the standing or permanent committees of the County Council, the Council participated in a number of joint committees, the most important being the Standing Joint Committee for the Police.[25] Valuations for rateable purposes were made for the geographical county, and so in 1890 a County Rate Joint Committee was formed, to carry through valuations of the county, to hear appeals and to deal with them. The twelve county council members of this committee also formed a County Rate Committee, which acted as a 'go-between' and presented the valuations arrived at to the County Council for adoption. Under the Rating and Valuation Act of 1925 a County Valuation Committee was formed but it did not function until 1929.

The County Council inherited from the justices four county lunatic asylums, situated at Lancaster, Prestwich, Rainhill and Whittingham; and two others were built at Winwick and Whalley. The asylums were administered by a joint committee of the Council and the Lancashire county boroughs, but under the Lancashire Lunatic Asylums and Other Powers Act of 1891 this committee was replaced by a Lancashire Asylums Board. At first the Board precepted for its expenses on its constituent authorities according to their rateable values. This was felt to be unjust, however, so from 1902 the precepts were made according to the user[26] of the asylums, and in 1913 representation on the Board was also made according to user. Under the Inebriates Act of 1898 an Inebriates Act Board was formed, with representatives of the Council and the county boroughs[27] on it. An Inebriates Institute was established at Langho near Blackburn, and had a chequered existence. The Board was dissolved and the Institute closed in 1923.

Besides the ordinarily accepted spheres of local government, Lancashire

County Councils became involved in river and sea fisheries. By 1889 three salmon fishery boards affecting northern Lancashire had been established;[28] these now became the concern of the county councils in whose areas their districts lay, and the boards became representative of these county councils. These boards – the Kent, Bela, Winster, Leven and Duddon Fishery Board, the Lune, Keer and Cocker Fishery Board and the Ribble Fishery Board[29] – appointed bailiffs, took legal proceedings over illegal fishing, executed works for the removal of river obstructions and the improvement of fisheries and issued fishing licences. Their accounts were audited and allowed by the county councils concerned.

Under the Sea Fisheries Regulation Act of 1888 Lancashire, Cumberland and Cheshire, on application to the Board of Trade, secured the formation of a Lancashire Sea Fisheries District stretching from Cumberland to Cheshire, and a joint committee was established in 1890. Then, in 1900,[30] the Western Sea Fisheries District was amalgamated with it to form the Lancashire and Western Sea Fisheries District, stretching from Haverigg Point in Cumberland to Pembroke, which was also administered by a joint committee.[31] As this was a large undertaking, the district was divided into four areas of sub-districts, each with bailiffs and in two cases assistant bailiffs, and the whole placed under a superintendent, assisted by a small clerical staff. A marine laboratory was established at Piel[32] in north Lancashire. The chief duties of the Joint Committee were to foster the development of sea and shore fisheries including shellfish, to make by-laws to regulate fishing, and to research into the food supplies, migration and reproduction of fish. The Joint Committee met quarterly at Chester, so that Lancashire County Council found it difficult to find members of the council willing to serve and, therefore, appointed some non-members as its representatives. The Joint Committee precepted for its expenses on its constituent authorities.

Two other joint committees formed in 1891[34] to act under the provisions of the Rivers Pollution (Prevention) Act of 1876 were the Mersey and Irwell Joint Committee and the Ribble Watershed Joint Committee. Each of these joint committees appointed a general inspector and sub-inspectors, and were concerned with effluents from sewage works and industrial concerns in their districts; their proceedings dealt with reports on these matters, and authorising representations to be made to local authorities and works over their findings. By patient and persistent effort the joint committees and their officials secured an improvement and the three rivers became less polluted. The Manchester Assizes Courts Committee was also a joint committee which was entrusted with the management of these courts.

The Annual General Sessions had appointed all committees on a Quarter Sessions area basis – the areas served respectively by the Quarter Sessions

Court held at Lancaster (Lonsdale Hundred), Preston (Amounderness, Blackburn and Leyland Hundreds), Manchester (Salford Hundred) and Liverpool (West Derby Hundred) – in order that each standing committee should be representative of each part of the county. The County Council, too, felt that it was right and proper that each committee should be a micro-cosm of the County Council and so continued the practice. The agreed ratio[34] was Lancaster 1, Preston 2, Salford 3 and West Derby 3, but when Liverpool was considerably extended, resulting in a loss of rateable value in West Derby Hundred in 1902, the ratio was amended to Lancaster 2, Preston 5, Salford 6 and West Derby 5. At the same time the ratio for county aldermen was also amended to Lancaster 3, Preston 11, Salford 12 and West Derby 9. The members of the Council for each sessions area formed a committee under a chairman, which yearly nominated its members to the various committees. The chairman of each area committee, by negotiation, tried to ensure that each member was appointed to a com-mittee for which he had special qualifications or an interest in its functions. This was not always possible, but yearly and also after a by-election an opportunity could arise for a member to change or exchange membership of a committee. This ratio was adhered to until 1920, when by resolution[35] it was suspended and thereafter kept for some committees and varied for others. The four sessions areas committees were abolished and replaced by one committee. The County Council automatically accepted all nomi-nations made. Most members of the Council served on two or three main committees, but some prominent members served on five or six.[36] Newcomers to the Council were usually initially appointed to only one committee. The Chairman and Vice-Chairman of the County Council were *ex officio* members[37] of all standing committees and the chairman of the Finance Committee was also a member of the main standing committees.

Most of the powers and duties of the County Council, except the levying of rates and the borrowing of money, were delegated to the various stand-ing committees, but all of them were required to report quarterly on the work done and to secure the Council's approval. In addition the Education Committee and the chief county officers made annual reports. The full County Council met only five times a year and its deliberations became ever more formal and its debates less frequent. Much business consisted in considering committee reports and confirming the recommendations contained therein; it approved estimates of expenditure, authorised the rates to be levied and loans to be raised, and had ultimate control over all county business.

County Finance

In its first year the revenue expenditure[38] of the County Council amounted to £408,782, and thereafter steadily increased to £675,000 for the year 1903–04. What caused a great increase in expenditure was the passing of the Education Act of 1902,[39] under which county councils became responsible for the costs of all secondary and the larger part of elementary education in their areas. In Lancashire expenditure for 1904–05 totalled £1,416,850, education accounting for 39 per cent of revenue expenditure. Expenditure decreased to £1,229,031 for the next year and was somewhat less for the next two years. From 1908–09 to 1917–18 expenditure steadily increased. Over these ten years the expenditure on roads increased by 15 per cent, on police by 23 per cent, on loan charges by 33.6 per cent and on education by 38 per cent; and new expenditure was incurred in respect of the County Council's tuberculosis scheme, which amounted to £61,701 for 1917–18. Total revenue expenditure for 1917–18 at £1,703,125 represented a four-fold increase during twenty-nine years.

After the First World War, as was to be expected, revenue expenditure took an upward turn, doubling itself in three years, and by 1928–9, at £4,771,232, represented an increase of 2.8 times that for the last year of the war. The increase recorded in these eleven years was not uniformly spead over county services. Road expenditure increased by some four times, as did also that for health and social services (still, however, a small percentage of county council expenditure), and costs for education and the police more than doubled. In these years expenditure on roads gradually replaced police expenditure as the second largest item of county expenditure, as can be seen in Table 3.1.

County revenue expenditure was financed from three sources – rates levied and orders precepted on the policed boroughs, government grants and other income. In Lancashire the system of rating involved much

TABLE 3.1
County Revenue Expenditure

	Education	Roads and Bridges	Police	Health and Social Services
1917–18	49.1	14.8	19.6	6.4
1928–9	47.6	21.7	16.3	9.3

differential rating. On the whole, administrative county rates were levied only for general purposes, higher education and the council's tuberculosis scheme. 'General purposes' covered the administration of justice, the maintenance and repair of county buildings, public health and the midwifery service, weights and measures, coroner's salaries and expenses, the County Architect's Department and, after 1921, the main roads. Previously each Hundred had been rated separately for its separate road costs.

In addition different rates for different purposes[40] were levied on areas less than the whole administrative county. The county police area excluded five non-county boroughs which had their own police forces. The police area rate met the costs of the police headquarters in Preston, and separate divisional police rates were levied to meet their separate divisional police costs. The county elementary school area excluded the Part III authorities. The boroughs of Clitheroe and Lancaster and the townships of Altcar and Winwick-with-Hulme were exempt from the county bridge rate. The Maternity and Child Welfare area excluded eighteen non-county boroughs and twenty-four urban districts, the Shops Act area nineteen non-county boroughs and forty urban districts, and the Advertisement Regulation Act area nineteen non-county boroughs and thirty-four urban districts. Townships within parliamentary boroughs were exempt from the rate levied under the Representation of the People Act; townships that had adopted the Public Libraries Acts were not rates for libraries; and the rate under the Gas Regulation Act of 1920 was paid only by townships for which the Council had appointed gas examiners. The Hundred of Salford was rated separately for the salary and expenses of the chairman of Salford Quarter Sessions, and the Manchester Police Division for the salary and expenses of its stipendiary magistrate. Lastly, the Hundreds of Amounderness, Blackburn and Leyland were also rated separately for the salary and expenses of the chairman of Preston Quarter Sessions.

The County Council yearly settled the rates in the pound to be levied for each of the purposes on their respective areas, and the total of these rates was returned as the county rate in the pound levied for the year to the Local Government Board and its successor the Ministry of Health. In the yearly issued booklet of county accounts, however, the county rate was shown as a total rate in the pound levied on each police division, and because of differential rating the rate in the pound was different for each police division. Up to 1927, county precepts or demands for county rates were sent to the twenty-six Boards of Guardians in the county; they were collected along with the poor rates by the overseers of the poor in each parish, sent by them to the clerks of the Boards of Guardians and by them remitted to the County Treasurer. In the case of rates not being paid, the Council authorised warrants for non-payment against the overseers of the defaulting parishes unless the rates were paid in the meantime. Arrears of rates unpaid reached a peak of £87,447 (4.9 per cent) in 1925 but decreased to £1371 by 1928. The first rate levied by the Council for the year 1889–90 was a modest 6.35d in the pound, and this was but little increased until the costs of education were placed upon the County Council, whereupon the rate rose steadily to 23.2d in the pound for 1913–14. After the war the rate levied rose sharply, 1921–2 being the peak year. The rates in the pound levied by Lancashire County Council, however, were comparable with those by the West Riding of Yorkshire, and were far below those levied by the Lancashire cities of Liverpool and Manchester, as is shown in Table 3.2.[41]

TABLE 3.2
Rates Levied by Selected County/Borough Councils

	Lancashire	West Riding	Liverpool	Manchester
1919–20	44d	44.25d	124d	115.75d
1921–2	68.4d	68.4d	173.75d	141.25d
1928–9	65.2d	60d	113.8d	122.2d

Rates were levied on the rateable value of land and property as valued for the poor rate up to 1896. In that year the Agricultural Rates Act in effect halved the rateable value of agricultural land, and rates were levied on the 'assessable' value rather than the rateable value: the administrative county lost £581,928 thereby in rateable value for the year 1897. More serious still was the loss of rateable value owing to the extensions of county boroughs to a gross amount of £3,141,734. Nevertheless, increases in the valuation of property and new property coming in for valuation afforded compensation for such losses so that the valuation made in 1917 at £8,998,244 was only 1.4 per cent under that for 1895. Under the Agricultural Rates Act of 1923, agricultural land was now rated at a quarter of its rateable value and rates were now levied on the 'reduced assessable value' of the administrative county. The new valuation made in 1928 at £11,058,132 was £750,029 less than the full rateable value of the administrative county. Up to 1925, the different valuations were carried through by the County Rate Joint Committee on returns made by the overseers of the poor to the clerks of the Boards of Guardians. The Rating and Valuation Act of 1925 made the eighteen county boroughs, nineteen non-county boroughs, eighty-two urban districts and nineteen rural districts the rating authorities in Lancashire. From 1927, therefore, valuation returns were made by the 138 local authorities in the geographical county, and county rates were collected from the 120 local authorities in the administrative county.

Government grants took several forms. Under the 1888 Act the proceeds of the local taxation licences and part of the probate duty were paid to county councils. In Lancashire the amount received in respect of local taxation licences was devoted to technical, including agricultural, education until 1903 when the sum received (from 1912 onwards a fixed sum of £31,037 2s 2d) was devoted to higher education. Out of the probate duty grant, as required by the Act, the County Council made payments to the poor law unions and other local authorities in the administrative county, payments towards the maintenance of pauper lunatics and an amount which met half the costs of the pay and clothing of the county police. Any surplus remaining was at the disposal of the Council, and from it grants were made towards main roads expenses and the residue, if any, was transferred to the general purposes account. These grants constituted the 'exchequer contribution' to the County Council. Under both Agricultural Rates Acts already mentioned, grants were made to compensate for loss of rateable value, and these were distributed over the general purposes, education and police accounts with small sums allotted to roads, sessions houses and prison pensions.[42] The main government aid came from direct grants, first from the Road Fund and then from the Ministry of Transport, the Board of Education, the Ministry of Health, the Ministry of Agriculture and Fisheries and the Treasury. Up to 1918, government grants met about one-third of revenue expenditure, but thereafter they were considerably increased (see Table 3.3).

TABLE 3.3
Government Grants as a Proportion of County Revenue

Average	Rates and orders	Government grants	Other income
	%	%	%
1889–1918	55.9	32.8	11.3
1918–29	45.9	44.8	9.3

Besides revenue expenditure, the County Council yearly expended sums on miscellaneous buildings, roads, plant – their renewal, reconstruction, and improvement – and on the purchase of land. The providing of such tangible assets, especially if financed from loans, became termed 'capital expenditure'. In the early years, apart from a new sessions house at Preston, capital expenditure was chiefly on new police stations. After 1904 new schools and roads accounted for most of the capital expenditure, which was not large, averaging, up to 1918, only 5.2 per cent per annum of gross (revenue plus capital) expenditure. After the war capital expenditure was more wide-ranging as, besides schools and roads, there was considerable expenditure on smallholding estates, tuberculosis dispensaries and the housing of employees. Even so, capital expenditure as a percentage of gross expenditure in the peak year 1921–2 only reached 10.8 per cent of that expenditure and averaged 7.9 per cent for the decade. Capital expenditure was financed from four sources – loans, current revenue, sales of surplus county property and, after the war, from government capital grants made by the various ministeries. In the same period loans provided 72 per cent of the finance for capital expenditure, government grants 23 per cent and only 1 per cent was financed from current revenue.

The 1888 Act required the county boroughs, removed from the jurisdiction of administrative counties, to negotiate financial adjustments with the new county councils, and on the extension of county boroughs similar financial settlements were made. In Lancashire by 1906 the county boroughs therein had paid to the County Council £480,806; by 1918 the total stood at £591,282 and by 1929 it had increased to £838,213. This constituted the 'capital monies' of the County Council, which the Council was required to invest on behalf of the several county services. Amounts were lent to County Council accounts and to Lancashire corporations, and small amounts were invested in government stocks.

The County Council inherited a loan debt from the justices which stood at £637,967 in 1890. At first, determined efforts were made to reduce this debt, and by 1902 it totalled only £181,251. Thereafter, the necessity to raise loans to build schools, improve and widen roads and construct new roads caused a steady increase in the county loan debt, which amounted to £721,018 in 1918. After the war that debt increased at an accelerated rate, reaching £2,551,608 in 1929, of which £820,026 was owed to its own capital monies. The capital money of the County Council served as a countervailing item on the county's loan debt and the interest paid thereon as an item in other income.

CHAPTER 4

Politics

As we have seen, county councils were first established by the Local Government Act of 1888. A development of this kind had been under consideration for a number of years, and in the discussions and debates that had taken place two major views about the purpose of the reform and the role and status of the new institutions had been expressed.

The Act was carried through by a Conservative government and its principal spokesmen explained that they were concerned, in the interests of administrative efficiency, to simplify and rationalise the numerous overlapping boards that ran local services. From their point of view, the new county councils were primarily administrative agencies for the central government at local level. Thus Lord Balfour of Burleigh, opening the debate on the second reading of the Bill in the House of Lords, argued its merits on the grounds that:

> there was a most pressing necessity for endeavouring to simplify our Local Government in England and Wales. The position of matters had been described by a high authority as 'a chaos of areas, a chaos of rates, and a chaos of authorities;' and he did not think anyone could say the description was overdrawn...[1]

and C. T. Ritchie, who as president of the Local Government Board was primarily responsible for piloting the Bill through the Commons, saw it as a response to:

> a real and substantial demand for a system of decentralisation by which many of the duties which are now performed by Central Departments, and in some cases by Parliament, might be entrusted to County Authorities, if they were constituted in a manner which should adequately represent the public.[2]

Radical Liberals, on the other hand, saw the Act in a rather different light. For them the reform was intended to be one aspect of the move towards the democratisation of all areas of government. The Bill planned by Dilke when he was president of the Local Government Board in 1883 would have given county councils full control over such critical matters as the Poor Law, public health and education. It would also have allowed women to become councillors. To the disappointment of the Radicals, the Act passed in 1888 steered clear of these controversial areas. Their only crumb of comfort came when an amendment giving the county councils some control over the police was carried against the government.

There were, then, two rather different perspectives on the purposes of local government. One saw administrative efficiency as the primary objective, whereas the other stressed the importance of local democracy. The clash between these two views has been a recurring feature of discussions about local government, and it will provide the main focus for our examination of the development of county government in Lancashire.

With this in mind, we organise our discussion around two of the principal themes that arose during the debates. The first is the question of democracy: to what extent did the institutions set up by the 1888 Act, and modified by later measures, provide an effective mechanism for local democracy, and to what extent were the fears of Radical critics, who thought that the Act did not go far enough, justified? The second is concerned with the role of political parties in county government. This was a subject that was rarely made explicit in the debates on the Bill except for expressions by various speakers of the pious hope that 'excessive party spirit' or 'party feeling' would not interfere with the proper running of county business. However, as we shall see, political parties did come to play a part in the development of the new councils, and we must try to assess their impact.

In this first section on the politics of Lancashire County Council we will be looking at the developments up to 1929. We start by looking at the first elections to the County Council and the creation of a new structure of government in the county. We shall then turn our attention to a number of the major trends in the forty years that followed.

As a preliminary, however, we must make some comments on the practical problems involved in a study of this kind.

SOURCES AND PROBLEMS OF EVIDENCE

The difficulties faced by students of the history of local government – and, in particular, of county government – can be brought out by considering the contrast with the study of national politics. In studying the latter the historian has access to verbatim reports of speeches and debates, extensive newspaper reports and commentaries, as well as the memoirs and biographies of the principal participants. In our case, however, virtually all of these sources are absent. Unhappily, newspapers have paid little attention to county affairs. For national newspapers the county has been too small to be important, and, because of the somewhat artificial nature of the county, there are no 'county' papers in the way that there are papers serving local urban communities. Furthermore, as we shall see, throughout its history the County Council has failed to capture the public imagination, and so even local newspapers have rarely felt that its affairs were worth reporting fully. The business of the Council, either in committee or in full session, has never been recorded in detail, and speeches by county leaders have rarely been given extensive coverage. Finally, in those cases where county leaders have been of sufficient standing to warrant the publication of biographies or memoirs, their activities at county level have been of relatively minor importance compared with their work in other spheres and have received correspondingly little attention.[3]

All of this means that, especially for the earlier part of this study, we have been forced to rely upon a very limited number of sources. Firstly, there are the records of *Proceedings of the Meetings of the Lancashire County Council*.[4] These formally record the attendance of members and decisions taken, and give some basic information about amendments to committee minutes and voting thereon. Printed with these are the reports of the various committees. Secondly, there are Lancashire's County Council *Yearbooks*, which provide valuable information about councillors, the membership of committees and electoral arrangements. Thirdly, we have had access to some useful unpublished material at County Hall in Preston and at the County Record Office. This has included in particular official returns of election results and committee minutes. Fourthly, a number of newspapers have been of some use, principally the *Lancashire Daily Post*, which usually gave brief reports of Council and important committee meetings and descriptions of election campaigns and the results. We have also referred to the *Manchester Guardian* and a number of local weekly papers. Finally, we have consulted some miscellaneous publications, such as the commemorative volume called *The Jubilee of County Councils*[5] and other occasional pieces.

For the later period we have been able to supplement these sources with interviews with Council members and officers and unpublished party records. But for the pre-1929 period, and especially for the years before the First World War, our information is of necessity limited. For this reason we have limited ourselves in this section mainly to a discussion of general trends. Even so, the interpretations that we suggest must necessarily be somewhat tentative.

Having briefly explained the difficulties involved in collecting information, we now return to our main themes, and we start by looking at the very early years of Lancashire County Council's existence.

The Setting Up of the New Authority

The various Acts and orders that governed the setting up of the county councils made provision for single-member electoral divisions and for the election of councillors every three years. Councillors in turn were to select aldermen in the ratio of one alderman for every three councillors. In Lancashire there were to be 105 councillors and thirty-five aldermen.

The first elections were held on Tuesday, 15 January 1889, in anticipation of the formal assumption of powers and duties in April of that year. The elections were contested in forty of the 105 electoral divisions but it is difficult to assess how much public interest there was. The *Lancaster Gazette* reported that 'in some cases great interest and excitement were prevalent, and the results were eagerly anticipated'.[6] However, this interest seems to have been confined to the mainly urban strip running from northeast Lancashire through the Manchester area to Liverpool, and was probably a reflection of the desire of the urban middle classes, critical as ever of the county gentry, to make their influence felt. In the Manchester area, in particular, there was a strong Liberal current, and the sort of Radical views that had been put forward during the debate on the Bill were frequently voiced. Mr L. Higginbottom, for example, an unsuccessful candidate in the Gorton division, argued that the appointment of aldermen was 'a sop to the landed gentry, intended to provide a back door to the County Council to those who were afraid to appeal to the electors',[7] and also complained that control of the police was still left partly in the hands of non-elected justices.

In the more rural districts in the north and west of the county there was much less interest. In these areas very few divisions were contested and the Conservatives had the upper hand.

One thing that is quite clear from this first round of elections is that those who hoped that party politics would have no place in the new counties were disappointed. The great majority of candidates declared a party interest and from contemporary reports we are able to arrive at figures for party strengths with a fair degree of accuracy. The Conservatives won forty-nine seats to the Liberals' forty-six, and there were also seven Liberal–Unionists and three who 'offered themselves to the constituents on non-political grounds'.[8]

The first meeting of the newly elected councillors took place on the 24 January 1889, and one of the first tasks was to choose thirty-five aldermen. After a vote (50 to 32) it was agreed that aldermen should be chosen from among the elected councillors themselves. This meant that thirty-five vacancies for councillors were created and by-elections were duly held on the 8 February. In these, eighteen of the thirty-five divisions were contested and the full Council met for the first time on 14 February. We are unable to be precise about the final composition of the Council in terms of party, but we do know that there were sixty Conservatives, sixty Liberals and seven Liberal–Unionists. Of the remaining thirteen, some were explicitly Independent but we have been unable to obtain any definite information about the rest.

What is clear in spite of this is that these first elections left the Council with a fairly close balance between the parties. It is in fact interesting that so many of the councillors did acknowledge a party affiliation, but it would be hasty to take this alone as evidence of any strong party conflict. Indeed, some of the Council's early actions point in the opposite direction. A prominent Liberal, Sir J. T. Hibbert, was chosen as the Council's first chairman, but C. R. Jacson, a Conservative, became the first vice-chairman. There seems to have been a similar attempt to keep a balance in the selection of aldermen, and when steering committees were appointed to set up the administrative structure Conservatives and Liberals were approximately equally represented on them.

In occupational terms the new Council was dominated by two major groups. On the one hand there were the gentry, landowners and farmers who comprised 23.6 per cent of the membership. But they were greatly outnumbered by manufacturers and factory-owners, who made up no less than 45.7 per cent of Council members. Over half of these were directly involved in the cotton industry and a number of others in subsidiaries. The rest of the Council consisted mainly of professional people (15 per cent) – lawyers, doctors, clergymen and so on – and small business proprietors (11.4 per cent).

Not surprisingly, perhaps, some groups in the community were not represented among Council members. The most obvious absences were those of manual and white-collar workers and, of course, women.

In its first few meetings the Council established the basic structures of decision-making and administration. It drew up and approved its own standing orders, appointed chief officers to run the services (sometimes not without dispute) and set up its various committees. Although there have, of course, been enormous changes, the basic structure set up at this time lasted throughout the Council's history.

POLITICAL TRENDS 1889–1929

Having briefly outlined the setting up of the Council, we now turn to an examination of the major trends in its political development during its first forty years.

Elections

As we have seen, one of the ideas behind the creation of the new county councils was that they would be a means of extending democracy. The election of representatives is of course a key element in any democratic system, but what is normally regarded as essential is not just that the formal requirement for elections is met, but that elections are contested and that a substantial proportion of the populace vote in them. Viewed in terms of these requirements, Lancashire County Council would surely have disappointed the hopes of Radical Liberals at least. After the initial flourish of enthusiasm in 1889, the proportion of seats that was contested fell sharply and did not recover until the late 1920s. The first election, indeed, produced the largest number of contests in the whole period. As Table 4.1 shows, for the most part the figure hovered around 10 per cent, falling to a derisory 1.9 per cent in 1907 and picking up only gradually after that. (During the First World War elections were suspended and the vacancies that arose were filled by co-option.)

It is quite clear that the County Council failed to arouse the sort of local

TABLE 4.1
Percentage of Divisions Contested

	%	(N)		%	(N)
1889	38.1	(40)	1910	8.7	(9)
1892	13.3	(14)	1913	11.5	(12)
1895	11.4	(12)	1919	7.8	(8)
1898	11.4	(12)	1922	18.4	(19)
1901	9.5	(10)	1925	17.5	(18)
1904	8.6	(9)	1928	21.9	(23)
1907	1 9	(2)			

interest that might have been expected. Complaints were continually being voiced in local newspapers about the very small number of contests and the apathy of the people towards the Council. For example, in 1913 the *Manchester Guardian* quoted a complaint that 'people are getting so tired of the whole thing that they don't care who represents them at Preston nor what is done at Preston'.[9]

The practical effect of all this was that, once an individual had been elected to the County Council, he could reasonably expect to remain a councillor until removed by death, voluntary retirement or promotion to the aldermanic bench. The number of sitting councillors who were defeated in contested elections was very small throughout the whole period. Even in 1928 when there were twenty-three contests only five incumbent councillors were defeated.

As we noted above, the Council took an early decision to select aldermen only from among councillors. For the purpose of nominating aldermen the councillors met separately in four committees representing the old Hundreds – Lonsdale; West Derby; Salford; and Amounderness, Blackburn and Leyland. This was intended to create a reasonable geographical balance in aldermanic representation, but a pattern was quickly established whereby promotion to the aldermanic bench became a reward for long service. This eventually developed into a fairly rigid seniority system with aldermanic elections rarely, if ever, being contested.[10] Once an individual became an alderman he could be sure of re-election for as long as he wished or as his health permitted.

This lack of electoral competition both at councillor and aldermanic level allowed a number of individuals to serve for lengthy periods without interruption. But it would be wrong to conclude that the overall picture was one of great stability. In fact, throughout this period there was a considerable turnover in council membership owing to voluntary retirement and death. Table 4.2 shows the percentage of new council members immediately following each of the triennial elections from 1892 to 1928.

TABLE 4.2
Percentage of New Council Members 1892–1928

	%		%
1892	28.6	1910	18.7
1895	35.3	1913	20.9
1898	33.6	1919	34.3
1901	28.6	1922	26.1
1904	22.9	1925	26.1
1907	27.1	1928	27.1

It can be seen that the proportion of councillors being replaced was rarely less than one-quarter, though the rate of renewal tended to fall in the years before the First World War.[11]

Apart from the growth of Labour representation in the twenties, which we will discuss further below, it is difficult to say with any precision much about the political complexion of the Council before 1928. After the first election in 1889, when as we have seen many candidates declared their party affiliation, information about the political loyalties of councillors becomes very difficult to obtain. To a large extent this is simply a product of the fact that very few elections were contested – there was no need for un-opposed candidates to declare their political allegiance. But it may also have been intentional – the product of a belief that party politics should not and need not enter into Council affairs. At any rate, for most of the period the political affiliation of over half the Council members is unknown. This in turn means that we can place very little reliance on any trends that may appear in the figures which are available. For what it is worth, however, the figures we have suggest that the proportion of Conservatives on the Council remained fairly constant, while the proportion of Liberals fell slowly but steadily.

Council Members

We saw above that the first County Council was dominated by two major social groups – landowners and manufacturers – and as such was not representative of the mass of the population. Table 4.3 shows that this situation changed remarkably little over the next forty years.[12]

TABLE 4.3
Occupations of Council Members

	1889	1898	1913	1919	1928
	%	%	%	%	%
Gentry and landowners	23.6	25.0	21.6	22.9	25.0
Manufacturers and owners of large concerns	45.7	36.4	36.0	30.7	21.4
Company directors and managers	0.7	2.1	3.6	5.0	9.3
Professional	15.0	15.0	18.7	17.9	16.4
Small business proprietors	11.4	20.0	17.3	11.4	12.9
All others	3.5	1.4	2.8	12.2	15.1
	(N=140)	(N=140)	(N=139)	(N=140)	(N=140)

Perhaps most surprisingly, the proportion of gentry and landowners remained very stable right up to 1928. Many of those in this category would of course not be the old county gentry but successful urban businessmen who had made their fortune in manufacturing and had acquired country estates. No doubt also there were an increasing number who used the term 'gentleman' more as a matter of aspiration than as an accurate description. By contrast, the proportion of councillors describing themselves as manufacturers or factory-owners declined quite markedly. This was no doubt partly a result of changes in the structure of industry itself. The days of the individual capitalist entrepreneur who had the wealth, time and inclination to devote himself to public service were passing, and in his place came the director of the joint stock company. But even the combined figure for manufacturers and company directors falls steadily. The numbers of professional men and small business proprietors remain fairly constant throughout the period, and together they account for thirty to thirty-five per cent of the Council. The residual category, 'all others', shows a quite large increase, rising to fifteen per cent by 1928. It includes a variety of occupational groups, such as white-collar workers, manual workers and trade union organisers, which were beginning to become more prominent after the First World War. We will discuss the impact of these new groups in more detail below.

One significant change in the composition of the Council is not revealed by Table 4.3 – the appearance of women in the Council chamber. The law, of course, did not allow women to participate in council elections, either as voters or as candidates, until after the First World War. The first woman elected to Lancashire County Council was Mrs Katherine Orme, who represented Clitheroe from 1922 to 1925. In that year two other women were elected – Miss Caroline Whitehead and Lady Audrey Worsley-Taylor. Both were to serve for a very long time and went on to become county aldermen. But the recruitment of women as councillors continued to be very slow, reaching only four in 1928 with the addition of Mrs Eveleen Lomax and Mrs Katherine Fletcher. Their election reflected another major change in the life of the council which was only just beginning to be significant, for they were both Labour councillors.

We have seen that, once elected to the Council, it was generally the case that an individual could stay there as long as he wished. The relatively high rate of turnover that took place seems to suggest, however, that for a substantial proportion of councillors either Council work was not very rewarding, or the costs involved in terms of time and travel etc. were too great. Further evidence for this can be found by looking at levels of attendance at Council meetings. Table 4.4 shows the average proportion of members attending full Council meetings in each three-year period. The

TABLE 4.4
Average Attendance at Council Meetings

	%			%
1889–92	74.4		1910–13	61.5
1892–95	65.7		1913–16	61.4
1895–98	64.5		1916–19	44.8
1898–1901	63.7		1919–22	59.3
1901–04	68.3		1922–5	62.5
1904–07	57.6		1925–8	68.6
1907–10	60.2			

attendance in the first three years was quite good, but then, with the exception of the years 1901–04, it fell to around just sixty per cent. The extremely low figure for 1916–19 is, of course, due to the war, but even in the twenties the figure rose only gradually and it was never higher than seventy per cent. It should of course be borne in mind that councillors received no allowance for travel and that road communications at this time were not well developed. None the less, the figures do not suggest a great deal of enthusiasm on the part of elected representatives.

As would be expected, this quite rapid turnover in Council membership is reflected in a fairly short average length of service for Council members. Table 4.5 gives details of lengths of service at four points during the period.

TABLE 4.5
Length of Service of Council Members

	0–3 years	4–9 years	10–21 years	Over 21 years
	%	%	%	%
1901	48.2	23.0	28.8	—
1913	32.4	25.9	33.1	8.6
1919	28.3	23.2	37.0	11.6
1928	39.3	25.7	20.0	15.0

The figures refer to the Council membership immediately after the elections in the years stated. It can be seen that in each case a considerable proportion of the Council were members of recent vintage, having been first elected either at the election of the year in question or at the one three years before. (The figure for the 1919 Council is artificially small owing to the fact that there were no elections between 1913 and 1919.) Generally, one-third or more of Council members had very short periods of service. On the other hand, the figures also show that, at the other end of the scale, there was a small but growing group of Council members with very long experience. By 1928, fifteen per cent of the Council had served for more than twenty-one years. These long-service members were, almost without exception, aldermen.

It would appear, then, that for a substantial proportion of councillors membership of the Council was a brief episode which was ended by their own unwillingness to continue, whether owing to lack of interest, lack of time, the expense or problems of travel. A smaller number, however, overcame these problems and accumulated considerable seniority. The question naturally arises whether, either as cause or effect, this group constituted an exclusive leadership. Contemporary newspaper comments lend support to such a view. For example the *Manchester Guardian* in 1931 remarked that 'Perhaps ... there is something in the suggestion that county affairs are managed by an inner circle over whom the ordinary elected members have comparatively little control', and reported a member of six years' standing as saying that 'he has found the control of affairs to be more or less in the hands of a small coterie of elderly gentlemen'.[13] We must now look at the evidence on this question.

The Leaders of the Council

It is perhaps inevitable that, in an organisation as large and complex as the County Council, a small leadership group, made up of those occupying key positions of authority, will emerge to control the formulation and execution of policy. But to assess the importance of this group we must see whether its members were able to maintain themselves in power for considerable periods of time, whether they were representative of the

TABLE 4.6
Length of Service on the Council of Chairmen and Vice-Chairmen

	0–3 years	4–9 years	10–21 years	Over 21 years	
	%	%	%	%	
1901	—	17.7	82.4	—	(N=17)
1913	—	11.8	52.9	35.3	(N=17)
1919	—	5.9	70.6	23.5	(N=17)
1928	—	—	23.1	76.9	(N=13)

Council at large, whether the group was socially or politically cohesive, and whether it controlled recruitment to its own ranks.

With these questions in mind, we have looked at the characteristics of those councillors and aldermen who were chairmen or vice-chairmen of the County Council or of one of its standing committees during the period.[14]

First of all, in Table 4.6 we show the length of service on the Council of chairmen and vice-chairmen at four points in time. If we compare the figures here with those given in Table 4.5 for all Council members it can be seen very clearly that the Council leaders had much longer service than average. In all four years well over eighty per cent of the chairmen had served for more than ten years, whereas for all councillors the figure never rises above fifty per cent. But not all long-serving members of the Council became chairmen. Although, as we have seen, most councillors served for a brief period only, there do seem to have been a number of councillors and aldermen who served for long periods without ever playing a very prominent role in council affairs. Thus in 1913, twelve of the twenty Council members who had served for more than twenty-one years were not chairmen. Similarly, in 1919 ten out of sixteen and in 1928 eight out of twenty-one senior Council members were not chairmen.

TABLE 4.7
Occupations of Chairmen and Vice-Chairmen

	1889–99	1899–1909	1909–19	1919–29
	%	%	%	%
Gentry and landowners	33.3	27.6	37.0	34.8
Manufacturers and company directors	26.7	34.5	25.9	34.8
Professionals	30.0	27.6	25.9	21.7
Small business	—	10.3	11.1	4.4
Skilled manual	—	—	—	4.4
Others	10.0			
	(N=30)	(N=29)	(N=27)	(N=23)

Simplifying a little, we can conclude from the figures that there were three types of Council member. Firstly, a substantial majority stayed on the Council for a relatively short time – one, two, at the most three terms. Secondly, there was a group of long-serving councillors who were content to play a back-bench role. Finally, a relatively small number of councillors achieved positions of authority and occupied them for long periods.

Was this last group representative of all Council members, and was it socially and politically cohesive? Table 4.7 shows the occupations of all those who held office in each of the four decades between 1889 and 1928, and it can be seen that, throughout, the leadership was dominated by three occupational groups – landowners, manufacturers and professional people. If these figures are compared with those given for all Council members in Table 4.3 it can be seen that, in this respect at least, the leadership group was representative of the whole Council, though 'professionals' were somewhat over-represented and manufacturers under-represented until the last period.

The other point worthy of comment in Table 4.7 is the stability of the proportions of the respective occupational categories that made up the leadership group. Only in the last period does any significant shift take place. This may of course be a reflection of the point we have just been discussing – the long service of chairmen and vice-chairmen. But in any case, we saw above that the occupational composition of the Council as a whole changed little in this period.

In party terms, the manufacturers tended to be Liberal and the gentry Conservative, though there were always exceptions. The professionals were fairly evenly divided. Thus the leadership group, like the Council as a whole, was always divided politically. This is capable of more than one interpretation. It may suggest a split leadership group, or it might be interpreted as showing that party was of minimal importance and did not affect the cohesiveness of the leadership.

We turn finally to the question of recruitment. How did councillors and aldermen become chairmen and vice-chairmen, and what, if anything, can be said about their career patterns? For these purposes, chairmen and vice-chairmen seem to fall into three broad types. First of all there were those who held office for a very short period and so can only very loosely be counted as leaders. Secondly, there were a number of councillors who respectively attained the chairmanship of one of the less important committees and held it for a long time. Finally, a few Council members rose from minor positions to become members of the small group of top leaders. We shall look at each of these types in a little more detail.

The average period of office for all chairmen and vice-chairmen first appointed between 1889 and 1929 was just under thirteen years. However, throughout the period there was a small number of chairmen who held office only briefly. Usually in terms of years of service these were senior councillors or aldermen who at the end of their period of service were briefly appointed to a fairly minor office. For example, William Sagar, after fourteen years of service, was appointed vice-chairman of the Main Roads and Bridge Committee in 1903 and held the position for just two years. However, there were also a number of short-serving chairmen in the first years of the council's existence. Thus of the eighteen chairmen and vice-chairmen appointed in 1889, as many as six served only until 1892, and by 1895 only six men retained the office to which they had been appointed in 1889. This phenomenon seems to have been a product of the uncertainties which were inevitable in the first years of a new body. The rate of turnover of chairmen slowed down considerably in later years, as can be seen from Table 4.8. Thus of those holding office in the decade after the First World War, over seventy per cent had held office during the previous decade.

TABLE 4.8
Proportion of Office-Holders in One Decade
Who Also Held Office in the Previous Decade

1899–1909	1909–19	1919–29
%	%	%
55.2	63.0	73.9

This leads us on to a consideration of the longer-serving chairmen. We suggested above that they fell into two groups. The first consists of those who served for long periods in the less important posts and were never really members of the innermost ring of leaders. It is made up almost entirely of men who specialised in one field and served for long periods, sometimes first as vice-chairmen and then as chairmen of a particular committee. For instance, W. J. Fitzherbert-Brockholes, a prominent landowner, started in 1905 as vice-chairman of the Diseases of Animals Acts Committee, became its chairman in 1912 and then went on to be chairman of the new Agricultural Committee that replaced it from 1919 to 1924.

We come lastly to the top rank of leaders. In this group we have included chairmen and vice-chairmen of the County Council and the long-serving chairmen of the major standing committees: Finance, Parliamentary, Main Roads and Bridges, Education (initially Technical Instruction) and Public Health and Housing. This gives us, for the period 1889–1929, fifteen individuals. Of these, seven were long-serving chairmen of major committees. Edwin Guthrie, a chartered accountant, was chairman of Finance from 1889 to 1904; Thomas Snape, an alkali manufacturer, was chairman of the Technical Instruction Committee from 1889 to 1901; Sir William Hulton, a landowner, was chairman of Main Roads and Bridges from 1889 to 1907; Robert Sephton, a surgeon, was first of all vice-chairman of the Public Health Committee from 1898 to 1901 and then was its chairman from 1901 to 1916; James Shuttleworth, a pawnbroker, was chairman of Main Roads and Bridges from 1907 to 1916; Sir John Aspell, a cotton manufacturer, was Shuttleworth's vice-chairman from 1907 to 1916 and then succeeded him as chairman from 1916 to 1931, and Samuel Taylor, a barrister, was chairman of the Parliamentary Committee from 1913 to 1933.

The remaining eight were all either chairmen and/or vice-chairmen of the County Council itself. Neither Sir John Tomlinson Hibbert, a barrister, the first chairman, nor Sir William H. Houldsworth, a cotton-spinner, who became vice-chairman after the early death of C. R. Jacson, had of course any previous service as a committee chairman. In the years that followed, however, a pattern was established whereby fairly long service as chairman of one of the Council's major standing committees was a prerequisite for promotion to one of the two top posts. For example, Sir Henry F. Hibbert was chairman of Technical Instruction and then of Education for eleven years before becoming vice-chairman in 1912, and Sir Henry Wade Deacon, fourth chairman of the County Council, served his apprenticeship as chairman of Finance from 1907 to 1927.

It seems clear, then, that one necessary, though not sufficient, condition for promotion to the highest ranks within the Council was long service. In particular, the composition of the central leadership group changed only slowly, and newcomers to it had always demonstrated their ability beforehand. One corollary of this was that the top leaders all served for very long periods – their average length of service on the Council was twenty-seven years, and their average period in office was just over twenty years.

What conclusions can be drawn from this discussion of the leadership group? First of all, two reasons for caution in drawing any conclusions should be mentioned. Firstly, our information is limited and in some cases fragmentary. Secondly, and partly because of this, we have been analysing a group defined in terms of formal positions of authority. We must not forget that formal authority and power are not equivalent, and in particular that there may have been individuals outside the leadership group as we have defined it – for example those who were important party figures but held no Council office – who were powerful.

Bearing those points in mind, however, the evidence we have presented does broadly support the view that, at least by the twenties, the Council was dominated by 'a small coterie of elderly gentlemen'. But it would be wrong to think that this state of affairs was widely resented. On the contrary, the following comments seem fairly typical: '... the domination of the old county families and the landed interest generally is not seriously challenged. No one, indeed, seems anxious to challenge it; the expense is too great and the need not too obvious.... The members, most of them Tories in national politics, carry on the county administration in a fairly enlightened spirit.... In the present system the work can only be carried on by men of a little means – county gentry, landowning cotton merchants, and, occasionally, trade union officials.'[15] In other words, it was an oligarchy, but a benevolent oligarchy. Those who sought to challenge it – in particular the Labour Party – found it difficult to make much headway, lacking not only the necessary organisation but, more importantly, a major issue over which they could challenge the establishment.

Issues

The nature of the issues that can arise in local government depends largely upon the powers and functions given to it. We have seen that, to the disappointment of the Radical Liberals, the 1888 Act deliberately withheld from county councils control over such controversial areas as education, the Poor Law and major aspects of public health. The independent policy-making powers of the county councils were further circumscribed by the conception of local government as an administrative agency of the central government which was embodied in the Conservatives' Act. All of this meant that a county council's room for manoeuvre was fairly small.

Inevitably, however, there were many areas of disagreement, though only a few matters were sufficiently important or controversial to warrant being called 'issues'. In exploring this subject we once again encounter the problem of inadequate information. We have been able to make some use of newspaper reports and other printed material, but we have relied heavily on information from the *Proceedings* about amendments moved in Council meetings. It seems likely that any matters that excited strong feelings would have been debated on the floor of the Council chamber, and the procedure that was used to force a debate was to move an amendment to a committee report or to introduce a notice of motion. Further, the standing orders of the Council allowed members to call for a recorded vote – that is, for the names of those voting for and against any resolution to be recorded in the *Proceedings*. One would expect that this procedure would be invoked only on matters on which councillors had exceptionally strong feelings.

We start by looking at the number of times these procedures were used. Table 4.9 shows that, for the whole period, there was a total of 147 amendments, but that these were not evenly distributed. There is in fact a fairly clear pattern. In the first few years, while the County Council was being established, the rate was quite high – indeed, the largest number of amendments in any three-year period occurs in 1889–92. Thereafter the rate fell sharply and remained at a very low level from 1898 until 1922, except for a period of greater activity between 1901 and 1907. In the twenties the

rate began to climb again. There were only five recorded votes in the period
and all of these took place in the first nine years of the Council's
existence.

When we examine the subjects upon which amendments were moved,
the explanation for this pattern also becomes fairly clear. In the first years
up to 1898 there were a number of problems arising out of the setting
up of the County Council itself and of the lower-tier district and parish
authorities. For instance, amendments were moved on the question of
which committee was to deal with railway and canal rates, or whether district
council chairmen should be JPs, or how the granting of theatre licences
should be handled and on the procedures which should be followed in
making various appointments. There were also a number of amendments
relating to the personnel of various committees and boards and some in
connection with the appointment of officers of the Council.

TABLE 4.9
Number of Amendments Moved in Council Meetings 1889–1928

1889–92	23	1904–07	11	1916–19	3
1892–95	13	1907–10	2	1919–22	9
1895–98	22	1910–13	5	1922–5	14
1898–1901	5	1913–16	3	1925–8	19
1901–04	18				

As an example, we may cite the controversy over the appointment of
a medical officer of health (MOH) which gave rise to the first two
recorded votes. In November 1889 the Public Health Committee proposed
that an MOH be appointed but an amendment was proposed that this be
deferred. When the vote was taken there were forty-five for and forty-five
against. The chairman then gave his casting vote against the amendment,
whereupon a recorded vote was called for. Somewhat surprisingly, a
number of extra councillors seem to have been found, for on the recorded
vote the amendment was carried by fifty-three to fifty-one. A similar amendment to a renewed proposal to appoint a medical officer of health was also
the subject of a recorded vote at the next meeting, in February 1890. On
this occasion it was lost by forty-four votes to forty-three. It is difficult
to know what precisely was at issue on this matter. However our party
affiliation figures, though incomplete, do suggest that there was something
of a party split in the voting, with most Liberals voting for the early
appointment of an MOH and most Conservatives voting against.

There were also a number of amendments in this early period on various
proposals for expenditure on roads – it should be remembered that at this

time the Main Roads and Bridges Committee was the principal spending committee – and on various matters to do with education, arising out of the Education Bill of 1896. But the only other subject of major dispute was on the question of the rates of pay and hours of work of men working for employers carrying out contracts for the Council. An amendment making it a condition that contractors should pay trade union rates was heavily defeated by fifty-three votes to nine in August 1892. In August 1894 a resolution was moved requiring contractors to pay 'the Standard Rate of Wages and to observe the Recognised Hours in the District in which the work is carried out'. However, an amendment refusing 'to sanction a Resolution which can only be beneficial to a section of Ratepayers' was carried by thirty-nine votes to twenty-five after a recorded vote. A year later, in November 1895, a further attempt to get a fair wages resolution passed was made, but a similar amendment was again carried, after a recorded vote, by forty-six to eighteen. Once again there seems to have been something of a party split with half of the Liberals favouring a fair wages clause and the great majority of Conservatives opposing it. This matter continued to be a source of conflict until February 1907, when a fair wage resolution was narrowly passed at the end of a meeting by twenty-six to twenty-four votes.

After this initial burst of activity the number of amendments slowed to a trickle, and then only on minor topics, until after the First World War. The major exception to this was the period just after 1902 when the new Education Act was the subject of considerable controversy. The details of this measure and its implementation are discussed in Chapter 5 of this volume, but the political controversy it aroused must be examined here.

The most controversial feature of the Act was that it involved giving aid from the rates to church schools, which were mostly Anglican. This gravely offended Nonconformists, and there was a bitter national campaign against the Act which involved the withholding of rates, among other things. The Liberal Party was strongly identified with Nonconformism and strenuously opposed the Act within and outside Parliament. The seriousness with which the County Council treated the matter is shown by the fact that a special meeting was held in December 1902 solely for the purpose of discussing the Act. At this meeting the Technical Instruction Committee was empowered to draft a scheme for the implementation of the Act, recruitment of temporary staff and so on. The first signs of dissension then appeared. An attempt was made to increase the membership of the Committee (which already had twenty-seven members) by nine. The nine names proposed included some very eminent figures – W. S. Barrett, E. Guthrie, W. W. B. Hulton, H. Wade Deacon and W. Sagar – and almost all of them were Liberals. This attempt was defeated.

At the next meeting of the Council, in February 1903, the Technical Instruction Committee reported back, and there followed a series of five amendments to the report. All were proposed by Liberals and they seem to have been designed either to delay or to thwart the plans of the Committee. They were all rejected. There followed a further four amendments suggesting small adjustments to the constitution of the new Education Committee. Liberals were again prominent in these moves. In this case three of the four amendments were carried, though this was probably because the changes proposed were relatively unimportant.

The Education Committee was finally established and its members chosen in May 1903. For a time the controversy continued. In February 1905, in a letter to the Council, Sir J. T. Hibbert wrote, 'I cannot conclude without a special reference to the earnest, unceasing and successful labours of the Lancashire Education Committee, who, amid some complaints and some obloquy, have had to carry out a most trying and difficult task.'[16] Amendments continued to be moved on questions arising out of the Act, but they had the air of being something of a rearguard action.

Clearly the whole question of the implementation of the Education Act was one that raised party passions, and it seems quite likely that it accounts for the higher attendance at Council meetings from 1901 to 1904, which is shown in Table 4.4. It is not clear, however, why education relatively quickly ceased to be a partisan issue. It may be that it was a result of purely local factors, or perhaps it was a product of the general decline in importance of religious issues at this time.

After the First World War the number of amendments started to increase once more. The reason for the increase was the activity of a small group of newly elected Labour councillors. Six councillors in particular were extremely active in proposing amendments: William Rogerson, Alfred Turner, Edgar Boothman, William Hughes, Robert Pownall and the Rev. Alfred Mitchell. Of the forty-two amendments proposed between 1919 and 1928 they were responsible for thirty-one. Rogerson, a full time trade union official, was the most prolific amender. He moved no less than seventeen amendments and seconded a further seven!

The amendments moved by these Labour members covered a wide variety of topics but most of them fall into one of four categories. They were opposed to salary increases for senior Council officials, in favour of better pay and conditions for junior staff and employees and of increased expenditure on various health and welfare projects, and they called for councillors' travelling expenses to be reimbursed. By and large they met with little success. Apart from the activities of the Labour members there were very few amendments in this period and those that were proposed related to minor and localised matters.

The general conclusion that can be drawn from this brief survey of subjects of explicit disagreement on the Council is that there were very few of them. The only major issue that arose during the period was education, and even this was short-lived. Why was it that education became an 'issue' whereas most other topics generated only minor disagreements?

We would suggest that, in general, for a subject to become an 'issue' it must have the following characteristics. First of all, the council must have the power to make policy in the area in question. Secondly, the matter must directly affect electors or special interests over the county as a whole. Finally, it must either be a matter on which different policy alternatives have importantly different material implications for various classes, interests or regions, or one on which significantly different policy alternatives arise out of differing philosophical perspectives. Matters that are outside the scope of the Council, are of purely localised concern, or cut across boundaries of class, interest and ideology are unlikely to become the subject of major and sustained dispute.

On the basis of these criteria the implementation of the Education Act was clearly likely to be an issue, but most of the other matters dealt with by the Council were not. Thus, for example, road schemes were likely to be of localised concern only; the Council's own procedural and administrative arrangements did not directly affect the electorate; and something like the reimbursement of councillors' travelling expenses was outside the Council's competence. Apart from education, only a few subjects came close to being issues – the fair wages question, the salaries of senior officials and councillors' expenses. All three of these had strong political overtones, but only the first two were within the Council's power and none of them very directly affected the population at large. It would seem, therefore, that, as we suggested at the beginning of this section, one of the causes of the low level of interest in the Council's work on the part of both councillors and electors was the absence of substantial controversial issues.

However there is one subject which, though not an issue in the sense that we have been discussing, was continually discussed throughout the period. This is the question of what was referred to as 'economy'. The term was used with two slightly different emphases – on the one hand it meant getting value for money; on the other it meant keeping spending, and therefore the rates, as low as possible. We have seen that very few elections were contested on party political grounds. Much more frequently, though, 'economy' was an issue. Commenting on the 1922 elections, the *Manchester Evening News* reported that: 'Very few of the seats are being contested on party grounds, the general motto of the candidates who are opposing the return of retiring members being economy and a saving in the rates.'[17] It is not surprising that the matter was one that was in the forefront of Council leaders' minds, or that Sir William Scott Barrett should single it out for attention in a brief pamphlet circulated shortly after he became Chairman of the County Council to mark its twenty-first year: 'The great desire of the Council is that the money spent shall bring in the largest possible result, and the principle that efficiency without extravagance in economy has been the guiding star of their deliberations.'[18]

The demand for economy was a recurrent theme throughout the period, but it could do little to make up for the lack of controversial issues that we have already noted or to raise the interests, let alone the enthusiasm, of the electorate. We have suggested that in some ways 'economy' was a substitute for party conflict, but in the following section we must examine how the paucity of issues and the lack of interest that resulted affected the role of the political parties.

POLITICAL PARTIES

We noted at the very beginning of this chapter that during the debates on the 1888 Act hopes were expressed that 'the poison of excessive party spirit' would not infect the new county councils.[19] In the course of our analysis in the last few sections, however, we have at various points seen that the political parties did play some part in the Council's affairs. In this section we will pull together the points we have made and try to assess the importance of party politics in the period 1889–1929.

In the first elections to the County Council most candidates fought as party candidates and a good proportion of the seats were contested. Thereafter, however, the number of contests declined sharply, as did the number of candidates whose political affiliation we know. We have warned that this last point must be treated with a little care, for it may simply be a product of the difficulty of obtaining information. However, we do not think this is the explanation – it is clear that many of the candidates in later elections simply did not state a political affiliation and some called themselves 'Independents'.

The interpretation that is to be put upon the rapid decline in contests is also unclear. J. M. Lee in his book on Cheshire County Council argues that 'it is a great mistake to believe that the decrease in the number of contested elections for the County Council [after] 1889 showed a decline in the influence of party in local elections'.[20] He goes on to show that there was a pact between the Conservatives and Liberals in Cheshire and that the parties limited the number of contests by mutual agreement. In Lancashire, however, we have no evidence of such a pact, or indeed that there was any central control of the parties' electoral efforts. The question, there-fore, must remain open, but it seems to us that the decline in electoral contests and in declared party allegiance in Lancashire are evidence of a very rapid decline in the involvement and interest of the parties in Council affairs. This interpretation is reinforced when we consider the role of the parties in the Council chamber itself.

Here there are three areas that are significant. First, there seems to have been from the very start some attempt to share major offices between the parties. As we have seen, throughout the period the chairmen and vice-chairmen of standing committees were drawn from the two parties. There is no evidence of a party using a majority on the Council to reserve for itself important chairmanships. Interestingly, although we are unable to say whether this was conscious policy or not, the positions of chairman and vice-chairman of the County Council were shared by men of different parties. Thus, for most of his period in office J. T. Hibbert, a Liberal, had as his vice-chairmen two Conservatives, C. R. Jacson and W. H. Houldsworth. Similarly H. F. Hibbert, a Conservative, served first as vice-chairman under a Liberal chairman, W. S. Barrett, and then when he became chairman in 1924 the vice-chairmanship went to a Liberal, H. Wade Deacon.

Secondly, there is no evidence of party conflict in the selection of aldermen. Within a short time after the Council's inception promotion to the aldermanic bench became almost exclusively a question of seniority. After some initial confusion, the election of aldermen was never a matter for dispute.

Thirdly, if party did play a major role in Council affairs we would expect this to come out most clearly in conflict over policy issues. We have seen that there is some evidence that this did happen. Most obviously, it occurred on the education issue, in which the national conflict between the parties was reflected on the Council. But this was something of an exception. Even in a dispute like that over the fair wages clause, which gave rise to two recorded votes, party lines were somewhat blurred. On both occasions some Liberals voted against such a clause and some Conservatives in favour. But contentious issues of this kind were few and far between. For the most part the Council's business went through smoothly without any hindrance arising from party conflict.

This evidence of the role of the parties confirms our initial interpretation. Generally speaking, party played a minimal role in the Council's affairs. For much of the time it was entirely absent, and when it was present the differences between the parties do not usually seem to have been of major significance. We find this interpretation being supported at various times by Council leaders. In his address to the Council in March 1898, Sir J. T.

Hibbert was reported as saying that 'in the past they had in this Council known nothing of politics and he hoped this state of things would continue',[21] and in 1910 Sir William Scott Barrett wrote: 'It is very satisfying to think that politics do not in any sense interfere with the election of councillors or with their work on the Council.'[22] Perhaps rather more surprisingly, it is interesting to find Andrew Smith, later to be a leading figure in Labour's rise to power, writing in 1928 that 'politics as such do not enter into County Council work, which can be said to be purely administrative'.[23]

THE SEEDS OF CHANGE

Throughout this chapter we have seen that there is a great deal of evidence suggesting that the politics of Lancashire County Council changed little in the period 1889–1929. But this was an age of political upheaval and rapid social change nationally, and towards the end of the period, especially after the First World War, these national trends began to work their way through into county politics. It would be wrong to conclude this chapter without giving some consideration to the signs of change.

National politics up to the First World War were dominated by the Liberals and Conservatives. Both were worried, however, by the increasing strength of the Labour movement. The Radical Liberals and the Lib-Labs of the 1880s and 1890s had given way to an independent Labour Party which had begun to make its weight felt in the general elections of 1906 and 1910. After the war Labour advanced very rapidly, forming a minority government for a short time in 1923–4, and coming to power again in 1929. These trends were somewhat delayed in their appearance in the County Council. Table 4.10 shows the number of Labour candidates and councillors elected from 1910 onwards. One or two Labour sympathisers had contested County Council elections before this, but without success. Albert Smith, a leading

TABLE 4.10
Labour Candidates and Councillors 1910–28

	1910	1913	1919	1922	1925	1928
Labour candidates	3	7	13	15	23	26
Labour candidates elected	1	5	11	10	16	20

Lancashire Labour Party figure and textile trade unionist, became the first Labour councillor when he was returned unopposed for Old Trafford in 1910. He was joined by four others in 1913 and thereafter the numbers rose fairly steadily. A number of difficulties hampered Labour's progress. Perhaps the most serious of these were the problems of the expense involved in fighting elections and in being a councillor, and the difficulty wage-earners faced in getting time off work. Thus Andrew Smith explained Labour's failure to contest one of the Nelson seats in 1928 on these grounds: 'considerations of expense alone prevented Labour from fighting both seats. County Council work is very expensive, as it involves much travelling, in addition to loss of work; and the Labour Party could not see their way to meet the extra cost...'[24] and more generally, the *Lancaster Observer* in 1925 ascribed the small number of Labour councillors and the continued dominance of 'the old county families' to the same problem of personal finance:

> A conscientious discharge of duties may involve a journey to Preston twice or even three times a week. To a man 20 or 40 miles away this entails a sacrifice that few, even among the wealthy, are willing to make. This work is done far from the limelight, and the councillor, unless he is prominent in other respects, can seldom hope even for the minor glory of frequent mention in the local paper. If expenses incurred in attending meetings were paid, as Labour members have advocated, there would be greater competition for a seat on the Council and a more serious attack from the Labour side.[25]

A second point of importance is that there was little immediate incentive for Labour to try to win seats on the Council. Both the apparently irremovable phalanx of country gentlemen and manufacturers who dominated the Council, and the largely administrative nature of county work, admitted even by Andrew Smith (as we have seen), deterred any concerted attempt to achieve increased Labour representation. The immediate aims of the Labour Party were more local, with efforts being concentrated in attempts to win control of boroughs, urban districts and the Boards of Guardians which administered the Poor Law. Representation on the County Council developed on an *ad hoc* basis, depending on the enthusiasm of local Labour Party organisations.

Finally, although as we have seen those Labour councillors who were elected made their presence felt, they were not without their critics. The *Manchester Guardian*, reviewing the situation at the time of the 1931 election, pointed out that Labour's progress compared unfavourably with other parts of the country, especially when it was remembered that Labour had captured forty-one of the sixty-six parliamentary seats in Lancashire in 1929. The article went on to attribute some of the blame for this to the poor performance of those who had been elected: '... it has been a group without a definite policy and its influence has been negligible. This is not altogether surprising, for there has long been something in the atmosphere of the County Hall at Preston that has minimised, if not altogether obliterated party distinctions.'[26]

However, the number of Labour councillors did grow steadily, and this had the important effect of beginning to widen the occupational structure of the Council. The problem of finance that we have mentioned made it extremely difficult for white-collar and manual workers to serve on the Council, but by 1928 there was a sprinkling of both, including two miners and two clerks. Significantly, the largest occupational category of Labour members in this period consisted of trade union officials and full-time Labour Party agents, of whom there were six in 1928. Their position gave them the time and the backing necessary for Council work.

How did the other parties respond to increased Labour representation? The Liberals on the Council, like the Liberals nationally, were already in decline. During the twenties the distinctions between the Conservatives and Liberals became increasingly blurred as they combined to face the common enemy. Both groups began to play down their differences and to emphasise the virtues of a non-partisan approach to local affairs. Both deprecated what they referred to as the 'introduction' of divisive party politics. In one respect they were correct, for the Labour Party brought to the Council a conception of the role of party in local government which was quite different from that held by either the Liberals or the Conservatives.

CONCLUSION

In this chapter we have been concerned with the representativeness of the County Council, the extent to which the system enabled democratic control of local affairs and the role of political parties in the work of the Council. We have seen that a small and exclusive group of men effectively ran the county and that, at least after the first few years, organised party politics was of little importance. What party conflict there was was fairly muted – the parties did not actively contest elections and did not seek to control the Council, and there were few issues dividing councillors on party lines. Councillors of both major parties shared a general view of how local authorities should be run, which we may call the 'consensus' view.

This view assumes that local politics is a matter of broadly like-minded

individuals overseeing the administration of local affairs. The personal
qualities of candidates and not their party should be the deciding factor
in elections; councillors should represent local communities and not a party
viewpoint; local government should not be seen as a means of initiating
new policy.

Between 1889 and 1929 a view of this kind was predominant and the
Council's politics can best be understood in terms of it. But it was already
beginning to be challenged in the late 1920s. The rise of the Labour Party
brought a new conception to local government and of the role of parties
within it. This 'party government' view sees local politics as simply a small-
scale version of national politics. Parties compete at elections for control
of the Council in order to implement their party policies. This view clearly
contradicts the consensus view and the clash between the two is a major
theme of our discussion of the politics of the Council in the years after 1929.

CHAPTER 5

Education

THE County Council assumed responsibility for one very important branch of education soon after it commenced its existence, when on 6 August 1891 the Technical Instruction Committee was formed as a standing committee of the Council.[1] Lancashire was one of numerous counties that reacted quickly to the promise of 'whisky money' for technical educational provision following the Local Taxation (Customs and Excise) Act of 1890,[2] and it is very noticeable that county councils generally took far more interest in this field than in the equally important one of public health.[3] However, Lancashire's need for trained workers in industry and agriculture was manifest, and in the November the Council confirmed the appointment of J. A. Bennion, a Cambridge graduate and barrister-at-law, as its director of technical education. His committee, meanwhile, received dedicated guidance from its chairman, Councillor Thomas Snape, alkali manufacturer of Widnes, although it is worth noticing that a minority of its members had direct experience of the needs of industry, judging at least by their occupations.[4]

Bennion's first detailed report[5] illustrates the great scope of the work undertaken by his small department, in the way of provision and encouragement of technical instruction classes in subjects as diverse as agriculture (always a major concern in English counties), cotton-spinning and weaving, watchmaking in Prescot, silk manufacture, mining in the Wigan district, horticulture and various branches of engineering. The teaching took place in school premises and their evening institutes, in mechanics' institute buildings and occasionally in the new technical colleges that were appearing in the municipal boroughs; courses and examinations were of necessity regulated by the Science and Art Department and the City and Guilds of London Institute. Non-county boroughs and urban sanitary districts received grants-in-aid for classes proportionately to rateable values, on condition that premises and equipment were provided by the local authorities.

Unfortunately, the county's campaign was severely hindered by a shortage of suitable instructors, by lack of support in many districts and, in the case of one borough (Chorley), apparent parochialism.[6] Although the County attempted to overcome the first of these problems by supporting a course for technical and science teachers, under the auspices of the University Extension Movement (in 1891),[7] the enrolments throughout both urban and rural areas of the county were relatively small, and during the first decade of the Committee's existence a part of its accumulated income remained unspent, a balance of over £28,000 in 1898 having grown up since 1890.[8] In a population for the administrative county approaching 1.4 million, there were 8764 enrolments for rural districts in 1897–8 but 18,670 for the non-county boroughs in the same period,[9] a figure that tended to increase in succeeding years. It should however be borne in mind that many classes were not strictly technical; domestic and commercial subjects occupied much evening class time and space, while evening continuation classes, in basic or elementary subjects, were relatively popular everywhere.[10] It is considerations of this kind that explain the sometimes curious pattern of distribution of grant monies, whereby Blackpool and Southport, hardly conventional industrial centres, received by far the largest sums in the early days.

In several spheres there were significant achievements. The county's Farm School at Hutton became one of the most important centres of agricultural education in the north; and there was, in addition, an Agricultural School at the Harris Institute, Preston. In 1899, meanwhile, the Technical Instruction Committee appointed a Cotton Industry Sub-Committee to further classes in spinning and weaving, although the furtherance of effective courses and classes proved to be hard work. During the 1890s there was an attempt to form district committees to encourage technical classes[11] – an interesting harbinger of later delegation schemes – and on the eve of the 1902 Act, Hundred Sub-Committees were formed with the same purpose in mind.[12] By that time, too, the Committee was even making grants for science teaching in endowed grammar schools throughout the county,[13] and there can be little doubt that, with a minimum of administrative staffing and expense, the county authority was doing a great deal for the practical education of adults and juveniles. It was, like many of the greater county authorities, more than half prepared for the massive administrative upheaval occasioned by the Balfour Education Act, in its involvement in what was really the borderland of secondary education. The world of technical education, however, brought other complications.

The reorganisation of local government, in which Lancashire had played such a notable part, had naturally strengthened the desire of county districts to levy their own rates for education and to provide their own education services. The growth of technical education since 1889 had only whetted this appetite, and the logic of administration, as forced upon parliaments and governments, seemed to point to counties as the main co-ordinators in the working of a rational system of education. Unfortunately, the same logic seemed to demand the abolition of school boards, some of which had an admirable record. Following the abortive attempt, embodied in the 1901 Education Bill, to satisfy all parties, Balfour's government, as is well known, succeeded in 1902 in placating the larger second-tier authorities by giving them the powers of Part III authorities and permitting them, on request, to administer elementary education within their localities. The school boards, which were at their strongest and most passionately supported in urban areas, were rather unwillingly (or disingenuously) abolished by Balfour's men. In the midst of the inevitable controversy, the Lancashire councillors awaited the outcome with a measure of complacency, a state of mind resting on a twofold advantage: the administrative county had very few strong school boards, or very few such boards of any kind; and it was manifestly in an excellent position to administer what was known as 'higher' education – secondary, technical, further or other non-basic form. The Technical Instruction Committee had already appointed a formidably qualified director of education, Dr Lloyd Snape,[14] and his *Report* for 1901–02,[15] published in the October, a few months after the 1902 Education Act had been passed (24 March), is a comprehensive document which, while refusing even to glance at the recent proceedings of Parliament, or even at the reception given by the county councillors to the new Act (1 May), shows the developing scope of the thinking of the county administration. The political reactions have been discussed in the second part of the previous chapter.

The task was in all conscience a massive one. The County Council now had the job of supervising seven hundred elementary schools in the administrative county, more than nine-tenths of which were run by Anglican, Nonconformist or Catholic managers. Indeed, the existence of so many church schools is a commentary on the social history of Victorian Lancashire. There was only one board school (Sandylands, Heysham) in the whole of Lonsdale South, just as there were only two such schools in the whole of the Fylde, outside (later) Part III areas. South-west Lancashire had the thinnest of scatterings of non-church schools, as did the eastern foothills near Blackburn and Burnley, while the peripheral districts of the Manchester conurbation were nearly innocent of them.[16] Many of these schoolbuildings, unsuitable, badly planned and inadequately heated, were to drag their inconveniences across the new century. The more populous districts, meanwhile, were already filing their claims to become Part III authorities, and ultimately the county of Lancaster, dotted with all-purpose county borough authorities, was to be obliged to accommodate no fewer than twenty-seven of the former in addition; it should be borne in mind, of course, that the county was to look after the steadily more important secondary education sector in each Part III district.

The county was left, as regards elementary schools, with the sprawling remainder. Nor did the school buildings provide the only problem. Pupil attendance left much to be desired, and there were the natural suspicions on the part of school managers and district councillors to be assuaged. As we have seen, Hundred Committees had already been formed before the Act; but during the period 1902–03, the newly formed Lancashire Education Committee set about a scheme of local representation and delegation, through thirty-five district committees, which has no parallel in any English county.[17] This not only engaged local interest, but left the main or county committee free to concentrate, through the earliest sub-committees, on policies in higher and elementary education respectively, on accounts and on scholarship awards. It was the Elementary Education Sub-Committee that planned the district committee system. The original planning body for educational reorganisation, however, was the former Technical Instruction Committee, with which Dr Snape, as director, had had a chance to become acquainted. The Director now had the backing of a dedicated chairman, Sir H. F. Hibbert of Chorley, who had himself experienced educational undernourishment in youth; and the two of them saw to it that the new Education Committee, which included sixteen county aldermen and thirty-eight councillors, as well as fourteen 'representatives of various bodies' and two women, consisted of people who knew, understood and cared about education.[18]

The new educational organisation was a phenomenal creator of work and committees. The most important sub-committee of the Education Committee was, understandably, that for Elementary Education, which met under the chairmanship of Alderman A. G. C. Harvey, and this body in turn gave forth no fewer than five sub-committees in 1905 alone: Accommodation, Attendance and Staff, Architectural, Religious Instruction in Council Schools, a separate one for Religious Instruction and Attendance of Children at Church During School, and a further sub-committee for Instruction of Children in Rural Districts.[19] Although mere lists of such bodies are of necessity tedious, the main sub-committees of the Education Committee do indicate the extent of the work of Dr Snape's department, and they are as follows: District Administration (1904), Farm (1904), Primary Education (1903), Pupil Teachers' Centres (1904), Scholarships (1903), Secondary Day Schools (1904), Teachers' Training Colleges (1904),

Architectural (1905), Higher Education (1903), Accounts (1903) and Evening Schools and Classes (1905). School Health and Horticultural Committees were subsequently added in 1908 and 1911 respectively.[20]

Nor was this all; members of the Lancashire Education Committee were expected to represent the interests of the central organisation on the thirty-five district sub-committees, which usually included between two and five nominees of the former. Naturally, too, such members might also be school managers; and some county members did in fact undertake a startling amount of committee work at the three levels, notably R. C. Assheton and W. J. Fitzherbert-Brockholes. The district committees, meanwhile, are by far the most interesting feature of the Lancashire educational system at this period. They included representatives of interested districts and parish councils, on a proportional basis, and varied in size from thirteen members (Brierfield, which was responsible for four schools) to thirty-seven members (Ormskirk, which had twenty-seven schools under its purview).

Lancashire was not, of course, alone in delegating much of its educational work to district committees, as permitted by the 1902 Education Act. Cheshire, the West Riding and Durham were among other counties that delegated in a similar fashion; but Lancashire was one of the relatively few English counties that found that delegation was thoroughly acceptable both to administrators and to the different interests represented at the local level. In fact, some counties, like Northamptonshire and Herefordshire, had even more district committees under their purview than had Lancashire, while others, like Cornwall and Derbyshire, gave their committees responsibility for a greater number of elementary schools individually. Lancashire, together with the West Riding, Durham and several smaller counties, had a really comprehensive system of devolution of responsibility, including that for school attendance, accommodation, budgeting, minor repairs, appointment of teachers (subject to formal ratification by the Education Committee) and the purchase of supplies. The system of district sub-committees, with local clerks, was estimated to cut central administrative costs by about half,[21] and such economies continued until the end of the 'old' Council in 1974. The post-1944 'divisions' simply inherited the experience and methods of the post-1902 system, and continued to use many of the latter's practices. There is, in any case, evidence of tactful handling from the centre; and where school boards had been involved, as in Kirkby Ireleth, Ulverston and Dalton-in-Furness,[22] representatives of the former bodies were brought on to the committee concerned. As the former school boards in other districts found their angry defenders, county policy there was less successful.

Each district had an average of two school attendance officers working in its locality; and, since regular sub-committee meetings on this vexed topic were the rule in every district organisation, committee members – as in the case of the Area Children's Committees of half of century later[23] – found themselves very much concerned with, if not always involved in, particular homes and families. School attendance remained a problem attributable to a variety of factors; distance from school in country districts, child labour in those same districts, lack of parental interest or downright resistance by parents, and of course the childish ailments which were rather more prevalent early in the century than later. The percentage of those attending school (as a proportion of children of all ages enrolled in elementary schools) rarely rose much above eighty-eight per cent, and it consistently remained below ninety per cent in the administrative county until 1936.[24] The implied problem, then, was not one to be easily solved by administrators, and probably the root causes changed over time. Perhaps the existence of the half-timer, who could spend half of the school week working part-time in the mill, set a bad example to some youngsters before 1920; these children, however, were fairly numerous only in districts like Great Harwood, Brierfield, Padiham, Ramsbottom or Royton, and even there they were fewer than twenty per cent of all the 'older scholars'.[25]

Many of the schools were not such as to encourage love of education, even though oral research[26] has shown that elderly Lancastrians have entertained happy memories of school days in poky church establishments. Kersley Ringley Wesleyan School (1905) had a Mixed Department 'carried on in one large room, measuring 50 by 36 feet, and in one classroom under the Chapel.... This classroom [went on a report] is dark and low, and is reached by descending some four or five feet below the surface of the ground'. Feniscowles CE School, near Blackburn, was little better, and besides having no cloakroom accommodation, it was situated 'under a steep bank sloping down to the River Darwen, and is, as a result, damp; it has dry rot in the floor and is not capable of being made satisfactory'.[27] Board of Education pressure led to the closure and (where possible) replacement of schools like this, or provided backing where the county authority needed it. Accordingly, the Education Committee followed the procedure of taking over schools by transfer where rebuilding was envisaged, or when a new district school was needed.[28] New council schools tended to be larger than the buildings they replaced. The County Council's record, in terms of pre-1914 days and in the earlier interwar period, is condensed into Table 5.1.[29] It will be seen that the number of voluntary schools was not notably diminished, although by March 1918 sixty-two of the former had in fact been transferred to the Council (thirty-three of them having been replaced afterwards). The numbers of certificated teachers rose only slowly, and already at the commencement of the period covered by the

TABLE 5.1

Elementary Schools Provided by or Maintained by Lancashire LEA, with Numbers of Teachers and Pupils per School, 1913–1928[a]

Year	Voluntary schools	Council schools	Total LEA schools	New schools built after 1903	Certificated teachers	All teaching staff	All pupils attending ('000)	Pupils per school	Teachers per school
1913[b]	578	126	704	44	2197	4534	134[c]	190	6.4
1919[b]	563	132	695	63	2342	4323	118	171	6.2
1924[d]	556	133	689	65	2611	4094	118	171	5.9
1928[d]	541	141	682	75	2757	4081	116	173	5.9

[a] Including uncertificated, supplementary, student and pupil teaching personnel
[b] Ending in March of year shown
[c] Average for six months of 1913 only
[d] In October of year shown

table there were complaints about the shortage of entrants to the profession in the county. Indeed, by 1920 the county teacher supply situation was 'worse than in the country taken as a whole',[30] and whereas the estimated Lancashire annual requirement was of the order of 700 new teachers recognised by the Board of Education, only 200 to 250 had come forward for several years past.[31] As the Board pointed out, the actual spectacle of unqualified teachers struggling with large classes was itself a deterrent to would-be members of the profession.

The Lancashire authority relied, as did education authorities generally, on the existing secondary education system for its supply of young teachers. Student teachers attended secondary school for one day a week, while bright elementary school pupils were given bursaries to enable them to pursue a secondary education and then become teachers; and after 1920 small but increasing numbers of Lancashire secondary school pupils were given scholarships to enable them to go to training colleges or to the elementary training department of a university. The secondary schools therefore played an essential part in the development of educational quality generally. It is well known that the 1902 Act was the 'first government measure explicitly to promote public secondary education (as distinct from the higher grade work of the board schools), and the Education Committee, through its Higher Education Committee under the chairmanship of Sir Henry Hibbert, conscientiously set about the planning of public secondary schools (1904–05) at Waterloo-with-Seaforth, Bacup and Rawtenstall.[32] By March 1913 there were fifteen county secondary schools under county ownership and municipal management, and nineteen endowed grammar schools assisted by the county authority. Of the latter, ten were wholly maintained by the County Council for running purposes, and the other received grants from the county. In the same year, fairly rapid progress was being made in the building of new secondary schools, several of which were, following further well-known provisions of the Act, joint secondary and technical institutions.[33] A total of 4838 pupils were in attendance at secondary schools throughout the administrative county, or 3.6 per cent of all elementary pupils. (A fairer comparison would of course be one with 'older pupils' attending elementary schools, and with those taking various technical courses; but even when such a proportion is considered, the relevant figure cannot have been high.) A further 1442 county pupils attended secondary schools in nearby county boroughs. The real tragedy, one of wastage of human potential, is contained in the following figures for January 1912, relating to children in Lancashire elementary schools:[34]

Total number on roll of all ages	153,363
Percentage on roll of 13 years of age	3.27%
Percentage on roll of 14 years of age	0.29%
Percentage on roll of 15 years of age	0.02%

This state of affairs was of course to be altered by the 'Fisher' Education Act of 1918, which by degrees stopped exemptions from school under fourteen years of age, and permitted the raising of the leaving age to fifteen. However, there was little hope of this last while such a shortage of teachers persisted, and the one bright feature of the war years, and those immediately following, was a continuing increase of pupil numbers in Lancashire secondary schools, leading inevitably to much overcrowding and contrivance in the schools concerned.[35] Unhappily, the war had put a stop to all but occasional council building, and the postwar depression years imposed further obstacles to the latter. Nevertheless, there were 11,044 children attending county secondary schools in March 1927.[36] It was fortunate that much essential building had been completed by 1914: the immediate postwar optimisms, curiously like those following 1944, and resulting in some brave experiments in day continuation and even in an emergency teacher training college at the Storey Institute, Lancaster,[37] soon began to pale before the economic stringencies of the age. In 1926–7 the County Council made its first major gesture in teacher training by taking over Edge Hill Training College, Ormskirk.[38]

The war years had imposed great strains on those responsible for elementary education in the county, and especially upon the Director of Education, Dr Snape, who was yet another casualty in the battlefield of county administration. As the Education Committee Report for 1917–18 put it, 'his conscientious devotion to his duties [have] resulted in a strain too great for his physical powers'[39] and his distinguished career thus culminated in his retirement (1918) at the early age of fifty-seven years. One of the leading members of the local authority education service, he was sometime chairman of the Association of Directors and Secretaries of Education, and his advice was sought by the Board of Education both on committees and informally.[40] He had worked closely and cordially with Sir Henry Hibbert, his chairman through his seventeen years of service, and Sir Henry retired from the Education Committee chairmanship only to undertake that of the Council Council in March 1921; the latter was then succeeded by J. T. Travis-Clegg, and Dr Snape gave way to G. H. Gater, who served the county until February 1924, and who went on to the only conceivably higher post in the same field, that of education officer to the London County Council.[41] (As Sir George Gater, KCB, GCMG, he was later a distinguished civil servant and under-secretary of state for the colonies, 1939–47.) Percival Meadon, who followed him until 1945, had been an assistant teacher before he became director of education for Essex, 1915–24; and in his time the teacher's lot improved, despite the economies of the crisis years.

By the end of the twenties, the Hadow Report had left a considerable impression in Lancashire, and there is plenty of evidence of goodwill in the LEA – 'the Committee have also continued their policy of grouping the senior scholars in the Elementary Schools with a view to the provision of more effective advanced instruction' (1926)[42] – even though such originality as the county had did not match up to its great resources. In 1919 there had been one 'Higher Elementary School'.[43] Perhaps the still rather conservative-minded councillors were too easily satisfied that, taking advantage of some fifteen types of scholarship or exhibition, or of junior technical schools and classes, the bright or moderately able boy or girl could still find a pathway to advancement – provided that his parents, or the economic conditions of the age, allowed him to do so. Ideas, as so often, came from the centre; local authorities do not produce many of their own, although their experiences make a fine seedbed. It was certainly pressure from the Board of Education that forced the Lancashire authority to face up continually to the fact that many of its elementary school buildings were defective: 'Comparatively few schools ... satisfied the Board's requirements' (1926).[44] The county could of course point to its pioneering work in agricultural education, or its adult classes, or its junior technical schools. But these excellent projects affected comparatively few people, and the age of secondary education for all was yet to come.

CHAPTER 6

Health

On 23 May 1889, a special meeting of the new Lancashire County Council resolved 'That a Health Committee be appointed'.[1] As in other matters, the background to the work of such a body must be considered before the subject becomes really meaningful. First of all, then, the future public health campaigners of the county authority were entering a field of conflict on which the battle, a grim and protracted one, was already more than half won. The great towns of the north had begun to conquer the 'problem of muck' in the mid-1870s, when the terrible death rates of the age began a modest but decisive turn downwards. The great Public Health Act of 1875 marked this first historic phase, and the setting up of rural sanitary authorities in 1872 meant that the town corporations received some slow and halting assistance in the fight. In addition, these two enactments of 1872 and 1875 gave power to the Local Government Board to set up urban sanitary authorities,[2] and it was in the 'twilight' areas of urbanisation, outside the boundaries of the great town corporations, and in smaller towns generally that the most serious health problems were later encountered.

The administrative county, then, was divided into both urban and rural sanitary districts, of which the former predominated, and each type of district had its special problems. Those of the urban concentrations were of a familiar kind, somewhat eased by the often belated measures of the sanitary authorities themselves; rural Lancashire, with special problems of water supply and sanitation, had virtually escaped the attentions of the sanitary reformer.

Dr Edward Sergeant was appointed medical officer of health for the county in June 1890, at a salary of £800 per annum, under the terms of Section 17 of the Local Government Act of 1888. He was to serve the county through nearly three decades, and was to play his part in the development of preventive public medicine and health education in an area that covered 129 county districts at the time of his taking office. His work was primarily supervisory, that of receiving periodical reports from the (usually) very much part-time medical officers for these districts; but he was of course enabled to give publicity to the more serious anomalies in the worst areas, and to mobilise constructive opinion as time went on. From the beginning, Dr Sergeant had no illusions. He remarked:

The small remuneration of many medical officers of health gives an idea of the value some sanitary authorities attach to the services of their chief officer. For instance, one medical officer of health is paid £10 annually for performing all the duties appertaining to his office in a district with an area of 6807 statute acres, and another authority grants the sum of £15 to their medical officer for looking after the health of their district, 3651 acres in extent, and a population estimated at 5180.[3]

Dr Sergeant, who had served his apprenticeship to public and preventive medicine in Bolton, commented on a 'densely packed' county population, 'too frequently badly housed, and with occupations laborious and inimical to health'. Yet, he found the county death rate 'not unsatisfactory'.[4] Dr Sergeant and his successor Dr Butterworth saw these death rates significantly reduced (Table 6.1),[5] and it was undoubtedly true that the contribution, in the way of health education, of his authority and its staff to the region, could count among the factors that brought this about. Part of this progress was more apparent than real, in that Lancashire's rates of population increase was falling, and in that fewer newly born and infant

TABLE 6.1
Lancashire: Crude Birth and Death Rates

Period	Crude live birth rate			Crude death rate		
		Urban	Rural		Urban	Rural
Five-yearly average	County	districts	districts	County	districts	districts
1889–94 (6 yrs)	30.42	30.98	28.63	18.70	19.18	16.91
1895–9	28.34	28.63	26.56	17.64	17.97	15.62
1900–04	26.51	26.67	25.37	15.89	16.13	14.21
1905–09	24.54	24.70	23.46	14.35	14.52	13.17
1910–14	22.26	22.40	21.38	13.90	14.09	12.69
1915–19	17.45	17.47	17.31	14.98	15.10	14.25
1920–4	19.13	19.13	18.29	12.61	12.73	11.87
1925–9	14.94	14.99	14.65	12.65	12.85	11.51

children were at risk – although there were also reassuring child mortality statistics.[6] By the end of the nineteenth century, many parts of the county were suffering losses by migration; and some rural districts, indeed, were exhibiting absolute losses of population.[7] In these circumstances, it is hardly surprising that birth rates were tending to fall. The fall in crude death rates is made up of a multiplicity of factors, in the working of some of which the county health service played a valuable part, notably in the spheres of improved midwifery and anti-tuberculosis campaigning.

The new County Council's first major health campaign was one with diplomatic overtones. The county had had many open sewers and public nuisances, and its rivers had long been in these categories. As the new medical officer remarked, 'the rivers of Lancashire are, with the increase of population and trade, becoming more and more polluted, and no action is taken because the local authorities whose duty it is to put the law in motion are themselves the greatest delinquents and pollute the streams in these districts more than anybody else.'[8] The Mersey received the tainted waters of the Irwell, Irk, Roch, Tonge and Croal, carrying waste and effluent from dye, print and bleach works as well as tanneries and paper mills. The Calder and Darwen polluted the Ribble, and, as was shown a few years later,[9] the remote and beautiful Lune could be rendered a menace to health by the one city on its banks.

An unfortunate technical misunderstanding with the Local Government Board led to a serious delay in the formation of a river authority to control the Irwell and Mersey, and not until 3 July 1891 was a provisional order for a joint committee confirmed. A similar order for the Ribble was confirmed as of the same date.[10] The creation of a nominal controlling apparatus, where the rivers were concerned, did not bring about magical changes, however, and pollution of varying kinds has remained a problem until the present day, despite vast achievements during this century. The local authorities of that period lacked an adequate monitoring system, and only the establishment in 1900 of a public health laboratory at Owens College (University of Manchester), could really indicate degrees of contamination adequately, as was shown in the case of the Lune, already cited.

Although the creation of urban and rural district councils in 1894 did something to help the Lancashire health authority's work, the problem of rural sanitation was a similarly intractable one. With sanitation went clean water supplies, often equally lacking, and Dr Sergeant could comment in 1889 that 'the drinking water of the village of Glasson was drawn principally from the canal basin'. The 'drains and water supply of Pilling and Stalmine' were defective, and in the case of Pilling there is a colourful description of its water-supplying ponds, used by dairy cattle (1894): the latter were 'contaminated with sewage, and the water is not fit for cattle to look at, let alone to drink'.[11] That conditions did not improve in spectacular fashion is indicated by the terms of a terse report by Dr Sergeant on nearby Cockerham in September 1900: 'Every summer, water is very scarce, both for human consumption and for farm purposes, and throughout the year the quality of the water is ... open to grave suspicion.' In this instance, Dr Sergeant referred the matter to the parish council.

His official duties were set out by the Public Health Committee in January 1890.[12] Besides those described, they consisted of the giving of assistance and advice to local authorities in the event of epidemics; the assistance of supervision of inspectors appointed under the Food and Drugs Acts; the giving of guidance in the making of by-laws for the suppression of nuisances; the performance of duties under the terms of the Artisans and Labourers Dwellings Improvement Act of 1874; and the overview of parliamentary Bills affecting the Council and dealing with sanitation, town extension, water supply and housing belonging to the Council. An actual work diary, in the form of a report covering three months of the summer of 1900 and tracing Dr Sergeant's activities during the whole of that time, is more revealing.[13] It should be borne in mind that he operated without the services of more than a tiny staff; his chief clerk, Mr J. E. Gee, handled office business in the course of the Medical Officer's almost continual absences in the field, dealing with correspondence from some 129 districts, all for a salary of £130 per annum.[14] That Dr Sergeant also earned £800 per annum cannot be doubted. During the three months of mid-July to mid-October 1900, he travelled about the county giving evidence in food and drug prosecutions, examined several cases of polluted water supplies, inspected isolation hospital sites and buildings, attended a sanitary conference in Aberdeen, and visited some eighteen places in the county.

In the prewar years the county had to face the task of providing a school medical service as its own educational responsibilities were augmented to huge proportions following the 1902 Education Act.[15] The condition of the schoolchildren attending the county's elementary schools was bound to attract the attention of its medical officers, and the Education (Administrative Provisions) Act of 1907 placed upon them the duty of providing for the medical examination of these children, and of acting in such manner as to protect – as far as possible – their health and to begin the health education of children and parents.[16] Accordingly, the Lancashire Education Committee in 1908 appointed Dr J. J. Butterworth (who became, in 1917, the second medical officer of health) as medical superintendent of schools, and soon afterwards six medical inspectors and six nurses were appointed to grapple with the problems to be encountered among some 160,000 children in 706 county schools. These officers and workers were to operate from centres with good railway facilities; and, indeed, in their first full year of inspection (1909) they managed to examine nearly 33,000 children and to perform their own clerical duties much of the time.

They succeeded in uncovering some sad social evils. In one composite group of girl pupils, the frequency of head infestation, in a large sample, (girls of twelve years), rose as high as thirty-eight per cent. Perhaps the saddest discovery of all was the high incidence of rickets, a disease most frequently found by the inspectors working in urban districts; well over a thousand cases were found in the first year of working. Corneal infections and opacities, not as numerous, were also revealed.[17] The inspectors soon realised that many children submitted to them were suffering from physical defects that actually interfered with their school progress. Where specific medical treatment was required, parents were recommended to see their own doctor, and the children would then be seen at school at a re-inspection. This follow-up work was found to be so beneficial that it was decided to increase the medical staff, so that by the end of 1914 the number of the latter had been increased to thirteen, and there were twenty-six school nurses, two being allocated to each doctor.[18] None of this is to deny, however, that there were serious elementary defects in the new service, and only forty-two per cent of children found in 1910 to need spectacles were actually provided with them, perhaps because of poverty and the inaccessibility of oculists and eye hospitals. Accordingly, the Education Committee arranged that a competent optician should supply spectacles of good standard quality at fixed charges lower than those paid by private patients, and although the scheme related to selected schools with barely over fifty prescriptions, this experiment was the forerunner of schemes that were to be greatly extended in years to come, and contained the seed of a concept of modern social welfare.[19]

Yet another legacy of the nineteenth century was the Mrs Gamp midwife, dirty and illiterate, and the Midwives Act of 1902 made the county the supervising authority for midwifery. This Act required the registration of practising midwives, and it laid down the necessary qualifications for such registration. Dr Sergeant, who now had yet another field to supervise, received an addition to his salary of £100 per annum, and his chief clerk, Mr J. E. Gee, received an additional £30.[20] By July 1904, 524 midwives had been certificated, whereas at the commencement of the work supervision, only one-sixth held certificates issued by various hospitals (152 in all), and no fewer than twenty-two per cent of the supervised women could not sign their own names. A survey of applicants for admission to the register of midwives in 1904 revealed another anomaly, the fortuitous and irregular distribution of these women, qualified and unqualified, place by place, so that Pemberton, for example, had twenty-one, Prestwich two, Turton ten and Ulverston two.[21]

The County Council appointed its first 'lady inspector' of midwifery in October 1902. Miss Edith Wright took the post at a salary of £104 per annum.[22] In the following three months she commenced her work of interviewing midwives, concentrating on the Preston and Chorley districts, and seeing that the women concerned understood the provisions of the Act of 1902, which laid down that deaths during childbirth were to be reported to the supervising authority, that medical practitioners were to be notified in all cases involving abnormalities in pregnancy, labour or lying-in, and that cases of puerperal fever or other infectious diseases were to be similarly notified. Miss Wright commented that, 'So far as I can judge, the majority of the women are anxious to properly carry out the requirements of the Act.... Most of the midwives looked clean in their person and have tidy homes, but very few carry bags of appliances or wear print dresses.'[23] Many years later, Miss Wright observed that 'At that time, only seventeen per cent of the practising midwives were trained; most had learned their trade by working ... with other midwives.'[24]

We now turn to the topics of sanitary control and control over housing. The former was a constant preoccupation of the county health authority, and the latter, in some of its aspects at least, was a responsibility of the Health Department. The 1909 Town Planning Act, a distant but historically interesting forerunner of mid-century planning legislation, had few repercussions for the county authority itself, but it did lead to the appointment of 'one Inspector to deal with the inspection of cowsheds and dairies ... and another Inspector to assist the County Medical Officer of Health in dealing with ... general sanitary matters arising under the ... Act.'[25] The second of these posts was soon afterwards (1912) filled by a farm and veterinary specialist, and the single remaining inspector, Mr Eginton, set about his herculean task. He did his best to deal with the 'nuisances' scattered round the urban and rural districts, but the beneficial work of dealing with them was held up by wartime shortages of labour and materials. As required by the Act, Dr Sergeant and Mr Eginton and their committee did attempt to bring pressure to bear on local authorities, but they had to contend with great inertia; and wartime conditions brought ready excuses, well exemplified in some correspondence between the Medical Officer for the County and the Clerk of Wigan Rural District Council.[26]

The wartime and immediate postwar years brought a much more significant development in the county's health services, one that put Lancashire's health administration among the outstanding pioneers in public medicine. From January 1912, cases of phthisis (pulmonary tuberculosis) became compulsorily notifiable for the first time, and in 1913 the Department launched a new scheme for the treatment of this disease.[27] A central tuberculosis officer and eight area officers were appointed, and the county was covered by a system of dispensaries. In the following year (1914), the scheme was administered by a separate Tuberculosis Committee, and within months there were special county sanatoria at High Carley and Elswick. The Tuberculosis Committee was detached from the main Health and Public Housing Committee in 1917,[28] during the first year of Dr J. J. Butterworth's period of office as medical officer of health. By this time, the clerical staff at the Central Tuberculosis Office had a complement larger than that in the main Health Department, and the scheme was under the guidance of one of the leading tuberculosis authorities in the country, Dr G. Lissant Cox, formerly of Liverpool. Once the totally unhelpful influence of the war had receded – county tuberculosis death rates climbed to a peak in 1918, whereas, significantly, they had tended to fall before 1914 – a more rapid decline in deaths from the disease within the administrative county went on uninterruptedly until 1930. Prewar experience clearly indicated that general social factors were playing some part in the battle against pulmonary and non-pulmonary tuberculosis, but Lancashire's highly organised fight evidently contributed to the steeper drop. By 1927, too, 'the tuberculosis death-rate was declining more rapidly than the general rate'.[29] Moreover, far more cases of the disease were being notified, and more people, accordingly, were receiving attention. General practitioners were working more closely with the staffs of dispensaries, and the skilfulness of treatment was itself enhanced by experience. Artificial light treatment was commenced early in 1925 at dispensaries, sanatoria and hospitals, and this gave most satisfactory results in non-pulmonary cases.[30] Specific results of this kind cannot be explained away, of course, by a complex of social and environmental factors, although the latter continued to work beneficially in the background.

After the School Health and Child Welfare Departments were amalgamated in 1919, it became possible to develop a more successful system of school clinics, which became centres for the treatment of visual defects, tonsilitis, deafness and a multitude of childish afflictions. In 1924–5 came the establishment of a pioneering orthopaedic scheme, whereby Dr Butterworth successfully sought the services of eminent consultants in Liverpool and Manchester (notably Sir Harry Platt), who could arrange for access to beds at the Ancoats Hospital and the Royal Liverpool Children's Hospital. In 1927 the County Council opened its own eighty-five bed orthopaedic hospital at Biddulph Grange in Staffordshire, where children could be educated as well as cured. The county authority also helped to provide extensive facilities for the care, training and employment of the blind under the terms of the Blind Persons Act of 1920, and the following decade saw many attempts, utilising new statutes, to improve the health and environmental services of the county. These ranged from improvement in the quality of milk supplies – and the all-important work of the County analyst, Dr G. D. Elsdon, calls for more than passing mention – through the registration and control of nursing and maternity homes to smoke abatement measures. Although the county's midwives were part-time workers, an increasing number had recognised qualifications, and it is worth noticing that, largely through improved maternity services, infant mortality fell from ninety-one per 1000 live births in the administrative county in 1920 to sixty-four in 1930.[31]

To sum up, then, a great local authority, operating in an economic and social climate that was decidedly cramping by mid-twentieth century standards, could yet deploy resources that had an appreciable effect upon public health. A smaller county, unable to command the services of outstandingly qualified physicians and organisers, probably could not have commenced to think of an onslaught on tuberculosis like that launched in Lancashire from 1913. The experience of later decades, which may yet teach us resoundingly that great administrative machines create ultimately insoluble problems, nevertheless should not obscure the fact that massive results can still be obtained in a situation of primary need, simply by the concentration of resources at the point of most effect.

CHAPTER 7

Roads

THE entire maintenance of the main roads within their borders, including their repair, improvement, enlargement and reconstruction, was assigned to county councils under the Local Government Act of 1888. In Lancashire, these roads had previously been under the control of the county justices who, acting through their Court of Annual General Sessions, were then the highway authority for main roads. These roads consisted chiefly of former turnpike roads – roads constructed by Turnpike Trustees who collected tolls for their maintenance – which by the Highways and Locomotives Act of 1878 the county justices had been obliged to take over and maintain free of tolls. At the same time the county justices were empowered to take over from the local highway authorities and 'main'[1] any road which, because of the volume of traffic on it or because it connected larger towns, was deemed of sufficient importance to warrant taking that step. The main roads were unevenly distributed over the administrative county; therefore the county justices declared them to be Hundred roads and not county roads, appointed each Hundred bridgemaster as surveyor of county roads within his Hundred, and levied road rates on each Hundred separately.

The new Lancashire County Council formed, as one of its standing committees, a Main Roads and Bridges Committee consisting of thirty-six members, and continued the system of roads administration set up by the county justices. Under this committee, there were in theory seven county surveyors of roads, seven county bridgemasters and seven Hundred bridgemasters, one each for the two divisions of Lonsdale Hundred and one each for each of the other five Hundreds.[2] By 1890, however, William Radford, a Manchester civil engineer, held all of these posts except those of county surveyor of roads and Hundred bridgemaster for West Derby Hundred. When Mr Radford died in 1897,

Lancashire County Council secured[3] an Act of Parliament, the Lancashire County Bridges Act,[4] which enabled them to appoint a bridgemaster for the whole administrative county, to separate the posts of county surveyors of roads and bridgemasters and to make two posts, of county surveyor of roads and county bridgemaster, each post to cover the whole administrative county. W. H. Schofield was appointed county surveyor of roads and W. H. Radford county bridgemaster, but on the latter's death in 1900 W. C. Hall became bridgemaster. Also in 1889, district surveyors were appointed, one for each of the three districts into which the county was divided for roads – northern, eastern and southern. A fourth district surveyor was appointed in 1892 and the districts reorganised on a Hundred basis – Lonsdale and Amounderness, Blackburn and Leyland, Salford, and West Derby – an assistant county surveyor was appointed in 1902 and a fifth district surveyor appointed in 1912, when the districts were further reorganised.

Initially the district surveyors were inspectors of roads, inspecting all the main roads in their respective districts monthly, reporting on necessary repairs and estimating their costs. Under the 1888 Act, any urban authority could claim to retain the power of maintaining and repairing the main roads or the portions of main roads within its district, but a county council was required to make payments towards the costs incurred. Then, under the Local Government Act of 1894, the highway boards were abolished and rural district councils, set up by that Act, became highway authorities in their districts. A clause in the Act allowed county councils to postpone abolition of these boards, so that it was not until 1899 that all highway boards were abolished in Lancashire. Some seventy urban authorities in the administrative county 'claimed' their main roads and carried out the actual maintenance and repair of these roads within their districts. The other main roads, though vested in the county council, were also maintained for the most part by local authorities. The maintenance and repair of some main roads were let to contractors, and up to 1912 the district surveyors were only responsible for the repair of some forty-seven miles of main road in rural districts which they effected by direct labour. Thereafter a policy of direct control of the repair and maintenance of the main roads by the county surveyor and district surveyors was rapidly extended.[5] The County Council was very cautious about 'maining' roads[6] except to secure good roads to the seaside resorts of Blackpool, Fleetwood, Morecambe and Southport and to the industrial town of Barrow-in-Furness. Any main roads not deemed to be really important traffic routes were 'dismained' and became secondary roads. When a diversion of a main road was completed, the portion superseded was, of course, 'dismained'. Instead the Council favoured the improvement and development of a secondary road system maintained by the local authorities but with grants towards their costs for repair and maintenance made by them. There was also a considerable mileage of district roads,[7] maintained by county district councils but also in receipt of Council grants.

The roads that the Council took over in 1889 were, for the most part, somewhat narrow roads and in places tortuous, constructed of water-bound macadam.[8] Some roads were formed of river cobblestones, some of boulders, and some paved or half paved with grit (sandstone) setts,[9] which were soon worn down by traffic. For some fifteen years a policy was pursued of road-widening and improvement in which tar macadam replaced water-bound macadam and worn sett roads. A new situation arose after 1905 with the increasing use of county roads by traction engines, heavy motor waggons and motorcars. Many roads and bridges were unable to bear such traffic, so that much damage was done to road surfaces – some subsidence occurred and bridges suffered fracturing. The heavy traffic also caused considerable dust nuisance on the roads. The decade 1905–15 saw the development of light railways and tramways, especially in the southern part of the county. In 1905 alone sixty-two such schemes were initiated. Although the railway and tramway undertakings were responsible for the road area between their lines, the roads along which they ran had to be widened to a minimum of thirty-seven feet.

Tar-spraying minimised the dust nuisance, and granite sett-paved roads replaced tar macadam on heavy traffic roads. Granite sett paving, however, was twice as expensive as other types of road surfaces. Therefore, on other roads grouted granite macadam roads were experimented with, which entailed applying boiling tar or pitch thinly with or without hot sand to granite road material. Artificial 'Durex' paving and 'Rocmac' (a patent road binding material) were also tried, while some tar macadam roads, too, were strengthened by placing granite cubes at random on the road surface. Just before the First World War some stretches of heavy-traffic roads in southern Lancashire were constructed of granite setts on a concrete foundation. Because of the difficulty of securing tar macadam as required, the Council established its own tar macadam works at Carnforth, operative from 1915. After 1909 the Road Board, established in that year, made grants to highway authorities towards the improvement of existing roads and the construction of new ones. At first Lancashire County Council made grants to the local authorities in the administrative county for the maintenance and improvement of the portions of main roads in their areas. Later it was found to be less expensive for the local authorities to raise loans for improvements to, and the widening and reconstruction of, these roads and then for the County Council to make annual grants to cover the whole or an agreed part of the repayments and interest on these loans. Expenditure on roads in the administrative county rose from £103,108 for the year 1890–1 to £274,657 for the year 1913–14.

The Main Roads and Bridges Committee met ten times per year, but in most years extra meetings were necessary. Its chairmen were: W. W. B. Hulton of Hulton Park near Bolton (1889–1907); James Shuttleworth, pawnbroker of Bacup (1907–13); and John Aspell, cotton manufacturer of Middleton (1913–34). The Committee formed only two sub-committees, one an Advisory Sub-Committee which had but that one function, and the other an Accounts Sub-Committee, which examined all accounts from local authorities as well as those of the surveyors and bridgemaster, and which were then passed to the Committee. The Committee itself dealt with all other matters. Much of the time was taken up in considering and sanctioning the grants to be made to local authorities and agreements to be entered into with them over the financing of their loans in respect of main roads. Decisions had to be taken over the 'maining' and the 'dismaining' of roads and the construction of new roads, and provisional and final orders had to be drafted for their implementation. Other matters claiming the attention of the Committee were contracts for road materials, for the repair and maintenance of some of the main roads and for the repair of bridges. From time to time, applications were drawn up to the Road Board for grants and to the Development Commissioners, set up by the Development and Road Improvement Funds Act 1909, for an order to acquire compulsorily land required for road-widening or a new stretch of road, which the County Council had failed to secure by agreement. Occasionally, too, the Committee drew up by-laws[10] under the Locomotive Act 1898, prohibiting locomotives from using certain county or hundred bridges or, in other cases, limiting the weights of vehicles permitted to cross them.

On the outbreak of war on 4 August 1914 there was government concern about unemployment in areas where local industries were likely to be adversely affected. A letter[11] was sent by the chief engineer of the Road Board, not to the Council but to the county surveyor, suggesting that schemes for road improvements should be initiated in densely populated urban areas in the administrative county to strengthen and improve important traffic roads, to widen carriageways and to improve corners and the drainage of these roads. In response the Main Roads and Bridges Committee drew up and recommended, and the Council approved, twenty-three schemes, estimated to cost about £130,000, for which the Road Board made a fifty per cent grant. As a result, expenditure on roads for 1914–15 rose to £305,000, a figure well above total receipts. In 1915, however, a circular letter[12] from the Local Government Board placed restrictions on capital expenditure on new works except those that were of pressing necessity. In these circumstances, the Council decided to complete all schemes where the work was well advanced, to stop schemes just begun and not to proceed with those not yet begun. In 1917 the Ministry of Munitions set up a Road Stone Control Committee which allowed local authorities only twenty per cent of the road materials used in 1913–14, and thereafter required them to obtain permission from this committee for further supplies and to give priority to roads bearing substantial military traffics. In Lancashire on roads other than these recourse was had to patching with tar macadam or sheeting[13] with tar-slag macadam. Inevitably road surfaces over much of the administrative county deteriorated.

After the First World War, as motor vehicle traffic increasingly replaced horse-drawn vehicles,[14] not only had a backlog of repairs to be coped with, but also a programme of widening and reconstruction undertaken and new roads built. Accordingly in 1919 a Ministry of Transport was formed to control all forms of transport, inland waterways, harbours and docks. The Road Board, established in 1909, was abolished and the general control of roads and bridges was transferred to the new Ministry, which established a Roads Department for that purpose. In the next year, the Road Act of 1920 transferred to county councils the collection of duties and licence fees on mechanically propelled vehicles and on carriages. After payments to local authorities, the residue of the sums so collected was paid into a Road Fund under the control of the Ministry, from which grants were made to highway authorities for the improvement of roads and the construction of new roads. The Ministry numbered the roads and classified all main roads into three classes – Class I, Class II, and Unclassified – paying grants of fifty per cent of actual costs on Class I roads, and twenty-five per cent on Class II roads. No grants were paid on unclassified secondary or district roads.

This more direct involvement of the Government in roads led Lancashire County Council to centralise its roads and bridges administration. In 1921 the separate posts of county surveyor and county bridgemaster were merged and W. H. Schofield,[15] the county surveyor, was appointed to the new post. Then, as from 31 March 1923,[16] in spite of opposition from the council members of the Hundred of Lonsdale,[17] all main roads and all Hundred bridges became a charge on the whole administrative county instead of on the six Hundreds separately as heretofore. The roads and bridges accounts became part of the general purposes account of the Council.

Under the Unemployment Relief Works Act of 1920, local authorities, with the approval of the Ministry of Health, could undertake schemes for works of public utility. Local authorities tended to opt for road improvements and construction, and so the Ministry of Transport, in addition to the Class I fifty per cent grant made for such schemes, for six years made grants to cover sixty-five per cent, for half the period of the loans, of the annual amounts for repayment of loans and interest thereon, in respect of approved schemes in areas of high unemployment. During these years the Main Roads and Bridges Committee undertook thirty-three schemes, costing £1,678,411, financed by government grants and loans.

In the construction of county roads, a policy[18] was established in 1922 of granite sett paving for heavy traffic roads, bituminous surfacing for fairly heavy traffic roads and tar macadam for light traffic roads. When through traffic or arterial routes were envisaged deeper foundations became necessary, often placed on a layer of compacted clinker ashes with a concrete foundation and a bituminous surface. The Council decided to have their own mechanical haulage and purchased motor tractors, waggons and trailers. In spite of recurrent losses the Council's tar macadam works at Carnforth was persevered with.

Under Circular 189 (Roads) of 1923 the Ministry of Transport offered seventy-five per cent grants for the resurfacing of roads in rural districts and the rural parts of urban districts to bring them up to the standard of main roads. The Main Roads and Bridges Committee in 1925 began therefore a programme of improvement of rural roads which, however, was not completed until the year 1932–3. Some 312 miles of these roads were resurfaced, chiefly with tar macadam, at a cost of £881,952. Many of these roads were 'mained' and became county roads, so that, together with new roads, the mileage of county main roads increased from 656 miles in 1921 to 981 miles in 1930. The bridges on these roads became county bridges. A policy was also initiated, which gathered momentum after 1929, of strengthening and widening canal and railway bridges, many of which also, on the payment of lump sums by the companies concerned to relieve them of liability for their repair and maintenance, became county bridges. As a result the number of county bridges increased from 552 in 1921 to 887 in 1930.

During the period 1920–9 traffic on Lancashire roads increased by some forty-six per cent and so a start was made to promote safety on the roads. Dangerous bends and corners were gradually eliminated, traffic signs[19] were erected and roundabouts (or 'circuses') began to make their appearance.

Further duties and powers under various Acts of Parliament were delegated by the Council to the Main Roads and Bridges Committee. The Public Health Act of 1925 and the Roads Improvements Act of 1925 involved the Committee in the making up of streets, decisions on improvement and the marking of lines on county roads. The regulation of advertisements on roads became a duty of the Committee under the Advertisements Regulation Act of 1925, and the control of petrol filling stations under the Petroleum Consolidation Act of 1928. These additional duties added to the administrative work of the Committee, since no additional sub-committees were formed.

As far as roads were concerned, the decade 1919–29 saw much improvement and reconstruction both of county roads and of bridges, in order to make good necessary work postponed or abandoned during the war period and as an attempt to cater for the ever-increasing motor traffic. Comparatively few new roads were built. Nevertheless revenue expenditure on roads more than doubled from £451,225 for the year 1921–2 (representing eleven per cent of county revenue expenditure) to £1,107,571 (twenty-three per cent) for 1929–30. This expenditure continued to be met by about half from government grants and other income, and the rest from county rates. Capital expenditure, except for small items, was financed from loans, which were increasingly secured from the Public Works Loan Board rather than from institutional and private sources.[20]

CHAPTER 8

Police

A COUNTY constabulary was established in Lancashire in 1840, as permitted by the County and District Constables Act of 1839, under the control of the county justices of the peace, exercised through their Court of Annual General Sessions, and administered by a Constabulary Committee. By 1888 the County Constabulary was a force of 1321 of all ranks (1:1062 of population) headed by a chief constable and an assistant chief constable, and the police area of the county was divided into police divisions, each under a superintendent. This force was regarded as one of the most efficient provincial police forces in the country.

The Local Government Act of 1888 transferred to the newly created county councils the administrative functions of the county justices, but the justices were not entirely deprived of their control of the County Constabulary. Provision was made under the Act for the exercise of county police functions by a joint committee – the Standing Joint Committee – consisting of equal numbers[1] of county justices, appointed by the Courts of Quarter Sessions, and of members of the Council. This Standing Joint Committee was not to be a committee of the Council but a separate statutory body employed to elect its own chairman. Its function was not only to exercise control over the county police, including the appointment of the chief constable,[2] but also to provide accommodation for the justices in Quarter Sessions and out of sessions; and it was also authorised to enter into contracts.

In Lancashire it was agreed that the Standing Joint Committee for the administrative county should have thirty-six members. At first the representatives of the county justices were appointed by the Court of Annual General Sessions, but on its demise in 1890 it was decided that each Court of Quarter Sessions in the county should elect or appoint members to represent their sessions area according to an agreed scheme.[3] The names of the justices appointed were sent to the Council before the end of the year preceding for which the Committee was to serve, and the Council in turn appointed its representatives. There was nothing in the Act to prevent members of the Council, who were also county justices and who had not been appointed as council representatives on the Committee, from being appointed at Quarter Sessions to the Committee as representatives of the county justices. Consequently, in Lancashire in most years two or more council members sat on the Standing Joint Committee as representatives of the justices, thus in effect giving to the Council a majority on the Standing Joint Committee.

The Committee met ten times a year but four or five additional meetings were always necessary to cope with the mass of administrative detail that came before it. At each meeting the chief constable made a return of the accessions, diminutions, promotions and reductions in the force, and put forward recommendations over the granting of pensions, gratuities and meritorious conduct awards and for increases in the police force. He also reported particulars of aid[4] given to and by the county police to and by other police forces. Quarterly the chief constable laid before the Committee the returns of crime for the quarter and estimates of police expenditure for the ensuing quarter.[5] The Committee had to authorise all payments from the county treasurer to the chief constable and by him to the county treasurer. Lastly, at each meeting reports from sub-committees, covering a variety of matters, were considered and acted upon. From time to time, too, the Standing Joint Committee considered the salaries of justices' clerks and yearly examined the accounts of private lunatic asylums.

The Standing Joint Committee at first formed two sub-committees, one to deal with accounts and the other, matters concerning justices' clerks. To these were added sub-committees for the police telephone service, increases in the police force, an Architects' Sub-Committee and, in 1912, a Mounted Police Sub-Committee. As far as possible, provided members were willing to serve, these sub-committees consisted of approximately equal numbers of justices' representatives and council representatives. The most important sub-committee was the Accounts Sub-Committee, to which all accounts were submitted for examination before being passed to the Standing Joint Committee. In addition, it was authorised to deal with all minor contracts and accept tenders for them. The sub-committees were small in number with two exceptions. The Justices' Clerks, Fees and Salaries and Police Fees Sub-Committee consisted of, as far as possible, one member representing each of the petty sessional divisions[6] in the administrative county. Similarly the

Augmentation of the Force Sub-Committee consisted of members to represent each of the police divisions.[7] In addition, yearly a number of temporary or special sub-committees, consisting of from two to five members, were appointed as the need arose to deal with such matters as the repair and improvement of existing police stations, the building of new police stations and the rearrangement of police and petty sessional divisions consequent on the extensions of boroughs. Each sub-committee enquired into the matter referred to it, made a report thereon to the Standing Joint Committee and, if action was decided upon, was re-appointed to see the work carried through. On its completion and report made of the fact, the appointment of the sub-committee concerned automatically lapsed.

The county police area, for which the Standing Joint Committee was the police authority, consisted of the administrative county of Lancashire less all the county boroughs[8] in the county except for the county borough of Bury, and also less five municipal boroughs,[9] which had already established their own police forces before 1889. Agreements termed 'consolidation agreements' were made with the county borough of Bury which, because of its relatively small size, decided not to form its own police force, and with thirteen municipal boroughs[10] that had not formed their own police forces, under which the county police policed these boroughs.

The Standing Joint Committee did not make any changes in the police organisation that had been set up by the county justices. The county police continued under the operational control of the chief constable and the twenty-one police divisions, each under a superintendent as before 1889. Extensions of county boroughs, however, compelled from time to time some rearrangement of the force within the divisions concerned, and a quite large extension[11] of the City of Liverpool caused the demise of the West Derby Police Division in 1895. At first, under the county justices police divisions coincided with petty sessional divisions, but as these increased in number police divisions were arranged within the framework of the several Hundreds of the county and were regarded as divisions of these Hundreds. The Council and the Standing Joint Committee continued the organisation devised by the county justices, and after 1895 the twenty police divisions were as follows: Lonsdale Hundred – Lonsdale North and Lonsdale South; Amounderness Hundred – Garstang and Kirkham; Blackburn Hundred – Blackburn Higher, Blackburn Lower, Church and Rossendale; Leyland Hundred – Leyland division; Salford Hundred – Bolton, Bury, Rochdale, Manchester and Ashton-under-Lyne; West Derby Hundred – Ormskirk, Seaforth, Prescot, Widnes, Warrington and Wigan. After the war the

Prescot and Widnes divisions were joined but operated as two portions of the Prescot division.

The manpower of the County Constabulary, as authorised by the Home Office, steadily increased from 1352 (1:1025 of population), all ranks, in 1889 to 1571 (1:1081) in 1899 and to 1983 (1:803) in 1918. By 1918 the county police included a mounted section of 51, all ranks. The urban divisions, too, had by that year plain clothes officers, often not more than a detective sergeant and a few detective constables. Nevertheless, their presence and the lowering of the ratio of police to population may have been connected with a considerable decrease in recorded crime between 1890 and 1914.[12] After the First World War, the county constabulary found itself no less than 396 under its authorised strength,[13] only slightly reduced by the use of fifty-one police pensioners from the first police reserve. Increased rates of pay adopted in 1919 took some time to take effect, but by the end of 1922 the force was only sixty-four under strength. This deficiency was partly made up by the use of thirteen police pensioners on the strength and over a score more for traffic duty on county roads during the summer months. Then the Standing Joint Committee came to the conclusion that, since headquarters staff and officers other than constables accounted for twenty-eight per cent of the total force, the county police was over-officered. From 1924, therefore, the headquarters staff was gradually reduced from eighty-eight to eighty-one and the number of sergeants from 368 to 319; and by 1929 the actual strength of the force at 2013 was but one under the authorised strength. In addition to the authorised strength, the Standing Joint Committee was also authorised to appoint twenty-four policewomen. Both the Committee and the Chief Constable agreed that there was need for women in the county force but only sixteen (one inspector and fifteen constables) were appointed, all suggestions from the Home Office that the full number authorised should be appointed being ignored. The Special Constables Acts[14] of 1914 and 1923 authorised regulations by Order in Council for the appointment of special constables to assist the police in times of emergency, and during the First World War fifty-five special constables were on stand-by duty in Lancashire. After the war the only considerable use of special constables was during the general strike of 1926, when again 500 special constables were enrolled.[15]

A matter that from time to time caused concern to the Standing Joint Committee and successive chief constables was the manning of the Weights and Measures Department from the county police, being especially manifest during periods when there was difficulty in keeping the county force up to its authorised strength. Any proposals to appoint men as inspectors of weights and measures from outside the police force were always opposed by the Council since it was thought that, because of the facilities that the county police had and the knowledge they possessed of the different localities, they were enabled to perform more efficiently the duties in connection with the Weights and Measures Acts than inspectors from outside their ranks.

Weights and measures inspectors had to deal with the stamping and adjustment of all weights and measures and to visit all shops and yards (within a two-year period) in their divisions. All inspectors, including the chief inspector, were under the control of the chief constable, who made recommendations as to appointments, transfers and dismissals of staff. These recommendations were passed to the Finance Committee, and all matters in connection with the purchase or renting and the furnishing of weights and measures offices[16] were also the concern of the Finance Committee. That committee made recommendations to the Council and the Council, if it approved, passed them as resolutions. The expenses of the Weights and Measures Department fell upon the county rates but were offset to the extent of about one-third by the receipts from stamping fees and penalties.

The probation officer service, set up as an ancillary to the police, was established by the Criminal Justice Act of 1925: probation officers were appointed for each petty sessional division by the justices of the division. The duties of these officers were the supervision of persons for whom supervision was required under a probation order made by a court of summary jurisdiction, a Quarter Sessions or a Court of Assize. In Lancashire in 1926 twenty-three probation officers were appointed for petty sessional divisions in urban areas and the service was gradually extended. The Standing Joint Committee had a duty to see that the Act was carried into effect, while the County Council as probation authority was responsible for the expenses of the probation service in its area, which however attracted a fifty per cent government grant. The Council delegated its powers in connection with the salaries of probation officers to the Finance Committee.

After the First World War, the Standing Joint Committee overhauled its system of sub-committees. The Accounts Sub-Committee was still the most important, followed by the Police Augmentation Sub-Committee, consisting of one member representing each police division. The Justices' Clerks, Fees, Salaries and Police Fees Sub-Committee now consisted of all thirty-six members of the Committee. A number of small committees were also formed for Police Scales of Pay (10), Police Pensions (9), Housing Accommodation (7), Police Houses (5), the

Telephone Service for Police (6) and Conveying of Prisoners to Prison (5). A Consultative Sub-Committee of ten members was also later added. This extension of the sub-committee system lasted until 1926 when the three main sub-committees were retained but the Justices' Clerks, etc. Sub-Committee was reduced to eight members. Of the other sub-committees only those for police pensions and police housing were retained for a time. The functions of those abolished were transferred to the Accounts Sub-Committee, which by 1928 dealt, besides accounts, with tenders for work; the purchasing, leasing or renting of houses; the granting of pensions, gratuities and awards for meritorious service; and the telephone service for police purposes. Further, the Standing Joint Committee delegated to this sub-committee its powers to give instruction or advice, at his request, to the chief constable on any urgent matter, to the Clerk of the Peace on appeal cases on which he desired instructions, and to the Clerk to the Standing Joint Committee. No other sub-committee had such a wide range of functions.

Although police expenditure rose from £183,713 for the financial year 1890–1 to £267,184 for the year 1913–14, and to £781,241 for the year 1928–9, education expenditure after 1902 replaced police ex-penditure as the chief item of county expenditure.[17] The costs of the county police were met from three sources – rates and orders on policed boroughs, government grants, and other income, which included charges made for the services of constables to industrial firms, private individuals and other police forces and payments for police services as inspectors under the Food and Drugs and Shops Acts and in connec-tion with the Diseases of Animals Acts. Government aid took three forms. From the Exchequer Contribution Account a grant was made to cover half the cost of the pay and clothing of the force. Under the Agricultural Rates Act of 1896 agricultural land was rated on half its rateable value, and under a similar act passed in 1923, on one-quarter of rateable value. To compensate for loss of rateable value grants were made to county councils under both acts. These grants were dis-tributed over several accounts including police accounts, but in Lanca-shire the police grants were small.[18] Up to 1919, on average, government grants covered over a third of police costs, other income about one-sixth and rates and orders precepted the remaining half. Then, under the Police Act of 1919 the Home Office made direct grants, so that government aid should cover half of ordinary police expenditure. In 1929, government grants met 45.8 per cent and rates and orders 44.7 per cent of police revenue expenditure. The Council made no change in the system of rating for police expenditure adopted under the justices.

The Standing Joint Committee was the police authority for Lancashire but the Council was responsible for financing the county police. Therefore all proposals for alterations and improvements to police stations and the building of new stations were sent as recommendations by the Standing Joint Committee, since the committee[19] did not report to the Council, but to the Finance Committee. Thereupon that committee included these recommendations in its next report to the Council, to be approved or otherwise by it. All payments in connection with the police were also sent by the Standing Joint Committee to the Finance Committee, and these were laid before the Council as recommendations at the request of the Standing Joint Committee. If approved, the payments were then authorised by resolutions passed by the Council and the county treasurer was authorised and instructed to make them.

Police forces have been subject to inspection by the Home Office inspectors of constabulary since 1856. This inspection, and also the fact that government grants towards police expenditure depend on forces being granted certificates of efficiency, has been not only the means of maintaining high standards in police forces but also a method of securing Home Office control when, under the Police Act of 1919, the Home Secretary was empowered to make regulations relating to the government, mutual aid, pay, allowances, pensions, clothing, expenses and conditions of service of the police. Every police authority was required by the Act to comply with those regulations.

PART III

Age of Transformation 1929-1974

CHAPTER 9

Economic and Social Change

THE forty-five years following the Local Government Act of 1929 witnessed profound changes in Lancashire life and industry, and some of these, in their turn, offered problems and challenges to local and national government. The most significant of these changes, the continued if fluctuating decline of the cotton textile industry, did much to alter ways of life in south and central Lancashire, accompanied as it was by a diversification of industrial activity in important areas of the county. These fundamental changes in the industrial base were accompanied by considerable internal shifts of population and by intensive growth of the latter, sometimes stimulated by deliberate housing and overspill policies. These, of their nature, created problems for the county's planners at Preston and elsewhere, just as the profoundly unsatisfactory environment left by the 'old' industrial revolution posed further problems for the planners and also led to additional strain on the health and social services of Lancashire.

The story of the slow failure of the Lancashire cotton industry is now a well-known one, and has been the subject of much careful study.[1] Following the First World War, there were already signs that the days of the cotton industry's greatest achievements were past. It had reached its respective peaks of productive capacity, employment and contribution to the national export market in the years immediately before the war, and some forty per cent of Lancashire's cotton products went to India. In 1917, however, the Montagu–Chelmsford reforms gave fiscal autonomy to India, the government of which imposed duties on imported cloth in 1921, 1925, 1930 and 1931. By the latter year, Lancashire's exports of cloth to India had fallen disastrously, with sad consequences to weaving towns like Darwen and Blackburn and to the coarser spinners of the Oldham area. The world crisis of 1929–31, bringing a shrinkage of international trade, inevitably affected Lancashire's remaining overseas markets, which were now being invaded by low-cost products from Japan.

While these developments were of the utmost seriousness for a number of Lancashire county boroughs like Oldham and Blackburn, their economic and social repercussions in the administrative county were somewhat less disastrous. The researches of the late Professor Wilfred Smith have shown that, despite the marked regional contraction of the industry in the 1930s, rural and suburban areas of central and eastern Lancashire were less affected than urban centres. Although the more recently built, modernised and extensive spinning mills (which tended to survive at this period) concentrated in towns, where they could easily find a suitable labour supply, weaving sheds were far more widely diffused.[2] These last tended to be smaller units, which could draw their work people from scattered and more diminutive communities; and in areas of finer weaving (e.g. Nelson and Colne) their survival record was tolerably good. This diffusion of weaving firms does not appear to have been directly connected with any rating advantages offered by given sections of local government, and the larger and smaller boroughs, together with the urban districts, enjoyed the advantages of industrial de-rating more or less equally.[3]

None of this alters the fact that the weaving section of the industry, largely situated in east Lancashire, suffered a greater relative decline than spinning, and that the weaving district as a whole had, in 1936, a greater percentage of unemployment than any other large area of the county (25.9 per cent as compared with 18.3 per cent for Lancashire as a whole).[4] This development had considerable repercussions for local government, although, again, the county boroughs were the main sufferers; Blackburn lost two-thirds of its mill employment between 1931 and 1951, while Nelson and Colne lost only half this amount, principally because fine weaving suffered less from Asian competition.[5]

Meanwhile, Lancashire's economy was based on the coal mine almost as much as on the mill, and in many areas the menfolk worked in the mines while their wives and daughters performed weaving and spinning tasks. The Depression ruptured the interdependent relationship of these twin forms of employment, so that in a (in this respect) typical Lancashire county district, Westhoughton, had a third of its insured population unemployed in 1934 and 1935.[6] Mining in Westhoughton had given work to 2200 men in 1929, but by 1947 the mining was dead, a state of affairs typical of the 'northern' part of the Lancashire coalfields around Wigan. Over the same period, textile employment in Westhoughton declined by one-half, and the total volume of work available in the town fell by forty-four per cent.[7]

Yet, while the now famous pen-pictures of darker Lancashire, represented by Walter Greenwood in *Love on the Dole* and by George Orwell in *The Road to Wigan Pier*, have their element of truth, the county was a region of sharp contrasts, so that Leyland, with its important motor industry, suffered minimal unemployment in the mid-thirties.[8] It remains true that the Council could not have taken responsibility for poor relief at a less auspicious time. Following the provisions of the Local Government Act, the functions of the Poor Law Guardians were transferred to the county authority as from 1 April 1930, and from that year to 1938 the amount of money spent by the Council on outdoor relief (known, by the latter year, as a sign of grace, as 'domiciliary assistance') virtually doubled.[9] Some 17,650 persons were in receipt of such relief on 1 April 1930, and 33,274 persons were receiving relief on the same date eight years later. An official statement remarked that the overall increase was 'no doubt partly due to the long industrial depression which has prevailed in many parts of the county'.[10] The significance of this development for the Council was twofold; it became more involved in what are dispassionately called the personal services, and the issue of public assistance, as is shown by Mr Hands and Mr Denver in Chapter 12,[11] became not only politically explosive in itself, but an issue conducive to the formation of, for the first time, sharp party alignments in the Council. It remains coincidental that the two most prominent spokesmen for those on public assistance, Councillors R. I. Constantine and Andrew Smith, represented a municipal borough (Nelson) which did not suffer the worst effects of the Depression.

A close and definitive study of the economic history of Lancashire in the thirties will undoubtedly reveal a state of great complexity, with economic development proceeding at the side of stagnation or decline in the staple industries. Even the cotton industry, meanwhile, enjoyed a brief upsurge of activity in the late thirties and again when war had broken out. The activities of the county authority itself, manifesting interest in technical and other education as carefully measured by Mr MacGregor-Reid in Chapter 11,[12] do not suggest decreasing public investment in the middle and late thirties, although it should be borne in mind that at least one major council activity of the Depression – the promotion of the East Lancashire Road – is to be seen as part of national public works policy to combat unemployment. Far more significantly, there is striking evidence of improvement in the health of Lancashire communities in the thirties and even in the twenties, and it is difficult to believe that this was wholly the direct result of more efficient public medicine, conscientiously administered though the latter was; it is probable that, notwithstanding serious unemployment, the standard of living (and thereby the health and environmental conditions) of considerable groups in the social structure of Lancashire was at the very least maintained if not improved. Hence, infant mortality in the administrative county showed a distinct decline in the twenties and thirties (one that was, however, carried on steadily through the wartime and postwar years); and, in the thirties and later, death rates from bronchitis, pneumonia and tuberculosis likewise dramatically fell.[13] As is shown in Chapter 14,[14] the better organisation of public medicine and the use of highly effective drugs has played a large part in these reductions, but social and industrial factors can never be discounted. It is well known, for example, that tuberculosis mortality and morbidity rates provide an index to living conditions in a given community; and it is also probably the case, as Hart and Wright showed, that real-wage movements have affected the rates concerned.[15] Meanwhile, the researches of Dr F. C. S. Bradbury, who was trained in Lancashire's fine anti-tuberculosis service, led to an intensified search for causal factors in tuberculosis, and his medical colleagues in the county pointed to operative predisposing influences in certain kinds of industrial employment, e.g. cotton-spinning (but not weaving) and coalmining, and in housing conditions in districts like St Helens.[16] In other words, it may well be the case that the steady elimination of Lancashire's great staple industries benefited the county's health.

The years following the Second World War saw both a marked contraction and some transformation of the regional textile industries, and the introduction of diversified industries – in many, not always the same, areas – in their place. The great mills were not left empty; they were taken over by engineering, clothing and many other kinds of firms in search of cheap and easily acquired accommodation, so much so that, in the words of one authority, 'A catalogue of the multifarious industries so housed would be an epitome of the standard industrial classification'.[17] There were, as Freeman and Rodgers point out, stimuli to firms other than cheapness; outside the postwar 'Development Areas', industrial building was strictly controlled in the region after 1945, and so there was an added incentive to the purchase and conversion of existing buildings.[18] Unfortunately, the transformation to new types of industry was not accomplished without human cost, and the county authority's efforts to plan industrial development as distinct from housing (described by Mr Daniels in Chapter 15) suggest that it was wholly inadequately equipped or directed.[19]

We must at this point discuss the economic and social transformation of Lancashire *in toto*, and its form and structure are best seen as based upon a geographical triangle – a southern axis base, which may be conveniently related to Liverpool, Manchester and the East Lancashire Road, and which may include a large part of the Lancashire conurbation stretching from Oldham to Leigh; the main industrial towns and districts of the east Lancashire valleys, mainly the weaving towns with their special problems; and the west Lancashire seaboard, including Southport and the Fylde resorts. The relationships of the histories of the three areas, or axes, are of much significance, and the former are reflected in population movements within Lancashire. There was, as is well known, an especially heavy stress on textile employment in the eastern area, and the effect of the Depression was to stimulate much out-migration and to diminish or inhibit population growth in large parts of east Lancashire both before and after the Second World War. In the base area of the geographical triangle (including, for the purposes of this discussion, parts of central Lancashire), there was considerably more diversity and industrial progress throughout the entire generation following 1930. Its cotton industry experienced a more gradual decline than in other parts of the county, and in the St Helens district the glass manufacturer has kept an outstanding reputation; while in Warrington and Widnes the development of a variety of industries, primarily chemicals, has hardly spelt depression. Employment in Lancashire chemicals approximately doubled between 1931 and 1959.[20] In Greater Manchester, mechanical and electrical engineering, especially in the Trafford Park Estate, have been partially matched by the postwar industries attracted to the Speke and Kirkby industrial estates in the Merseyside conurbation, but the latter has suffered more economic and other problems than the Manchester district. Great motor firms like Ford have been directed, at the behest of the Board of Trade, to set up works on Merseyside (Halewood), and equally great aircraft establishments have appeared at Chadderton and in the Bolton and Preston areas.[21] It is hardly surprising to find, therefore, that the 'metal and engineering' group of employed workers in Lancashire doubled in numbers between 1931 and 1959,[22] and all of the main industries touched upon here (engineering, vehicles and electrical goods among them) were giving steadily increased employment in the fifties.[23] There were, it is true, exceptions, so that railway and textile engineering suffered a decline from fairly obvious causes; but in general these economic growth areas have had the greatest significance for local government. As Freeman and Rodgers have put it, 'these industrial trends are the root causes of ... great changes in population distribution',[24] and the latter, in turn, have caused local government structures and areas to be questioned increasingly in the last three decades. As these authorities stress, the industrial transformations of the present century have reversed many of those of the original industrial revolution, and now the great growth localities are to be found in the plain of south and west Lancashire.

On the other hand, 'a clear and sharp contrast can be seen between the textile province of the east and the newer industrial areas of the west and south.... Almost all the cotton towns suffered heavy losses of employment during the period [1952–8], which rose as high as fifteen per cent per decade in the worst affected areas.'[25] It may be added that the effects of the new industrial transformation are to be qualified in a threefold sense as relates to this axis of the Lancashire 'triangle'. Firstly, the shock of the Depression of the thirties, and the unemployment that accompanied it, led to 'heavy and sustained migration southwards to more prosperous areas',[26] which has been continued (although not in any recognisable correlation with periods of slump in textiles). Again, those industries that sought roots in the old textile districts, by virtue of their use of empty cotton mills, often failed to introduce sufficient new employment to counterbalance the losses of jobs incurred in the older industry, and the failure was accentuated by slowness of diversification of industry in many parts of north-east Lancashire, and by further unemployment in the cotton industry of that area in the fifties.[27] The result was that an old established weaving area like the Calder–Darwen Valley (which included as many as a dozen local government districts of the administrative county) remained substantially dependent upon cotton manufacture until about 1960.[28] It is true that a North-West Lancashire Development Area, to cover this district, was designated in March 1953, but this was successful only in relation to the poor record of other neighbouring textile localities. As Mr Daniels shows elsewhere (Chapter 15) the attempts by the Lancashire County Council planning authority to introduce trading estates in this sub-region were circumscribed to say the least.

Before discussing the third or western axis, that of the Lancashire seaboard, it will be in place to stress that in two other parts of south-west Lancashire there were government-sponsored designations of 'Development Areas' – South Lancashire (1946), which resulted in the development of trading estates at Lamberhead and Parr near St Helens, and Merseyside (1950), with consequent growth of trading estates at Kirkby and Speke. Meanwhile, Kirkby became a key area for the reception of overspill from Liverpool (which lost population as a result), but it should be emphasised that, notwithstanding the spectacular growth of overspill centres of this kind, a great part of the south-west of the county was also one of high natural increase, a tendency that was enhanced in the sixties. Freeman and Rodgers attribute this in part to 'strong Catholic communities ... chiefly but not wholly of immigrant Irish origin'.[29] This is in some measure borne out by the relatively large number of

Catholic schools in the south-west aided by the Lancashire Education Authority, and by the great and sometimes unpredictable numbers of children of school age in the new towns and overspill areas (see Chapter 13). Nor was this the only problem for local government; the new settlement areas, Skelmersdale as well as Kirkby, created vast social problems which are now fully recognised if not always adequately discussed. It remains true that the Lancashire County Council, obliged to cater for the populations and sometimes the employment problems of the great towns, was placed in a most invidious position.

Nor was this all; the fifties and sixties brought a growing suburbanisation and settlement of many central western rural and fringe areas of the administrative county, and a greater rate of population increase as the new industrial transformation began to bring social and demographic consequences in its train. There was an upswing of the crude birth rate of the administrative county as a whole in the fifties and early sixties; and this, taking effect against a stable crude death rate,[30] ordained that those central and western areas mentioned enjoyed a powerful element of natural increase as well as migration; not only Kirkby; but Rainford, Whiston and Golborne, and even places in the old Wigan coalfield area like Ashton-in-Makerfield, Billinge and Winstanley.[31] Much of this growth was planned for, as at Worsley and Middleton, but a great deal was not.

Meanwhile, the western seaboard had long been a growth area; but it was, as a whole, one with a markedly different demographic history and set of characteristics. It was here that population growth was consistent in the four decades before 1974, with a stress on the earlier part of the period; between 1929 and 1947, for example, there was an increase of sixty-three per cent in the coastal areas from Formby northwards to Morecambe (including, of course, the Fylde resorts in general and Blackpool in particular).[32] Since then, the growth has continued at a lesser rate, so that the Fylde as a whole grew in population by only eight per cent from 1951 to 1961. This figure was almost entirely the result of inward migration and settlement by the elderly; otherwise there would have been an absolute loss of population, for, not surprisingly, a community heavily weighted towards the older groups produced more deaths than births.[33] Yet it would be a mistake to regard the seaboard as simply a settling ground for the retired, although it has, indeed, an historic role of that kind, as the comfortable Victorian roads of residential Southport and Lytham St Annes clearly testify. Parts of the coastal areas were regarded, more than two decades ago, as 'not only attractive for residents, but also ... for industrial development'.[34] This, moreover, is to ignore the existence of the greatest of Fylde industries, the tourist and entertainment industry, which has been supplemented by light engineering in the Blackpool district and in Southport, and by clothing and food and drink factories also.

The significance of the coastal axis for the Council was twofold; its elected (or opposed) representatives were often men of a special stamp, whether as members of their district councils and municipal boroughs, or as members of the council chamber in Preston; and the large retired population and seasonal holiday industries for which they sought to speak tended to create problems for the postwar county health services. (There was a shortage of home helps in the summer, and the large elderly population, both in west and in east Lancashire, meant that more of the resources of the health service were devoted to the problems of the aged and their accommodation.) The councillors from these seaboard localities, meanwhile, often had strongly marked characteristics. Meticulous, contentious, economy-minded, these representatives could act as valuable (or voluble) watchdogs or could simply be, in the words of a widely experienced local government official, 'shopkeeper-minded'. Their territory of retired people of means, commuters and small businessmen produced distinctive types of spokesmen as consistently as inner rural Lancashire produced gentlemanly Conservatives. The urban and suburban districts of the south and east nurtured a greater variety of types of councillor and 'public person'; and straightforward occupational analyses, such as we give in Chapter 12, cannot claim to do full justice to their diversity of background. It will be enough to add that, as time went on, business and professional people were rather more likely to represent rural or semi-rural districts than before.

The fifties and sixties, then, saw both an invasion of the countryside and an extension of suburbia, tendencies that were sharpened in the decade 1961–71. A county statistician, commenting on some trends shown at the time of the 1961 census, remarked that there was some evidence of two distinct population movements in the county – 'one from the centres of high density, mainly County Boroughs, into neighbouring county districts, and the other westward from the areas in East Lancashire long dependent upon the textile industry'.[35] The first of these conclusions is strikingly confirmed by the Census of 1971; suburban and rural districts like Fulwood, Longridge, Blackburn Rural District, Walton-le-Dale, Garstang and Lunesdale all showed markedly higher growth rates for the previous decade than for 1951–61, and higher ones than the county average.[36] The distinction between town and country was continually blurring, and people who worked in the great Lancashire towns lived more and more in the administrative county. Meanwhile, the great towns themselves, before Lancashire County Council had in some measure halted the tendency by acting as a general caterer for overspill populations, continually sought to nibble at county territory. Hence, during the post-1929 period, Blackpool had gained boundary extensions at the expense of the administrative county in 1934 and 1955, Preston in 1952 and 1956, Blackburn in 1934, Bootle in 1940 and 1951, Liverpool in 1932 and 1952, Manchester and Rochdale in 1933, and St Helens in 1934 and 1954, while Warrington also gained an extension in 1954. Such pressures had the effect of throwing into question the value of some of the county's traditional administrative boundaries, although it should be borne in mind that the combined county boroughs of Lancashire had to face an even more powerful lobby formed by a working alliance of county districts and county council.

To a planner, anxious to see the best use made of land and green spaces, this balance of power and splitting of function between a great county authority and nearly a score of county boroughs – each of which had an autonomy of planning powers – made fairly palpable nonsense. Professor J. R. James, writing of south Lancashire in 1969, expressed an increasingly fashionable opinion when he commented that:

> It is clearly nonsense to think that a dozen or so planning authorities can act as independent units and produce a coherent plan for so closely meshed an area. No authority, acting on its own, can face the challenge of the future and plan for growth and change on so large a scale. Again, therefore, an overriding regional agency is required which can carry on the work of Lancashire County Council and Central Government in designing new towns as at Skelmersdale and Leyland–Chorley and giving overall form and direction to this great urban entity. Yet beneath this piece of regional or provincial machinery one must recognise that Liverpool is very different from Manchester and Wirral from Wigan.[37]

Lancashire County Council had, of course, propounded its own solution of splitting the 'old' county into three, with Liverpool and Manchester each taking the headship of a Riding or a metropolitan county, and the history of this basically realistic project is outlined in Chapters 10 and 16.[38] It is moreover suggested, there and elsewhere, that Lancashire managed to plan without outraging local susceptibilities. Mr Daniels probes the strengths and weaknesses of this planning in Chapter 15, and the question is inevitably posed – can a measure of democracy and local involvement maintain an easy partnership with effective regional planning?

CHAPTER 10

The Years of Transformation

UP to the time of the Local Government Act of 1929, county government altered little in scope and style. There were, as we have seen,[1] important developments in educational provision, but so great was the impact of the Education Act of 1944 and the National Health Service Act of 1946, structurally and organisationally, that the apparently gentle tempo of inter-war administrative growth seems to belong to prehistory. Yet, as we shall see, there is enough evidence of both vision and momentum in the interwar years to suggest that, in certain areas, the interruption of the Second World War acted as an untimely impediment to the forward movement of some aspects of social welfare and environmental planning. For the postwar social, health and welfare services to bear their hope of real success, a great groundswell of political vision – the aftermath of the war itself – was not enough; they had to have administrators who were at least partially persuaded that what they were doing was right, and that the means to achieve their ends were feasible.

A generation of officers and councillors (as of civil servants and national representatives) had first of all to identify problems and then to face them. Where major social ills were concerned, traditional county government, before 1930, had been largely concerned with the more remote and unseen kind of environmental service, or with the direct administration of law and order – with the magistrate and policeman just as much as the road-mender. The education and school health services, like the tuberculosis service, brought officers and councillors closer to the problems of the relatively defenceless or deserving; and the vast human problem of the public relief of poverty not only served to educate the post-1930 County Council, but also brought a new urgency into the Council's debates.[2] This, however, was not simply a matter of politics. Officers themselves had to confront, or be confronted by, major challenges, and it was they who suggested tactics and solutions. Acts of Parliament, indeed, 'determined' what would happen in time and place, bearing in mind that those enactments, like the Local Government Acts, were often very largely created by the needs and experiences of local government itself; but the soldiers in the local battlefields decided the outcome. Lancashire was a very large battlefield, and was often to be an influential one.

In the field of increasingly intractable challenges, over and beyond poverty and its effects, the motor vehicle was already moving into a significant position. It was already far too fast, destructive and ill-adapted to winding and unsuitable roads to be ignored, or to be held in check by negative legislation and by-laws, and it was increasingly important to industry and commerce, and also to the revenue. The national and local remedy was vastly improved main roads; and Lancashire became, and remained, a civil and traffic engineer's laboratory of prime importance. The thirties saw the birth of the idea of the motorway, drafted in Lancashire with Ministry of Transport approval – and the M6 follows what is broadly the line of the north–south route through the county which was then surveyed.

In many other and more subtle ways, the county of the thirties was experimenting with measures and forms of administration that were to be useful testing grounds for the medical and welfare services of mid-century. The Midwives Act of 1936, to the details of which a Lancashire Medical Officer of Health, Dr Hall, made a significant contribution, produced a maternity service so greatly improved as to require little alteration in the 1950s. Lancashire, with its great administrative area, was once again an important laboratory where almost any problem of large-scale organisation was concerned, and the problem of decentralisation into administrative divisions was always a very real one. Even though control was invariably centralised at County Hall, personal-service fieldworkers increasingly operated through localised machinery and premises; and the working foundation, if not the supposedly democratic control, of later divisional delegation was laid in these years. Meanwhile, as county government acquired new powers by central legislation, so the necessity for continual consultation with county district authorities became imperative, and a further foundation for ultimate delegation was thus created.

The 1929 Act affected county government in a number of fundamental ways, and one of these at least had profound administrative repercussions for the future. On 1 April 1930, the functions of the Poor Law Unions and the Guardians in the administrative county were transferred to the County Council, which then administered public assistance in the whole of that area. This work was the responsibility of a Public Assistance Committee of fifty-six members, which in turn supervised new Guardians'

Committees for each of sixteen areas. The County Council, which had always shown sensitivity to the views and opinions of district authorities in its territory, arranged for nine representatives of the county district associations[3] to take their places on the Public Assistance Committee, while each of the Guardians' Committees had a very strong representation of nominees from district councils from within the area supervised by that committee – indeed, these far outnumbered the direct nominees of the Council, whose strength included, as a matter of course, councillors from the county electoral divisions within the same area.[4]

This was plainly both sensible and politically expedient; the original Guardians' bodies and their unions had had a long history and deep local connections, and the most sweeping reorganisation that the County Council dared attempt was that of combining a number of town and country Poor Law Unions, arranging at the same time that each new committee met alternately month by month at the original places of meeting of the unions affected. In the majority of cases, the old union boundaries, shaped out of the combined boundaries of old ecclesiastical and administrative parishes (which also shaped the outer boundaries of the county districts), were still utilised. In each area, meanwhile, there was one or more former union 'institution' or workhouse, the medical wards of which were taken over (under the terms of the Local Government Act (1929)) by the Health Department of the County Council, and which were by degrees transformed into general purpose hospitals or refuges for the aged, infirm and sick poor. This transformation, much needed and historically significant though it was, did not remove the deep public hatred of the idea of the workhouse at a stroke, nor did the buildings themselves lose their associations.

Meanwhile, the geographical situations of the 'institution' hospitals remained crucial, for when thirteen of these hospitals were transferred to the regional hospital boards in the immediate postwar period, the seventeen Lancashire health divisions formed in consequence of the National Health Service Act of 1946 owed part or all of their respective shapes to the Guardians' areas, and, through them, to the Poor Law Unions – largely because the divisional areas were also designed to be hospital catchment areas. Hence, the Ulverston Health Division, formed in 1947, was also the area of the Ulverston Union of former generations; and Burnley, Wigan and Ashton-under-Lyne Unions left their shapes on the entirety, or nearly so, of Lancashire's Nos 6, 8 and 11 Health Divisions. Most of the others contained a substantial number of the parishes and districts formerly in one or more unions.[5] The health divisions, however, aimed at a somewhat more equitable distribution of population – so that the Leigh and Warrington areas were split into separate divisions in 1947 whereas before they had been combined (however inappropriately) into one Guardians' area. The Council had the good sense to realise that these, and many other Lancashire localities, had a deep sense of identity; and there was the further problem that the very heavy representation of the districts in matters of public assistance (in 1929) was not repeated in 1947, if only because room had to be made for hospital management nominees, those of local health authorities, and those of divisional education executives.

The separation of the hospitals from county or other directly answerable government has sometimes led to wonderment, and has been regarded by at least one leading county officer, with long experience of major responsibility,[6] as something of a disaster, resulting from the more general inability of large and small authorities (and their associations) to work together to the requisite degree. However, it should be borne in mind that the hospitals of the thirties were part of an 'administrative tangle'[7] of voluntary and public organisations, so complex and so deep-rooted in its traditions that only a major act of surgery could deal with it. Our point here is that, however indirectly, the 1929 Local Government Act did in fact permit experimentation, and did create precedents that paved the way to the administrative upheaval of 1944-8. Its effect on the health services as such was not great; the latter developed under their own momentum and with their own rationale, while behind them, a slowly changing attitude to social welfare was manifesting itself.

Before the outbreak of war, however, it should be borne in mind that the Guardians' Committees could exert political pressures, which tended to be cushioned, as regards their impact on the Council's Central Relief Sub-Committee, by the traditional difficulties of administering poor relief in England. There were, it is true, many straightforward cases of able-bodied unemployment, as from 1931 more and more workers, forced from unemployment into the receipt of transitional payments, had to seek outdoor relief. But many unemployed suffered from ill health, and relieving officers, like the administering committees, found the classification and relief of individual cases technically difficult, as they involved dependent children, the sick, the aged and of course widows. Removal cases, the bane of every Poor Law administrator from time immemorial, still vexed and worried committees, principally because the old union boundaries entered county boroughs. In matters of humanity and principle, local Guardians might still press for improvement, as for example when the Barton-on-Irwell Area Committee in 1933 demanded 'a more generous scale' for outdoor relief in winter. There were, indeed, some angry demonstrations outside meetings of the Central Relief Sub-Committee, which contained eminent old-style members like Travis-Clegg and

Assheton as well as rebels like Constantine of Accrington and Mrs K. M. Fletcher, and which by the later thirties, despite a doubling in the number of cases dealt with, came to interpret the needs of poor persons more liberally and to spend greatly increased sums on 'domiciliary assistance'.[8] (Some political aspects of this subject are dealt with by Mr Hands and Mr Denver in Chapter 12.) Welfare-mindedness, then, was forged from political conflict in considerable measure, but one must also take into account the field of experience of doctors, health visitors and relieving officers, whose work, like that of their colleagues who dealt with schools and education, took them into the midst of human problems, and took county government closer to human beings.

The schools and their children had compelled the Council's attention to a mass of problems, social and medical; even in the thirties, the three major providers of personal services, Public Assistance, Health and Education, carried within them the seed of yet another important and humane development, the Children's Department of the postwar years. The Ministry of Health-approved constitution for the Public Assistance Committee gave that body the right to 'arrange in suitable cases for the rights and powers of parents in respect of children to be vested in the Council under Section 78 of the Poor Law Act, 1927', and also permitted it 'to arrange in suitable cases for children being boarded out'.[9] The adoption of children, however, was under the control of the Education Department, under the terms of the Adoption of Children Act (1926). By the end of 1936 there were 457 cases 'in which the Education Committee [had] been appointed by the Courts as Guardian *ad litem* since the Act became operative'.[10] Even at this stage, the field officers in the personal services were tending to collaborate when cases of extreme need, as with those involving orphan or abandoned children, came to their attention.

The later history of the county's educational service is discussed elsewhere,[11] and it will be enough to say that in the thirties, too, there were plenty of signs that pointed towards a more generalised concept of secondary education, although it would be foolish to claim that the County Education Authority moved ahead of much in current thinking. It was, like the others of its kind, influenced by the Hadow Report and central government, and it had emerged from that Dark Age of which half-time education for some young mill-workers was an all too memorable symbol. It was responsible for the training of teachers, but its work was mainly centred on Edge Hill Training College, Ormskirk. Lancashire's vast area called for devolution of supervision of schools; and there were, in the thirties, local Committees for Higher and Elementary Education, aiming at the co-ordination of the elementary and secondary stages and, in the words of the *Jubilee History*, at 'equal educational opportunities for all pupils'. This was the language of a later stage also; but it did not help to make some of the village schools, really run by the parson and the local headmaster together, less bad in buildings and conditions.

It is of course both difficult and dangerous to judge certain commitments in monetary or quantitative terms. Particularly is this so in the case of the Lancashire County Library, created as a responsibility of the Lancashire Education Committee in 1924–5. In 1930 the County Librarian, working from a former private house near County Hall, had only eight persons on his staff, and much of his work consisted of the distribution of books by box to service points throughout the administrative county – in which a system of branch libraries, sometimes staffed by part-time assistants, was gradually established during the thirties.[12] However, one should judge the library service not so much by its staffing, which had risen to 101 full-time and thirteen part-time workers by 1939, and which had roughly doubled a decade after that,[13] as by the millions of books that came to hand to fill, enrich or enliven the hours of hundreds of thousands of Lancastrians. The books repeatedly did the 'work' after the assistants had given their labours, often in places that would never have been reached by other kinds of book-distributing enterprise. Progress was of course gradual, and the branch libraries themselves (there were forty-three full-time and part-time branches operating by 1940) were often seriously inadequate as places to browse. In 1935–6 the book issues topped the three million mark,[14] an achievement that must have given satisfaction to the County Librarian, Mr Raymond Irwin, who had taken over from the pioneer officer, Mr J. D. Cowley, in 1934, and who was given administrative space in County Hall in the same year. It is an interesting, and perhaps a significant, commentary on the power and standing conferred by great organisations and large wage and salary bills, and also on the values of public administration, that subsequent occupiers of the librarian's office were not invited to be members of the chief officers' committee which met in the postwar years. The record implies that those in positions of responsibility and power are apt to forget that books are as important as policemen or good road surfaces.

In other matters, there are many instances that show that the Council and its officers were more concerned with human beings and humane values than the bare facts might suggest. One important aspect of the 1929 Local Government Act had to do with the more effective and centralised administration of road maintenance and construction, which had hitherto been under the control of municipal boroughs and county districts, with the county – as described earlier in these pages[15] – responsible for main roads (and for some district roads by special arrangement).

The real reason for this organisational upheaval was the ever-growing influence of the motor vehicle, which, despite the more than adequate warn-
ing of its advent as a social factor, still succeeded in bursting upon the
world in the thirties as a frightening and destructive phenomenon as well
as an economically portentous and valuable one. It did so while using
roads that were anything but well adapted; in Lancashire, many main
roads were still cobbled and fissured with tram tracks, or twisting and
otherwise unsuitable – not least the A6, the main route through the county.
Both cyclists and pedestrians were increasingly at risk, and the accident
rate was higher *pro rata* than at any time since, despite the enormous
toll of the postwar years. The Ministry of Transport, meanwhile, was
already coming to regard the county, with its vast industrial needs, as
a suitable area for experimentation in road and traffic engineering (as
well as in relief work for the unemployed); and by 1930 the Liverpool–
East Lancashire Road, eventually opened in July 1934 at an approximate
cost of £3 million, was already under construction.[16]

The Highways and Bridges Committee, under the chairmanship of
(Sir) Percy Macdonald, discovered to its consternation in 1937 that, where
such a busy highway crossed or was joined at frequent intersections by
secondary or other roads, passing inevitably in or through seats of population, pedestrians and cyclists were being killed and injured with some
regularity, especially near the intersections themselves. Some 270 persons
were killed or injured on the East Lancashire Road in 1935 alone. The
Committee considered various remedies; signs, bollards, traffic lights. It
even saw the force of the then slender and ineffective Town and Country
Planning legislation, which, if enforced, would prevent access to the road
itself. Eventually, however, it was obliged to consider total segregation
and abolition of intersections in the case of any further new major trunk
road, and while this counsel of perfection could not be – and never has
been – applied to the East Lancashire Road, it could be applied experimentally in the future on what was then known as 'the north–south route'.

In this way the idea of the motorway was born. It was decided to
remove the access of pedestrians and non-motorised traffic to the new
trunk route, for

> On a modern arterial road the traffic should not be impeded or made
> dangerous by numerous road intersections. Provision should therefore
> be made for existing roads of lesser importance to cross either under
> or over the new route, and only a very limited number of entrances
> should be made to accommodate traffic to or from large centres of
> population.[17]

Although the Committee was obviously unable to visualise an age in which
the numbers of vehicles had multiplied five-, six- or seven-fold, their

entire planning policy showed quite remarkable prescience. This was an age that already understood the nature of traffic queues and congestion, and which was determined to overcome them if it could.

The county's engineers went farther under Ministry of Transport guidance, and planned a motorway which, in general design and externals, including its occupation bridges, was a model not so much for the M6 as for the M1. It followed the line of the present M6 in the county with quite remarkable faithfulness, and was approved in principle by the Minister of Transport (Mr Leslie Burgin), who had, no doubt on the advice of his permanent officials, in 1936 travelled along the A6 from Preston to Warrington, 'and after doing so expressed himself as being satisfied as to the difficulties of improving the existing road'.[18] It is not clear how much influence the Minister himself had on the course of events;* his ministry certainly provided advice as to straight-line flyover intersections, which were eventually superseded by the US and continental-type clover leaf or curved junction approaches. Most of the planned access points (e.g. Carnforth, Halton, Galgate, Broughton, Samlesbury and Bamber Bridge) were those in use a generation later.[19]

Roads, traffic, communications – these massive factors in modern life affected yet another great organisation administered by the county authority, the constabulary. The Standing Joint Committee, one of the county's most important bodies, has had a shadowy existence made more so by the absence of particulars within County Council *Proceedings*, and by the similar absence of separately published Chief Constable's Reports. We are therefore obliged to turn to other sources for some basic information covering this period.[20] The Lancashire Constabulary, then, reacted to the growing flow of motor traffic, which carried criminals as well as businessmen and tourists, by building its own traffic fleet, which had commenced with a squadron of motorcyclists as early as 1920. These, even when supplemented by MG sport-type cars more than a decade later, were not a highly effective arm when the force itself was bedevilled by a system of private telephone communications which ordained that a message could take as long as two hours to pass from one end of the county to the other. The desperate difficulties thus occasioned, up to and before 1930, led to experiments from 1926 onward in radio transmission. After 1935, under Chief Constable (Sir) A. F. Hordern, the Lancashire force became one of the pioneers in the use of VHF radio. This was not only used (from four fixed stations in the county) in the pursuit of criminals; mobile radio telephone systems were put into opera-

---

* Probably not a great deal. An unkind but authentic story, from a local surveyor who became one of the country's leading road engineers, suggests that the Minister could not read a surveyor's plan or map.

tion in traffic control, so that, at large race meetings for example, an observer in an aeroplane could note the state of traffic on the main roads below and give directions to motor patrols. Lancashire's role in this field of traffic direction was often that of innovator or experimenter, and in 1938 it was one of five constabulary bodies to try out, with Home Office approval, the experimental motor patrol scheme involving the use of the so-called 'courtesy cops'. Meanwhile, the county's peculiarities created pressures and counter-pressures, which led in the end to amalgamations of forces. The Lancashire county boroughs resisted absorption until the late sixties, but 1947 brought the non-county borough forces of Lancaster, Accrington, Bacup, Ashton-under-Lyne and Clitheroe into the County Constabulary.

The thirties, then, were marked by experiment, by ideas that were to reach their fruition in the generation to come. The local government service had already established a very real tradition in its upper echelons, although that tradition was not in any way geared to rapid change and improvisation. The even tenor of administrative work was reflected in the staffing of the Clerk's Department (at the beginning of the period known, appropriately, as the Clerk of the Peace's Department, and changed to Clerk of the County Council Department in 1931 when the two offices were combined), which increased by very little in the thirties under the paternal rule of (Sir) George Hammond Etherton, who could still know all the people on the County Hall staff by characteristics, name and reputation. His staff of committee clerks serviced no fewer than sixteen council committees, innumerable sub-committees and a number of joint bodies; this meant not only much minute-taking and agenda preparation, but also a detailed knowledge of continually growing statute law. Hardly six months went by without the appearance of some important enactment affecting one or other of the main committees; and some examples will make the point clear. The early thirties brought the Town and Country Planning Act (1932), the Local Government Act (1933) and the Road Traffic Act and the Unemployment Assistance Act of 1934. The year 1936 brought a Midwives Act which had profound repercussions for the county medical service (see Chapter 14), an Education Act, a Trunk Roads Act and a Public Health Act, while 1937 brought a Local Government Superannuation Act, a Livestock Industry Act (as well as the usual parliamentary orders affecting agriculture), another Road Traffic Act and a Rating and Valuation Act. Each of these had to be discussed at length with committee chairmen and vice-chairmen. None of these enactments was especially far-reaching, or in itself involved the imposition of heavy financial or manpower commitments, but the paperwork involved was always heavy. Even in the general atmosphere of the later interwar years, already sultry with the threats from Europe, the senior officer, little used to any major reformations of local government, could be a man who needed much animal energy to keep on top of his job.

County government, then, although still somewhat restricted in scope and very conservative in its style, nevertheless gained enough in experience and practical experiment to face up to the exacting problems of the immediate postwar years. Likewise, the spirit of election time, so long dimmed by lack of public interest and of contests, was entering into a resurgence, and debates in the Council chamber were gaining edge. Little of this was evident in the style and background of the county's leaders, whether chairmen or chief officers; they conformed to the pattern of the social leaders of an earlier age, dedicated servants of the public though they were. Sir James Travis-Clegg, chairman of the Council from 1931 to 1937, commented at the time of his appointment on 'the county reputation for efficient and economical local government',[21] and this was very much in the spirit of the national administration of the time.

Sir James, at his introduction to the chair, was at fifty-seven much younger than the new chairmen who had preceded him. Indeed, he had only failed to reach this high office earlier because of his comparative youth, and it should be borne in mind that he had begun his service as a local councillor at the age of twenty-two. He was nearer in origin than most to the (in Lancashire) minority of leisured-gentleman county councillors, his father, John Travis-Clegg, having been a county magistrate resident at High Crompton in south-east Lancashire. Sir James differed from most of his colleagues in that he was an Old Etonian, although like most of them he had leisure enough to perform public service, taking up such work 'after leaving school'.[22] Like Sir Henry Hibbert, he had strong local interests, and for one period he served as chairman of Crompton Urban District Council. This experience was undoubtedly important, because it gave the new chairman real insight into the problems of district councils; moreover, his chairmanship coincided with an acceleration of the 'suburbanisation' and speculative building sprawl touched upon in Chapter 15, and accordingly with an increase of applications for boundary changes by county boroughs and county districts. Section 46 of the Local Government Act (1929) had laid upon the County Council the duty of reviewing county district boundaries, and this made it necessary to organise conferences with no fewer than 140 urban boroughs, rural and parish councils by 1 April 1932. The Parliamentary Committee of the Council had to apply for an extension of the time required, and was still engaged in recommending boundary changes in the following year.[23]

Despite such inundations of unrewarding labour, the chairmen maintained his deep interest in education, his first love among the county services. When not engaged in attending the more than a round dozen of committees to which a chairman was obliged, *ex officio*, to give attention, Sir James (he was knighted in 1933) lived in the pleasant seclusion of Bailrigg, near Lancaster. It is one of the ironies of history that he died in October 1942, without having means to know that his private landed estate would become the ground on which the new University of Lancaster would be administered and built just over twenty years later; and that his own Council would do much to further its creation.

Sir James retained the chairmanship until March 1937, during which time the normally unruffled calm of the council chamber was increasingly disturbed by some of the protesting and other amendments mentioned in Chapter 12. The last chairman of the interwar period, Sir William Hodgson, was, again, an immensely experienced member of Council who, like his forerunner Travis-Clegg, had served on a district council, in this instance as chairman of Poulton-le-Fylde Urban District in 1900. As though to make up for the wild aberration of Sir James's relative youth, Sir William was seventy-nine when he took over the chairmanship. He had been a member of the county magistracy since 1896, and was therefore imbued with all the deeper traditions of county leadership. Not surprisingly, he had served on a great many county committees – no fewer than twelve main ones over a total Lancashire service of more than forty years.[24] The resolution confirming his appointment was carried unanimously in March 1937, and although it was seconded by Alderman W. M. Rogerson of the Labour Party (Hodgson was a life-long Conservative), there was a sharp and, in the face of later events, significant dispute over who should be vice-chairman, concerning a demand for a free vote in the election of aldermen and vice-chairmen. The members of the aldermanic bench were nominated proportionally by Quarter Sessional divisions, and had been so nominated since 1889; the new proposal was that such positions should be awarded in open vote and on considerations of pure merit. Although the councillors of 1937 hardly realised the fact, a new broad principle was only awaiting a future re-emergence, albeit one of political expediency rather than 'pure merit'. The long-cherished sense of consensus before the overriding duties of county service was in jeopardy.

Yet on the surface, the long-established procedures and style remained. The war came, shattering the old ways and the newer hopes at one blow; and an octogenarian chairman and a deeply traditionalist clerk, on the edge of his own retirement, had to face the manifold demands and duties of wartime organisation. Sir George Etherton became county civil defence controller, and the world of local and national government, sensing the dangers of the future, had been planning air raid precautions since 1936. Lancashire County Council had asked for a report from its Special Committee on Air Raid Precautions in 1937, and referred the whole subject to the Standing Joint Committee and the chief constable.[25] Accordingly the County Constabulary came to play a major part in civil defence.

But the experiences of wartime amounted to more than a mere watershed between one age of local government and a later one; they cemented relationships, as no other form of activity or legislation had done, between county districts and the county authority. It is a commonplace that the war effort inspired innumerable sections of the community into joint efforts of enterprise unthinkable in any other context; and when Lancashire, with its great cities of Liverpool and Manchester under real or threatened air attack, had to organise evacuation of schoolchildren on a massive scale, it was the county districts of Lancashire that played a vital role under the general direction of Sir George Etherton and County Hall. Likewise, those other duties that fell like hailstones upon county and district officers – air raid precautions, national savings, army welfare, food registration, fuel rationing, Red Cross collecting (a voluntary activity which was nevertheless willingly undertaken by the rural districts in the 'rural pennies' campaign) – tended to lead to continual consultation between the rural, urban and non-county borough districts (and their associations) on the one hand, and Sir George Etherton and his county officers on the other. As a leading officer of the Rural District Councils Association put it:

> On matters of new legislation and policy, the Lancashire County Council invariably consulted the three district associations; invited their representatives down to talk – this was particularly so in Civil Defence, before, and during the war, and continuing [the policy] into the post-war period, because the process of consultation had become established by then. In consequence, representatives of each of the associations were invited down to County Hall once a year before the budget was announced ... to hear from the Chairman of the Finance Committee the details of the forthcoming year's expenditure, and to ask questions. ...[26]

The war, then, further consolidated county policy towards the constituent districts, in such a manner as to produce an approach and a style that were ultimately distinctive. Accordingly it was possible for the next clerk, R. H. Adcock, to pursue this policy with unwavering consistency, and to adumbrate it in a now well-known article in *Public Administration* (vol. XXVI, 1948).

Sir George Etherton, whose legacy this style was, retired on 2 November 1944, and died on 3 December 1949. It is to be hoped that he was enabled to appreciate what excellent foundations he had lain for the solution to many complex administrative problems of the postwar upheaval. Sir William Hodgson, who had also (quite incredibly in view of his advanced age) borne the strains of wartime office, died in harness on 26 February 1945. The passing of these two distinguished and deeply traditionalist leaders marked the end of one phase of county administration and the commencement of a new one. It was Sir George, however, whose work linked the two phases together; properly, indeed, for it was in the world of administration, rather than that of representative rule, that the stirrings of the future were to be found before 1945.

The war's own legacy was a series of Acts of Parliament which now stand out in every textbook of social, economic and political history. The wartime coalition government produced the Butler Act, the Education Act (1944), and the consequences of this are described in Chapter 13. In addition, the postwar political upheaval gave forth the National Health Service Act (1946), which caused the transfer of the functions of thirty-three autonomous county district health authorities to the Council, and which led to the acquisition of an ambulance service and a district nursing service by the Health Department – which at the same time lost the extensive hospital service which had been largely built on the old Guardians' institutions. The latter went to the newly created regional hospital boards. Meanwhile, the National Assistance Act (1948) abolished the former public assistance administration and made the county into a welfare authority, with the duty of providing a wide range of services for the aged and the handicapped. In a more than nominal sense, an administrative revolution was thereby completed; the Poor Law had long shown a somewhat gentler profile in its attitude to the sick and weak; and this Act, in intention and in practice, completed the transformation in so far as slowly adjusting official attitudes permitted.

Much of this is well known. It is sometimes forgotten that the postwar period brought a range of totally new functions to county and county borough authorities, and it is the impact and nature of these with which much of this section of the volume is concerned, and which also forms much of the subject matter in the present chapter. Not only did the county administer a fleet of ambulances, but it had to build a fire brigades service under the terms of the Fire Brigades Act of 1947, which allotted the administration of this service to the counties and the county boroughs. Here again was a legacy of wartime, and its work is described hereafter.

The same postwar period saw the development of two more totally new departments, the Planning Department and the Children's Department. As will be seen, these departments and services did not add greatly to the numerical strength of the county professional staff, but they did add very considerably to its range of professional expertise and enterprise. In terms of numbers, all such services tended to be dwarfed by the massive proportions of the Education Department. Yet their organisation and construction was no easy task; a new professional corps had to be built up in each case, and a new generation of planners and social workers had to be trained or nurtured. A significant part of the increased work derived from this fact fell upon the Clerk's Department, which was responsible for staffing and salaries, and this period of accelerated growth and intensive organisation threw its strains upon a new and powerful clerk, R. H. Adcock, who had joined the county staff from the City of Manchester, where he had served as town clerk from 1938 to 1944.[27] His period of office saw a steady building of the services mentioned, and an equally significant development of the common service departments (which of course included the Planning Department), such as Finance and County Architects. In May 1945 James Drake, an equally dynamic figure who was to be one of the country's pioneer motorway-builders, was appointed county surveyor and bridgemaster.[28] In the previous March the former Highways and Bridges chairman, Sir Percy Macdonald (1934-41), became chairman of the Council, but he held office for one year only (1945-6), to be succeeded by an able former solicitor and County Court registrar from east Lancashire, Sir James Aitken, the first Liberal to hold office since Sir William Scott-Barrett, who had retired in 1921.

Sir James Aitken, who held office during what was plainly a period of administrative turmoil, was distinguished for his interest in education, marked in his case by a period as president of the Association of Education Committees. Like nearly all his chairman colleagues, he had had a significant period of service on a second-tier authority, in this instance the municipal borough of Nelson, where he had held the office of mayor between 1925 and 1927. He had served a total of twenty-seven years as a member of the Council, and was sufficiently knowledgeable and experienced to hold the new office in this especially difficult period. Nevertheless, he died after only two years of service in the chair, in March 1948;[29] Alderman Harry Hyde (who was knighted in 1953) acted as Council chairman during the remainder of his term of office. He then served an additional year in the chair. Hyde was another prominent Conservative from, in this case, Ashton-under-Lyne.[30] He was succeeded in April 1949 by one of the most memorable figures of the postwar period, (Sir) Alfred Bates, who had been clerk and solicitor to the old Heysham UDC from 1921 to 1928, before its amalgamation with Morecambe. Much in the legalistic and procedural nature of county government gives such personalities scope for their talents, and the growing pressures and rough-and-tumble of this particular phase, with its enormously multi-plying problems affecting second-tier authorities and divisional organisa-tions, and its flood of new legislation, seemed to call urgently for a chairman of both experience and relatively youthful energy.

Both Sir Harry Hyde and Sir Alfred Bates held office during a period of political storm; like most of their fellow-chairmen, they were Conser-vatives who had the job of putting into effect the legislation of a Labour government, at a time when the Council was itself changing in composi-tion, and when the basic forms of a two-party system were taking shape in the council chamber. It is clear that Alderman Bates's relative youth influenced his appointment (he was fifty-one, and Harry Hyde was then seventy), and when Andrew Smith seconded his nomination he added, pointedly, that there was a growing belief that the arduous position of chairman was one for a younger man.[31] Up to that period, the Council had accepted the notion of seniority, with its corresponding emphasis upon gerontocratic leadership, almost without question.

As party formations developed, it remained true that there were never two counterposed sets of detailed party policies regarding the priorities of the main county departments, except, perhaps, in matters of the broadest principle, and touching only on subjects like comprehensive education. This apparent consensus is all the more striking because the full impact of Aneurin Bevan's 'vermin' speech was felt in Lancashire political circles; he attended a banquet at County Hall on the following day, in an atmosphere of some hostility and embarrassment.[32] The breakage of the *political* consensus was a fact in postwar county politics; but it never reached far down into the administrative subsoil.

The ethos of county government, in any case, was in conscientious and efficient administration. In a great many matters, there was little freedom of choice to permit of the formation of detailed alternative policies, and the information that would have made elaborate technical alternatives a reality lay mainly in the hands of officers and chairmen. Accordingly, manifestoes at election time tended to be spirited but nebulous. 'They went through the motions of hating each other,' remarked a senior officer, 'but they were the best of friends the following day.' Although the politic-ally dedicated may see in this evidence of wholesale denial of faith, the fact is that the individual services and their administration offered much that was immensely absorbing to the layman. It was not so much that a committee member or chairman needed to derive a sense of possibly corrupting self-importance from his work; the importance of his involve-ments was self-evidently there, and could be demonstrated at every turn. A competent officer, for his part, would always try to make his committee members feel involved in major decisions; these decisions could affect thousands of people and commit the Council to an expenditure of many hundreds of thousands of pounds. The officer could also make his committee associates feel that their amateur position conferred upon them a special status, given in turn by the fact of public representation, and that even the most formal decision, hedged as it was by statute law and its interpretation, was a sacred discharge of duty.

It is probable that these psychological attitudes changed little even when political lines were consolidated. Much depended upon the nature and size of committees; some of them, like the Education Committee, were much too large for anything but the formal discharge of business and the occasional party debate or wrangle, but the sub-committees of all the standing committees were a different matter, and a sense of involvement was stronger there. Local interests, too, were often touched upon, and a substantial proportion of the councillors were also district council members. Experiments, instigated by officers themselves, which rubbed against common sense or popular prejudice, would sometimes lead to sharp comment and make clear that the relevant committee was not being led by the nose.[33]

The remainder of this chapter will include accounts of developments in several of the new postwar departments, and will attempt to show that, in areas of work that were not long-established and controlled by precedent, the work of both officer and councillor had its excitements. The survey will commence by showing the relative strengths of the main departments in staffing terms, and will dwell upon the sheer size of some of them, a consideration that led in turn to the furtherance of the 'Three Shires' idea, that of splitting Lancashire into three main areas or Ridings. The early burgeonings of this plan will also be discussed.

A straightforward representation of the staffing of the education service in Lancashire, compared with other main services, will demonstrate very clearly how vast such a commitment could be (see Table 10.1[34]). The full-time and part-time staff totals include teachers, the most numerous of all county employees, but in the case of the Health Department they also include home helps. As the figures in Table 10.1 show, an increasing proportion of the county employee total was represented by the staffing of the education service. Of the 12,113 full-time education employees in January 1947, 8383 were teachers and the remainder were administrators and clerical staff at County Hall and in the thirty-five education divisions and two excepted districts that were formed, as shown in Chapter 13, following the 1944 Education Act. The anxious negotiation that resulted in the formation of Lancashire's network of education divisions was to a lesser degree reflected in the creation of the seventeen health divisions some two years later (1947). As has been seen, the latter were often based upon, although they were not always co-terminous with, the old Poor Law Unions; hence, since the county district boundaries that made up the divisions were generally the same as before, they frequently followed the district, parish and Hundred boundaries of earlier history. In other words, the collective requirements of groups of districts were consistently the main Lancashire consideration, and functional requirements and total populations could always be adjusted to the former.

TABLE 10.1
County Staff Totals by Departments

	1939	1947	1951	1955	1960	1965	1970	1972
Education								
Full-time	5,995	12,113	14,904	15,819	18,517	21,620	26,821	30,017
Part-time	648	4,147	6,411	11,485	15,268	21,659	30,328	32,277
Totals	6,643	16,260	21,315	27,304	33,785	43,279	57,149	62,294
Health (including welfare and environmental services)								
Full-time	2,698	4,852	3,297	3,482	5,643	7,530	8,640	10,291
Part-time	522	314	874	2,022	—	—	—	—
Totals	3,220	5,166	4,171	5,504	5,643	7,530	8,640	10,291
Highways and bridges								
Full-time	1,392	1,624	1,650	1,822	2,009	2,945	3,034	3,147
Part-time	—	2	5	6	8	10	8	8
Totals	1,392	1,626	1,655	1,828	2,017	2,955	3,042	3,155
All departments								
Full-time	13,173	22,081	25,582	27,613	33,172	40,540	43,317	48,363
Part-time	1,263	4,579	8,178	15,000	17,004	23,675	31,635	33,589
Totals	14,436	26,660	33,760	42,613	50,176	64,215	74,952	81,952

It may be significant that the period 1945–7, the time of these remarkable experiments in divisionalisation, was also the period of a dialogue of the Council with the Local Government Boundary Commission. The initial impulse of the discussion, however, was provided by a series of proposals by Lancashire county boroughs to extend their own boundaries into the massive conurbations of south Lancashire. The Commission reacted to these suggestions by proposing that the county boroughs, especially in the area of Manchester, might take a second-tier position under anything up to five shire or riding divisions of the original Lancashire county, each with a top tier on county council lines.[35] It is certainly true that the boundaries of individual communities, under the effect of suburbanisation, were either losing or had totally lost their former relevance, and this fact was much emphasised in the official enquiries of the following twenty years.

The County Council's predictable reply[36] was a stout defence of the principle of two-tier government; and a suggestion that if Manchester was to form its own 'county' then the same arguments should apply to Liverpool and its area. Lancashire could be split into three shires if the rateable value of each was not to fall below £10 million, the rateable value of the *geographical* county being £35,893,754. The reason for this apparently arbitrary figure of £10 million was that the Council thought that the high standard of officer required for Lancashire 'circumstances' and services could not be provided for an area of lesser value. The Council's remarks on the optimum populations (and thereby areas) for the most effective administration of given services are of great interest, for they were to be directly related to practice in a number of instances; education, for example, called for a divisional executive area of at least 60,000, which figure the Lancashire Education Authority had adopted only two years previously after recommendations from the Ministry of Education, and after itself trying to create much smaller divisions. However, the Council did afterwards pursue this optimum fairly consistently, and it also pointed out that a population of 300,000 was needed for the proper administration of further education, teacher training and regional technical colleges; a shrewd blow at all but the great cities! Health divisions ('second-tier units') called for a population of 100,000, which could engage medical services with skilled advisers for divisional sub-committees, which could result in 'complete co-ordination', and which was surprisingly close to the populations of the urbanised health divisions then forming (perhaps, therefore, not a coincidence).

In the matter of the police, the Council could see 'no maximum population that a police force should control',[37] and the good sense of its observations was tested out in the next two-and-a-half decades. In the matter of highways and bridges, the Council merely recommended 'power to delegate', and its comments were perhaps coloured by its then highway policies; it did however (very wisely) comment on the massive works which a second-tier authority might have to undertake. Its comments on town and country planning (which referred to 'advisory joint committees') also owed something to the local discussions of the period, and its suggestions for a fire services area explored the realms of very high population minima indeed. Once more, the recommendations showed realistic judgement, and in later pages of the present chapter a brief study of the Lancashire Fire Brigade may indicate what could be gained organisationally by a very large unit.

The Council then added its figures together to see how large the two-tier authority should be, and suggested 300,000 population as the minimum total, with a travelling time of roughly thirty minutes maximum for an official or councillor driving from the outer extremity to County Hall. This corresponds strikingly to the administrative Lancashire of the mid-seventies; yet it is a bizarre fact, as will be shown elsewhere,[38] that district authorities at the end of forty or fifty miles or more of indifferent road from Preston, namely in Ulverston and Mossley, saw no particular disadvantage in belonging to such a vast county as the old Lancashire. The County Council recommendations to the Boundary Commission ended with a characteristic flourish; one-third of the new top-tier authority's members might be 'nominated by County Districts, the balance being directly elected'.[39]

The Three Ridings Scheme, as it came to be known, was put into cold storage because it proposed to reduce a mass of jealously independent county boroughs to second-tier status – and even the postwar upheaval never really aspired to this. It remains true that local government bodies will always try to justify their own functions and operations, and Lancashire's claims, to be fully tested, would call for exhaustive case studies which go beyond the scope of a general history. County government must be judged not only by the effectiveness of the grass-roots contacts of the main services, as seen through the work of committees and sub-committees, but also by the impact of a great many other types of contact with the public, by field staff as well as councillors, and by the palpable effectiveness of all the personal and some environmental services. To pass comprehensive judgement on such a complex phenomenon can hardly be valuable at this stage, and all we can do here is to outline the growth, working problems and achievement of three distinctively postwar services, the Fire Brigade, the Police and the Children's Department. It will be noticed that the problems of delegation of powers did not seriously beset these county organisations. Meanwhile, it will be proper also to mention the work of a 'common service' department like the Treasurer's and to refer also to the further development of the County Library.

The relative magnitude of the major services can be judged by expenditure figures for each as seen over the postwar years (see Table 10.2[40]). These figures were, of course, subject to inflationary pressures which are measured by Mr MacGregor-Reid in the following chapter; but they represent a startling growth in the scale of operations of all the departments listed, and a great increase in capital expenditure on, e.g., schools, offices, police houses, fire stations and, above all, roads, as well as in the staffing of each of these departments. (The staff figures for Education, Health/Welfare and Highways Departments are given in Table 10.1 above.) It is not suggested that these growth phenomena and pressures were peculiar to Lancashire; they were, as Mr MacGregor-Reid suggests, country-wide and in general conformity with the national trends, despite the local characteristics inevitably encountered. The Treasurer's department, responsible for the administration of these vast sums, had a staff of 138 in 1939, 210 in 1947, 295 in 1951, 323 in 1960 and 487 in 1970.

TABLE 10.2
Expenditure, Before Grant Relief, by Lancashire County Council Departments

	1947–8	1954–5	1959–60	1968–9	1972–7
			(£ millions)		
Education	9.52	18.3	33.34	88.15	150.77
Health (all services and welfare)	1.28	3.35	5.44	12.55	26.46
Highways	1.76	2.86	6.58	13.04	19.10
Police	1.76	2.93	4.50	10.61	17.27
Fire	—	0.77	1.22	2.80	5.70
Children	0.13	0.47	0.60	2.40	—

The County Treasurer (Mr Alan Beal) was responsible for the introduction of punched card equipment in 1948 to replace overloaded keyboard machines for main accounts and cost accounting. Yet, in the view of the Department, the increase in its staff would have been far greater had it not been 'for major strides in the use of non-manual methods'.[41] Under the county treasurership of Mr Norman Doodson (1951–69) there was a move into electronic data processing, when a plugged programme computer was installed to deal with monthly and weekly payrolls; and two more computers were installed in 1963, followed by the introduction of multi-programming in 1966, by which time computerisation had already been extended to the non-financial work of county departments.[42] By the early seventies, computer services were being provided for eleven Lancashire district councils, and the facilities of the computer section in the Treasurer's Department were subject to two-shift working from 1968 onwards.

All this makes a spectacular enough record of experiment; what value did the public get for its money? Unfortunately, the general public itself has few comprehensive means of assessment, and it will for this reason be fair to describe one of the most obviously useful services, the Lancashire County Fire Brigade. This, immediately after the war, was a totally new venture as far as county government was concerned; Lancashire county and municipal boroughs and districts had had their own fire brigades until the Fire Brigades Act of 1947, which put the responsibility for this service into the hands of counties and county boroughs specifically. Fortunately for all concerned, the National Fire Service (NFS), from which men and gear were inherited, had formed its own skills and traditions under the stresses of wartime; its senior personnel had to be appointed to the new local government staffs *en masse*, and for this purpose multiple appointment sessions took place at London County Council offices.[43] Accordingly, the former NFS divisional officer for Lancashire, Mr Herbert Blackledge, took up his post as chief fire officer for the county as from 1 April 1948.[44]

The suitable equipment and accommodation of a partly seasoned staff was a different matter. Men 'serving at stations like Atherton or Tarleton, which were of the converted air-raid shelter type, counted themselves lucky in that their machines did not have to suffer the conditions under which those at Swinton were housed',[45] and Leyland UDC had the distinction of handing over the oldest vehicle, a 1922 Leyland Pump Escape.[46] While these are undoubtedly extreme cases, dormitories, messes and recreation rooms frequently occupied prefabricated huts, and a vast programme of capital expenditure, the true nature and purpose of which was evident almost exclusively to a few elected representatives and officials, and the members of the service themselves, occupied the next twenty-five years. Hence the Brigade was, between its inception and 1974, the justification for the expenditure of over £2 million on buildings alone.[47] It is difficult to say how far the Brigade came to exhibit the advantages of economies of scale, because it had many stations in areas of high fire risk. Nevertheless, it cost the population of Lancashire roughly £1 a year per head to run in 1965–6,[48] and was certainly not markedly more expensive than the brigades of smaller counties. In addition, it was undoubtedly one of the most innovative and best organised in England.

By 1967 the Lancashire Brigade had over 1800 personnel working from sixty-one fire stations, all as far as possible strategically sited with regard to density of population and degree of fire risk. Statistics for the inclusive years 1964–6 indicate that each station was likely to handle some 150 'incidents' in a working year, or three to four a week; that every couple of weeks was likely to bring a malicious false alarm and a well-intentioned false alarm; and that grass fires, often started by the mischievous young, occupied an alarming proportion of the Brigade's time, reaching the total of 3765 in 1965.[49] These did, of course, depend upon weather and season; and for the rest, chimney fires, and fires caused by 'children with matches', took up much brigade time. Major fires (those involving over ten jets per incident) came to a total of only six in 1966.[50] Nevertheless, the existence of the Fire Brigade probably prevented losses of property and capital equipment considerably greater than the cost of the Brigade itself, although the precise extent of any benefit is impossible to estimate. (By the same token, the achievement of the health service in 'preventing' diseases it had helped to eradicate is equally conjectural.)

Finally, the Brigade undertook in 1953 a rather resented task of running the Council's direct labour scheme, the Centre Vehicle Maintenance Unit, which was responsible for the maintenance of ambulances and other vehicles belonging to the authority (except those belonging to the Police and the Highways and Surveyor's Department). The scheme, which in the opinion of brigade officers 'did little to promote the efficiency of the Fire Service', was jettisoned with relief on their part in 1967.

The Fire Brigade Committee was perhaps rather low down in the hierarchy of Council committees. Yet it controlled a major spending service, and it was chaired by (later) leading personalities in both contending political parties – (Sir) Henry Lumby, later chairman of the Council (1967-74) was chairman of the Committee in 1947-52 and again in 1955-61, representing the Conservative side, and he had Alderman T. Hourigan of the Labour Party (chairman of the Fire Brigade Committee in 1952-5 and also a Health Committee chairman) as his vice-chairman. It is certainly the case that, unlike the old-established services, the Brigade, by the very nature of its expansion and accompanying efficiency-seeking ethos, tended to encourage an involvement and pride in visible skills and equipment that was lacking in other spheres of council-controlled work. Despite the mundane nature of much fire station work, the organisation never lost its romantic associations. The average committee member could understand, or thought he could understand, its problems, however technical they might be.

The County Fire Brigade had a special responsibility for road accidents involving inflammable materials, and thereby worked in close collaboration with the County Constabulary in these and in innumerable other routine matters. Unlike the police, however, it had no public relations problems, and unlike several of the other major services, it pursued activities that were appreciated by district authorities without incurring any desire on their part to demand local control of its work. Like the police, the Children's Department and the education service, the Fire Brigade was subject to central inspection, in its own case from the Home Office. It was most decidedly an innovative service and, with Home Office encouragement, it established a training scheme which was a model for the country at large (during the sixties), and which aimed to increase job satisfaction.

The Fire Brigade Committee and the Chief Fire Officer saw no need for 'a tiresome Annual Report', which would serve little purpose in the county;[51] the shining 'appliances' of the developing service, with their flashing lights and sirens, were in any case sufficient advertisement. The Standing Joint Committee, the body controlling the police, had shunned any kind of publicity during the first two generations of its existence, and had shrunk so far from it that, as we have seen, its deliberations were omitted from the Council's annual *Proceedings*, although its sub-ordination to the Finance Committee was recognised in occasional minutes or resolutions of that body. The Committee consisted of thirteen aldermen, three councillors and seventeen county magistrates, and was renamed the Police Committee in 1964–5, when it contained thirty-six members. Essentially an undemocratic organisation, it limited council participation to the senior 'establishment' for the most part, and was probably totally uninfluenced by passing political phases, except in so far as these filtered through the Home Secretary's own policy and staff.

Yet, by the sixties, this rigid and deeply traditional body, and even more the senior police staff, found itself under some considerable publicity, and public, pressures. These were not all negative or derived from animus against the police, for the latter began to feature heroically, but in a realistic and well-documented way, in BBC television features, in series with a recognisable Lancashire or Merseyside background. The casual viewer began to learn something about police politics as well as patrol cars, and even a little about the administrative effects of county and county borough boundaries. He might even be reminded that criminals ('villains') raced out of Lancashire on the newly constructed motorways, and returned just as quickly. It was not unreasonable that Lancashire should provide a scenario for a motorised fight against crime, for the county, as has been noted, was one of the pioneers in the development of road patrols. It had also suffered from a multiplicity of police forces for a century, and the remaining five non-county borough forces, already listed,[52] were absorbed into the County Constabulary as late as 1947, sending the total strength of the latter from 2494 (the 1939 figure) to 2800 including postwar recruitment. Thereafter the strength of the county force rose gradually but considerably, until in 1968 it had nearly doubled the 1947 manpower and womanpower total. The crime and misdemeanour rates rose more rapidly, however, and roughly followed the track of the growth rate for fires.

The work of the force was in reality, and necessarily, much more prosaic than the most realistic television representation. The remainder of its story falls into several fields, some familiar, some of them not; that of a long and successful project to improve working accommodation and housing, the building of a policewomen's section, that of a great improvement of training (both in service and at regional centres), and that of the development of more sophisticated beat and field techniques. It is these that have attracted most interest, notably the use of personal radios by foot and motorised police, and of mobile patrols working in combination with beat constables. In addition, the Lancashire force was among the pioneers in the use of radar, frogmen, white and 'day-glow' coloured police cars and women's police motor patrols. Chief Constable T. E. St Johnston, who served in that office during the greater part of this crucial period (1950-67), remarked[53] of the introduction of personal radio that 'This has revolutionised the work of the man on the beat. It has made his daily tour much more interesting and efficient'. At the same time, it was recognised that rapid communications and motorisation were not in themselves enough, and so, after an experiment at Accrington in 1966, the unit beat policing scheme was devised.[54] The principle here was that a foot policeman, with a limited regular solo beat and close contact with the public, was essential as a supplier of information into a network of supervision. Each such beat policeman was known as 'the area constable', and was in practice in the old tradition of the village 'bobby'. He was, however, directly linked to mobile patrols responsible for several beat areas, and where necessary to detectives distributed through such areas.

To the policeman himself, relief from clerical and routine duties by a growing section of civilian employees could be of even greater significance, and even where he had this valued help, too many station premises were sub-standard and ill-designed. Living accommodation remained a constant problem. The war, and its immediate aftermath, interrupted plans by the Joint Committee to build more police houses. By 1950 nearly 300 standard houses were completed; in that year, nevertheless, the Chief Constable could speak of housing for the force as 'very poor'.[55] With the help of the County Architect and his staff, and that of the Housing and Welfare Branch of the County Constabulary (set up in 1951), the number of purpose-built police houses more than doubled from 1012 to 2501, by 1966. However, progress was slow, and St Johnston remarked in 1964 that the county borough policemen of Lancashire could buy their own family houses when appointed to the service, but that the county police were still less well off.[56]

Amalgamation, the great fact of the sixties, obviously assisted the co-ordination of action so necessary to deal with the rapidly moving criminals, especially the motorway-borne element.[57] An enquiry into the total amalgamation of the Lancashire county and county borough forces commenced in 1967, and the date for their combination was set at 1 April 1969, when twelve county borough forces came together with the Lancashire Constabulary. It was then possible to divide the whole of Lancashire into five districts with a total of fifteen divisions, each based on a major town. Something of the rationale of local government reorganisation, Redcliffe-Maud style, had already taken effect. One of the advantages of this new pattern lay in the feasibility of the 'task force' idea, yet another method of work made familiar by the television screen in recent years; the new (April 1969) Lancashire Constabulary formed three such task forces of eighty men apiece, consisting of detectives, dog handlers and uniformed mobile crime patrols, any one of which could now invade a given piece of county territory without incurring more than a modicum of misgiving from fellow policemen.

There is little question that the Lancashire force, in common with other British police bodies, went through something of a revolution in public relations at this time. Chief Constable St Johnston commenced the practice of giving published *Annual Reports* in 1964, but Chief Constable W. J. H. Palfrey (who held office from 1967 to 1972) had far more publicity sense than his predecessors, although his knack was not always to appeal to the more liberal-minded elements in society. There is no doubt that he understood some Lancashire instincts and prejudices, and that the need for a closer relationship between police and public was fully appreciated. In the year of Chief Constable Palfrey's retirement, the force was working satisfactorily as one body; but it learned, when Chief Constable Stanley Parr took over (1972), that the administrative county was to be split into three segments, and that much of the reorganisation work had been in vain. The realisation of the Three Ridings Scheme had come at the wrong moment for the police; unfortunately, too, some of the new boundaries created by local government reorganisation were about to cut across existing police divisions, and when members of the county force were asked to state whether they wished to join the old remaining Lancashire or one of the new metropolitan counties, a majority opted for the former – far too many to be accommodated.[58]

Yet it is likely that the short-lived and in some ways rather wasteful experiment in massive amalgamation was not without its valuable lessons. It was, for example, decided in the light of experience that some of the post-1969 police divisions, which had had over six hundred men each, were too unwieldy.[59] It is possible that any dis-economies of scale had their roots in pre-amalgamation (i.e. pre-1969) days, or rather that the continual need for up-to-date equipment (under the just as continual pressure to keep a rather under-strength force covering many urban areas at full effectiveness) made the Lancashire Constabulary, the largest police body in provincial England, somewhat more expensive to run *per capita* of population policed than a number of roughly comparable counties. The selected figures and years in Table 10.3[60] show trends with approximate fairness.

Comparatively few Lancashire councillors and 'public persons' had much to do with the running of the police service, and not many more had experience of helping to administer the Fire Brigade. With the personal, as distinct from the protective, services there was much more public involvement, and both the Education and the Health and Welfare administrations had the effect of drawing in the participation of many scores of local representatives. A most important spiritual offshoot of both of these departments was the Children's Department. Both the Education and Public Assistance Committees had, in prewar days, some legal responsibility for the boarding out or adoption of children,[61] but as so often

TABLE 10.3
Rate-Borne Expenditure on Police Services

	Gross expenditure	Rate-borne expenditure	Population	Gross expenditure per 1000 of population	Rate-borne expenditure per 1000 of population
	£	£	£	£	£
1950–1	2,189,064	977,940	2,047,010	1,095	489
1953–4	2,678,564	1,215,986	2,044,400	1,339	608
1956–7	3,658,562	1,662,464	2,091,000	1,843	831
1959–60	4,500,633	2,070,628	2,151,000	2,092	963
1963–4	6,902,984	3,174,780	2,268,060	3,044	1,400
1966–7	9,666,324	4,316,911	2,366,020	4,086	1,825
1969–70	11,151,371	5,611,016	2,457,280	4,538	2,283
1971–2	15,580,541	7,853,818	2,513,400	6,199	3,125

happened it was the impact of wartime experiences that accelerated or crystallised comprehensive legislation designed to protect children without secure home backgrounds. The wartime evacuation of children revealed the relatively large number who were deprived of a settled home life, and this was the stimulus to the Interdepartmental Committee (1945) under the chairmanship of Dame Myra Curtis, which enquired into the methods of caring for such children, and which led to the Children Act of 1948. The latter empowered local authorities to appoint children's officers, with staff, to 'exercise their powers with respect to [the child] so as to further his best interest and to afford him opportunities for the proper development of his character and abilities'. It will be seen that the Children Act was very much in the stated spirit of the Education Act of 1944; in fact, it shines out as one of the most humane and useful pieces of legislation of the century, being straightforwardly directed to achievable ends. The method to be used was the extensive provision of carefully chosen foster homes, with adoption as a basic aim and the provision of residential accommodation as a temporary measure.

As in other significant cases, there was in Lancashire a striking degree of anticipation of what was to come, and considerable preparation for the Act (and the subsequent Children's Department) had been made. On 17 April 1946 the first meeting of the Children's Welfare Committee took place, the Council already having under its care about a thousand children of whom fewer than three hundred were in foster homes. The Committee, under the chairmanship of Alderman Mrs K.M. Fletcher, included nominees of the Council, the Education Committee, the Public Assistance Committee and the then Midwives, Maternity and Child Welfare Committee, which was responsible, *inter alia*, for remand homes.[62] The Children's Welfare Committee, which was already responsible for evacuee orphans and for two children's homes, appointed Mr H. R. Irving as children's officer for the county as early as July 1946.[63] Moreover, there was already a Lancashire Children's Committee, derived from the body already described, in existence in September 1947, considerably before the placing of the Children Act in the statute book in the following year.

Its work, then, was mainly concerned with the provision of temporary accommodation in reception centres. The Education Department, meanwhile, remained the parent department for the time being (maintaining legal records of adoption cases until 1950), and provided the children's officer and his staff with records of neglected children.[64] The acquisition in 1947 of a small staff, comprising forty-seven persons in all, together with central offices led logically to the establishment of seven area offices by September 1948, with the then winding-up of the Public Assistance Committee providing office space and furniture.[65] As cases became more numerous, the areas were increased to a total of fourteen by 1954, and staffing increased accordingly, to 287 in 1951 and 369 (full-time and part-time) in 1955. At first, the area offices were little more than sub-offices of the central office, but by degrees the areas acquired more independence, especially when area Children's Committees, consisting of county councillors, district councillors and representatives of voluntary bodies and statutory services, were established beginning in 1952. These dealt with a large number of routine cases of adoption and boarding out, and ultimately only technically or personally difficult cases went to the central office or main Children's Committee. Although the children's officers worked closely to the letter of the statute, and were being trained by universities and the Home Office to do so, much delicate personal judgement entered into the actual handling of cases, and there was a sense of involvement on the part of committee members (who often knew details of cases, even though children were never mentioned by name) lacking in almost any other level of council activity, local or county. Human judgement and human problems often took the place of dry technicalities and purely formal decisions, and the work of the committees was, on the whole, limited to these problems.

Under the chairmanship of W. J. Throup, the Children's Committee carried on a drive to find foster homes. Not only did the number of children in care and boarded out increase steadily, reaching 1904 in February 1955[66] (from 1100 in 1946); the Children's Department found its work expanding on a self-regenerative principle, through the success of its officers in mounting experiments in areas and through the effectiveness of short-stay and other boarding-out arrangements for children in care. In other words, only a comparatively small number of children cared for (at this stage) by the Lancashire authority were put in institutions, even for a short period, and not far short of a thousand children were boarded out by the authority's officers by 1958.[67] In obviously suitable and happy instances, children were adopted by those who had given them a temporary home.

Even at this rewarding stage of the Department's history, however, there were difficulties. The recruitment of field officers was never easy;[68] training was provided under Home Office auspices, but the qualities of personality needed were both clearly definable and complex, and the supply of suitable people by degrees ceased to match the demand. In addition, much of the work of the Department had a judicial basis, and had to do with juvenile court proceedings or with court reports on children. In 1962 the responsibility for authorising court proceedings was delegated to area committees and offices, and this meant that the officers themselves had to be highly businesslike and well organised, and yet capable of exercising acute human insights at the same time.

The period 1963-71 was one of great expansion of the Department, largely as a consequence of the Children and Young Persons Act of 1963. The latter had the worthy (and logical) aim of attempting to prevent the types of family crisis that resulted in children coming into care by providing help for families in need, so that the family unit might be kept intact wherever possible. The pursuit of this goal meant the appointment of a large body of fieldworkers, as can be seen in the staffing statistics given in Table 10.4. The administrative 'boom' of the sixties is shown very clearly in these figures; indeed, in 1963 the Children's Committee authorised the appointment of eighteen field officers and eleven assistant area officers to develop family work. At the same time, the broadening of the social welfare concept of the Department's work meant that the latter could now make use of trained social workers from allied fields; and a separate category of officer, the family caseworker, was utilised in consequence. Meanwhile, the authority was attempting to overcome the shortage of suitably qualified children's staff by the development of in-service training, combined, where appropriate, with university professional training courses. In the period 1963–6 the family caseworkers managed to pick up the more general skills of departmental work so effectively that their title was dropped, but this did not in itself provide a complete solution to the shortage of qualified staff. What did begin to appear all over the country was the realisation that social work could be too narrowly confined within a particular field or department, although it is also doubtful if the then advocates of larger, multi-purpose administrative bodies (who were certainly in line with the prevailing drift of thinking) realised what was entailed in transformations of this kind.

TABLE 10.4
Children's Department, Full-time and Part-time Staffs

	1951	1955	1960	1965	1970
Full-time	287	295	274	406	891
Part-time	—	74	104	75	118

The Children's Department, then, passed out of the halcyon or pioneering days of the fifties into a much more complex and stressful period. During the sixties there was increasing pressure on residential (i.e. institutional) accommodation, and in consequence the Department embarked upon a drive aimed at the acquisition or conversion of suitable houses for this purpose and the building of specially designed accommodation, so that, for example, a special unit for twenty-one seriously disturbed children was opened near Chorley in 1967, using local educational and psychiatric facilities. Another means of lightening the pressure on children's home accommodation was the family group home, whereby an adjacent pair of council houses was turned into a small residence; as a consequence of this type of project, some district housing authorities agreed to make council houses available to foster parents who would accept several children on the Department's behalf.[69] At the same time, the Children's Department and Committee took steps to encourage the speedier professionalisation of residential staffs, whose members had incurred much criticism but who had often had to carry burdens beyond their capacity. The Committee in 1963 approved the appointment of a 'homes adviser', whose job it was to 'support and advise residential staff in the care of children in their Homes'. It is startling to note that the residential staffs had not previously had a qualified spokesman at the central offices on any permanent basis.

As we have seen, the trend of thinking was by this time strongly towards family welfare, and where possible towards returning the child to his parents or family background after a short or a long period in official care. By 1965, meanwhile, the Seebohm Committee on the Social Services was already deliberating, and its thinking, which was reinforced by the national trends which Lancashire merely reflected, affected the Council enough to cause the latter to appoint a Social Services Co-ordination Sub-Committee. The latter reported to the Council in May 1967 on the problem of homeless families – chiefly those evicted or likely to be evicted from local authority housing.[70] In other words, a steady flow of problems, and persons requiring help, from families with serious rent arrears could be expected in the future, and this was yet another attempt to deal with a source of work for field staff. It was now only a matter of time before the expected findings of the Seebohm Committee, in its Report of 1968, speeded the process towards the setting up of a comprehensive Social Services Department.

The latter experiment (1972) is too much with us and too close to the historian to be a fit subject for generalisation or judgement here. All that can be said is that pioneers among the early fieldworkers of the Department regard with much reserve the grouping of social work functions into one great administrative unit. These were employees of the Department who remembered the straightforward but stimulating and rewarding work of the fifties, and who, in contrast, most felt the upheavals of the sixties. Informal (but not necessarily inefficient) relationships at area level were replaced by much larger office staffs and groups of officers, with a tendency towards more complex work patterns. Much of a fieldworker's case load kept its original character, but the organisational concomitants did not, and eventually (from 1966) 'computerisation' was invoked by a newly appointed statistical officer. The emergence of the generic social worker was in any case regarded with some misgiving by those who had developed expertise within a narrower sphere. The new Social Services Department, which incorporated mental welfare staff, old people's welfare personnel and members of the Children's Department, could claim fairly to look after every member of a problem family from the cradle to the grave.

Yet this tendency to create larger administrative units in what was already an enormous county administrative machine – the result of external and governmental pressures of an entirely generalised kind – was not without logic, if only because the social and personal services themselves had a natural affinity to each other. This was partly the result of a changing view of the human being who was the subject of their attentions, and more directly the result of the many-sidedness of his problems. The multiplicity of the agencies dealing with those problems, at local govern-

ment and related levels, was manifested in startling fashion in the Annual
Report of the Lancashire Medical Officer for 1953, which was describing
conferences on the subject of the neglected child, held in Health
Divisions of the county:

> Conferences, presided over by divisional medical officers have been
> held in all health divisions, to which representatives of all interested
> bodies have been invited. These include, in addition to officers of the
> County Council, such as assistant divisional medical officers, assistant
> superintendent health visitors, health visitors, home help organisers ...
> area children's officers, divisional education officers, school attendance
> officers and police, representatives of county district councils (clerks,
> medical officers of health, sanitary inspectors, housing managers),
> magistrates' courts (assistant magistrates' clerks), probation officers,
> hospitals (almoners), Ministry of Pensions (area offices), N.A.B. (area
> offices), and voluntary organisations (N.S.P.C.C., and W.V.S., Diocesan
> Moral Welfare Societies)....[71]

The Medical Officer added that such conferences were useful because
'they help officers with a common aim to get to know each other'. It
was the special skill of the pre-reorganisation Children's Department staff
that they could negotiate through and with all these persons and bodies;
perhaps a much larger organisation would have had rather less facility
to do so. We cannot now tell; what is certain is that the Children's
Department, a small group, played a significant part in securing interdepartmental collaboration. Will a greater one tend ultimately to establish
much sharper boundaries of its own? The point may one day be worth
pursuing.

The Children's Committee chairmanship tended to be the province of
women council members. Alderman Mrs K. M. Fletcher had, as has been
noted, played a pioneering role, and she remained an active member;
she was succeeded by Alderman W. J. Throup during the period 1952–5.
He in turn was followed by Alderman Mrs Winifred Kettle, Councillor
Dr Mary K. Hall and Councillor Mrs C. M. Pickard, the Committee
being replaced by the Social Services Committee after 1971. Likewise the
Committee itself contained a high proportion of women members as
compared with other council committees. It is not clear whether this
happened because the male membership of the Council (and Selection
Committee) saw this field as 'women's work', or because the women
councillors were drawn towards something in which they could take a
keen interest. The work of the Children's Department was not only a
personal service developing human relationships; it interacted with the
general public in a unique way, securing the collaboration and services of
hundreds of foster parents, and it certainly made a powerful impression

on individuals with whom it dealt, not least delinquent children, neglectful parents and innumerable voluntary workers.

It remains true that the Children's Department was one of the smaller spending departments, and for this reason and that of its newness (and despite its cross-departmental role) the children's officer was only lately a member of the informal committee of chief officers chaired by the clerk of the Council; in other words, he had to submit to the type of value judgement already (and traditionally) passed on the county librarian – another officer whose staff and department continued to interact with the public in a profoundly valuable but not easily measurable way.

Successive county librarians did, however, have the satisfaction of seeing their service grow in an almost spectacular fashion; from 1958 to 1974, some seventy-seven purpose-built libraries were erected as part of a systematic plan to provide all county populations of approximately four thousand or over with a full-time branch library, generally a single central branch. At the end of the old Council's existence in April 1974, as many library buildings again still remained to be erected in the area of the former administrative county. The County Library was for long guided by a sub-committee of the Education Committee (it was, for example, responsible for the provision of school libraries in and after 1947); but an independent Library Committee was set up by the Council in 1966,[72] a recognition of the growth of the librarian's organisation. Miss F. E. Cook, unique among senior officers by virtue of her sex, was county librarian from 1946 to 1966, and Mr Alan Longworth took over what had become a considerable service by the latter year, with a total full-time staff approaching four hundred and part-time staff reaching towards three figures.[73] It had an expenditure on salaries, premises, books and establishment costs which was soon to outstrip the £1 million mark annually,[74] and was the largest library organisation of its kind in Britain. Its users enjoyed a great many amenities – new, pleasantly designed libraries in many a nondescript corner of Lancashire, mobile book vans which reached out into the remotest country districts, collections of books in hospitals, old people's hostels and prisons, as well as specialist collections in music and drama, and technology and science built up in the Preston headquarters. The music and drama collection was the means of sending sets of plays and scores to the local dramatic societies and music circles which are a noticeable feature of leisure-time life in many northern urban areas. These remarks, which must seem to labour the commonplace, are probably all the more necessary because library services are taken for granted, as indeed they should be in a civilised society. But it is proper to stress their contribution here. A large-scale, divisionally organised county library could make experiments in computerisation, as

Lancashire's did from 1972; but, leaving aside the not always certain benefits of electronic aids, it is clear that a county-wide organisation could provide amenities that most purely town-located libraries would not hope to rival, even though the former might be somewhat more costly to equip and administer in a period of rapid growth.

'Rapid growth' was indeed the keynote of the postwar period in all services. How did this affect the Council and its conduct of business? Such a fundamental question is difficult to answer satisfactorily, but the following comments may suggest where the answer lies. The number of Council committees, in the first place, did not increase; indeed, the latter were reduced in number between 1953 and 1973, when the increase in council staff and spending was greatest. This increase – seen in a fourfold one of full-time and part-time employees combined – meant that the Council now became an employer on an unprecedented scale, beyond that of most of the great industrial firms and approaching that of a nationalised industry. The creation of an Establishment Committee and staff officer post in the early fifties was a response to this massive growth, but it was also in conformity with current fashion, as was the acquisition of Organisation and Management (O and M) teams subsequently. The internal administrative problems thus examined were often beyond the grasp of the generality of elected representatives. The councillor's problem, too, was that of having time to absorb increasingly elaborate agenda, and 'homework' was impeded not only by the business of earning a living, which more and more representatives in this age were now doing, but by the long list of regional committees on which a councillor might in his turn be expected to serve. The proceedings of the Selection Committee show the range of possibilities here; consultative councils for nationalised industries, regional hospital boards and hospital management committees, school management committees, national insurance advisory committees, local valuation panels, war pensions committees, territorial and auxiliary forces associations, joint management committees dealing with overspill populations, the Lake District Planning Board (in which Lancashire had a territorial interest),[75] as well as historically rooted bodies like the Lancashire River Board, the Lancashire and Western Sea Fisheries Committee and the Mersey River Board. This is to ignore membership of district council associations, the Association of County Councils and the Association of Education Committees, and to ignore the fact that a large element among the representatives were also district councillors. This elaboration of committee membership became a much more serious problem in the postwar decades, and some Council committees were reduced in size, although the difference made cannot have been a significant one; a body like the Road Safety Committee, created near the end of this period with twenty-two members, must have taken up the 'slack', if any indeed was left.

It will be noticed that the motor vehicle still dominated much of the Council's work; not only did several of its services rely largely on the internal combustion engine, or provide facilities for its users, but council officers and councillors themselves relied upon it. Appropriately, the Council's Local Taxation Department, which administered Road Fund licences until 1973, issued over £6 million worth of private car road licences in 1968-9.[76] This flourishing section in Stanley Street, Preston, was a curious historical development of the Council's early (1888) privilege and obligation as a beneficiary from local taxation licences and probate duty grants,[77] and the next and logical step was to restore it to central government and computerdom.

The 'O and M' campaign of the early fifties brought with it an experiment in co-ordinated purchasing (May 1953) leading to the formation of a Contracts Committee as distinct from the Finance Committee. The experiment lasted three years, and some advantages were claimed by the new committee,[78] although there was comment on 'difficulties and irritations' experienced by administrators – principally, perhaps, because the chief officers' meeting had to allot bulk purchases to departments irrespective of the direct utility of a given commodity to the department concerned. This Committee continued to operate subsequently as a sub-committee of the Finance Committee. Continually rising prices made it almost impossible to prove that the system gained the Council and the public any great advantage, and the quantities of goods involved were so large and difficult to supply from one source that some types of tender had to be 'regionalised'; e.g., fruit and vegetables supplied to county establishments (amounting in 1954-5 to an annual total of £190,000) had to be obtained through eight tendering groups in different parts of the administrative county.[79] Coal and coke, likewise, were purchased through education divisions.[80] The co-ordinated purchasing system continued to operate throughout the sixties, and its chief merit lay probably in the fact that contracts were subject to regular review by Finance Committee members. Serious complaints as to the quality of goods could be acted upon; the real problem, however, was often simply that of finding firms that could meet demands regularly. When a reliable supplier was found, his contract was often renewed.[81]

The Finance Committee was a senior body to which the most experienced and qualified councillors graduated. Nevertheless, the quality of its work depended on a supply of well-equipped and experienced representatives; and the work of other committees could be just as complex. In such cases, the qualities called for, both at senior officer and senior representative level, were akin to those required in the management of a great business enterprise or nationalised industry. Management training is of course provided in universities and polytechnics; there is no such training for senior committee men in a great public authority, perhaps because amateurism is prized as part of a mystique of government. Unfortunately, the amount of spontaneous 'in-service training' also diminished, because the turnover of councillors intensified during the postwar decades and the proportion with long experience was accordingly reduced.[82] The probable result of this was to throw more of the burden of ultimate (if not constitutional) responsibility on to senior officials, who of course developed their own professionalism to a high degree during the same period.

It should be stressed that such tendencies were probably common in all larger local government bodies of the period. Lancashire merely exemplifies, in startling fashion, the sheer scale and complexity of the machinery that had to be administered and initially guided. It is assumed that, because a large authority administers services by statute, and because innumerable controls exist to further the acceptable running of those services, it really exercises very little freedom of choice. In matters of detail and management this is certainly untrue,[83] and it is obviously important that elected members should understand what is taking place in a given area. There is less chance of this when the average length of membership of a Council is reduced by events.

It is an irony that, in the relatively tranquil days before 1930, long service and high experience were commonly encountered on the part of the nominally leisured industrial and county leaders who contributed so largely to the work of the Council. The post-1930 period saw the beginning of a social revolution in council membership, which continued decisively into the fifties and sixties, but also of an administrative and governmental transformation which left the newer councillors in charge of a massive, complex and still growing machine. The general understanding of this machine required considerable and prolonged experience as a councillor. Few considerations of this kind, in so far as they related to many great authorities, seem to have troubled Lord Redcliffe-Maud's Commission.

It is another irony that two of the most distinguished chairmen of the Council during this period of social revolution exemplified the seniority principle to a remarkable degree. Sir Andrew Smith (chairman 1952–5, 1958–60 and 1960–1) and Sir Fred Longworth (chairman 1964–7) were both septuagenarians on taking office. Both Labour leaders in the Council, they had served their apprenticeships in the classic manner, with senior membership of district councils preceding election to the Council, on which they had had between twenty to thirty years' service before elevation to the chairmanship. The Labour Party, as is explained elsewhere,[84] brought new life into council debates; but it did little to transform the mystique of leadership which in turn grew from many years of saturation in the specialist mysteries of a number of departments and committees.

CHAPTER 11

Expenditure and Finance

THIS chapter* deals with the development of Lancashire County Council spending and with its financial policy and activities since 1929, necessarily covering the areas of responsibility of the Council's Finance Committee and its Treasurer's Department. Lack of space does not permit a full consideration of financial policy; therefore discussion of such matters as policy towards cash balances, the budget formulation process and forecasting have had to be omitted.

CURRENT ACCOUNT EXPANDITURE[1]

Trends in Council spending, as well as providing a reflection of the development of its activities, also provide an essential backdrop to the ensuing discussion of Council finance. The main themes of this discussion will be the explanation of the Lancashire experience and the relating of this experience to events in the United Kingdom local government sector (UKLGS) as a whole. The comparative analysis of spending trends for Lancashire and the UKLGS provides a basis for an approximate assessment of the Council's relative performance in making service provision. It also provides a method of assessing the role of the purely local factors in influencing council spending. Broadly speaking, inflation and the force of government, through its statutes, financial powers and ministerial involvement in local government administration, can be regarded as the main

* A particular debt of gratitude is owed to Mr J. G. Barber-Lomax (Lancashire County Council Finance Committee chairman, 1967–74) and to Mr J. Conway (county treasurer 1968–74) for the advice and help they provided towards the writing of this chapter.

factors influencing the spending of the UKLGS as a whole; whereas demographic structure and other specifically local factors, such as the degree of poverty and the level of unemployment, council attitudes and local political forces, can be regarded as the factors specific to each local administration area, producing, as in the case of Lancashire, divergence between local and UKLGS spending behaviour. Of these, the role of government is overwhelmingly the most important factor in explaining service development and 'real', as opposed to money, expenditure growth. Through statutes that define the obligations and limitations of councils, through powers of financial audit, but most importantly of all through the relationship between government departments and councils, control is exercised most explicitly.

In the 1930s the inspectorial system, together with grant and loan-sanctioning powers, provided the main means of control. After the Second World War, most Lancashire County Council services had become the full statutory responsibility of ministers who had an obligation to use their wide-ranging additional powers to ensure that council service development plans conformed (as a minimum) with government service provision norms and that the day-to-day administration of council services was conducted in a competent manner. The implication of this high degree of ministerial involvement, coupled with the force of statutory obligation, was to leave relatively little room for Council discretion in spending. What the actual degree of discretion was is difficult to estimate. Some authorities use grant share in total finance as an indicator. The Council itself on occasions, particularly after the Second World War, presented its own estimates of the share in its total spending of its discretionary spending. For example, in 1951 it estimated that it had full power (i.e. discretion) over 12.1p in every £1 of its spending.[2]

Our first task is to provide a broad account of what happened. Anticipating later results, it is worth stating at this point that the key characteristics of all Lancashire County Council spendings, over the entire period between 1930 and 1973, was that they followed very clearly defined trends of exponential growth. Consequently, our explanation of council spending development, a markedly continuous and orderly process, must be primarily concerned with the location and description of trend influences.

The basic statistics describing Lancashire County Council current expenditure are contained in Table 11.1. Firstly, for selected years, it presents gross and per capita spending figures for Lancashire County Council and per capita spending statistics for the UKLGS as a whole. Secondly, it presents the trend growth rates[3] for per capita and gross spendings for the periods 1930–8 and 1946–73 and, for Lancashire County Council only, for the whole period 1930–73.[4] Each growth rate is followed by a symbol signifying the percentage of annual variation explained by the trend (see Table 11.1, n.2).

Table 11.1 reveals a number of interesting features. Firstly, there is the already cited exponential growth and correspondence to trend. It is indeed surprising that the sequence of parliamentary Acts that at frequent intervals extended and adjusted county council responsibilities, the forces of inflation and demographic change, the four major restructurings of the system of social finance and the frequent changes in political administration (since 1952), should have produced as their net effect so orderly a pattern of spending development. This orderliness is shown very clearly by graph AA in Figure 11.1. The main fluctuations from trend were relatively unimportant and can be attributed very directly to government action. For example, the slight surge in spending in 1930–1 was attributable to the

TABLE 11.1

Lancashire County Council and UKLGS Current Account Expenditure[1]

Levels of expenditure	1930–1	1938–9	1946–7	1959–60	1972–3
Lancs CC total current spending (£ million)	6.7	8.7	16.9	53.5	226.5
Lancs CC total current spending *per capita* (£)	3.67	4.76	8.76	24.87	89.36
UKLGS total current spending *per capita* (£)	5.76	6.55	10.72	28.63	105.83

Trend growth rates	*Rate of growth of trend* $(\%)$[2]	
(i) *Total expenditure*	*Lancs CC*	*UKLGS*
1930–73	8.7[a]	n.a.
1930–8	3.9[b]	2.2[c]
1946–73	10.1[a]	9.0
(ii) *Expenditure* per capita		
1930–73	7.8[a]	n.a.
1930–8	3.6[b]	1.8[c]
1946–73	9.1[a]	9.0[a]

[1] Sources are described in the Appendix to this chapter.

[2] The proportion of the total annual variation accounted for by the trend rate of growth can be measured by a statistical coefficient designated by R^2. In the table the following ranges for the value of R^2 were found: [a] 99% and above; [b] 90–98%; [c] 80–89%.

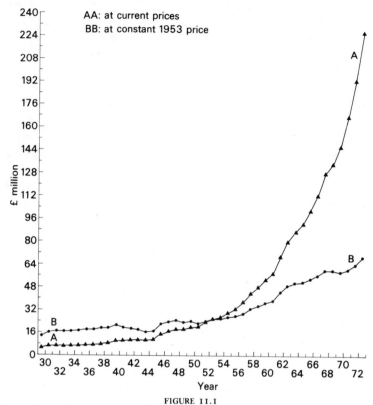

FIGURE 11.1

Lancashire County Council Current Account Expenditure

transfer of Poor Law administration to the Council under the Local Government Act (1929), and to a lesser extent to increased highways responsibilities under the same Act. The small downturn over 1931–3 was consequent upon the economy cuts imposed on the Council by the Government following the 1931 national crisis. Salary cuts were imposed on the police, on school teachers and on council officials, which together with other economies reduced spending to some small extent (by £289,000 between October 1931 and September 1932, for example).[5] These measures were not removed until July 1935. The gentle acceleration in spending growth over the early war years was due to council responsibility for wartime expenditures. The scale of these expenses can be seen by a reference to 1940–1, in which air-raid precautions and fire precaution expenditures alone comprised some twenty per cent of total spending. The sequence of postwar Acts of Parliament following the 1944 Education Act transferred full responsibility for certain services, such as education, from the county districts to the County Council, created new responsibilities such as child welfare and the ambulance service, and transferred services such as hospital care and national assistance from the Council to government boards. The consequences of all of these changes was to cause a rapid though rather unsteady acceleration in the growth rate of Council spending. The cycles over the the late 1950s and 1960s were associated with the phasing of the motorway programme, which the Council implemented as agents for the Government. Finally, the slight slackening in the rate of growth after 1968 was due to economy cuts in services, such as the demise of the Auxiliary Fire Brigade and the putting of civil defence on a care and maintenance basis, measures imposed by the Government in the interests of national policy.

The second interesting feature is a substantial divergence between Lancashire trends and national trends, indicating a major role for the local factors already defined. For purposes of comparison, the 1930s and the postwar era are considered separately. For both periods Table 11.1 shows that Lancashire County Council *per capita* spendings were always substantially lower than their UKLGS counterparts, but that the trend growth rate for Lancashire County Council spending was higher than that applying nationally, the difference between the Lancashire and the national growth rate being less pronounced in the postwar period.

Demographic factors were of some importance in explaining both the growing trends in expenditure and this difference between the Lancashire and national experiences. Over both periods population grew exponentially. Over the 1930s the rate of growth was slow and virtually the same in Lancashire as in the United Kingdom as a whole (0.3 and 0.4 per cent per annum respectively), so that we must really look to other factors for the explanation of the prewar differences. After the war, not only did population grow faster than hitherto but the rate of growth in Lancashire exceeded that for the United Kingdom as a whole, being approximately twice as fast – the rates of growth were 1 per cent and 0.49 per cent respectively. This faster growth in population in Lancashire would be expected to explain some of the postwar differences in the overall expenditure growth between the Council and the UKLGS in general. Indeed, Table 11.1 shows that the postwar trend growth rates in *per capita* expenditure were virtually the same for Lancashire as they were at the national level. It is tempting to conclude from this that the different rates of population growth were the most important cause of this divergent experience of expenditure development after the war. However, analysis of the expenditure trends of individual services (presented later in this chapter) suggests a somewhat different conclusion, and even if one accepts this conclusion one is still left to explain the relatively low levels of postwar expenditure *per capita* in Lancashire.

The prime reason for this relatively fast population growth rate in Lancashire was that the Lancashire County Council administrative area received overspill population from county borough areas. Over most of the postwar era Lancashire County Council actively encouraged overspill schemes, taking a strong initiative in this field despite the absence of grant aid and (apparently) help from the county boroughs which were losing the overspill population.[6] The scale of these population movements was large and can be gauged by reference to the fact that, between 1945 and 1960, 100,000 people were resettled into the overspill reception areas of Worsley, Middleton, Leyland and Kirkby, implying an additional major need for spending on council service provision (e.g., over the same period 34,000 new school places were provided as a direct response to overspill) as well as on increased water supply and sewerage precepts and financial aid to the affected district councils. Furthermore, as the overspill population was essentially made up of young families with a high proportion of school- and preschool-age children, who received a disproportionately large share of Council services, this form of population growth had a disproportionately strong effect on Lancashire County Council's expenditure.

Probably the most important cause of spending growth in Lancashire however (and in the United Kingdom as a whole) was inflation. While the price index of public authority goods and services was relatively steady over the early 1930s, from around 1937 until the present day it has increased at a steadily accelerating rate. There is no doubt at all that this consistent inflationary experience explains the major part of Lancashire County Council spending expansion, and is therefore the main trend-determining factor. Re-estimating the trend in council spending between 1930 and 1973 at constant 1953 prices, we find stable exponential growth in real spendings, but at the lower mean annual rate of increase of 3.6 per cent. Bearing in mind that spendings at current prices grew annually at 8.7 per cent, we see that the trend contribution to spending growth of inflation was 5.1 per cent per annum, or very nearly 59 per cent of the mean annual rate of growth. The development of real current spendings followed its trend of exponential growth very closely (over 95 per cent of its annual variation being explained by its trend), implying that the factors making for real spending growth, almost synonymous with service expansion, were also acting with remarkable long-term consistency (see Figure 11.1, curve BB). Carrying the analysis one stage further, we see that, because the trend growth rate in *per capita* spendings at 1953 prices lay at 2.75 per cent per annum, something like sixty-eight per cent of the trend growth in Lancashire County Council current spending (at the mean annual growth rate of 8.7 per cent) is attributable to the combined effects of inflation and population growth and thirty-two per cent (i.e. the 2.75 per cent per annum) remains to be explained in terms of the influence of the Government and other local factors.

But what of the roles of these factors other than inflation and population growth? Insights are gained by considering the four main areas of Council spending in turn. The spending categories used here conform to a functional classification and do not always conform to the classification based on committee responsibilities. (The functional classification is described in the Appendix to this chapter.)

TABLE 11.2
Lancashire County Council and UKLGS Education Expenditure[1]

Levels of expenditure	1930–1	1938–9	1946–7	1959–60	1972–3
Lancs CC current spending on education (£ million)	2.3	2.7	6.9	26	125.8
Lancs current spending on education per capita (£)[2]	1.21	1.42	3.51	11.87	47.51
UKLGS spending on education per capita (£)[2]	2.0	2.3	3.52	12.02	44.74

Trend growth rates

	Rate of growth of trend (%)[3]	
(i) *Total expenditure*	Lancs CC	UKLGS
1930–73	10.2[a]	n.a.
1930–8	2.4[c]	2.4[c]
1946–73[2]	10.9[a]	10.0[a]
(ii) *Expenditure* per capita		
1930–73	9.4[a]	n.a.
1930–8	2.1[c]	2.0[c]
1946–73[2]	9.8[a]	9.5[a]

[1] Sources are described in the Appendix to this chapter.
[2] For purposes of comparison the postwar statistics are presented net of interest payments.
[3] See n. 2 in Table 11.1.

Education was the principal council service throughout the period discussed in this chapter, making up forty per cent of total spending in 1930, declining to twenty-five per cent by 1940, then growing very rapidly to reach forty-five per cent by 1950 and fifty-five per cent by 1973. The key statistics describing Lancashire County Council education spendings are contained in Table 11.2. (The format of this table follows closely that used in Table 11.1.) Much of the analysis for total spendings applies also to education spending; it manifested stable exponential growth between 1930 and 1973, with faster growth after the Second World War than before. But before as well as after the war there is a remarkable correspondence between the trend growth rates for *per capita* education spendings for Lancashire County Council and for the UKLGS as a whole. (In this case there is a much closer correspondence between Lancashire and national expenditure *per capita* trends than between the expenditure trends.) The faster growth in *per capita* spendings in Lancashire after the war is probably explained by the fact that the overspill phenomenon in Lancashire was increasing the school-age population at a faster rate than that which applied nationally. Assuming that inflation had more or less the same role to play in the development of education spending as it did in the case for total spending, then this uniformity in *per capita* trends at the Lancashire and the national level suggests that the dominant cause of growth in real education spending was government policy and that the only factors causing variation in experience between Lancashire and the UKLGS were differing demographic structures and population growth rates (the role of population growth being crudely indicated by the difference between the gross and *per capita* spending trend growth rates).

However, *per capita* education spending was lower in Lancashire than it was nationally until well into the postwar era. The division of responsibility between the County Council and the district councils before the implementation of the 1944 Education Act explains some, but not all, of the prewar discrepancy, and we are also left with the explanation of a relatively low *per capita* spending rate over a major part of the postwar era. Chapter 13 argues that this is explicable by the high degree of cost-effectiveness in this Council service.

The welfare services make up the second most important component of Lancashire County Council spending, its share in total spending varying (since 1931) between sixteen and twenty-six per cent. Its exact composition has varied considerably over the years. Essentially it includes all council aid to needy persons, such as personal or poor relief subsidies, and domiciliary and hostel care. The Council's main responsibilities in this area were initially defined under the Local Government Act (1929), which transferred the administration of the Poor Law from Boards of Guardians to the Council, taking effect in 1930–1. In 1940 the Old Age and Widow's Pension Act transferred responsibility for cash aid to pensioners to the Government,[7] and in 1948 the National Assistance Act transferred responsibility for domiciliary public assistance and assistance to blind persons to the National Assistance Board. The effect of the 1948 Act was to reduce welfare spending by approximately £1.5 million between 1947–8 and 1948–9, reducing the share in total spendings from twenty-five per cent to ten per cent. It was not to regain its 1947–8 spending level until 1954–5. The ensuing years saw an expansion in council welfare service provision, in terms of the care of children and young persons, the aged and the mentally handicapped, so that spending more or less kept pace with the expansion of total expenditure and maintained an eighteen per cent share of the total expenditure.

TABLE 11.3
Lancashire County Council and UKLGS Welfare Services Expenditure[1]

Expenditure levels	1930–1	1938–9	1946–7	1959–60	1972–3
Lancs CC welfare expenditure ($£$ million)	1.3	2.2	4.3	10.4	4.1
Lancs CC welfare expenditure *per capita* ($£$)[2]	0.74	1.15	2.21	4.8	15.79
UKLGS welfare expenditure *per capita* ($£$)[2]	0.44	0.33	1.38	2.61	13.6

Trend growth rates

	Rate of growth of trend (%)[3]	
	Lancs CC	UKLGS
(i) *Total expenditure*		
1930–73	8.5[b]	n.a.
1930–8	19.1[c]	2.3[c]
1946–73[2]	9.5[b]	9.7[b]
(ii) *Expenditure per capita*		
1930–73	7.7[b]	n.a.
1930–8	18.8[c]	1.8[b]
1946–73[2]	8.4[b]	9.2[b]

[1] Sources are described in the Appendix to this chapter.
[2] For purposes of comparison the postwar statistics are presented net of interest payments.
[3] See n. 2 in Table 11.1.

Table 11.3 provides the key spending statistics for this service. It shows that, despite the major changes in its fortunes, its spending closely followed a trend of exponential growth between 1930 and 1973. The table reveals two important facts. Firstly, there was a striking difference between the Lancashire and UKLGS experiences over the prewar and to a lesser extent over the postwar period. Secondly, Lancashire County Council welfare expenditure *per capita* was always higher than that applying to the UKLGS as a whole. The general implication of these facts is that the growth in Lancashire County Council welfare spendings as measured in real terms was heavily dependent on local influences and that the Council had a relatively high degree of discretion in this area of spending and gave it a high priority. The main local factor that suggests itself is the relatively high level of need for this type of spending in Lancashire. Demographic factors do not seem to be important in explaining these Lancashire–UKLGS differences, the trend growth rates for *per capita* spendings, both prewar and postwar, being more divergent than those for spendings in gross terms.

The rapid growth in Lancashire County Council welfare spending over the 1930s can be attributed to the effects of the 1929 Act, which would have had a greater impact on the welfare spendings of the Lancashire County Council, as a county council, than upon those of the typical United Kingdom local authority. On the other hand, for the six years following the completion of the transfer of Poor Law responsibilities, Lancashire County Council welfare spendings *per capita* continued to grow rapidly, while at the same time those for the UKLGS declined. This can be explained by reference to factors specific to Lancashire. The character of Poor Law spendings was such that they varied positively with the level of unemployment and the incidence of poverty. The economic and social history of Lancashire indicates that over the 1930s it was prone to. both of these problems, so it is not surprising that Lancashire County Council should have given such a relatively high priority to welfare spendings over those years. The consequence of this was to make welfare the main area of spending growth over the 1930s, and it was this phenomenal growth in welfare spending that was the main cause of the already cited divergence between Lancashire County Council and UKLGS total expenditure growth of the 1930s.

After the war, the trend growth rates in spending in Lancashire and for the UKLGS were very similar, with that of the latter being somewhat larger, so that *per capita* spending levels converged with the passage of time. This suggests a postwar growth in the influence of government departments over welfare expenditure, but it was also associated with the radically changed nature of welfare spending after the 1940 and 1948 Acts. These Acts had the effect of transferring the responsibility for unemployment and poverty relief to government departments, so that Council welfare expenditure became composed mainly of the care of the aged, of children and of the mentally handicapped. Social needs levels, defined in terms of this changed nature of local authority social service responsibility, were in closer relationship in Lancashire and in the United Kingdom as a whole than they had been under the 1930s system, so it is not surprising that there should have been a convergence of trend growth rates in the postwar period.

Measured by share of spending, highways was the third most important Council service, its share ranging from seven per cent (in 1945–6) to nearly thirty per cent (in 1929–30). Table 11.4 shows that while highways spendings grew exponentially over the 1930–73 period, it did not lie as closely to its trend as did other forms of spending, fluctuations about the trend (and in its share of total expenditure) being more marked in the case of highways expenditure than for the other expenditure types. These fluctuations were mainly caused by the irregular phasing of major road-building programmes, such as occurred on the motorways agency account (which produced major road expenditure peaks in 1958–9, 1962–3 and 1967–8).

TABLE 11.4
Lancashire County Council and UKLGS Highways Expenditure[1]

Expenditure levels	1930–1	1938–9	1946–7	1959–60	1972–3
Lancs CC highways spendings (£ million)	1.2	1.3	1.7	6.6	19.1
Lancs CC highways spendings per capita (£)[2]	0.78	0.67	0.86	3.04	7.14
UKLGS highways spendings per capita (£)[2]	1.17	1.1	1.26	2.36	5.79

Trend growth rates

	Rate of growth of trend (%)[3]	
	Lancs CC	UKLGS
(i) Total expenditure		
1930–73	7.5[b]	n.a.
1946–73[2]	10.5[b]	6.3[a]
(ii) Expenditure per capita		
1930–73	6.7[b]	n.a.
1946–73[2]	9.5[b]	5.8[a]

[1] Sources are described in the Appendix to this chapter.
[2] For purposes of comparison the postwar statistics are presented net of interest payments.
[3] See n. 2 in Table 11.1.

There were important differences between Lancashire County Council and UKLGS highways spending trends. Table 11.4 shows that until the late 1950s Lancashire County Council *per capita* spending was significantly lower than the national average, but that subsequently the position was reversed, because the Council's postwar highways' expenditure increased at a trend growth rate nearly double that for UKLGS as a whole. This was attributable mainly to the motorways building programme undertaken by the Lancashire County Council as agents of the Government. However, even when agency expenditures are excluded from *per capita* road expenditure there seems to be little correspondence between national and Lancashire postwar spending trends. This suggests a major role for local influences and a high degree of local discretion as far as expenditure on roads, other than under agency arrangements, was concerned.

Law and order, including the police force, adult probation and administration of justice, was the fourth most important spending area, its share in total spending declining steadily from fifteen per cent in 1930 to nine per cent in 1972–3. Table 11.5, as well as showing that expenditure under this

TABLE 11.5
Lancashire County Council and UKLGS Expenditure on Law and Order Services[1]

Expenditure levels	1930–1	1938–9	1946–7	1959–60	1972–3
Lancs CC law and order spending (£ million)	0.9	1.1	1.6	4.9	19
Lancs CC law and order spending per capita (£)[2]	0.48	0.6	0.82	2.2	7.49
UKLGS law and order spending per capita (£)[2]	0.54	0.63	0.59	2.32	9.08

Trend growth rates

	Rate of growth of trend (%)[3]	
	Lancs CC	UKLGS
(i) *Trend growth rates*		
1930–73	7.4[a]	n.a.
1930–8	2.6[c]	2.5[b]
1946–73[2]	9.1[a]	10.6[a]
(ii) *Expenditure per capita*		
1930–73	6.5[a]	n.a.
1930–8	2.3[c]	2.1[c]
1946–73[2]	8.1[a]	10.2[a]

[1] Sources are described in the Appendix to this chapter.
[2] For purposes of comparison postwar statistics are presented net of interest payments.
[3] See n. 2 in Table 11.1.

heading closely followed a trend of exponential growth, shows also that, with the exception of the war and immediate postwar years, *per capita* spendings in Lancashire were significantly lower than in the UKLGS as a whole. The trend growth rate over the 1930s was much the same in Lancashire as in the United Kingdom as a whole, but after the war it was relatively low in Lancashire. The low spending rate prewar can be explained to some extent by the separate administration of police services by five non-county boroughs. The police service did not become a full Council responsibility until 1949.[8] This, however, does not explain the generally low rate of postwar law and order spending. Dr Marshall's analysis in Chapter 10 suggests that Lancashire's police service was relatively cost-effective, and that this provided the main reason for the relatively low level of spending *per capita* on this service in Lancashire.

The discussion of the four major county services, embracing the bulk of peacetime spending, shows clearly that conclusions based on total spending do not tell the whole story. While there was little difference in the postwar trend growth rate of *per capita* spending on all services in Lancashire and in the UKLGS (suggesting a high degree of central control), important differences existed in the case of individual services, indicating an important role for local influences other than the demographic factor and also for Lancashire County Council initiative. The discussion shows the remarkable stability of postwar spending trends. Certainly the shares of the spending categories in the total were changing, but changing gradually and consistently; the one exception to this – highways – being explicable in terms of the phasing of the motorways building programme. It is this stability that suggests the unimportance of local political factors and financial structure.

This still leaves the basic question of the interpretation of the generally relatively low *per capita* spending levels in Lancashire (e.g. on education and law and order). Was Lancashire more cost-effective? Certainly the Council was constantly searching for ways to reduce the costs of a given service provision. This is evidenced by the establishment in the 1950s of a Contracts Committee to gain bulk purchase economies, by the use of radio schemes to reduce the costs of the ambulance and police services and by the early introduction of computer facilities to reduce administration costs.[9] In addition, it was constantly aware of the need to minimise the cost of borrowing[10] (an objective it achieved relatively well, as is argued below), and in particular to control personnel costs. Given the general scope of this chapter it is impossible to give a firm answer one way or the other as to the general efficiency of the Council. But reference to evidence on the education and police services suggests a picture of efficiency. Should this conclusion be extended to the other main services, and should lower *per capita* spendings levels be regarded as a sign of efficiency rather than a relatively low level of service provision? These must remain open questions as far as this chapter is concerned, as must the related question of the precise degree to which Council spending policy was the result of local initiative as opposed to government control.

What is clear from this discussion is the apparently inexorable nature of the force for growth of the trend influences on expenditure. The futility of government-inspired short-term economy measures seems to be indicated by the stability of the expenditure time series discussed above, as well as by statements made by council members (see n.2). The Council realised early on in the postwar era how potentially damaging such policies might be in terms of the forced loss of high-priority spending, particularly on capital account, and sought ways to protect its priorities (such as the instituting of long-range capital account planning, discussed below). Knowing its own situation best, it was well aware of how little real control it had over its current expenditure. Loan charges were determined by decisions taken over a period of years and could not easily be changed quickly. The Council could not dismiss employees at will, nor did it, in general, have the power to reduce wage rates or salary levels. Finally, a demand by the Government for expenditure cuts was likely to find the Council in the impossible situation of having to prune expenditures which it had already sanctioned and was in the process of implementing. The probable effect of a government economy drive (backed up by grant cuts) would not be to reduce expenditure, but to increase the rate call. Realising all this the Council sought long-term measures such as those cited in the previous paragraph for achieving economy. An efficient council would be less likely to be discommoded by government-imposed economy measures.

The most important component of the Council's cost-reducing strategy was its personnel policy. Personnel costs (wages, salaries, superannuation and employers' national insurance contributions) were always the largest class of cost met by the Council. Table 11.6 gives basic information on employment and personnel costs, showing how their growth followed the development of council spending. They also show the importance of wage inflation as a cause of expenditure growth between 1955 and 1974. With personnel costs growing in trend at a mean rate of 9.8 per cent per annum and the number of employees at 4.1 per cent, we see that 42 per cent of the average increase in personnel costs was attributable to a growth in numbers and 58 per cent to wage inflation.

While the Council's concern with the control of personnel costs is well documented, what really were the effects of all this activity? The information in Table 11.6 yields two important indications as the answer to this question. Between 1955 and 1974 part-time employment grew in trend at a faster rate in the average year than total employment. Now this had been a process commencing in the 1930s and may have been a reflection of the changing nature of council services, in those services characterised by part-time employment grew faster than others. On the other hand, it might have also been due in part to conscious policy. An economical use of labour would require, wherever feasible, the employ-

TABLE 11.6
Lancashire County Council Employment[1]

	1929–30	1939–40	1947–8	1955–6	1963–4	1971–2	1972–3
Total employees ('ooo)	n.a.	14.5	26.7	42.6	55.2	77.1	87.2
Total part-time employees ('ooo)	n.a.	1.3	4.6	15.0	20.8	31.4	34.9
Part-time/total employees (%)	n.a.	9	17	35	36	41	40
Personnel costs (£ million)	2.34	n.a.	n.a.	16.6	38.25	81.38	119.4
Personnel costs total expenditure (%)[2]	43	n.a.	n.a.	50	45	44	40

Growth rates 1955–1974[3] (%)

Total employees	4.1a
Part-time employees	5.4a
Personnel costs	9.8a
Total expenditure[2]	10.5a

[1] See Appendix to this chapter for statistical sources.
[2] For purposes of analysis estimates of expenditure are used here.
[3] See n. 2 in Table 11.1.

ment of part-timers, so that the Council had a more flexible and therefore controllable labour force, saving money by not paying under-
utilised personnel. Secondly, we note that the 1955-74 period saw a
reversal of the earlier trend (of an increasing share of labour costs in total
costs), the growth rate of personnel costs proceeding at a significantly
lower level than that for total expenditure. It is hard, in these times
of wage inflation, to see this as anything else than a response to a
conscious policy of economy in personnel costs.

FINANCE OF CURRENT ACCOUNT EXPENDITURE

The very rapid development of Council current spending had to be
financed from local resources, such as the rates, or from central government aid. The main categories of government aid included block grants,
specific grants and reimbursements. Block grants were those not allocated
to any specific purpose and could be used, at the Council's direction,
for any legitimate purpose. Specific grants, on the other hand, were given
as a contribution to the finance of specified approved spending.
Reimbursements were paid to the Council to cover the costs arising from
its activities as agent for the Government. Before discussing these various
forms of finance in detail, the Council's experience in terms of the broad
aggregate of rates and grants is considered.

   Table 11.7 presents Lancashire County Council and UKLGS income
statistics for selected years, together with their trend growth rates. The
table shows that all of the income variables conformed very closely to
trends of exponential growth over time. Comparing Lancashire Council
per capita income receipts with those of UKLGS, clear differences emerge.
Per capita income derived from local sources was lower for Lancashire
County Council than nationally, suggesting that Lancashire County
Council had a relatively low rate burden,[11] and *per capita* grant receipts
were typically lower in Lancashire's case too, with the exception of the
period 1958-66. Over the 1930s the ratio between Lancashire County
Council and UKLGS *per capita* grants was typically 0.6. The ratio increased towards unity in the 1950s and reached a peak of 1.4 in 1961-2.
Thereafter it declined towards 0.8 over the 1970s. These differences were
attributable partly to the already discussed lower *per capita* spending
levels for Lancashire County Council, partly associated with the
working of the grant system and partly caused by Lancashire not being
a housing or trading authority, and therefore having a relatively low level
of non-rate local income.

The trend growth rates in the income variables other than grants were very similar for Lancashire County Council and UKLGS. It is highly significant that Lancashire County Council grant income grew much faster than it did at the national level. The table also indicates that the govern-

TABLE 11.7
Lancashire County Council and UKLGS Current Income[1]

Lancs CC total income (£ million)			1929–30	1946–7	1957–8	1955–6	1972–3
1. Locally derived	(i) Rate		2.15	6.51	12.17	27.79	58.05
	(ii) Non-rate		0.58	2.1	3.48	7.58	17.5
2. Grants			2.69	7.93	28.68	64.71	153.66

Income per capital (£)							
1. Locally derived	(i) Rate	Lancs CC	1.19	3.37	5.77	11.94	22.9
		UKLGS	3.79	6.24	12.64	25.34	46.91
	(ii) Non-rate	Lancs CC	c.38	1.09	1.65	3.26	6.9
		UKLGS	2.21	2.7	6.69	14.33	30.29
2. Grants		Lancs CC	1.48	4.1	13.59	29.81	60.62
		UKLGS	2.8	5.32	12.83	27.32	78.47

Trend growth rate

		Rate of growth of trend (%)[2]	
		Lancs CC	*UKLGS*
		I *Total income*	
1. Locally derived	(i) Rates	7.0[b]	n.a.
	(ii) Non-rate	7.2[b]	n.a.
2. Grants		9.9[a]	n.a.
II *Income per capita*			
1. Locally derived	(i) Rates	6.2[b]	6.1[b]
	(ii) Non-rate	6.4[b]	6.1[b]
2. Grants		9.1[a]	7.3[b]

[1] Sources are described in the Appendix to this chapter.
[2] See n. 2 in Table 11.1.

ment share in the finance of Council spending increased in trend over the period of study, and furthermore that this worked to displace the rates component of local resources more than the non-rate component (this last point did not apply at the national level). These observations follow from the fact that the grants trend growth exceeded that for total current spending at 8.7 per cent (Table 11.1), which in turn exceeded that for non-rate local income, which itself exceeded the trend growth rate for rate income. So that, while rates were typically the most important component of Lancashire County Council income over the 1930s, by 1940 the grant share exceeded the rate share and by 1949 government grants provided the major proportion of current account finance. These conclusions are not surprising, as much the same pattern of change in the structure of finance for UKLGS as a whole is shown in the table and has occasioned much comment.[12] What is surprising, and interesting, is the relatively rapid and extreme way in which the processes occurred for Lancashire County Council.

Figure 11.2 shows the fractions of Lancashire County Council current

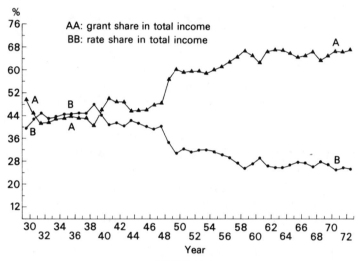

FIGURE 11.2
Lancashire County Council Rates and Grants

expenditure met out of grants (AA) and rates (BB) between 1930 and 1973. The behaviour of the Lancashire County Council grants share conformed in its general movement to that pertaining to UKLGS as a whole, which in turn reflected the changing attitude of the Government to local government finance – which was generally antipathetic towards the rating system. For UKLGS the grant share remained fairly constant at around thirty-one per cent over the 1930s. During the last war, with the growth of heavily grant-aided wartime spending, it increased to a peak of forty-four per cent in 1942, and then declined to 40 per cent by 1945. The changes in the grants system of the late 1940s (discussed later) created a permanent displacement of the local resources element in UKLGS financial structure, so that the grant share did not revert to its prewar level but maintained a fairly constant level at 40 per cent until 1965. The rates-displacing provisions contained in the 1964 Rating (Interim Relief) Act and the Local Government Act (1966) caused the grant share to increase steadily towards the 50 per cent level reached by 1974.

The Lancashire County Council grant share shown in graph AA of Figure 11.2, although conforming in general pattern to UKLGS experience, did not conform in detail. The Lancashire County Council grant share was always much higher than that applying nationally. The decrease over 1929–31, the very rapid increase over the late 1940s and the less rapid increase over the late 1950s were not parallelled at the national level. Finally, the increase in UKLGS grant share after 1965, owing to the workings of the 1964 Act and the Domestic Element of the Rate Support Grant after 1966, was not evident in the case of Lancashire County Council. The Council, not being a rating authority, did not receive compensation for the rate rebate schemes or the domestic element of the Rate Support Grant. These postwar differences are attributable to the way in which Lancashire County Council spending development proceeded (which has already been shown to be at variance with the national experience), and to the special impact that the changing grant structure had on finance for county councils in general but Lancashire County Council in particular. While the full explanation of these differences must be postponed until a later, more detailed, discussion of grant-aid their main implication is clear. If local political and decision-making autonomy from government control had been related to the share of locally derived resources in overall finance, then Lancashire County Council would have had less autonomy and furthermore would have lost that autonomy faster and to a greater degree than may have been the case in the UKLGS as a whole.

Starting with the county rate, attention is now directed towards a more detailed consideration of the components of Council income. The Council was not at any time a rating authority. It derived its revenue by precepting on the rating districts, which actually collected the rates. Before the Local Government Act (1948), which made valuation for rating a responsibility of the Inland Revenue, it had some powers to appoint to the County Rate Committee, which was responsible for considering appeals against valuation; but this role in the valuation process was lost under the Act. Thus the only formal control the Council had over its rate yield was on the setting of its annual rate poundage (the rate charged per pound of rateable value), the rate yield being in principle the product of rateable value and rate poundage.

The Council precepted a general county rate, levied equally on the whole administrative county. It also precepted special rates for services provided under the Special County Purposes Account to areas outside the Council's administration area (such as the police service and certain courts) or to part of that area. The Council also precepted, temporarily, a differential education rate between 1945 and 1948, to enable the merging of the elementary education services of certain county districts with the Lancashire County Council education service, under the Education Act (1944), to be accomplished in a fair manner.[13] The importance of special rating declined after the war. In 1929-30 the Special County Purposes Account included courts, the police, elementary education, bridges and libraries, as well as maternity and child welfare, which together made up 45 per cent of total council current expenditure and on which were precepted 47 per cent of total rate income. By 1973-4 the county library service was the only one of any size under this account and it contributed 4 per cent of rate income to finance only 1 per cent of total expenditure.

Having control only over the poundage rate, the Council, along with other local authorities (including rating authorities after 1948) was in the position of being a taxation authority with no control over the definition and value of the base on which it levied taxation. Rateable value (the taxation base) and its derivative, the product of a penny rate, changed over time as national revaluation of property took place, according to the Government's variations in the definition of liability for rates and finally through natural causes such as changes in the stock of property.

Probably one of the most serious problems facing the Council was the relative stagnation of its rate product.[14] Despite the provision for five-yearly, countrywide, revaluations of property contained in the Rating and Valuation Act (1925), very few actually took place. These occurred in 1956, 1963 and 1973, but it was not until the 1963 revaluation that current rental value was used as the valuation basis: the 1956 revaluation had domestic premises in effect partially derated by having them valued on a 1939 rental value basis.

Government policy until 1958 worked to undermine the rating system. Thus, under the Local Government Act (1929), agricultural land and premises were fully derated and industrial premises were 75 per cent derated, so that the Lancashire County Council lost 20 per cent of its rate product. Again, the Local Government Act (1948) derated public transport and electricity industry premises, and the Rating and Valuation Act of 1957 derated commercial premises by 20 per cent, reducing the Lancashire County Council rate product by 5 per cent.[15] A reversal of policy took place under the Local Government Act (1958), the derating provisions for industrial premises being cut to 50 per cent and those contained in the 1948 Act being removed altogether. Finally, by 1964, all derating provisions other than those pertaining to agricultural land and premises had been removed.

These changes in rate product caused by variations in the definition of the liability for rates and by revaluations occurred infrequently. Thus the growth in the Lancashire County Council rate product was due in general to 'natural' causes and was therefore taking place relatively slowly over a typical year. The pattern that emerged was one of generally slow growth with extreme changes taking place at irregular intervals, as shown in Figure 11.3.

This experience of the rate product was far from the ideal, suggested in the 1930s, that rate product should increase in line with the benefits (and costs) of provision of the services provided by the Council.[16] If rate yield was to have been kept in step with growing expenditure, it would have been necessary to increase the rate poundage charged by the Council in the typical year by a proportion nearly equal to the rate of growth

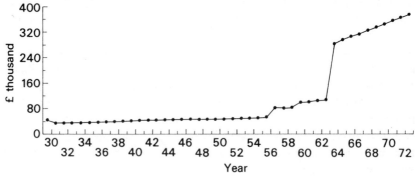

FIGURE 11.3
Lancashire County Council 1d Rate Product

of expenditure. This was not the policy followed. Despite the irregular progress of the rate product, and the problems of estimation that this must have posed at times, the Council followed a policy of increasing the rate yield by a remarkably steady 'norm' of 7 per cent per annum in trend (Table 11.7), which fell considerably short of the expenditure's growth rate of 8.7 per cent (Table 11.1).

The Council chose to accept the falling rate share for a number of reasons. The rate poundage increases needed to keep a constant rate share would have probably proved politically unacceptable and morally undesirable, particularly before the introduction of the low-income person rate relief provisions in 1964 and 1967, because of the regressive nature of the incidence of the rates.[17] The most important reason lay in the very generous grants policy of the government, which reduced the need to use rate finance.

Turning now to the grants structure, the block grant is considered first. The changes in the grant system in the United Kingdom over the period of this study favoured not only grants as a whole, displacing locally derived income, but also the block grant in relation to specific grants. The Local Government Act (1929) dismantled the 1888 Goschen System of assigned revenues and replaced it with a block grant, called the General Exchequer Contribution Grant. This formula grant was seen not only as replacing assigned revenues, but also as replacing a number of small grants, mainly specific to health spending. It also included a component compensating the Council for 75 per cent of the loss of rateable value owing to derating. It constituted a break with the assigned revenue system in that grants were allocated according to the needs of councils rather than in direct relationship to the rateable value of council areas.

The Local Government Act (1948) introduced the Exchequer Equalisation Grant which, like its predecessor, had an element to compensate local authorities for the loss of rateable value owing to derating, but this time of electricity and transport premises. It differed from the 1929 system in having an exchequer equalisation grant, the old formula grant system being abolished. The equalisation grant was paid to local authorities with a rate product per head of weighted population less than the level for the whole of England and Wales.

The Local Government Act (1958) abolished the grants that compensated councils for derated property, but kept the equalisation grant and introduced a General Grant. This was calculated on a formula basis and replaced the major proportion of the specific grants paid to councils until this date.

The Local Government Act (1966) saw a continuation of the process of the displacement of specific grants. The Rate Support Grant introduced under this Act had three components. The equalisation grant was maintained as the Resources element. The General Grant was enlarged, replacing most of the specific grants remaining after the implementation of the 1958 Act. The new grant system's third component, the Domestic Element, was an innovation. It was specifically designed progressively to displace rates in the local government financial structure, and was paid only to rating authorities. It was therefore not directly relevant to Lancashire County Council finance.

Apart from the growth in the share of block grants in total grants after 1958, their development had some further important implications. Firstly, the loss of rate products through derating was matched by increases in block grants and vice versa. Here, then, was a very direct substitution of grants for rates. Secondly, Lancashire County Council, with a relatively low rate product per head of weighted population, gained substantially from the introduction of the equalisation element into the block grant. The growth in grant share from 1948 to 1950 for Lancashire County Council was attributable in large part to the working of the equalisation element and to a lesser extent to the compensation for loss of rate product through derating, contained in the 1948 block grant system. The postwar revaluations that took place also worked to the benefit of Lancashire County Council. In the 1956 revaluation Lancashire County Council rateable value increased by 56 per cent, while that for England and Wales as a whole increased by 72 per cent.[18] In 1963 the revaluation increased rateable value in Lancashire by 162 per cent and in England and Wales by 170 per cent.[19] Thus Lancashire County Council's entitlement to equalisation grants increased, and this contributed to the growth in the Lancashire County Council grant share, particularly after 1956. The Council's experience of block grants is summarised in Table 11.8. Used in conjunction with Table 11.7, it shows that the trend growth rate for

TABLE 11.8
Lancashire County Council Block Grants, 1930–73[1]

	1929–30	1946–7	1957–8	1956–7	1972–3
Lancs CC block grants (£ million)	0.12	1.29	5.01	46.33	129 51
Rate of growth of trend (%)[2]	13.22[b] *g*				

[1] For sources see the Appendix to this chapter on statistical sources.
[2] See n. 2 in Table 11.1.

block grants substantially exceeded that for total grants, so that their share in total grants increased. This was true nationally too, but the growth in the block grant share was much more marked in Lancashire's case. In 1946–7 the block grant share in total grants was 16 per cent in Lancashire and 28 per cent nationally. By 1972–3 the shares had increased to 84 per cent and 87 per cent respectively.

The grant systems over the whole 1930–59 period were dominated by the specific grant element, with the 1950s as the heyday of this type of grant. The 1960–6 period, on the other hand, was dominated by the block grant, but major specific grants accrued to highways and to law and order expenditures. After 1966 the main grant to highways was abolished. Reimbursements remained unaffected by these changes.

Council services benefited to different degrees from the specific grant systems. Police spending was approximately 50 per cent grant-aided throughout the entire period 1930–74. Over the 1930s highways were, typically, 25 per cent grant-aided with rates meeting 73 per cent of expenditure. Over the 1950s and until 1966, however, the typical year had grants meeting 45 per cent and 50 per cent of expenditure.

In contrast, health and welfare expenditure were 80 to 90 per cent rate-financed over the 1930s. Over the 1950s health expenditures were typically 45 per cent grant-financed and 50 per cent rate-financed. On the other hand, welfare expenditure was typically 63 per cent rate-financed over the same period. Of the main expenditure categories, welfare and the fire service (after 1949) had the least grant aid over the 1950s: fire service expenditure was typically 70 per cent rate-financed.

Education expenditure was relatively heavily grant-aided. Over the 1930s it was, on average, 47 per cent grant-financed and 45 per cent rate-financed. The typical year over the 1950s had specific grants meeting 60 per cent and rates 33 per cent of expenditure. It is interesting to note that Lancashire, with a relatively low rateable value per head of population, received favourable treatment under the education formula grant systems of the 1930–59 period.

The Council's high and relatively fast-growing degree of specialisation in the heavily grant-aided education service provides the main reason for the untypically high level of and fast growth in postwar grant aid to the Council: education's share in total expenditure in 1945–6 was 41 per cent in Lancashire and 33 per cent nationally, and by 1972–3 the shares were 53 per cent and 42 per cent respectively.

The fast growth in heavily rate-financed welfare expenditure and its growing share in total expenditure explains the increase in the rate share in total council finance over the 1930s. Furthermore, the losses of heavily rate-financed health and welfare expenditures after 1948 partly explain the growth in grant share in council finance in the late 1940s (which was not evident at the national level). Finally, the Council's reimbursements on account of agencies, particularly under highways, grew very rapidly after the war and contributed significantly to the relatively fast growth in the role of government finance and council spending.[20]

Given that council services benefitted to different degrees from the grant systems, did the patterns of council spending reflect in any way the pattern of service grants?[21] Were heavily grant-aided services being favoured in relation to those with little or no grant aid? The foregoing service-by-service discussion of financial structure pinpoints education as the most heavily grant-aided of the main services and welfare services (other than the children's service) and the fire service as the most heavily rate-financed over the 1950s, a period dominated by specific grants. The other main services were placed in intermediate positions with a roughly equal grant–rate share in their finance. Certainly, education was the largest and fastest-growing service over this period, which suggests an affirmative answer to the question. On the other hand, welfare services were not in general heavily grant-aided, and yet the Council gave them a high priority. Again, the progressive abolition of the specific grant system in 1958 and 1966 had no detectable effect on the progress of council spending development: services (excluding highways) that were heavily grant-aided and those that were heavily rate-financed before 1958 continued to grow at much the same annual rates throughout the 1955–73 period. In fact, police spending showed, temporarily, a small but distinct slackening in its growth rate between 1967 and 1969 and this was one of the few areas of spending to which a specific grant accrued after 1966! The movements in highways expenditure over the 1955–73 period, although relatively extreme, were associated with the phasing of the motorway programme and cannot be associated with the changing grant systems. This suggests that, at this level of aggregation at least, the grant structure had little or no effect on the structure of spending. The documented evidence on the Council's attitude to the grants–expenditure issue presents an ambiguous picture. Sometimes we find pressure exerted to spend so that grant aid should not be lost.[22] At other times the opposite picture presents itself, with the Council apparently rejecting the gaining of grants as the basis and justification for making expenditure.[23] Often the loss or absence of grants, although regretted, did not deter the Council from continuing to spend in areas with diminished grants or no grants at all.[24] Clearly, grants policy ought to have had some effects on the direction of council spending, but one is forced to conclude that, if they existed, they were of a subtle nature, working at a much lower level of aggregation than is used here and requiring a fuller and more detailed investigation than has been possible in these pages.

CAPITAL EXPENDITURE

The essential difference between capital spending and current expenditure as far as council finance was concerned was that the former involved loan finance whereas the latter did not. Council capital spending, though small in relation to current spending, constituted an important dimension of the Council's financial activities.

The relationship between the Council and the Government was quite different in matters pertaining to the capital account than it was in the case of the current account. Here we come to the vexed question of central government control over local government. This control is at its most evident in the matter of capital expenditure, which is directly influenced through the allocation of building programmes or through the issue of loan consents. There was conflict between attempts to economise, on the one hand, and the demands of centrally stipulated building regulations on the other. An example of Council concern with this problem is seen in Councillor T. Atkinson's statement of 1950: '... further economies could be made if the [Building] regulations [for Schools] were less ambitious ...'.[25]

Another point concerns the changing attitude of the Finance Committee to capital budgeting. Whether or not the Government's short-term-orientated economy drives had any effect on council capital formation, they do seem to have had some influence, together with the factors of the sheer growth in council capital formation and debt, on the Council's attitude to capital planning. In the 1930s there was little evidence of any cohesive capital plan. It must be assumed that the various service committees had the main responsibility for this function, and the Finance Committee followed a comparatively passive policy of, in the main, accepting their proposals.[26] The late 1930s, however, brought the beginning of the administrative and policy upheaval that is described elsewhere in this volume, and, not surprisingly, we find the need for a capital budget discussed for the first time during this period.[27] The tremendous growth in capital spending in the late 1940s and early 1950s caused the Council to form a long-run forecast of capital payments and to use it as a basis for ensuring that priority spending should not be part of an economy drive.[28] In this respect the Council seemed to be anticipating the policy recommended by the Institute of Municipal Treasurers and Accountants (IMTA) and other concerned bodies in the late 1960s.[29]

The 1930–1 period is seen as one of fast growth in capital expenditure as the Council met the additional responsibilities consequent on the transfer of highways responsibilities, following the 1929 Local Government Act, and embarked on unemployment relief road projects, such as the Liverpool–East Lancashire Road. This growth was cut short by the economies following the financial crisis facing the National Government in 1931. Spending declined between 1932–3 and 1935–6 when the needs of the education service initiated an upturn. Spending then continued to grow until 1939–40, when wartime conditions and controls reduced it to negligible proportions. There was a fast recovery in the late 1940s, following the 1944 Education Act, after which spending, mainly under the heading of education, grew spasmodically, but according to an underlying trend of exponential growth, at a mean annual rate of 17.8 per cent. The postwar growth in traffic densities eventually led to a growth in

TABLE 11.9
Capital Account Expenditure[1]

	1929–30	1939–40	1952–3	1957–8	1962–8	1967–8	1973–4
Lancs CC capital formation (£ million)	0.78	1.13	3.5	5.4	9.2	19	34
Composition: Education (%)	28	47.8	74	71	73	47.6	52
Highways (%)	67.3	43.3	1	12.5	9.1	29.3	30
Lancs CC capital formation *per capita* (£)	0.43	0.59	1.7	2.5	4.1	7.9	13.3
UKLGS capital formation *per capita* (£)[2]	2.33	—	2.4	3.8	6.5	10.8	21.9

[1] See Appendix to this chapter for sources.

[2] These statistics have been made comparable to those for Lancashire by the exclusion of housing and trading enterprise expenditure.

capital account highways spending in the late 1950s, which became most marked over the 1960s and 1970s. Most capital expenditure took place under the education and highways headings. Table 11.9 provides the key statistics for capital expenditure and Figure 11.4 reveals the rather uneven development of council capital expenditure (graph AA).

Both current and capital spendings appear to have been subject to much the same forces, although capital spending was for the more rigidly controlled. This created problems for the Council and was a source of irritation, as was indicated by J. Selwyn Jones's comment in 1966: 'An anomaly inherent in the problem of capital finance [is] that Local

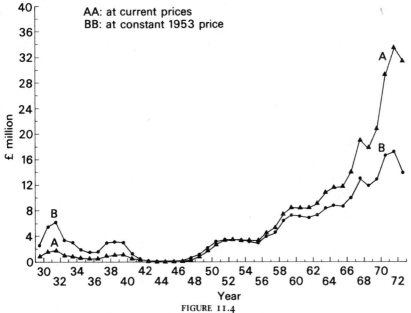

FIGURE 11.4
Lancashire County Council Capital Expenditure

Authorities, though acting in many respects as agents of the government, are left to their own initiatives in borrowing....'[30] This problem was widely recognised in local government circles.[31] Council capital spending at 1953 prices is shown as graph BB in Figure 11.4. The divergence between the graphs AA and BB gives an indication of the role of inflation in forcing spending growth. Over the period 1946–73 annual capital expenditure at 1953 prices grew at 14.3 per cent per annum (which in association with the growth rate in capital expenditure at current prices (at 17.8 per cent), suggests that 20 per cent of the postwar expansion in annual capital expenditure was due to inflation. The effects of inflation became particularly noticeable in the late 1960s and the early 1970s).

In fact, while currently valued spending is shown as increasing between 1971–2 and 1973–4, in real terms it shows a quite marked decline.

The postwar growth of capital spending as shown in graph AA of Figure 11.4 proceeded in four-yearly fluctuations. There is some correlation between the timing of these cycles and that of the published building programme and forecasts of capital payments, suggesting that they were attributable to the influence of long-range budget planning. If these fluctuations were the result of effective planning (and long-range forecasting), the actual facts of council financial administration do not appear entirely to support the idea. A comparison of spending on works in progress and completed in estimate (as published in the *Building Programmes and Capital Payments Forecast*) and in actuality (as given in the *Annual Abstract*, published subject to audit) for a given year reveals large disparities. For example, for 1973–4 the forecast for capital payments was £44.35 million,[32] while according to the *Abstract* for that years the actual figure was less than £35 million. On the other hand, the main cycles in the growth of capital spending were closely associated with the timing of the schools and roads construction programmes of the 1950s and 1960s, which were planned developments.

On the basis of council statements, one would have expected the Government to have played a role in causing cycles in capital spending. There were frequent references, made by successive Finance Committee chairmen, to the use of loan sanction denials and also to the refusal of building licences by the Government to curb Council capital spending in the interests of national economic management.[33] But how does one square statements of capital spending cuts in the Budget Speeches with the contrary picture presented by information in the *Abstracts*? For example, the £2 million cut in capital expenditure cited in the Finance Committee chairman's speech of 1966[34] did not seem, according to the actual capital formation statistics, to have had much effect at all. Spending continued to grow at an accelerating rate between 1965–6 and 1966–7 and between 1966–7 and 1967–8. Likewise the £2.5 million cuts for 1956–7 cited in the Budget Speech for 1957,[35] consequent on the virtual moratorium on loan sanctions over 1956–7,[36] had a negligible reduction in capital spending associated with them. At the national level, in the preceding year the reduction in spending had been quite dramatic, particularly in those areas of capital spending for which Lancashire County Council had responsibility.[37] Council capital formation had been static for three years before these controls were announced, so that the only possible effect (if any) of these restrictions would have been a postponement of a planned expansion in capital formation over 1956–7.

All of this leads one towards the conclusion that it was not so much government action, in the interests of national economic management, that made the progress of council capital spending uneven, but something inherent in the nature of council long-range capital planning. This view is supported by the diverse natures of Lancashire County Council and UKLGS trends in capital expenditures. There seemed to be little correlation between the timing of the frequent changes in the rate growth of capital spending in Lancashire and the timing of those occurring in the UKLGS as a whole.

How did Lancashire's record of capital spending compare with the national record? Table 11.9 shows that, even when areas of spending for which Lancashire County Council had no responsibility (such as housing) are excluded from the national statistics, the Council tended to spend considerably less *per capita* of population than was true nationally. On the other hand, annual rates of council capital spending *per capita* grew faster (at 16.8 per cent per annum) after 1946, than did national capital spending (at 12.95 per cent), so that Lancashire and national *per capita* spending rates were converging over the postwar era.

CAPITAL ACCOUNT FINANCE

This rapid growth in capital spending posed serious problems for the Council. We have already seen that the Council, although strongly controlled by the Government through building regulations and at the mercy of loan sanctions, was left largely to its own devices in the raising of capital account finance (the Government gave some capital grant aid towards highway expenditures). The Council financed the major part of its capital spending by borrowing, and a major theme of this discussion must be its search for new borrowing sources, in particular internal sources. Another theme is the growing use of revenue account resources to finance capital spending. Underlying all of this was the drive to minimise loan charges while at the same time undertaking necessary capital expenditure programmes.

While there have always been small-scale transfers of current financial resources to the capital account, in some cases termed revenue contribution to capital outlay, they did not reach significant proportions in this latter form until 1950.[38] The attitude of the Council to this form of capital finance was clear at this time. The concern over growth in current spending requirements over 1950–1 led to a reduction in 'revenue contributions' and to the use of loan sanctions to meet the £0.25 million worth of capital spending they would otherwise have financed.[39] That

TABLE 11.10

Debt[1]

	1929–30	1947–8	1953–4	1963–4	1966–7	1972–3
Lancs CC debt (£ million)	3	5.11	15.65	53.43	67.95	115.63
Lancs CC debt *per capita* (£)	1.65	2.61	7.66	23.56	28.72	45.62
Lancs CC debt composition						
(i) PWLB (%)	—	5.8	53.8	12.7	25.6	30
(ii) Internal (%)	29	26	28.4	25.6	23.6	35.4
(iii) Other external (%)	—	68.7	17.8	61.7	51	34.6
UKLGS debt *per capita* (£)	—	39.8	77.4	161.3	212	—
UKLGS debt composition						
(i) PWLB (%)	—	24	56	31	34	—
(ii) Internal (%)	—	13	7	6	4	—
(iii) Other external (%)	—	63	37	63	62	—

[1] Sources: Hepworth, N.P., *op. cit.*, p. 139. See also the Appendix to this chapter.

is, in the interests of current account economising, the Finance Committee was prepared to allow small projects to be financed by borrowing, even though the overhead costs of this way of financing, in terms of administrative and brokerage costs, would be relatively high.

By 1956 Council policy was changing. The Finance Committee was examining the questions of the efficient finance of small projects and the appropriate policy concerning the use of revenue resources in the finance of capital projects. On the basis of its recommendations, a new policy was to apply from the beginning of 1957-8. All projects costing no more than £2000 were to be financed from revenue. An exception was made in the case of education, which was subjected to the limitation that its total annual use of revenue contributions should not exceed the product of a 2d rate.[40] The motivation for this change in policy was the avoidance of high overhead costs of borrowing to finance small projects as well as the avoidance of interest costs. Although the revenue finance of capital spending was an important component of Council financial strategy and a fast-growing source of finance over the postwar era, its contribution to total finance remained quite small, averaging 14 per cent of annual capital spending since 1950.

The scale of the financial problems posed to the Council by its fast growth in annual capital spending can be gauged from the debt statistics given in Table 11.10. Although debt per head of population was much lower in Lancashire than nationally, it grew much faster in Lancashire over the postwar era (increasing ninefold between 1947 and 1966, as opposed to the national fivefold increase). This was largely a reflection of the much faster growth in capital spending in Lancashire than nationally. It is not surprising that the Council was preoccupied with the problem of capital finance.

The main ways in which the Lancashire County Council extended its internal borrowing resources beyond the traditional County Capital and Superannuation Funds was to introduce borrowings and to institute a separate County Capital Fund. Revenue borrowings provided a fast-growing source of new finance, growing from £1 million in 1958 to over £29 million in 1972-3. Effectively they were borrowings of unapplied funds in the county's current account on which a rate of interest was paid. This rate fluctuated fairly widely, reaching 10.5 per cent in 1972-3.

The Capital Fund was set up in 1962-3 under the Lancashire County Council General Powers Act (1951). Initially (that is, from 1 April 1962) the annual contribution from the revenue account equalled a 3d rate product, no project greater in capital cost than £5000 could be financed from it, and the unapplied balance of the fund had not to exceed a 1s rate product. It was therefore another means of financing low-cost projects without incurring high overhead costs. It was modified in 1965-6, so that from 1 April 1965 it was governed by the Local Government (Miscellaneous Provisions) Act (1953). This had the effect of increasing the maximum annual contribution from revenue to the fund to the product of a 5d rate. Annual contributions from revenue to the fund have ranged from approximately £0.35 million in the year of its foundation to over £1 million in 1972-3. Spending committees were loaned cash from the fund and charged a rate of interest of five per cent per annum. From its very small beginnings it had grown rapidly as a source of finance, so that by 1972-3 it financed nearly £12 million worth of small capital projects.

The Council's reliance on internal borrowing pinpoints an important difference between Lancashire and national experience (as shown in Table 11.10). This difference is due in part to the fact that the Council had greater capital resources than the typical local authority in the United Kingdom, but it also indicates the conscious policy of the Finance Committee in augmenting these resources.

The extension of external borrowing sources has been a theme present in the Council finances since the early 1930s. The growth in capital spending under the highways and bridges service following the 1929 Local Government Act, coupled with the high costs of borrowing to meet this growth, had caused the Council to go beyond its traditional sources, the Public Works Loans Board (PWLB) and insurance companies, and to borrow from the general public. These loans were in the main small and involved a high administrative overhead cost. To avoid this problem it was proposed for the first time that the Council should borrow in larger amounts by the issue of county stock, when the money markets were favourable to such a policy and once the necessary consolidation of the county loan service had taken place.[41] The government restrictions on capital expenditure following the 1931 crisis and over the war years prevented further innovation in this direction, and it was not until the Government again allowed local authorities access to the money markets in 1952 that the Council was able to widen its external borrowing sources.

Since this date various issues of county bonds of varying maturities, and even county bills (for revenue-financing purposes) have been made,[42] As well as widening the Council's borrowing sources, they have enabled it to keep loan charges down, mainly by borrowing at the shorter-term end of the market at times when long-term interest rates were high, in particular when PWLB rates were considered to be excessive. At times when interest rates were not only considered to be high but were expected to fall, this greater flexibility in borrowing enabled the

Council to borrow on short term, so that the debt could be funded at some future time, at a lower rate of interest.

As a large local authority, the Council has suffered more than most in being denied access to the PWLB (as Table 11.10 shows). From a postwar situation in which the PWLB was the only permitted source of external finance, access became restricted, so that by 1955 the PWLB was a 'lender of last resort' to local authorities. Between that year and 1963 access was opened and closed periodically with, in general, freer access being provided to the smaller authority. After the new financial policy of 1963, access has been slowly widened, but again with freer access being given to the smaller authority. The Lancashire County Council experience over this period is reflected in the statistics provided for selected years in Table 11.10. The share of total council debt held by the PWLB expanded rapidly until the mid-1950s. It was reduced far more severely than was the case for the typical authority following 1955, and began to expand again following the free access permitted under the post-1963 policy. Quite apart from government restrictions on the Council's access to the PWLB, the Council itself frequently chose to borrow elsewhere because it could raise loans at a lower rate of interest than that charged by the PWLB.[43]

How successful was the Council in its policies of capital account finance? One criterion, but by no means the only one, is the cost of borrowing. Were the interest charges paid by the Council low by national standards? The postwar trend in council interest charges was one of exponential growth at a mean rate of 10.1 per cent per annum. This growth rate did not exceed that applying nationally (7.6 per cent) by as much as would have been suggested by the differences in capital expenditure growth rates over the postwar era (at 17.8 per cent for Lancashire and 8.1[44] per cent nationally) had the Council not funded its capital programmes by efficient means.

EPILOGUE

The reorganisation of the local government structure in 1974 ended the eighty-six-year life span of Lancashire County Council. This chapter has shown that, certainly since 1930, its record has been a proud one. Its policies of sound financial management in a context of growing complexity and its willingness to innovate in the interests of efficiency were recurrent themes in its history. The policies espoused in 1973 in the framing of its final budget epitomised that council attitude so often shown in the past – its fundamental commitment to the maintainance of the continued wellbeing of Lancastrians.

Against a backdrop of imminent demise by reorganisation, rapid inflation and government-imposed financial stringency, the Council chose to set itself two difficult tasks. On the one hand it was determined to ensure the continuation of its policies of service provision and on the other to provide its successor authorities with a sound financial basis on which to commence their operations. Towards this end the Council precepted a 1½p rate to provide the new authorities with an estimated initial balance of £3.5 million, and it budgeted for a closing balance of £7.5 million.[45]

When the books were finally closed on the Council's last financial year, it was revealed that expenditure on the current account had topped £266 million, exceeding the budget estimate by £7 million (mainly because of wage inflation). Despite this, the Council was able to bequeath to its successor authorities a very welcome closing balance of £17.5 million.[46]

APPENDIX: STATISTICAL SOURCES AND METHODS

I

Lancashire County Council statistics were derived from the following annually published sources:

1. *Abstract of Accounts* (Preston, 1930–74)
2. *Lancashire County Finance* (Preston, 1947–74)
3. *Handbook* (Preston, 1930–41)
4. *Budget Statement* (Preston, 1929–73). This was published in the *Proceedings* until 1946 and separately thereafter.
5. *Budget Speech* (Preston, 1939–73)
6. *Personnel Budget* (Preston, 1952–73)

United Kingdom local government statistics came from:

7. C. Feinstein, *National Income and Expenditures* (London, 1970) for the 1930s and
8. *National Income and Expenditure* (*Blue Book*) (London, 1946–73) for the postwar era.

    (a) Lancashire population statistics were Census figures or Registrar General's estimates contained in (1) and (2) above.
    (b) Personnel statistics came from (5) and (6) above. For the period before 1952 they came from unpublished council sources.
    (c) The composition of county debt came from (1) and (2) above.

(d) Estimates of expenditure came from (4) and (5) above.

(e) All other Lancashire County Council statistics came from (1) above.

(f) Price deflators for capital goods and for public sector goods and services were constructed from series contained in (7) and (8) above.

II.

1. Lancashire County Council accounting conventions changed on a number of occasions, and the statistics used in this chapter have been constructed in conformity with the post-1953 system. Grants paid to the county districts by the Council on behalf of the Government are excluded, as are the transitional hospital and national assistance boards agencies of 1948.

2. The functional spending categories were constructed as follows:

(a) Education included all Education Committee expenditure less school health, school meals and milk expenditures and aid to pupils.

(b) Highways spending included all Highways Committee expenditure on roads and bridges as well as highways agencies and road lighting.

(c) The law and order category included all police service, courts and adult probation expenditure.

(d) The welfare services category included all Public Assistance, Health (Welfare) and Children's Committee expenditure. In addition it includes aid to pupils and school milk and meals expenditure. It has variously included some spendings listed by the Council under the health heading such as the non-clinic expenditure on the case of mothers and young children.

CHAPTER 12

Politics

IN Chapter 4 we saw that party politics played little part in the early years of Lancashire County Council's history, especially before the First World War and during the 1920s. From 1929 onwards, however, the picture was very different. Party politics became increasingly important, and for the last twenty-five years of the Council's existence it was organised on the basis of an explicit two-party system. In this chapter we will try to show how and why these changes came about and to estimate their significance.

Our discussion falls into three parts. In the first, which covers the period 1929–46, we will show how the trends that were already apparent in the late twenties were reinforced by the Local Government Act of 1929. The second part looks in detail at the crucial years between 1946 and 1952 when the clash between the consensus and party government views, which were outlined at the end of Chapter 4, came to a head. Finally, we consider the years after 1952, when a *modus vivendi* was worked out between the Labour and Conservative groups which enabled the Council's business to be carried on smoothly.

Information about this last period, is, of course, much fuller. We have had access to unpublished party records and have been able to interview a number of individuals who were closely involved in the events we discuss, and from whose comments we quote below. One further source deserves special mention. This is the *Nelson Gazette*,[1] a weekly newpaper which appeared from 1927 to 1962 and was edited for most of this period by Andrew Smith, leader of the Labour group on the Council and the Council's first Labour Chairman.

THE RISE OF LABOUR: 1929-46

From a political point of view the most immediately important feature of the Local Government Act of 1929 was the reform of the Poor Law. Up to 1929 poor relief had been administered by locally elected Boards of Guardians. The 1929 Act swept away this structure and placed full responsibility for poor relief on the county and county borough councils.[2] In Lancashire, a Public Assistance Committee was set up at the end of 1929 to carry out the Council's duties under the Act, and a county-wide network of local 'Guardians' Committees' was appointed to carry out the detailed administration of the Act.

The importance of this change lay in the fact that it created an 'issue' at county level. In the circumstances of poverty and unemployment existing between the wars the question of poor relief was highly controversial. Throughout the twenties, particularly in areas of heavy unemployment, it divided communities very sharply, and it was a major focus for the activities of the Labour Party and other working-class organisations. Before 1929 these activities had been concentrated upon the Boards of Guardians, but with the passing of the Act attention shifted to the county councils.

After 1929 the administration of poor relief had all the characteristics of an issue as we described them in Chapter 4,[3] touching on a fundamental ideological division between Labour and the other parties. In the years immediately after the First World War, Labour lacked both the organisation and the incentive to make a strong challenge to the established groups on the Council. This new issue provided the incentive, and the luke-warm interest of the 1920s quickly gave way to greater enthusiasm.

As late as 1928, Andrew Smith felt that 'Politics, as such, do not enter into County Council work, which can be said to be purely administrative. The presence of a few Labour members will not at present alter the predominantly Conservative composition of that assembly'.[4] But by the time of the 1931 triennial election Labour's attitude was entirely different. Smith now favoured much more aggressive tactics:

> Recently, the Public Assistance duties of the Council have immensely increased its importance, particularly to the workers; and this is one of the reasons why Labour is out to increase its strength on the Council ... the paramount issue, in Nelson at any rate, will be the attitude of the County Council on Public Assistance.... Nelson Guardians on the old Burnley Board of Guardians put up a constant fight on that body for the sick and defenceless for many years: now

that fight is being transferred to the County Council.... The only thing left for the local Labour Party is to make an attack on the stronghold of reaction – the County Council itself. The issue must be fought out on the floor of County Hall at Preston.[5]

This illustrates clearly the change in Labour's attitude towards the Council. There was, generally speaking, a much greater awareness of the need to contest county elections, and throughout the thirties the question of public assistance continued to be the major stimulus for Labour Party activity at this level. It was invariably the key issue around which Labour candidates fought their campaign, and it was a recurring theme of election addresses and newspaper reports of campaigns. Thus, in Ashton-under-Lyne in 1934, the County Council was reported to be 'under fire from all quarters', and Labour's victory in Ashton West was attributed to their having 'vigorously attacked the County Council's interpretation of the means test'.[6] And after the same elections the *Nelson Gazette* promised: 'a keen fight will be put up on poverty questions in the future. Some of the new Labour members are going to the Council specifically for that purpose'.[7] In 1937 Sidney Silverman, the MP for Nelson, joined in, asserting that 'the Lancashire County Council, under its Tory majority, is notorious throughout the land for its meanness, its cheese-paring, its grim selfishness'.[8]

Elections, Candidates and Councillors, 1929–46

The first and most obvious effect of Labour's new-found enthusiasm was an increase in the proportion of electoral divisions contested in the triennial council elections. Table 12.1 shows the percentage of seats

TABLE 12.1
Percentage of Electoral Divisions Contested

1928	1931	1934	1937	1946
%	%	%	%	%
21.9	24.8	30.5	34.2	66.7
(N=105)	(N=105)	(N=105)	(N=120)	(N=120)

contested from 1928 to 1946. After 1928 there was a steady increase in the proportion of seats contested up to 1937. Although the figure for that year was still modest, the proportion of contests was roughly twice what it had been in the early twenties. There is little doubt that it was

Labour's entry into county politics that increased the number of contested seats. In the three elections in the 1930s there were Labour candidates in 78 out of the 99 contests.

As had happened during the First World War, elections were suspended between 1939 and 1945, vacancies being filled by co-option. The first postwar county elections were held in 1946, the year after Labour's overwhelming general election victory, and for the first time Labour made a broadly based electoral challenge, breaking out of its pre-war urban and industrial strongholds to fight seats in the less heavily populated areas. The effect of this was a dramatic increase in the number of seats contested to two-thirds of the total, the largest proportion in the County Council's history to that date. Table 12.2, which shows the

TABLE 12.2
Number of Candidates, 1928-46

	1928	1931	1934	1937	1946
Conservative	41	45	52	75	87
Labour	26	35	38	49	96
Liberal/Progressive	18	18	15	17	17
Independent/Others	14	21	25	11	—
Unknown	31	19	16	—	—
Total	130	131	142	166	211

number of candidates put forward by the various parties between 1928 and 1946,[9] reflects these changes. By 1946 Labour had more candidates than any other party. (Interestingly, there was a parallel increase in the number of candidates identifiable as Conservatives.) This increase might be accounted for partly by the decline in the number of candidates whose political affiliation is unknown, but more generally it is indicative of the increasing importance of political parties.

Labour's increased electoral efforts did not, however, bring quick results in terms of seats won. In 1931, despite having an increased number of candidates, Labour lost two seats. This almost certainly was caused by the national situation at the time, as the Labour Government floundered in the face of economic crisis. Eight Council seats were gained in 1934 and a further four in 1937, but these still left Labour very much in a minority, with only thirty councillors. Throughout the thirties problems persisted for the Labour Party. Their support remained very localised, concentrated in the mining areas around Wigan, the industrial areas around Manchester and Salford and in the Calder Valley. In 1937 Andrew Smith was still lamenting the unco-ordinated Labour campaign, the problems of finance, the inadequate number of contests, the frustrations of having to leave potentially winnable seats uncontested. The relative lack of progress came out most strongly in contrast with London, where Labour had won control of the Council in 1934, and Smith complained that:

> Instead of the well-knit, well-organised, central body which Labour in London has built up, Labour in Lancashire is dependent almost entirely on purely local effort and organisation. In many divisions the local party takes little interest in the County Council; and the Lancashire Federation of Labour, which was formed a year or two ago, has but little influence and less real power.
> The result is that Lancashire Labour, whilst more active in County elections than formerly, makes no serious effort to secure a majority.... [Even] if every Labour candidate had been returned ... the Tory majority was never in danger.[10]

In the 1946 election, Labour might well have expected great things. As we have seen, they fielded more candidates than any other group, but the results must have been something of a disappointment. They made a net gain of nineteen seats, but they failed to gain control of the Council or even to become the largest party.

Table 12.3 summarises the election results for this period. In the

TABLE 12.3
Councillors Elected, 1928–46

	1928	1931	1934	1937	1946
Conservative	31	42	39	64	55
Labour	20	18	26	30	49
Liberal/Progressive	15	15	12	13	14
Independent/Others	9	11	13	13	2
Unknown	30	19	15	—	—
Total	105	105	105	120	120

course of these years the party situation on the Council gradually became more clear-cut. The political affiliation of almost forty per cent of councillors in 1928 is unclear, but by 1946 there were only two councillors who did not belong to one of the three main party groups. Indeed, had it not been for the continued presence of a small but signicant group of Liberal councillors (backed up by a sizeable group of Liberal aldermen) a two-party situation would already have existed by 1946.

Party Politics on the Council

Labour brought to the Council a new conception of the role of party in local affairs – what we called the 'party government' view. We must now see what effect this had on the workings of the Council.

In some respects the prevailing convention of consensus was extended to include Labour, and Labour accepted this. Thus, for example, the seniority method of selecting aldermen was not disturbed. As they acquired the necessary seniority Labour members were duly promoted to the aldermanic bench. By 1937 there were seven Labour aldermen. Labour seems to have been happy to go along with the seniority system in the early thirties, voting along with everyone else for those whose 'turn had come'. At the annual meeting in 1937 some objections were raised, particularly by R. I. Constantine, an outspoken Labour member from Accrington, but even so Labour members voted in accordance with the convention. It was not until 1946 that Labour launched a full-scale attack on the seniority system, but we will return to this below.

Similarly, although Labour was in a fairly small minority, Labour members were allowed to play their full part in the working of the Council. Thus, on the committees in which one would expect them to have been most interested, Labour was well represented. On the Public Assistance, Education and Public Health and Housing Committees in 1937 Labour actually had more representatives than they would have been entitled to on the basis of strict proportionality.

Nor were Labour members entirely excluded from formal positions of authority. Among those who were appointed to important positions in the thirties were Edgar Boothman (vice-chairman and then chairman of the Tuberculosis Committee, vice-chairman of the Public Health and Housing Committee); William Spofforth (chairman of the Co-ordination Committee); and Robert Barrow (vice-chairman of the Co-ordination Committee). Labour members also held a number of the chairmanships and vice-chairmanships of the important sub-committees of the Public Assistance and Education Committees.

This is not to say, however, that Labour was accepted into the ruling group on the Council. Labour did not get any major chairmanships, and on the centrally important Finance Committee there were, in 1937, only five Labour members out of thirty-three. Although Labour's presence was recognised, the Council continued to be controlled by a small group of Conservatives and Liberals. Most of the chairmen of important committees were Conservatives and of the four dominant figures in the thirties and early forties – Sir James Travis-Clegg, Sir William Hodgson, Sir Percy Macdonald and Sir James Aitken – three were Conservatives and one was a Liberal.

Labour's opposition to the establishment comes out quite clearly when we look at the issues that divided the Council in this period. Once again we have taken the number of amendments moved in Council as a rough indication of the level of political conflict. As Table 12.4 shows,

TABLE 12.4
Number of Amendments Moved in Council, 1928–46

1928–31	1931–4	1934–7	1937–40	1940–3	1943–6
19	23	13	28	26	27

the level in the thirties and early forties was much higher than it had been previously – the average number of amendments per annum between 1928 and 1946 was in fact double that between 1889 and 1928. And the procedure whereby a recorded vote could be demanded, which had not been invoked since 1895, began to be used with some regularity. Between 1928 and 1946 there were no fewer than twelve recorded votes.

As we would expect, the greatest source of dissension was public assistance. Over a quarter of all the amendments in this period (39 out of 136) were directly connected with this topic, as were ten of the twelve recorded votes, and quite a number of other amendments were indirectly related to it. The Labour Group's attacks on the public assistance question were persistent and vigorous, being aimed both at the Government's general policy and at the Council's Public Assistance Committee for the way it applied the regulations governing the administration of relief. Thus in February 1932 there was a recorded vote on the motion:

That this Council learns with regret that the Public Assistance Committee has declined to make more provision for meeting the needs of persons applying for Public Assistance ... and that the Public Assistance Committee be asked to at once reconsider this matter and make recommendations that will adequately meet these needs.[11]

In February 1934 anger was directed against the Government in a motion proposing: 'That this meeting ... enters an emphatic protest against the financial clauses of the Unemployment Bill which bear heavily on Local Authorities, and urges the necessity for expenditure in relief of unemployment being made a national charge.'[12] And at the following meeting, Labour members returned to a similar theme and made a specific proposal in an amendment to the budget: 'That the Council agree to increase the estimates by £100,000 which must be used only to provide work for the unemployed.'[13]

The other major subject that gave rise to a large number of amendments during this period was the appointment and conditions of service of senior and junior staff. There were eighteen amendments concerning junior staff, but most of these occurred between 1940 and 1946 and dealt with problems specifically arising out of the war. On the other hand, the fourteen amendments concerning senior staff again had a somewhat ideological flavour. Labour members sometimes opposed the appointment of senior staff and frequently opposed the fixing of their salaries at what they considered exorbitant levels, arguing that such expenditure could not be justified at a time when the unemployed were not being adequately provided for.

The activity of the Labour Group does not seem to have been reduced or diverted to any great extent by the war. The number of amendments moved remained very close to the prewar level, and when we look at their subject matter the same themes recur – public assistance, the appointment and salaries of senior staff, conditions and pay of junior employees and a variety of procedural matters. Nor were Labour members afraid of making the conflict explicit by calling for recorded votes – there were four between 1940 and 1946, all on matters relating to public assistance.

TABLE 12.5
Average Attendance at Council Meetings, 1928–46

1928–31	1931–4	1934–7	1937–40	1940–3	1943–6
%	%	%	%	%	%
76.4	76.8	77.9	80.8	72.6	79.5

The increased level of political conflict as reflected in the increased number of amendments and recorded votes was clearly a product of Labour's efforts. Over two-thirds of all the amendments and ten of the twelve recorded votes were moved by Labour members. Their efforts were rarely successful, for the great majority of their amendments were defeated, often very heavily. But Labour members certainly made their presence felt. As the *Nelson Gazette* commented in 1934, 'the Labour councillors made a gallant attempt to infuse life and reality into the proceedings which, heretofore, have often been of a purely formal nature'.[14]

As a final indication of the increasingly 'political' atmosphere on the Council we give in Table 12.5 figures for average attendance in each three-year period between 1928 and 1946. We suggested in Chapter 4 that, as the Council became an arena for conflict and as the business became more controversial, one would expect attendance to rise. Although this had already begun to happen by the late twenties, the average attendance between 1919 and 1928 was only 63.5 per cent. It can be seen that it was much higher after 1928, rising steadily throughout the thirties to a peak of 80.8 per cent.

It is clear, then, that the period from 1928 to 1946 saw the beginnings of a major change in the political life of the Council. There was a steady growth in Labour representation and, as a result of this, an increase in the level of political conflict. It would be wrong to exaggerate Labour's advance, for the party's successes were in no way dramatic. It still faced great difficulties of organisation and finance; and, in spite of the public assistance question, the basic problem of apathy among the electorate remained.

By the outbreak of the war, however, Labour had made real advances and was preparing to challenge the ruling oligarchy. The postwar surge in Labour support, marked by Labour's victories in the 1946 election, at last brought the challenge to a head.

Labour's Challenge: 1946–52

In many ways, the years following the Second World War were the most important in the Council's history. In the first place, it was a period of major reform. The Attlee Government, brought to power by a landslide victory in the spring of 1945, carried through a series of important measures, which directly affected the Council. Thus a great part of the Council's time in the late forties was taken up with planning and setting up of new administrative structures and sorting out the problems that arose.

The late forties also have a crucial significance for the politics of the Lancashire County Council. We have suggested that Labour's adherence to a 'party government' view was bound, sooner or later, to lead to a clash with the more traditional 'consensus' view of the established parties. This clash, though perhaps in a rather more muted form than we might have expected, came shortly after the war. By 1952, when Labour won an overall majority for the first time, a new two-party system had been established and the two major parties had gone a good way to working out a compromise that would last for the remainder of the Council's existence. We must now examine these events in detail.

1946–9: The Clash over Aldermen and the First Agreement

The first triennial election after the war, and the first full election for nine years, was held on 4 March 1946. Labour made a great effort, fielding 96 candidates – almost twice as many as in 1937. Especially after the party's sweeping success in the general election of the previous year, Labour were somewhat disappointed at the outcome. The final figures, given in Table 12.3, show that, even though Labour's representation jumped to 49, there was still a solid phalanx of 71 Conservatives, Liberals and others.

Following these results, the years from 1946 to 1949 saw a further increase in party conflict. The average attendance at Council meetings was 80.9 per cent – just above the prewar peak – and though there were no recorded votes, the number of amendments was the highest ever at thirty-six. It is important to note, however, that there was a marked change in the range of subjects on which amendments were moved. For the first time in many years there were no amendments at all on public assistance, no doubt partly as a result of the much lower level of unemployment in the years after the war. Instead, the great majority of amendments were on procedural issues. The largest number, concerned with specific appointments of council members to committees and outside bodies, arose directly out of the clash between the parties. The second largest category, concerned with the procedures and standing orders of the Council, was partly a reflection of the administrative revolution that was going on.

Immediately after the 1946 election there were signs that the ruling oligarchy envisaged things continuing as before. At the first meeting of the new Council on 21 March 1946, Sir Percy Macdonald, the Conservative chairman of the Council, resigned after only twelve months in office, apparently finding the work uncongenial. He was replaced by Sir James Aitken, the leading figure in the Liberal Party, who had been a prominent committee chairman since before the war. His election as chairman by a predominantly Conservative Council suggests that the Conservatives and Liberals felt that things had not changed. But Labour had other ideas, as immediately became apparent when the meeting moved to the selection of aldermen.

We have seen that in the first years of the Council's existence a pattern was established whereby aldermen were selected from among councillors on the basis of their seniority within the Quarter Sessional Hundreds. When there was an aldermanic vacancy, the councillors for the Hundred in question met and nominated their longest-serving member, and this nomination was then confirmed by the full Council as a matter of course. Promotion to the aldermanic bench became an automatic reward for long service, and once selected an alderman might expect to retain his seat unchallenged for as long as he wished. Labour councillors had benefited from this convention as much as any others, and it had never been seriously challenged.

This method of selecting aldermen clearly conforms fairly well with the 'consensus' model of local politics. It is based on the view that what is important in choosing an alderman is a person's seniority and the experience that goes with it, and not his party allegiance. Equally clearly, the seniority system was bound to be challenged as soon as the 'party government' view gained a strong foothold. Aldermen, as full voting members of the Council, were politically as significant as councillors, and a party's total voting strength on the Council – and in some cases its majority – would depend on its aldermanic strength.

This challenge came in 1946. Previously, Labour's members had been divided among the four Quarter Sessional divisions in such a way that they were in a minority in all four, and could therefore do nothing to break the seniority system. However, following Labour's successes in 1946, they now had majorities in the Salford and West Derby Hundreds and were determined to use them. When the result of the election became clear, a request was sent to the Conservatives that the principle of proportional representation by party should be introduced in the selection of aldermen. This was discussed at a Conservative Group meeting on 7 March, but, as the minutes of the meeting put it, 'the suggestion was not agreeable to the Conservative Party'.[15]

Faced with this refusal, Labour proceeded to force the issue into the open. It used its majorities in the Salford and West Derby Quarter Sessional Divisions to secure the nomination of ten Labour councillors for aldermen, as well as the two (Aldermen McLean and Rigby) who were retiring and due for re-nomination. Thus at the meeting of the Council on 21 March, thirty names were put forward for twenty aldermanic vacancies – the twelve Labour nominees plus the eighteen Conservatives, Liberals and Independents who would in any case have come up under the seniority system. For the first time in many years the vote was more than a formality. The Conservative, Liberal and Independent nominees all received between 69 and 73 votes – the combined strength of these groups being 71 councillors – and were elected. The twelve Labour nominees all received between 46 and 49 votes – total Labour strength being 49. But only two of the Labour nominees, Mrs Clephan and Mrs Fletcher, got the full 49 votes, and so they were elected. The remaining ten, including the retiring Aldermen McLean and Rigby, got 48 votes or less and were therefore unsuccessful.

The direct outcome of all of this was perhaps not all that significant. Whether as the result of an accident or as a deliberate manoeuvre, two senior Labour aldermen were replaced by two Labour councillors.[16] Otherwise the seniority system was maintained. However the departure from the normally smooth workings of the Council seems to have been regarded as a minor fiasco. And it was followed immediately by Labour's second challenge to the consensus system. Andrew Smith, the Labour Group's leader, was nominated for the vice-chairmanship of the Council in opposition to the new Conservative leader, Harry Hyde. In the vote that followed, Hyde won.

So Labour succeeded in creating a good deal of fuss at the meeting of 21 March 1946, but there was little practical result to show for it. However, the more farsighted leaders of the Council were impressed. They realised that a Labour Group with a total strength of over fifty members could, if it wished, create considerable difficulties. Some working arrangement between the parties was clearly needed, and a meeting of Group leaders was held on 8 April 1946 to see what could be worked out. This in fact proved to be only the first of a long series of meetings which eventually led to the signing of an agreement between the Conservatives, Liberals and Labour on 5 February 1948.

The initial meeting seems to have been called by Sir James Aitken, acting in his capacity as chairman of the Council. But thereafter, in spite of the objections to any change in the seniority system that had been expressed at their meeting on 7 March, the Conservatives seem to have taken the lead. At a group meeting at the end of May 1946, the Conservatives elected Harry Lord as their secretary and set up an Advisory Committee of leading members. It was Lord, with the aid of the new Advisory Committee, who steered the talks to a successful conclusion over the following two years.

By the beginning of 1947, the Conservatives had worked out a set of basic principles to cover the selection of aldermen and appointments to committees. These were approved, though not without a division, by a group meeting on 12 February 1947. There then followed a further five meetings between the Group leaders during the course of 1947, and after the necessary resolutions had been passed by Council the 'Agreement', in the form of a four-page printed document, was signed by the representatives of the three parties and witnessed by the Clerk on 5 February 1948.

In the Conservative Group minutes, Harry Lord rounded off his carefully kept record of the negotiations with the following comments:

> So ended a long and delicate series of negotiations and it is sincerely hoped that the closer relation between the political parties and the principles accepted and acknowledged in the signed agreement will lead to smooth working amongst the members of the County Council and a consequential benefit to the people they represent.[17]

This hope was to prove somewhat optimistic, for it was ten years before the Agreement, in a revised form, could be made to work. How the initial Agreement broke down and had to be renegotiated we shall see below. However we must pause at this point to assess the significance of the 1948 version.

The Agreement[18] had three provisions. First of all, the appropriate number of aldermen for a party was to be determined by the number of councillors it had, on the basis of a 3 to 1 ratio. But aldermen were to 'remain in office and be re-elected at the expiration of their period of office' unless their party decided not to nominate them for re-election. Only as vacancies occurred through death or resignation would a party be able to make up its appropriate aldermanic strength. Secondly, the parties were to be represented on committees in proportion to their overall strength on the Council. Committee appointments would be made by a new Selection Committee, consisting of four representatives from each of three political parties. Thirdly, the members of the Selection Committee, meeting informally, would also consider the appointment of chairmen and vice-chairmen of committees. In doing so, they would 'primarily have regard to the suitability of the individuals concerned', but they would also 'have due regard to the principles of proportional representation of the Parties'.

These provisions seem to have been designed to combine an acknowledgement of the new importance of party with the minimum disturbance to the Council's established procedures. As such, they must have been fairly satisfactory for the proponents of the consensus view of local government. But an agreement of this kind seems inconsistent with the party government view. Indeed, it is rather difficult to see why Labour accepted it. What Labour gained was the acceptance of the principle of proportional representation of parties on committees and in aldermen. But in practice this principle was so hedged about with conditions that it was of little value.

Proportional representation on committees was not unimportant, but in assessing its significance three points must be remembered. First of all, committee recommendations are of course always subject to revision and amendment in full Council. Secondly, the basis of committee representation took into account aldermanic strength and not just councillors, and was therefore bound, initially at any rate, to be biased to the Conservatives and Liberals. And thirdly, proportional representation on committees was, for Labour, only a slight improvement on the existing situation – indeed, on some important committees Labour already had more than its proportional share of places.

The provision of the Agreement with reference to the appointment of chairmen were vague – they only required the members of the Selection Committee to 'have due regard to the principles of proportional representation'. And again it should not be forgotten that Labour already had some chairmanships. Since 1946 Mrs Fletcher had been chairman of the Children's Committee, and Labour members had also become vice-chairmen of the Parliamentary, Health, Co-ordination, Children's, Mid-wives Act, and Planning Committees.

Finally, on the question of aldermen, it is difficult to see how Labour could have been satisfied. The requirement that progress towards proportional representation would be made only as vacancies occurred through 'natural wastage' meant that there was bound to be a very considerable lag in achieving proportionality. A party winning a majority of councillors at a triennial election could well be prevented from having an overall majority on the Council before the next triennial election came round.

If the Agreement offered them so little, why did Labour sign it? It seems probable that this was a sign of despair or frustration. We have already seen that Labour's advances in the thirties had required considerable effort. In 1946 the party had made a major assault in what must have seem the most favourable possible circumstances, and they had still failed to make a major breakthrough. Not surprisingly, many Labour leaders came to feel that they could never win control of Lancashire, and it may well have been that the terms of the Agreement were thought to be the best that could be hoped for, a way of making the best of an unfavourable situation.

Shortly after the signing of the Agreement Sir James Aitken died, and at the next Council meeting, on 11 March 1948, Harry Hyde was elected chairman of the Council. In the spirit of the new Agreement, Andrew Smith was elected vice-chairman. This nicely symbolised the whole episode. By those taking the consensus view, it could be seen as the first fruit of the Agreement and as formally marking Labour's replacement of the Liberals as the junior party in the governing élite. By opponents of the Agreement within the Labour Party it was seen as proof of the fact that the Labour leaders had been seduced by the temptations of power and that the party had lost the impetus that had brought it into Council affairs. The *Nelson Gazette* clearly anticipated this sort of criticism, and felt that it was necessary to justify Smith's acceptance of the vice-chairmanship:

> There are many in the Labour Party who declare it is a futile compromise to accept offices of government when one's own party backing is in a minority. In many cases, this argument may be true; but, as in all things, there are exceptions to the rule.
>
> We believe Vice-Chairmanship of the County is one such exception. It gives its occupant power to act independently in many situations and enables him to make personal decisions which will affect the welfare of widespread numbers of people. In future we shall have the satisfaction of knowing that these acts and decisions will spring readily forward from a true Socialist conscience. . . .
>
> And, as for Alderman Smith himself, he is an exception to any rule. . . . He is beyond the corruptive power of high office. Compromise is out of the question. Those who hope that his new office will blunt his political outlook are indeed heading for a disappointment. We know for certain that he will carry his Socialism wherever he goes.[19]

Opponents of the Agreement might have noticed the irony of the fact that, shortly after this, unsung and unrecorded, the Public Assistance Committee ceased to exist as its functions were taken over by the central Government.

1949–52

The events of the years 1949–52 tend to conform our interpretation of the Agreement, for in most respects they suggest a slackening of Labour's efforts. The results of the 1949 election were a setback for Labour, though this was probably more a reflection of the declining popularity of the Labour Government. Labour lost 14 seats, and were reduced to 35 councillors. The Conservatives gained 15 seats to give them a total of 73. The Liberals were reduced to 12, and for the first time there were no independent councillors.

Perhaps more significantly from our point of view, Labour put forward only 89 candidates compared with 96 in 1946. This was the first time that Labour had fielded fewer candidates than in the previous election. On the other hand, the Conservatives seem to have worked hard for their victory. They fielded no fewer than 104 candidates – as compared with only 87 in 1946. Also significant was the fact that Conservatives were returned unopposed in 29 seats whereas Labour won only 5 without a contest. Overall, the number of contests rose by five, to 85. The overall turnout was also considerably higher – 41.7 per cent compared with 33.2 per cent in 1946.[20]

In thise circumstances, there was no difficulty in applying the Agreement. The retiring aldermen were all re-elected unanimously, and proportional representation was applied in the appointment of committees. Labour members became vice-chairmen of seven standing committees, and Andrew Smith was confirmed as vice-chairman of the Council.

But in some ways the most interesting and important feature of the first meeting of the new Council was the replacement of Harry Hyde as chairman by Alfred Bates. This seems to have been the result of a palace revolution within the Conservative Group. All that we know for certain, however, is that at the Advisory Committee meeting on 11 April 1949 the names of Hyde and Bates, together with those of W. J. Garnett and Sir Henry Hancock, were put forward, and that 'After a long discussion and ballots it was finally unanimously resolved that Captain Bates be invited to accept nomination for the position'. At the full Group meeting two days later Hyde himself formally proposed Bates as chairman of the Council, and this was carried unanimously.[21]

The reasons for the change are not clear, though there are grounds for informed speculation. To start with, Hyde was already seventy years of age in 1949, and the chairmanship was clearly becoming a much more important and onerous post. It is also surely significant that Hyde had had remarkably little experience of major office. On becoming vice-chairman of the Council in 1946 he had never been chairman or vice-chairman of a standing committee. Bates's experience was also somewhat limited. However, he had been chairman of the Parliamentary Committee since 1944 and before joining the Council he had been clerk to Heysham Urban District Council. Furthermore, Bates had already shown the characteristics of drive, organisational ability and firmness that were to allow him to dominate the Conservative Group for the next fifteen years. Interestingly, though, Hyde did continue as chairman of the Conservative Group until 1955.

The relatively rapid succession of Macdonald, Aitken and Hyde as chairmen of the Council between 1945 and 1949 was unusual. Between 1889 and 1945 there had been only six chairmen, with an average length of service of over nine years. With the election of Bates as chairman in 1949 and Andrew Smith as vice-chairman in 1948 things settled down once more. For Smith, like Bates, was to dominate his Group until the middle sixties. It was these two men who were to ser the tone for the long period of stability that followed Labour's victory in the 1952 election.

In other respects the 1949–52 Council also showed the cooling of political conflict we have referred to. Although there were five recorded votes, the total number of amendments fell to only seventeen – less than half the number in the three previous years. With the removal of public assistance from the Council's control, and with the Agreement working fairly smoothly, there seems to have been a scarcity of contentious issues. There were four amendments on the old topic of officers' salaries, and three of these led to recorded votes, but most other amendments were on fairly minor matters. One new trend is worth noting – the development of what might be called 'ideological issues'. These were issues which in themselves seem fairly minor, but which gave rise to considerable controversy between the parties because of their ideological significance. In the 1949–52 period two such issues were the subjects of recorded votes. One concerned the setting up of a Central Vehicle Maintenance Unit for the servicing of the Council's vehicles. This was to be a recurring topic in years to come and was dear to Labour's heart because it involved the principle of direct works. The other seems to have been almost purely ideological – it concerned a proposal that the Council's banking should be done through the Co-operative Society.

Finally in this section, let us look briefly at the 1952 election. Labour's victory in that year may be thought to contradict our argument that political conflict on the Council was on the wane. But, though we shall see later that the result did re-invigorate Labour, at the time it took them, and everyone else, by surprise.

The results themselves were remarkable. Labour made a net gain of no fewer than 29 seats, giving them a total of 65 councillors. They won back all of the seats lost in 1949, but also went further, breaking into new territory in areas like Chorley, Clitheroe and Lancaster. The Conservatives lost 23 seats, leaving them wth 50 councillors, and the number of Liberals was halved to 6.

When we look at the numbers of candidates put forward by the parties these figures are even more surprising. The Conservatives again made a big effort, putting forward 102 candidates – only two fewer than in 1949. But the number of Labour candidates fell still further to 79, which was then fewer than in 1949. The total number of contests fell to 66, the lowest figure since before the war. The Conservatives took no fewer than 38 seats without a contest, and won only 12 of the seats where they were opposed. On the other hand, Labour retained only 13 seats without a fight, but took 52 of the 66 that were contested. The average turnout rose quite sharply to 47 per cent, and there was a swing of roughly 6 per cent to Labour across the county.

How is this to be explained? The most obvious answer seems to be that it was a reaction on the part of the voters to the Attlee Government's defeat in the general election of 1951 and the new Conservative administration. There had already been signs in 1949 that the county election results reflected national rather than local trends. From 1952 onwards this pattern became very clear. Our information about the campaign run locally by Labour supports this view. The further reduction in the number of candidates does not suggest that Labour was making a special effort, and Labour leaders were clearly surprised by their success. Ellis Wood, who was secretary of the Labour Group from 1948 onwards, said, referring to the late forties, 'At that time it was never envisaged that Labour would *ever* have power'; and Edwin Roscoe, who came on to the Council at a by-election in September 1949, described his and his colleagues' reaction as follows: 'That was the greatest shock of our lives, to tell you the truth. We were all absolutely astounded.... I just picked my *Guardian* up through the door that morning ... and I couldn't believe my own eyes that we were in.... It was as big a shock to every member as it was to me.'

Thus it seems clear that Labour's victory in 1952 was not really the climax to a continuing effort to win power. All the evidence suggests that Labour won in 1952 in spite of, rather than because of, the campaign they organised.

We have argued that, as well as being a time of extensive change in the powers and functions of the Council, the years 1946-52 also saw a climax in its politics. Throughout the thirties a clash had been in the making between the consensus view of local government, as held in particular by the Conservatives, and Labour's party government view. The clash came following Labour's gains in the 1946 election, but the challenge was unsuccessful.

Then shortly afterwards, in 1948, Labour made an Agreement with the Conservatives and Liberals whereby the Labour Group effectively abandoned some key elements of the party government view in return for formal acceptance into the governing élite. And in the elections of 1949 and 1952 there were signs that the steam had gone out of the Labour Group's efforts. Smith himself summed the situation up well. In the course of the negotiations for the 1948 Agreement he was reported as saying that 'there was the choice of making the Council an administrative body, in which each party took its fair share of responsibility, or of running the Council on Parliamentary lines, when the predominant party would take all the offices and responsibility.'[22]

There seems little doubt that before the war Labour would have favoured the latter view. But by the late forties, perhaps in despair at the seeming impossibility of their task, they were willing to accept the former. We must now see what effects Labour's unexpected victory in 1952 had on the situation.

THE RETURN TO STABILITY: 1952–74

The results of the 1952 election could hardly have been better designed to expose the weaknesses of the 1948 Agreement. In the conventional sense Labour won the election, ending up with sixty-five out of the 120 councillors. But to ensure overall control of the Council Labour needed at least sixteen of the forty aldermanic seats. At the time of the election, Labour had only eleven aldermen, and the Agreement stipulated that aldermen would be re-elected unless they or their party decided they should retire.

Thus the Labour leaders faced a clear choice. Either they could abide by the Agreement and sacrifice control of the Council, or they could break the Agreement, take the necessary number of aldermanic seats and re-assert the doctrine of party government. They chose to do the latter. Immediately after the election there were talks between the Labour and Conservative Group secretaries, and a possible amendment to the Agreement was worked out. But the Labour Group would not accept it, and at the first meeting of the new Council, appropriately enough on May Day 1952, they took sixteen of the twenty aldermanic seats. The Conservatives could do no more than protest.

It is one of the characteristics of the party government position that once it is adopted by one powerful group, it is bound to spread to others. A consensus can be maintained only if the various parties support it. Thus it is not surprising that the Conservatives increasingly, if reluctantly, abandoned their old standpoint and organised themselves on party government lines. In 1955, when the triennial elections returned them to power, they in turn took aldermanic seats from Labour.

Thus by the early 1950s the party government view seemed to have become established as the prevailing ideology of the Council. The pattern of election results over the next twenty years, which kept the two main parties well balanced in strength, helped to maintain it. All the outward signs at least suggested that Lancashire County Council was now run as a two-party system on parliamentary lines. Officers and party leaders even referred to the two parties as 'the Government' and 'the Opposition'.

In the rest of this section we will examine the politics of Lancashire County Council between 1952 and 1974 and ask two questions: to what extent did the party government model really apply – was it any more than

skin deep? And, to the extent that party government did prevail, did it
live up to the claims of the proponents? As a preliminary let us make explicit the main points of a party government model:

  (a) Elections are fought over the whole authority by organised political
      parties.

  (b) Candidates stand as party candidates, not as individuals.

  (c) Voters vote for a party rather than an individual.

  (d) Parties seek to gain control of an authority in order to implement
      party policies.

  (e) The role of officers is primarily that of executing the policies deter-
      mined by the controlling party.

A system of this kind, it is claimed, secures efficiency together with a
maximum of democracy. How well did party government in Lancashire fit
this pattern?

Elections 1952–74

The regularity with which control of the county changed hands between
Labour and the Conservatives after 1952 is remarkable. Table 12.6 shows

TABLE 12.6
Seats won in Triennial Elections, 1952–74

	1952	1955	1958	1961	1964	1967	1970
Conservative	50	71	49	70	54	93	92
Labour	65	46	66	47	66	29	32
Liberal/Progressive	6	2	1	—	3	1	1
Independent	—	2	6	5	2	2	2

the number of seats won by each of the parties in each triennial election
between 1952 and 1970. Until the last election in 1970, the pendulum

TABLE 12.7
Percentages of Councillors Elected in Contested Divisions, 1952–70

	1952	1955	1958	1961	1964	1967	1970
	%	%	%	%	%	%	%
Lancashire CC	54.6	60.3	59.0	56.5	63.0	72.8	74.0
All county councils	44.6	25.9	39.1	38.8	50.1	52.6	50.3
County boroughs in Lancs	89.2	88.8	84.5	90.7	91 5	97.3	98.3

swung with complete regularity, each party having three years in power and then three in opposition. The pattern was broken only in 1970, when the Conservatives were able to retain the very large majority they had won in 1967. Table 12.7 shows the proportion of seats contested at each election and for comparison also gives figures for all county councils in England and for county boroughs in Lancashire in the years in question.[23] It can be seen that the proportion of seats contested remained fairly large throughout the postwar years. The proportion of contests in Lancashire was always a good deal greater than in other English counties, but was considerably smaller than in county boroughs in Lancashire.

Why was this? Part of the explanation can be derived from the figures in

TABLE 12.8
Candidates put Forward by Each Party, 1952–70

	1952	1955	1958	1961	1964	1967	1970
Conservative	102	100	94	97	92	106	113
Labour	79	90	91	86	97	98	94
Liberal/Progressive	7	4	3	—	16	17	10
Independent and Others	3	3	7	14	7	12	17

Table 12.8, which shows the number of candidates put forward by each of the parties at each election. It is immediately obvious that the great majority of candidates – in fact over ninety per cent – came from one of the two major parties. In effect, the number of contests in any year was determined by the number of candidates fielded by Labour and the Conservatives.

The number of candidates put forward by the main parties seems likely in turn to reflect two further factors. First of all, the marginality of divisions is important – clearly, parties will be keener to contest winnable seats. Secondly, the general level of party organisation in an area is significant – if there is no party organisation locally, the recruitment of a candidate and the mounting of a campaign will be very difficult; while if party organisation is good there may be keenness to fight a seat even if it is unlikely to be won.

The differences shown in Table 12.7 can be understood in these terms. On the one hand, Lancashire was much more marginal than most other counties – hence the higher proportion of contests. On the other hand, the even higher proportion of seats contested in the county boroughs seems likely to be a product of the relative strengths of party organisation in urban areas. It is hardly surprising then that the proportion of seats contested in the extensive rural parts of the county should be lower than in places like Preston, Blackburn, Salford, Warrington and Wigan.

Table 12.9 gives figures for turnout between 1952 and 1970.[24] The figures for Lancashire show a steady decline from 1952 to 1961, something of a recovery in 1964, and then a further decline. The trends for all county councils in England and Wales and for all county boroughs in Lancashire are roughly similar. But of course the really striking thing about all of these figures is how low they are – turnout in Lancashire never approached fifty per cent.

TABLE 12.9
Turnout in Elections in Various Authorities, 1952–70

	1952	1955	1958	1961	1964	1967	1970
	%	%	%	%	%	%	%
Lancashire CC	46.5	39.8	36.3	33.7	39.2	36.6	32.2
All county councils	43.2	36.5	33.3	35.7	40.7	38.4	33.4
County boroughs in Lancs	51.7	44.6	39.4	40.3	39.6	38.7	37.4

Information on turnout in elections before the war is fragmentary, so we are not able to make any strict comparison with earlier periods. But the lack of interest that was lamented by the local press in the 1920s and 1930s clearly continued. If one takes account of uncontested seats as well, the proportion of the total electorate of the county that participated in council elections never rose much above twenty-five per cent in the whole of the postwar period.

Finally, we return to the question of party choice. In Table 12.6 we gave details of the seats won. Table 12.10 shows the share of the votes received

TABLE 12.10
Party Share of the Vote in Triennial Elections, 1952–74

	1952	1955	1958	1961	1964	1967	1970
	%	%	%	%	%	%	%
Conservative	41.9	51.3	44.9	52.4	44.3	56.5	54.8
Labour	56.7	46.6	51.7	44.2	47.1	36.0	40.5
Liberal/Progressive	0.1	0.1	1.6	—	5.6	5.3	2.3
Other	1.4	2.1	1.8	3.4	2.9	2.2	2.4

by each party in each election and the figures for the Labour and Conservative parties are represented graphically in Figure 12.1.[25] The figures bring out very clearly the regular 'swing of the pendulum' between 1952 and 1967, and they also emphasise the extent to which the politics of the county was dominated by the two main parties.

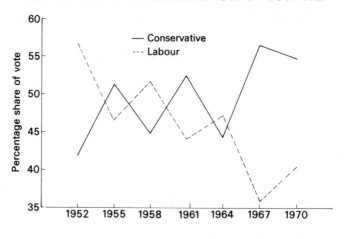

FIGURE 12.1
Share of Vote in Triennial Elections

The 'pendulum' theory of elections suggests that in a two-party system the party in power is bound to make more enemies than friends, and that it therefore gradually creates discontent among the electorate which will result in its defeat at the next election. Thus as a result of what they do, or omit to do, the two parties will alternate in power. Is this the explanation for the situation in Lancashire? Unfortunately (for the theory, if for no other reason) this seems unlikely. Figure 12.2 shows why. The graph demonstrates the Conservative lead over Labour in triennial elections (as a percentage of the total votes cast) and of the Conservative lead nationally taken from the

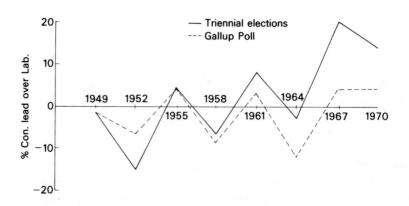

FIGURE 12.2
Conservative Lead Over Labour in Triennial Elections and in Gallup Poll

nearest Gallup Poll.[26] It can be seen that the relationship between the two is very close.

What this suggests is that the way the parties fared in the county council elections had little to do with how they had performed on the Council in the previous three years, or with the kind of election campaign they ran. It was the national popularity of the parties – determined by national and not local affairs – that determined the amount of support they got. Who won the triennial elections was very much a matter of chance depending on the timing of the elections in relation to national events. The neatly symmetrical swings, first in favour of Labour and then back to the Conservatives, do not after all seem to have been a product of the way the Council worked, or of any innate political canniness of the Lancashire electors – it was simply a freak. The way Lancashire voted was a reflection of the way voters throughout the country felt at the time of the elections.

One further feature of Figure 12.1 is interesting. From 1952 onwards, every swing of the pendulum to Labour is less strong than the previous one, and every swing away is stronger, culminating in the disastrous result in 1967 from which there was hardly any recovery in 1970. There was not an absolute decline in the Labour vote, but the Conservative vote increased markedly and, relative to it, Labour's proportion dropped steadily. Similarly, Figure 12.2 shows that, after being slightly ahead of its national showing in Lancashire in 1952, Labour's local performance gradually slipped further and further behind.

This trend seems to have been confined to the county elections, for when we examine the parliamentary results in Lancashire and the results of elections to borough and urban district councils there is nothing comparable. This suggests that there was no genuine swing towards the Conservatives in Lancashire. Rather it suggests that in the county council elections they were increasingly successful in getting their supporters to vote, while Labour was increasingly unsuccessful. We will try to explain why this was the case below.

We have seen then that, on the surface at any rate, there are signs that the party government model was working in Lancashire – the regular swing of the pendulum between the two parties, the relatively high proportion of seats contested, the fact that the electorate voted in party terms rather than for individuals, and the fact that the main parties fought campaigns on a county-wide basis. But there are other features of the situation that suggest that, in so far as this was party government, it was not working properly – in particular, the level of interest displayed by the electorate was low, and those who did vote seem to have done so not on the basis of the performance or programme of the parties at County Hall but in accordance with national trends. The situation was one in which the parties wanted to play, and as far as elections were concerned did play, the party government game, but in which the electorate was not interested and did not respond. The inability of the parties to arouse the interest and stimulate the participation of the voters, and indeed of their own local membership, was partly a result of organisational difficulties, and we must now consider these.

Party Organisation and Election Campaigns

After the Second World War the two major parties always fielded a large number of candidates at elections, with the result that there were usually contests in well over half of the seats – a figure that was high by comparison with most other county councils and with Lancashire's own previous experience. However, in spite of their clear intentions to fight the triennial elections in a co-ordinated cross-county campaign – modelled on general elections – both parties ran up against considerable difficulties. Their structures were poorly designed to cope with county elections.

In the Conservative Party there were three relevant levels of organisation. First of all, there were the Constituency Associations. The party's organisation was designed principally for fighting parliamentary elections, and the Constituency Associations therefore formed the basis of the whole structure. They were to a large degree autonomous and were responsible for all of the party's activities within their constituency. In particular, this meant that they had charge of county council elections for divisions lying within their area – there was no level of organisation corresponding to the county council division.

Secondly, there was the Area Association. The North-West Area covered Lancashire, Chesire and Westmorland, and had an Area Council made up of MPs and prospective candidates, officers and representatives of constituency associations. This body was deliberative and advisory and was of relatively little importance. The Area Office on the other hand was more significant. It consisted of an Area agent and staff, financed by and responsible to Central Office, and had general responsibility for party organisation in the Area.

Thirdly, there was the Conservative Group on the Council. To be strictly accurate, this was not a part of the party organisation – it had no official powers or responsibilities. Indeed, both party literature and party workers go out of their way to stress that the councillor (at county, borough or district level) is responsible only to his constituents – the party organisation has no control over him and he is not answerable to it. That is the theory; in practice of course the Group did have considerable power over its members and assumed responsibility both for the formulation of Group policy within the council and for certain aspects of organisation outside it.

What is clearly absent in all of this is any level of organisation specifically designed for the needs of the county as a whole – this is of course part of the reason why the county Group came to exercise important functions. The problems inherent in the situation are clear. On the one hand, there were the powerful Constituency Associations, which had responsibility for county elections but generally speaking were more interested in their own constituency affairs or in those of boroughs or districts lying within the constituency; while on the other hand, there were the Group and Area Offices which had the interest in, and some responsibility for, county affairs but lacked the power to do a great deal. But further, because there was no county-level organisation, the county Group not only came to carry out the necessary functions, but did so to a large extent unchecked, operating to all intents and purposes autonomously. How this affected Conservative performance at the county level we shall see below. We must now, however, examine the ways in which Labour's organisation differed from that of the Conservatives.

In general, there are two major differences between Labour and Conservative organisation, which reflect Labour's origins as a mass movement outside Parliament. First of all, the Labour Party has a level of organisation corresponding to each elected authority. And secondly, and as a partial corollary of this, Labour's representatives are regarded as being answerable not just to their constituents, but also to the party organisation. Having said this, however, the fact is that in practice Labour's organisation with respect to Lancashire County Council differed remarkably little from that of the Conservatives.

Like the Conservatives, Labour had powerful constituency organisations, called Constituency Labour Parties, and lacked any organisation specifically at the level of the county division. Their intermediate organisation also differed in name, but otherwise followed the Conservative pattern fairly closely. The Regional Office was financed by and responsible to Transport House. The Regional Council, made up of representatives from constituency parties and affiliated organisations, was, like the Conservative area council, fairly insignificant. R. T. Mackenzie's comment on regional councils seems apt for both parties: 'they are so nearly powerless that it is difficult to see how they succeed in holding the interest of those who attend their meetings'.[27]

The main difference lay in the existence, as part of the Labour organisation, of a County Committee. This was a committee of the Regional Council and consisted of two delegates from each constituency within the county. It had the power to arrange the general conduct of elections, and to draw up the panel from which candidates were selected, and the responsibility of ensuring the proper functioning of a Labour Group containing all representatives elected under the party's name. In practice, the Lancashire County Committee met only once a year, its meeting being held on the same day as the annual meeting of the Group. Although it served as a forum for airing criticism of the Group, it seems to have had little power and little effect. In practice, the Group, like its Conservative counterpart, seems to have been remarkably autonomous, and indeed it was the Group rather than the County Committee to which Labour councillors were in practice accountable.

In assessing the role of these organisations in elections, we will look at four main aspects of their work: the selection of candidates, finance, the drawing up of the policy statement or programme and the organisation of the campaign.

The problem of candidate selection was not just one of getting the right candidate: it was more often one of getting a candidate at all. We have already mentioned the unattractiveness of being a county councillor. Although by this period travelling expenses and loss of earnings were refunded, the costs were still considerable.[28] On the other hand, the rewards were few. It was difficult to make one's mark in a body of 160 people, and even if one did the press and the public were pretty uninterested. The politically ambitious could make more of a stir, and have more of a sense of controlling events, on their local borough or district council. Not surprisingly then, both parties had some difficulty in getting candidates, Labour perhaps slightly more so than the Conservatives. Moreover, the decision on whether to fight a division lay, as we have seen, with the relevant constituency organisation. Whether a seat was contested, therefore, depended on the enthusiasm of the local party organisation and its workers. The regional offices of both parties regarded it as part of their responsibility to see that as many seats were fought as possible, but they had no means of forcing a constituency organisation to put up a candidate. They could use moral pressure, and they could offer to subsidise the campaign, but that was all. As a result, even winnable seats were sometimes not contested.

The other point that has to be borne in mind is that no amount of pressure from the regional office could make any difference if party organisation did not exist locally. In particular, in the very rural areas Labour was weak and had its work cut out to fight district, let alone county elections. The Conservatives faced a similar problem in some parts of the boroughs, though things were not usually so difficult for them.

On the selection of candidates the regional offices had virtually no say. The Conservatives left the matter entirely in the hands of the Constituency Associations and their branches. Labour's arrangements were more complex. Prospective candidates had first to be nominated to a panel supervised by the County Committee, and Constituency Parties then selected their candidates from this panel. In practice, this was usually a formality, because a constituency would simply select the individuals it had itself nominated to the panel, and in any case it was not difficult to bypass the procedure altogether. Thus, in spite of a feeling in both regional offices that candidates were not always of the right calibre, there was little they could do about it.

The financing of elections was again the responsibility of the constituency organisations and most of the money was raised locally by them. Some Labour candidates might attract donations from their unions, but generally speaking the main source of outside funds was the regional office. In practice both parties used two methods of subsidising local organisations. First of all they arranged for the printing of a broadsheet or election address, and made it available to the constituencies relatively cheaply. This was an important method of assistance, because the election address would usually be the principal item of expense in a campaign. Second, as a more specific inducement to weak or struggling constituencies, the regional offices might give cash grants of anything up to £50. On the Conservative side much of this money was raised by the Group itself, both by means of individual subscriptions from councillors and by means of a county ball which was held every three years in the run-up to the elections. The Labour Group was less active in this respect, and any cash donations came directly from Regional Office.

In the drawing up of the parties' policy statements, the Conservative Group again seems to have played a slightly more independent role. A sub-committee of leading members of the Group would draft the statement some time before the election and it would be discussed at a number of 'briefing conferences' of councillors, candidates and constituency workers in the run-up to the campaign. It could then be revised to meet criticisms and suggestions before being printed. The local government agent from Area Office would sit in on the original sub-committee, but it was stressed that the job of party officials was to provide advice and liaison and not to make policy. Labour's arrangements were a good deal less formalised. In practice, what seems to have happened is that one or two of the leading figures in the Group got together with the regional organiser, and they drew up the policy statement together. However, it was apparently not unknown for the matter to be left entirely in the hands of the regional organiser.

When it came to the organisation of the election campaign the same difficulties reappeared. On the one hand the constituency organisations tended to be concerned only with their own area, while on the other the regional offices and the Groups wanted to get a campaign mounted that was co-ordinated across the whole county. It cannot be said that either party was particularly successful, though once again the Conservatives seem to have managed a little better. Their 'briefing conferences' were held at various centres across the county, and were designed to get across policies and generally to boost morale. As far as the actual machinery of the campaign was concerned, however, this had to be left to the constituency associations. Labour attempted a similar sort of procedure, but seem generally to have been less well organised.

There are two points that stand out. First of all, both parties were working against the basic handicap of an organisational structure that was not well designed for county council elections. The constituency organisation had the power but lacked the interest; the regional offices had the interest and the responsibility but lacked the means to back them up. This problem of course, reflected the artificiality of the counties themselves – a point to which we will return below. Secondly, in coping with these problems the Conservatives seem to have been rather more successful than Labour, though their formal structure was, if anything, less adequate. The key to the matter seems to have been that the Conservative Group was itself more active and had a better relationship with its area office. Their superiority in this respect seems likely to have been one of the causes of the Conservative's success in breaking the swing of the pendulum in 1970, and it also helps to account for the slight but steady long-term decline in Labour support from 1952 onwards.

Backbenchers and Leaders, 1928–74

We now turn to look at the characteristics of the men and women who served on the Council, and in this section, for purposes of comparison, we go back to 1928.

Table 12.11 shows the occupations of councillors and aldermen at six points between 1928 and 1970. As we suggested in Chapter 4, some care must be taken in interpreting these figures because they are based on Council members' descriptions of themselves. There is also a further problem in the period after 1952, since from then on changes in the composition of the Council may reflect not long-term trends, but simply the fact that different parties won majorities at successive elections. However, bearing these points in mind, a number of important features stand out.

The occupational composition of the Council remained remarkably stable between 1889 and 1928, but from 1928 onwards there were a number of clear and steady trends. The two most striking are the steady decline in the proportions of gentry and landowners and of manufacturers. However, as we have noted before, the decline in the latter is to a con-

TABLE 12.11
Occupations of Council Members

	1928	1937	1946	1952	1961	1970
	%	%	%	%	%	%
Gentry and landowners	25.0	18.1	15.0	6.9	8.6	7.1
Manufacturers	21.4	10.6	8.8	9.4	3.0	2.4
Company directors and managers	9.3	11.2	11.9	11.3	17.3	20.1
Professional men	16.4	21.3	15.6	11.3	14.2	17.2
Small businessmen	12.9	12.5	11.9	15.6	9.9	10.7
White-collar workers	5.0	6.9	12.5	12.5	12.4	8.3
Political agents and trade union organisers	2.9	4.4	5.0	6.3	5.0	2.4
Manual workers	4.3	7.5	9.4	13.8	13.6	8.9
Housewives	2.9	6.9	8.8	10.0	10.5	13.6
Retired people	—	0.6	0.6	3.1	5.6	8.9
Other	—	—	0.6	—	—	0.6

siderable extent made up for by the steady rise of directors and higher managerial staff. The other clearly middle-class groups – professional and small business – again remained very steady, making up just about the same proportion of the Council in 1970 as they had in 1889.

Among the lower–middle- and working-class occupations the slow upward trend continued. The proportions of white-collar and manual workers were over 10 per cent by 1961, though both clearly suffered from Labour's poor showing in the 1967 and 1970 elections. Political agents and trade union officials continued to make up a small but important part of the Labour representation.

The two remaining categories – housewives and retired – are both to a certain extent residual, for they do not include women who stated an occupation or retired people who gave their occupation before retirement. Complete figures showing the proportion of women on the Council are given in Table 12.12. It can be seen that the number of

TABLE 12.12
Proportion of Council Members who were Women, 1928–70

1928	1937	1946	1952	1961	1970
%	%	%	%	%	%
2.9	6.9	9.4	11.9	13.6	16.6

women grew only very slowly and that, as at all levels of political life, women were considerably under-represented.

All these trends reflect changes that were going on throughout British society. But there are two more specific points that should be made. First of all, the costs of being a councillor – in terms both of travel and time – were still a considerable impediment, particularly to potential Labour representatives. Even though travel costs and loss of earnings could be claimed by this time, this undoubtedly affected the occupational composition of the Council in the fifties and sixties. Those who were able to get time off work easily and could do so without harming their career or employment prospects were most favourably placed – hence the large numbers of directors and managers, small business proprietors and professionals. But most obviously this accounts for the relatively large numbers of housewives and retired people.

TABLE 12.13

Proportion of Council Members Serving on other Local Authorities, 1931–70

	1931	1937	1946	1952	1961	1970
	%	%	%	%	%	%
All council members	52.1	52.5	53.2	53 4	53.7	48.5
Conservatives	45.1	46.7	40.2	34 3	39.8	47.5
Labour	76.2	69.2	73.6	69 4	71.0	53.1

The second point follows to a certain extent from this and is in fact the central theme of J. M. Lee's book on Cheshire County Council.[29] Lee shows how control of county affairs in Cheshire gradually passed from a group of 'social leaders' – broadly, wealthy landowners and manufacturers who became involved in Council affairs as an amateur pursuit arising out of an ethos of social responsibility – to a group of 'public persons' – a much more specialised breed, who were involved in local government because they were interested in politics and for whom their involvement constituted almost a full-time occupation. A change of this kind is also apparent in Lancashire, marked in particular by the decline of the landed and business élite – or, at least, of its involvement in local affairs. The group that replaced it cannot be identified so easily on a class or occupational basis. It was now membership of and activity in political parties that was the major precondition of becoming a councillor, and this was not confined to any one class or occupational group.

Two other characterisitics of the Council as a whole are worth commenting on – the proportion of council members who served on other local authorities, and the age and length of service of councillors. Table 12.13 shows the proportions of all members of the Council, and of Conservative and Labour members separately, who were at the same time elected members of other local authorities in Lancashire.[30] Two points are worth noting. First of all, throughout the period, around half of all county councillors and aldermen were members of other authorities. Given what we have said on several occasions about the onerous nature of council work, the figure is remarkably high and suggests that for many county councillors involvement in local government was virtually a full-time activity. Even more surprising perhaps is the remarkable consistency of the figure over the forty-year period. Secondly, there is a marked and stable difference between the major parties. Consistently, Labour members were much more likely to be members of lower-level authorities than were Conservatives. How this is to be accounted for is not at all clear, but two possible lines of explanation may be suggested. It is possible that Labour members tended more than the Conservatives to be 'public persons' of the kind we have just described. On the other hand, the difference between the parties may simply be a product of Labour's difficulty in finding the large number of candidates necessary to fight local government elections at all levels.

The question of the length of service of councillors requires more detailed discussion. In the period 1889–1928, the proportion of new council members after elections was regularly around twenty-five per cent and a substantial proportion of Council members stayed on the Council for only one or two terms. The percentage of new members after each election between 1931 and 1970 is shown in Table 12.14. It can be seen that the proportion rose somewhat after the Second World War, and was considerably higher in the last three elections.[31]

TABLE 12.14
Percentages of New Council Members
1931–70

	%		%
1931	24.3	1955	31.7
1934	22.9	1958	32.1
1937	31.9	1961	32.1
1946	5.9	1964	49.4
1949	34.4	1967	40.8
1952	34.4	1970	51.5

Table 12.15 shows the length of service of Council members at six points between 1931 and 1970. The proportion of council members with

TABLE 12.15
Length of Service of Council Members

	0–3 years	4–9 years	10–21 years	Over 21 years
	%	%	%	%
1931	38.1	25.9	20.9	15.1
1937	45.9	22.6	23.9	7.6
1946	45.9	27.7	21.4	5.0
1952	43.8	24.4	21.3	10.6
1961	37.0	25.3	30.9	6.8
1970	38.5	23.7	23.7	14.2

three or fewer years service was always fairly large – never much below forty per cent.

We have suggested that in earlier years short service was an indicator of lack of interest on the part of councillors. But in the thirties and after another reason became important. As Labour's strength increased, more and more seats became marginal and could not be held by the same party for more than one or two elections in a row. In fact, in some ways it is surprising that the figure for short-serving councillors is not higher after 1952.

A closely related characteristic is age. However, the collection of information about council members' age is far from easy, and we have not been able to get figures for more than about half of any one Council. For what they are worth, however, we show in Table 12.16

TABLE 12.16
Age of Councillors and Aldermen

	0–44	45–54	55–64	65 and over	
	%	%	%	%	
1946	—	13.5	51.4	35.1	(N=37)
1952	6.9	20.6	31.5	41.1	(N=73)
1955	8.0	14.7	26.7	50.7	(N=75)
1958	9.0	11.2	28.1	51.3	(N=89)
1961	7.1	9.4	28.2	55.3	(N=85)
1964	6.1	16.1	25.9	51.9	(N=81)
1967	10.6	21.3	19.2	48.9	(N=47)

details of the ages of councillors between 1946 and 1967. If these figures are anything like an accurate reflection of the Council as a whole, it is clear that it was predominantly a body of old men – after 1955 consistently around half of those for whom we have information were sixty-five or over. If we consider Tables 12.15 and 12.16 together, this suggests that a relatively large proportion of councillors must have been first elected when they were already quite old, and more detailed analysis confirms this. This, and our general impression of the agedness of councillors, is supported by many observers. For example, Andrew Smith remarked in 1941:

> Judged only by the number of deaths amongst its members, member-ship of the Lancashire County Council should be classed as a dangerous occupation. Rarely, indeed, do we start a meeting without sympathetic reference from the chair to the recent demise of one, two or even three County Councillors.... The reason is, of course, that the average age of County members is somewhat high. We have a handful of youthful members; but we have far more who have passed their allotted span; and most men are well beyond middle life before ever they join the Council.[32]

To summarise this picture of the Council as a whole in the postwar period we can make three points. First, though it was more broadly representative of the electorate as a whole, the Council still included a more than proportionate number from the business and professional classes. Second, there was a tendency for those occupations and categories that could most easily allow the time required to be strongly represented. And third, the Council had a heavy preponderance of elderly men. One woman who was for a short period a member of the Council told us that, when asked for her opinion of the Council by Richard Crossman, the then Minister of Housing and Local Government, she had replied: 'If you want the truth, it's a mausoleum full of old stuffed mummies of the male sex.'

In this period, as in the earlier years, the majority of council members played a fairly minor role. The real influence lay with a small group of leaders, and we now turn our attention to them. Up till 1946, the Council was effectively run by a benevolent oligarchy consisting of the leading members of the two parties which then dominated the Council, the Conservatives and the Liberals. We must now look at the postwar period.

Table 12.17 shows the occupational composition of the leadership group in each of the four decades from 1929 onwards. We have again defined the group as consisting of chairmen and vice-chairmen of stand-ing committees of the Council. From the late forties the division between leaders and back-benchers was to a certain degree institutionalised, for both of the main party groups set up small executive committees, called Advisory Committees, to help with policy formation, and these groups usually consisted of chairmen and ex-chairmen.

TABLE 12.17
Occupations of Chairmen and Vice-Chairmen

	1929–39	1939–49	1949–59	1959–69
	%	%	%	%
Gentry and labourers	21.1	14.3	8.5	10.4
Manufacturers	18.8	11.9	10.6	10.4
Company directors etc.	—	11.9	17.0	14.6
Professional men	34.4	28.6	14.9	12.5
Small businessmen	6.3	16.7	10.6	6.3
White-collar workers	—	—	10.6	10.4
Political agents and trade union organisers	3.1	4.8	12.8	10.4
Manual workers	3.1	2.4	6.4	16.7
Housewives etc.	6.3	9.5	8.5	8.3
	(N=32)	(N=42)	(N=47)	(N=48)

A comparison between Tables 12.17 and 12.11 shows that changes in the leadership group reflected those in the Council as a whole, though the figures for the fifties and sixties are partly a product of the entry of Labour into leadership, as a result of the Agreement between the parties of 1948 and of Labour's victories in the election of 1952 and after.

TABLE 12.18
Length of Service of Chairmen and Vice-Chairmen

	0–3 years	4–9 years	10–21 years	Over 21 years	
	%	%	%	%	
1931	—	21.4	21.4	57.1	(N=14)
1937	—	20.0	40.0	40.0	(N=15)
1946	—	22.7	54.6	22.7	(N=22)
1952	—	48.0	40.0	12.0	(N=25)
1961	—	18.5	59.3	22.2	(N=27)
1970	4.2	12.5	41.7	41.7	(N=24)

Table 12.18 gives details of the length of service on the Council of chairmen and vice-chairmen. Comparison with Table 12.15 shows that,

once again, the length of service of chairmen is very much greater than that of all councillors. Whereas around sixty-five per cent of all councillors regularly had less than ten years' service, the corresponding figure for chairmen and vice-chairmen was usually around twenty per cent.

However, this kind of analysis becomes less satisfactory after 1952, when the alternation of power between Labour and the Conservatives meant that there were effectively two leadership groups alternating in office. On the matter of chairmanships, the 1948 Agreement, though it was not very precise, seems to have operated fairly successfully. What happened was that the party in power took the majority of the chairmanships and gave the vice-chairmanships to the opposition. But a number of chairmanships was always left for the opposition – and not just the minor ones. Thus, for example, in 1952 Sir Thomas Tomlinson and Harry Lord, both Conservatives, continued as chairmen of the Public Health and Housing Committee and the Health Committee respectively, and in 1955 William Bannister, a Labour member, remained as chairman of Planning and Development.

In the period from 1949 onwards both parties went through two generations of leaders, marked on the Labour side by the succession of Sir Andrew Smith by Sir Fred Longworth in 1964 and on the Conservative side by the succession of Sir Henry Lumby to Sir Alfred Bates in 1965. The contrast between the two generations is very interesting and worth examining a little further.

Andrew Smith was, as we saw earlier, a key figure in Labour's rise to power, and especially after George Tomlinson's departure into national politics, he was the undisputed leader of the group and the obvious choice for Labour's first chairman of the Council in 1952, although he was already seventy-two years of age. Smith's experience in local government went back to pre-First World War days. He had been a leading Labour representative on Nelson Borough Council between the wars, and in the twenties on the Burnley Board of Guardians. He was manager, editor and a major contributor to the Labour-owned *Nelson Gazette* from the late twenties onwards and this kept him at the centre of local politics in north-east Lancashire. As a leader he was widely respected and generally agreed to be both knowledgeable and authoritative on local government matters. Although physically a rather frail figure, Smith had a very forceful personality – he had strong views and as often as not got his way. He kept firm control of the Labour Group and, in the view of one former clerk to the Council, 'he ran the show in a benevolent sort of way'. But though he was respected it seems that Smith was not liked – he was a rather severe man and was described to us as being 'a bit tetchy' and 'a bitter politician'. A member of his own party commented: 'Andrew wasn't "nice".... He was a strong character and firm.... As a leader the Tories were afraid of [him] never mind the Labour people; the officers were afraid of him, everybody.'

Although the majority of Labour members came from the south of the county, Smith's base was Nelson; and, on becoming chairman of the Council in 1952, he gathered around him a team that included several figures from north-east Lancashire. Cameron Doodson, who had represented Colne West as a councillor, became chairman of Highways and Bridges; W. J. Throup, the elder of the well-known Throup brothers from Nelson, became chairman of the Children's Committee; and William Bannister, who had succeeded to Smith's own seat in Nelson North when Smith became an alderman, became chairman of Planning and Development. Other prominent figures in the early fifties were Mrs Katherine Fletcher of Atherton, who became chairman of Education, Joseph Eastham from Worsley, Ellis Wood, the group secretary from Abram, and Tom Hourigan from Leigh.

Labour's return to power in 1958 saw few changes in this leading group. Selwyn Jones, who had been vice-chairman of Finance from 1952 to 1955, Smith himself having been chairman, now took over the chairmanship. J. W. Thorley came in as chairman of Public Health and Housing, and Mrs Winifred Kettle took over as chairman of the Children's Committee. The other notable newcomer was Fred Longworth, who became chairman of the new Road Safety Committee.

In 1964 Andrew Smith, by now eighty-four, at last resigned the group leadership. He was by this time in very poor health. He had become 'a doddering old man clinging to office', and came into meetings 'virtually on crutches'. As he got older he seems to have become more dogmatic. Despite his poor health he insisted on taking the chairmanship of the Education Committee in 1964 – and he got his way.

There was no obvious successor to the leadership and a ballot was held. There were four candidates: Ellis Wood, Tom Hourigan, Selwyn Jones and Fred Longworth. Hourigan was thought by some people to be likely to win, and he did later become leader of the Labour Group, but there is some suggestion that on this occasion his being a Roman Catholic weighed against him. Jones was widely regarded as in some ways the most able – he was certainly a good debater – but he also had an unfortunate knack of making enemies. A colleague in the Labour movement described him as 'a cantankerous Welshman ... [who] couldn't get on with people'. Longworth, who won, was less well known but none the less highly respected. He was an ex-miner and NUM official and a prominent Methodist lay preacher. At seventy-four years of age he was also much the oldest of the four candidates. But most surprising, perhaps, he had had very little experience of office, having been chairman only of the relatively minor Road Safety Committee since 1958.

Although Longworth's victory was unexpected, he seems to have been a successful leader. He was modest and unassuming and impressed officers and fellow councillors alike as 'a very moderate, very level-headed and a very sensible man'. A typical assessment of his leadership was that given by a senior Conservative who said 'Sir Fred Longworth ... who to the astonishment certainly of our party emerged as leader ... was an absolute find ... he made a wonderful leader.' Longworth's team contained many of the old faces. Apart from Jones, Hourigan and Wood, Smith himself, as we have seen, remained as chairman of Education and Doodson and Mrs Kettle also retained their posts. But there was some new blood – Bob Foulkes, Jack Martin, T. G. Harrison and Franklin Ainsworth.

The overriding impression one gets from looking at the Labour leaders in this period is one of age. Many of these men and women were already well into their sixties by the time they first took office and many continued in office until well into their seventies if not beyond. Thus, in 1964, Andrew Smith was eighty-four; Joshua Mawdsley, chairman of the Small Holdings and Allotments Committee, was eighty-one; Longworth was seventy-four and Doodson was seventy-eight. Selwyn Jones, at sixty-three, was a relative youngster.

On the Conservative side, Sir Alfred Bates, their leader until 1965, had a personality that was in many respects similar to that of Sir Andrew Smith. He was a strong character; he expected and usually got his own way. His control over the Conservative group was very firm, and indeed in some people's view it bordered on the dictatorial. 'He was a very strong leader of the party. In our group meetings he brooked no nonsense – very firm indeed ..., he kept a very firm hand on things.' Again like Smith, Bates's grasp slackened somewhat as he got older and he suffered from ill health and the effects of overwork. After a third period as chairman of the County Council from 1961 to 1964, his poor health finally forced him to resign in 1965.

In 1955 the leadership group around Bates included Robert Guymer (Finance), Thomas Hargreaves (Highways and Bridges), Sir Thomas Tomlinson (Public Health and Housing), John Welch (Education) and Harry Lord (Health). R. E. Mottershead was chairman of the Establishment Committee and Henry Lumby was chairman of the Fire Brigade Committee.

In 1961 Lumby was promoted to chairman of Finance, and a number of new figures were brought in – F. L. Neep, J. R. Hull, H. M. F.

Carrington and Dr M. K. Hall. By 1965, when Bates retired, Lumby had emerged as the natural successor and he had two years as vice-chairman of the Council before the Conservatives took control again in 1967. In contrast to Bates, Lumby was very actively involved in the Conservative Party in Lancashire. In line with this he viewed his role as being that of leading a party team rather than of directing policy himself. His approach was characterised by great thoroughness and conscientiousness and by a concern to carry his colleagues with him on controversial matters. Like Longworth, and to some extent in contrast with Bates and Smith, he was popular with elected representatives of both parties and with officers. On becoming chairman in 1967, Lumby brought in some more new faces – J. G. Barber-Lomax, who became chairman of Finance, W. D. Cooper, Traviss Carter, Mrs M. M. C. Kemball, Mrs C. M. Pickard, B. Greenwood and others. But, like Labour, the Conservatives had something of an age problem. By 1967 Harry Lord, still chairman of Health, was seventy-seven and R. F. Mottershead, still at Establishment, was sixty-nine. In 1967, with this problem in mind, they introduced an age limit of seventy for chairmen of the main committees.

As a matter of general impression, it seems that the Conservatives handled the problems of an ageing leadership group better than Labour. The lines of promotion were rather clearer and there was a steadier flow of new men. On the Labour side, either because new, younger, talent was simply not available, or because the established leadership did not make use of it, the picture seems to have been one of gradual ossification.

This discussion of the leadership groups in the fifties and sixties beings out one important general point. Normally, proponents of the party government model would claim that one of the important benefits of party competition is that it keeps the parties vigorous and alert. In Lancashire, however, the even balance between the parties and the high degree of marginality of the Council seem to have had the reverse effect. The large number of marginal divisions enabled the leadership groups in each party to become more strongly entrenched. The councillors in safe seats and the aldermen were in an unassailable position and could build up considerable seniority. The new and younger members, on the other hand, because their seats were always at risk, could never build up the experience and seniority necessary to challenge the established leadership. Thus, in spite of the overt party political competition of these years, the leadership situation was in many ways similar to that in the old days of consensus.

Parties and Policy-Making

The central feature of the party government view is policy-making; the idea is that parties fight elections on the basis of a clearly worked out and stated programme in order that the party that wins power should then use it to implement that programme. We must now see how far things in Lancashire conformed to the model in this respect. First of all, however, it should be remembered that the model is worked out with central government very largely in mind, and it is clear even at a superficial level that the policy-making possibilities in an organisation like the county council are much more restricted. The primary reason for this is that the powers of county councils are statutorily defined – they may only do what central government empowers them to do. They have no residual powers.

In what ways, then, could a political party affect the County Council's policy? There are, very generally, four possibilities:

(a) It might secure the more efficient operation of a particular department or service.

(b) It might alter the emphasis given to different services – for example the development of some might be speeded up at the expense of others.

(c) It might alter the proportion of resources being spent on a department or service.

(d) In areas where the Council had freedom of action, it might choose whether or not to pursue active policies.

The attempt to assess how far a political party did affect policy in any of these ways faces considerable difficulties. First of all, the major influence on policy is always central government, and it is therefore difficult to decide whether changes are a result of local or of central influence. Secondly, it is never sufficient to compare what happened in a particular period with what happened in the previous period; rather we must compare it with what would have happened if another party had been in control. Thirdly, it is always unclear whether policy initiatives come from the party in power or from the full-time officers of the Council. And fourthly, it is in any case extremely difficult to assess the efficiency with which services are run.

We must, however, try to make some assessment of the parties' role in policy-making in the postwar period. One obvious place to start is Labour's first period in control, 1952–5. Here, if anywhere, one might expect to see party government clearly in operation – a party coming to power after a long period in opposition might be expected to want to implement some fairly important changes. As we have already seen, on winning the 1952 election Labour reasserted the party government view by breaking the 1948 Agreement in order to secure control of the Council. Let us see what happened in the following three years.

During the election campaign, Labour concentrated on attacking the incumbent administration for its extravagance and also for the sort of economies that they expected the Conservatives to propose. Addressing a meeting of Labour candidates and workers on 23 February 1952, Smith argued that if Labour gained power they would

> administer County services much more economically than the Conservatives. But we would not do it at the expense of the children, nor of the aged.... We are faced as we were in 1931 with people in power whose only accepted method of economy is to inflict hardships on the aged, the children, the helpless. That is not Labour's way. Economy we must have – but not by methods such as this.[33]

The sort of economies that Labour had in mind involved a reduction in the numbers and salaries of officers, the re-rating of industry and a change in the Council's banking arrangements. In general Smith wanted to see an end to what he referred to as 'de luxe' administration.

At the budget meeting on 6 March 1952, just before the election, an *ad hoc* committee was set up 'to consider County Council expenditure generally and to report ... as to ways of reducing or at least preventing further increases in the cost of County administration'. In the event, the committee proved to be a useful means for the Labour leaders to initiate some of their new policies after the election. It reported twice – in July and November 1952. Some general economy measures were proposed and accepted. In addition, a number of more specific schemes were proposed: the setting up of a 'controlled purchasing scheme' to supervise bulk purchase; the setting up of a Central Vehicle Maintenance Unit to service the Council's vehicles; a change of the Council's banking arrangements to the Co-operative Wholesale Society (CWS) Bank; and the setting up of a central printing unit.

Some economies were achieved, but they were soon engulfed by generally rising costs, and the rate had to be raised by 6d for the year 1953–4, and by a further 8d for 1954–5. The specific items are more interesting from our point of view, for they were all 'pet schemes' of Labour and were more controversial. None of them involved particularly large amounts of money, but two of them touched on an issue of principle – that of 'direct works' versus 'private enterprise' – which divided the parties. The 'controlled purchasing scheme' was approved by the Council on 5 February 1953, and a new Contracts Committee was set up to direct it. The setting up of a central printing unit was also agreed at the same meeting. Although there had already been objections from 'employers and employees in the printing trade',[34] and an attempt was made to get the matter postponed to consider these, the scheme went ahead.

Labour had already supported the setting up of a Central Vehicle Maintenance Unit in May 1950 when the matter had been the subject of a recorded vote. This topic was always a particularly sensitive one which aroused party spirit on both sides. At the Council meeting on 6 November 1952 the Conservatives made an attempt to delay the progress of the scheme, and then moved the reference back of the detailed proposals at the 5 February 1953 meeting. The scheme went ahead, but there was a string of reports in the following months justifying and defending it.

The last of the specific schemes proposed by the *ad hoc* committee – the transfer of the Council's banking arrangements to the CWS Bank – was quietly dropped in July 1953, on the grounds that the terms offered 'would be less favourable to the County Council than the terms now operating'.[35]

All four of these schemes were, in a sense, political, and in the case of two of them Labour used its majority to force them through against Conservative opposition. However, it must also be said that none of them was of particularly great moment. The most controversial, the Central Vehicle Maintenance Unit, only involved savings estimated in February 1953 as being in the order of £3110 per annum.[36]

One of Labour's long-standing criticisms of county administration, which as we have seen had cropped up again in the 1952 campaign, concerned the level of senior officers' salaries. Shortly after coming to power they took advantage of a national review of officers' salaries to propose what amounted to reductions in the salaries of senior officials. This proposal was rejected by the officers concerned and a protracted period of negotiation followed. Eventually in November 1953 the matter was resolved, with the Council backing down and agreeing to higher rather than lower salary scales.

What further signs are there that Labour carried out a clear party policy? An examination of the distribution of resources among the various committees from 1951 to 1955 does not suggest that Labour radically altered the pattern of expenditure, though the detailed analysis that would be necessary to establish this point firmly is beyond the scope of the present study.[37] Otherwise there are only two areas in which significant developments seem to have taken place. First of all, the Children's Committee, under Willie John Throup, carried out a successful experiment, which was later considerably extended, to increase the number of children in its care who were boarded out with foster families. Secondly, quite a lot of work was done in connection with land reclamation, overspill housing and industrial development. In both of these cases, however, it is difficult to know to what extent they were initiatives on Lancashire's part, and, if they were, whether they came from the controlling group or from the officers.

Our general conclusion on the years between 1952 and 1955 must, then, be that there is little evidence of a specifically Labour programme being implemented. The great majority of the Council's services continued to operate along the same lines as before – the assumption of power by Labour was marked by few, if any, major switches in policy. From the outset Labour's principal concern seems to have been to run the machine more efficiently and economically than its opponents. This interpretation is supported if we look briefly at the performance of the Conservatives in opposition. If Labour had been pursuing a strongly partisan programme, we would expect to see this reflected in a high degree of political activity from the Conservatives. But there is little sign of this. Although the average attendance at Council meetings rose to 83 per cent, the number of amendments between 1952 and 1955 fell to only eight, the lowest number for any three-year period since the First World War, and there were no recorded votes. Most of the amendments concerned the topics we have discussed – the central printing unit, the Central Vehicle Maintenance Unit, other direct works schemes and senior officers' salaries. There is no indication of other policy issues giving rise to serious party conflict in this period.

So those who expected Labour's first term in office to demonstrate the party government model at work must have been disappointed. Although all the outward trappings were there – elections contested on a party basis, Labour's taking aldermanic seats to secure its majority, the appointment of major chairmen from the controlling party and so on – the practical effects were slight. Labour's successes were in relatively minor matters. They do not seem to have attempted many major changes of direction in council policy, and even in some small matters they were unable to implement their ideas.

We have examined the 1952–5 period in detail because it seemed likely that these years would provide the clearest example of party government at work. In fact, our discussion suggests that even in these years the role of party in policy-making was very limited. From 1955 onwards, however, party became still less important. As we shall see below, shortly after the 1955 election the Agreement was patched up, and from then on relations between the parties were smooth and amicable. There seems to have been a more or less conscious attempt by both parties to 'de-politicise' much of the Council's business. There were questions on which the parties disagreed, and some – notably comprehensive education – had the characterisitics of 'issues'. But the regular change in political control of the Council did not lead to regular changes in its policies, and the potential 'issues' never became a source of great controversy. Indeed, both parties seem to have concentrated on making general claims that they could run the Council's services more efficiently rather than on developing and implementing distinctive party programmes.

There were some matters on which party control did have an effect, however. For example, when the Conservatives took over in 1955 they shelved plans for extending the Council's direct works activities which Labour had been developing; and in 1967 the incoming Conservative administration stopped negotiations for the purchase of Aintree race-course, which Labour had wanted to bring into public ownership. But examples of this kind are few and far between. More heat seems to have been generated by issues such as the fluoridisation of water, which led to a lengthy debate in February 1966, but did not divide the Council along party lines.

TABLE 12.19
Amendments, Recorded Votes and Average Attendance, 1952–74

	1952–5	1955–8	1958–61	1961–4	1964–7	1967–70	1970–4
	%	%	%	%	%	%	%
Average attendance	83.6	80.7	79.8	81.3	82.6	87.4	85.4
No. of amendments	8	7	1	—	4	6	9
No. of recorded votes	—	—	1	—	—	1	1

Table 12.19, which gives details of amendments and attendance from 1952 onwards, confirms our interpretation of the role of party in this period. Although the level of attendance remained very high, the number of amendments was very low – falling to nil in 1961–4. In the whole period there were only three recorded votes. An analysis of the subjects of amendments and recorded votes does not reveal any major issues. Most were on minor or isolated points, though there is some sign from 1967 onwards of Labour members pressing amendments and notices of motion on more controversial matters – the deduction of trade union contributions from wage packets, free school milk, family planning etc. Surprisingly, there was only a single amendment, in July 1964, on the reorganisation of secondary education. The reason why this potentially explosive issue never really became prominent seems to have been that, from a fairly early date, the Conservative leadership accepted the principle of com-

prehensive education, and were able to contain opposition from some of their own back-benchers.

Further evidence for the limited impact of the parties on Council policy and about the relations between the Groups comes from our interviews with leading figures in county affairs. Several of them, when asked what matters had been affected by Group policy, found it difficult to suggest any. Others candidly admitted that the influence of party had been slight. Thus for example, one official in the regional organisation of the Labour Party said that 'No matter who was in power at County Hall, the same things got done'. Another commented: 'Looking back, it's very difficult to demonstrate that the Labour Party as such really achieved very much more in control of the County Council than the Tories achieved.' Similar views were expressed by two senior officers of the County Council:

> There wasn't all that huge a difference between the parties ... the issues affected by the parties were comparatively minor things ... [there was] no difference on major issues, only on spending.

> Actually it made little or no difference to what was done. The policy didn't change. The machinery was there ... they were the greatest friends, both parties. They went through the machinery of hating one another and kissed the day after – that's a bit of an exaggeration.

As might be expected, the practising politicians tended to see the differences between themselves and their opponents as being somewhat more important. But even most of them did not regard the differences as fundamental. A senior Labour chairman, commenting on the work of his committee, said:

> I can assure you, when we took over, there was no change fundamentally, for the Tories ... had a progressive outlook on the implementation of [the] Act. The only difference between him [his Conservative opposite number] and me – perhaps I was a little more impetuous in getting on with the programme quicker. There may have been a change in emphasis when I came in, but on fundamental policy, no.

This sort of view was echoed, in a more general context, by a senior Conservative:

> As for the influence of party politics on the administration of the County ... it was largely a question of speed of development, and also slightly the direction. The Labour Party always wanted to advance the welfare services much more quickly than the Conservative Party. We agreed on the aim, but one party wanted to rush it much more swiftly than the other.

The evidence, then, suggests that the political parties' influence on policy for the most of the postwar period was fairly slight. How can this initially rather surprising fact be accounted for?

Part of the explanation, as we suggested above, lies in the fact that the County Council had relatively little control over its own policy. This point deserves to be emphasised. It was a frequent complaint of council leaders that the Council was restricted far too much by central government. As early as 1910 a conference of all local authorities in Lancashire passed a resolution stating

> that the time has now arrived for a united and strong stand to be made by local authorities against the tendency of the Board of Education and other Government Departments to endeavour gradually to transfer the real direction and control of expenditure out of rates to a bureaucracy in London, and so undermine the principles on which local administration has been founded.[38]

The same point was made even more directly by Tom Atkinson, when chairman of the Finance Committee, in his budget speech in 1951:

> The County Treasurer has recently ... estimated that the Government exercise full or partial control of 17/7d in every £ of County Council expenditure, and the County Council has full control over the remaining 2/5d in the £. The reason behind this is largely that the government meets 62% of our gross expenditure ... and ... 'He who pays the piper calls the tune'.[39]

This situation got worse rather than better over the years as the County Council became increasingly reliant on central government finance to cope with expanding health, welfare and education services.

However, some part of the explanation for the parties' lack of control must also be found in the way in which the Groups themselves operated. In organising themselves to make policy the Groups faced a number of obstacles. To start with there were the usual problems faced by lay representatives in coming to grips with the technical complexities of administration. Many councillors must have found a good deal of the business hard to grasp. On top of this, the difficulties of travel again caused problems. We have already seen how they affected individual Council members and created difficulties in recruitment. However, they also led to special problems in policy-making. Because many members had to travel long distances to meetings at County Hall, Group meetings could not be called frequently. Both Groups, therefore, held their meetings immediately before Council and committee meetings. The Groups met at 10.45 am before Council meetings which started at 11.30 am, and the party members on committees met half an hour before committee meetings to go through the agenda. This had two drawbacks. In the first place, the time available was very limited. Secondly, because meetings were always taken up with consideration of the agenda of the following meetings, there was rarely an opportunity for discussion of new policy proposals. As a final factor, there was one other difficulty – the sheer size of the Groups. The Group in control would be over eighty strong. A meeting of that size was poorly equipped for the task of policy-making.

The result was that what effective control of policy there was passed into the hands of a smaller group of leaders. Committee chairmen were in a particularly powerful position. Their appointment usually presupposed that they had the time available to devote to the job, and if initially they lacked expertise they could usually rely on making up for it by experience gained over a number of years. The relationship between a chairman and his chief officer was crucial. The officer was in many ways in a better position to control events – he was a full-time employee; he had a large staff at his disposal; and he had the advantage of expert knowledge. None the less, long-serving chairmen could also build up a position of considerable authority – one thinks of men like Hourigan, Lord or Doodson, who were chairmen or vice-chairmen of their respective committees for many years. One suspects that where lay members did exercise significant control over policy, it was through the work of vigorous and powerful individuals like these, rather than through the party groups.

The task of co-ordinating party policy fell upon the party leaders, and although different leaders had different styles they operated in roughly similar ways. Both party Groups had 'advisory committees'. These were small executive committees, consisting of senior chairmen, ex-chairmen and other leading figures, which were intended to carry on the day-to-day business of the groups between quarterly meetings. However, less formal methods of co-ordinating policy tended to develop. In each party there was usually a small group of experienced men who were consulted regularly by the Group leader and who formed a kind of 'inner cabinet'. These men would be chosen on the basis of their administrative experience, their political influence or simply because they were trusted friends or colleagues of the leader.

Sir Henry Lumby described to us in some detail how he arranged things. The Advisory Committee did meet regularly during his term of office, but he made considerable use of what he called his 'cabinet'. This was a small group of senior Conservatives with no fixed membership which met about half a dozen times a year, usually over dinner, to discuss general policy, priorities and current problems. The exact composition of the 'cabinet' at any meeting would depend on the issues to be discussed, but it was a mechanism whereby Lumby was able to ensure that there was a consensus among senior members of his Group.

Informal arrangements such as these provided one of the main opportunities for elected members of the Council to influence the general direction of policy. They further worked to reinforce the tendency for influence to be concentrated in the hands of a small group of senior members of the two parties. In these circumstances the possibility of distinctive party policies emerging clearly depended on the attitudes of these leading members. This leads us on to our third point.

We have suggested that the parties' lack of impact on policy was partly a result of the fact that the Council's services were largely determined by central government, and partly a result of the problems of organising the groups for policy-making. But it was also to some extent due to the attitudes of the party leaders themselves. We return inevitably at this point to the Agreement between the parties, for it clearly reflected the leaders' views on the role of the Council and the part that party politics should play in its work.

First of all, however, let us complete the story of the Agreement. We saw that the Agreement signed in 1948 was broken by Labour after the 1952 elections, when Labour needed extra aldermanic seats to secure its overall majority and took them. In other regards Labour kept to the Agreement, but the events of 1952 clearly caused a certain amount of bitterness, and when the Conservatives won the 1955 election they took five of Labour's aldermanic seats, even though this was not necessary for them to secure an overall majority. The whole matter was the subject of a slightly acerbic correspondence between Alfred Bates and Andrew Smith, but eventually a basis for compromise was found, and a renegotiated Agreement was signed on 25 July 1957.

The new Agreement differed from the old in two major respects. The position of aldermen was again safeguarded – they would not be displaced to make up party strength. However, the number of places a party got on committees would now be determined by the number of seats it had won at the triennial elections and not by its total strength (councillors and aldermen) on the Council. Secondly, it was agreed that, if a party had an overall majority on the Council as a result of having a disproportionate number of aldermen, it would not use that majority to overturn decisions carried in committee by the party having the majority of councillors. In the words of the first clause of the Agreement:

the Political Party having the greatest number of County Councillors at Triennial Elections shall *control* the County Council *for a period of three years* following the Triennial Elections regardless of the effect of the operation of clause (3) (ii) [safeguarding the position of aldermen] ... and of the effect of the result of any Bye Election during that time.

In this final form the Agreement lasted for the rest of the life of the County Council, and worked fairly smoothly. The kind of situation that might have put the Agreement under severe strain – if for example the result of a triennial election had been so close that by-elections might have affected control – never arose, though it was with some difficulty that the rank-and-file of Conservative members were restrained by the leadership from throwing over the Agreement when they won their huge majority in 1967.

Although the Agreement was the subject of heavy criticism from party workers on both sides, party leaders regarded it as a considerable achievement. All of the leaders to whom we spoke clearly felt that the working out of a smooth relationship between the parties had been a major success. Thus, for example, J. G. Barber-Lomax, Conservative chairman of the Finance Committee from 1967 to 1974, commented on the Agreement as follows:

> So much of the work of the County Council and its Committees was purely administrative, and the parties had recognised the need to have a 'second eleven' in waiting should there be a shift in political power. The opposition party, by taking the vice-chairmanships, and its members enjoying proportional representation on committees, shared in the work and were fully cognizant of the responsibilities and complications of a very big organisation. This system made for continuity and took the bitterness out of party politics.... This is not to imply that the Agreement meant power-sharing; it meant involvement, and where political policy was not paramount, it meant shared responsibility on common sense lines in the interests of the ratepayers as a whole.

Another senior Conservative summed up the Agreement's benefits as follows:

> The great thing about the County Council and the thing which is responsible for its efficiency more, I think, than anything else was this unique Agreement between the parties.... It was forged out of strife and, because of that, it was very binding and very loyally adhered to.... The party headquarters didn't really like it – certainly the Conservatives didn't. It was impossible to get it across to them – the tremendous benefits to local government which accrued from that Agreement.... It removed strife, bickering and arguing.... It was a wonderful Agreement.

Labour members were, on the whole, a little more sensitive when questioned about the Agreement, and emphasised that it didn't involve compromising their principles. As one Labour member put it:

> We realised the Agreement was the correct thing to do. It was good for the community and good for the Group. But it didn't alter in any way whatsoever – I want to stress this – the policy. Some people had the silly idea that we were all joining in together as one bandwagon. But I assure you that this was not true.... There were one or two dissensions, but we soon realised it was the best thing.

Another leading Labour member explained the Party's attitude to the Agreement in rather more detail:

> There were one or two who objected to [the Agreement].... There are the left wing in the Labour Party always, all over the country [who think] 'if you get control, sweep the deck – the chairmanship, vice-chairmanship, a majority on every committee, and all the rest.' But the moderates ... won the day ... and it went on year after year.
>
> From time to time, there was criticism about it – younger members coming on didn't like this set-up at all. But it was maintained. The senior members of the Group always insisted on honouring it and the Tories the same.
>
> [Q: And do you think on the whole it was beneficial?]
>
> Oh yes, I think so. You retain the men of ability, men of leadership in chairmanships ... you had continuity all the time.

These quotations illustrate the way in which the leaders of both groups viewed the Agreement and something òf their attitude to the role of parties on the Council. They clearly regarded the Agreement as a major achievement which was valuable because it minimised party conflict and secured the stability and continuity that they regarded as essential to the efficient operation of the Council's services.

But the effects of the Agreement were more far-reaching. Perhaps inevitably, it created a situation in which the leaders of the two Groups came to be on very friendly terms. In the words of one leader, 'it created harmony, goodwill and friendship between the parties'. In such circumstances, the pursuit of partisan policies was bound to be inhibited.

To conclude this section, let us briefly summarise our argument. We started from the premise that a key feature in the party government model was policy-making – the model requires that policy should be made by the controlling party on party lines. We have seen that both parties did make an attempt to fight elections with this end in view. Both drew up policy statements and, within the limits imposed by the nature of the county itself and their own organisation, fought co-ordinated campaigns. In spite of this, and in spite of the fact that political power did change hands regularly, there is little evidence that the parties significantly changed the direction of county policy when they came into power. This was partly because of the difficulties that the groups faced in organising themselves to make and control policy; but it was also partly due to the attitudes of the leadership of the two groups. These attitudes were, perhaps, specific to Lancashire. A senior officer of the Council suggested that:

> The Lancastrian has an enormous capacity to compromise.... The Lancastrian way of learning to live together produced an amicable solution ... [the parties] developed this relationship of putting their heads together to find out what was best for Lancashire. They were first Lancastrians ... and politicians second.

Conclusion

We must now look back over our discussion in this chapter and Chapter 4, and see what general conclusions can be drawn about Lancashire County Council and its politics.

At the end of Chapter 4 we made a distinction between what we called the consensus and party government views of local government. We argued that up to 1929 the government of the county was predominantly consensual, the leaders of the Conservative and Liberal Parties forming an oligarchy administering county services. In the thirties and forties this oligarchy was challenged by a group of Labour members whose involvement in county politics resulted initially from the transfer of responsibility for public assistance to the county councils by the Local Government Act of 1929. Labour's view was that the Council should be run on party lines, and after Labour's victory in the 1952 election the Council displayed all the outward signs of party government. But it gradually became clear that the change was more apparent than real. The Agreement between the parties symbolised a return to a more consensual approach – behind the façade of party politics, the leaders arranged things so that the county's business was carried on smoothly.

How are we to account for the failure of party government to develop fully in Lancashire? Two reasons seem important – the performance of the political parties, and the nature of county government itself.

There seems little doubt that some part of the explanation for the way in which Lancashire's postwar politics developed must be sought in the way in which the Labour and Conservative Parties adjusted themselves to the new circumstances. The Conservatives had been the traditional upholders of the consensus view of local politics, but after their initial resistance to the notion of party government immediately after the war they seem to have adjusted fairly well to the situation and to have made the most of it. They conceded the form of party government, but managed to avoid what they saw as its worst excesses. In their organisation both inside and outside County Hall they seem to have been moderately successful.

The same cannot however be said for Labour. Already in the signing of the first version of the Agreement in 1948, and its subsequent rejection in 1952, there were signs of some indecisiveness. The evidence suggests that the Group became steadily more and more cut off from its grass-roots organisation and that the party machinery in the county was not particularly well designed and did not work very well. All of this was reflected in Labour's declining electoral support. After 1952, Labour seems to have become increasingly absorbed in the problems of efficiently administering a vast organisation rather than implementing specifically Labour policies.

Even more important than the performance of the parties (and in part the explanation for it) were the problems arising from the nature of county government itself. Party politics could not thrive in Lancashire because the necessary conditions did not exist. There were two main problems. First of all, the county was not in any real sense a community. There were no shared interests that distinguished people living in Lancashire from those living elsewhere. Of course, many people thought of themselves as Lancastrians, but in material terms there was little to unite a man living in Furness with one living in north-east Lancashire or west Lancashire. The sheer size of the county meant that its citizens did not share the same concerns. Their feelings of loyalty tended to be directed towards much smaller and more compact units – cities, towns and villages.

Compare, for instance, the administrative county with medium-sized towns like Accrington, Chorley or Lancaster. The latter are small and compact and have a recognisable identity. Issues are likely to arise in them that affect people in all parts of the town. And they have the institutions that are typical of small communities – in particular local newspapers – which tend to sustain local identity. Lancashire on the other hand was a huge, artificially defined area with a heterogeneous population and nothing to bind it together except the institutional structure of the Council itself. The net result of this was that the Council was very remote. The ordinary elector knew little and cared less about what went on at county level.

The second major problem was one we have referred to several times already – the restricted control that the Council had over its own services. The predominant influence of central government meant, as we have seen, that the Council's powers were severely circumscribed. And this problem was exacerbated by the pattern of administration that was developed. Generally speaking, the Council favoured, or was required to develop, highly decentralised administrative structures involving a considerable degree of participation by first-tier authorities. Thus, for example, two of the potentially most 'political' areas – education and health – were administered through divisional committees. Even the collection of the rates was decentralised. The effect of these arrangements was once again to focus attention and interest on the local community and the first-tier authority, and away from the Council.

If party politics is to thrive and be successful it is not sufficient to have party organisations and workers eager for the fight – there must also be something for them to fight about. If there are no controversial issues then political conflict will soon be seen to be pointless and it will wither. This to a considerable extent is what happened in Lancashire. It is notable that, in the two periods when party politics did get a foothold, such issues did exist – public assistance in the thirties and, for a brief period at the turn of the century, education. In the fifties, sixties and early seventies the number of controversial issues was not sufficient to allow party government anything more than a halting and fitful existence.

If our argument is correct, then, it suggests that the basis of county government was ill-conceived. We saw in Chapter 4 that the debate on the 1888 Act had exposed a clash between the view of the county councils as an administrative extension of central government and the view that they should be an exercise in local democracy. Lancashire's experience suggests that this ambiguity was never resolved. The machinery of elections and lay control set up by the 1888 Act invited a political approach to county government; the restricted powers of the new bodies and the size and heterogeneity of Lancashire made the full development of such an approach impossible.

CHAPTER 13

Education

EDUCATION was not only the major Lancashire service during a great part of the Council's life-span; it was the field of activity that both strengthened and reflected the humane and civilised values, and one that caused the county's councillors to become even more deeply involved in the problems of their particular localities than they might otherwise have been. The work of Lancashire's divisional executives represents a fascinating aspect both of the county's own history and of local government in general. After the problem of public assistance in the thirties, education was the next most contentious field, as regards potential political differences in the council chamber itself; although, in the late sixties, comprehensive education ceased to be such a sparking point for intense debate and became instead a matter leading to considerable bipartisanship of viewpoint.

It was an enormous generator of administrative problems and workloads, and it caused the county to become an employer not only of many thousands of teachers, but of hundreds of administrators and ancillary staff, on a scale hitherto unknown. It reached out into a vast and varying range of activities and commitments – adult education, village drama and music-making, the youth service, further and technical education, a great and comprehensive library service, the provision of scores of school and college buildings, a county youth orchestra, evening institute activities of many hundreds of different kinds and, of course, the administration of just as many hundreds of schools and other institutions, including teacher training colleges, agricultural colleges and a nautical school. To deal adequately with all these variants of the work of the county education service would be quite impossible, and every one of them requires its own historian. Indeed, it should be one of the functions and purposes of the present volume to stimulate such research. The present account, is, for fairly obvious reasons, largely restricted to the major functions of the educational service, the provision of primary, secondary and further education.

Despite the sheer size of the different Lancashire educational organisa-tions, the administrative costs of the county's machinery appear to have been low compared with those of most other counties. As Mr MacGregor-Reid explains elsewhere,[1] education was the principal county service between 1930 and 1974, making up forty per cent of total spending in 1930, forty-five per cent by 1950, and a huge fifty-five per cent by 1973. Spending over the period, as is there demonstrated, followed the path of national *per capita* rather than gross spending, if only because postwar Lancashire had to cater for great overspill populations in its industrial or residential border areas in the west, south and east. It was in these localities that the most spectacular feats of accommodation and school-building took place. Yet, as Mr Reid shows, Lancashire did not spend lavishly on education *per capita* of its population either in the prewar or the postwar years, and it continued to suffer, despite heavy commit-ments to the building or improvement of schools, from inadequate schools in inconvenient places. Its problems were compounded by the strong voluntary school element in the county's educational history, and the necessity to deal diplomatically or gently with the religious groups or opinions that were represented by these schools. Accordingly, the first requirement of a Lancashire chief education officer was that he should be a diplomat for the county authority, dealing tactfully with both the members in county district authorities and with church or diocesan bodies. A county so concerned with elaborate schemes of representation and delegation could not innovate with effect in other directions; this would have been impos-sible, and, in the circumstances, probably undesirable.

ELEMENTARY AND SECONDARY EDUCATION IN THE THIRTIES

In 1928, as was shown in Chapter 5,[2] the county had 541 voluntary schools, some, by government standards, with defective buildings. These were, of course, geared to the concept of 'elementary' education, to use the jargon of a past age, and many of the same buildings were adapted to infant and junior school (or primary school) work in the post-1944 years. The Church of England provided roughly seventy per cent of the voluntary schools, and the Roman Catholic Church a further twenty per cent. By contrast, the county authority owned some 190 schools, but far fewer of its buildings were of a kind considered as 'defective' by the Board of Education; this meant in practice that the managers of the voluntary schools had to seek means of improvement, and this was achieved by close co-operation between the county architect's department and the school managers concerned, with the result that, between 1925 and 1929, thirty-one schools, principally voluntary, were removed from the 'defective' list. Surprisingly few voluntary school committees of management or church bodies offered their schools to the county, however.

The campaign for the improvement of defective premises was coupled with a movement for the reorganisation of elementary education on the lines recommended by the Hadow Report, which stimulated an effort to provide more effective instruction for pupils of eleven years and over through the establishment of senior schools. By 1929, twenty-five such schools were drawing pupils from ninety-eight elementary schools, and such a simple fact in reality indicates a great deal of patient negotiation with a large number of voluntary school managers. Nor was it easy to find sites for these senior schools in a county broken into thirty-five elementary education districts (each with its own area committee), and the process of reorganisation was thereby protracted. Meanwhile, many of the elementary schools were small ones, with the result that a single senior school might have to accept pupils from up to a dozen of the former. In 1931, the administrative county (excluding the Part III authorities) contained 948 elementary school departments, each with separate head teachers, 447 of which had fewer than one hundred pupils in attendance, sixty-four between thirty and forty pupils and fifty-two fewer than thirty.[3] In rural areas the problem was especially acute, in that some children had to travel more than ten miles to their senior schools. Not surprisingly, parents objected, and even in towns it was difficult to find central sites for senior schools which included adequate space for playing fields. In 1931 the Education Committee commented on the substantial amount of time and energy expended on reorganisation.[4] It was, of course, unable to add that much of the work done, and the successful negotiation achieved, was the result of the patient endeavours of Percival Edward Meadon, the chief education officer, and his immediate colleagues.

Until 1932, reorganisation proceeded rapidly, so that by that year there were forty-three senior schools in existence, drawing pupils from 166 elementary schools. After 1932, and the crisis period, however, the pace slowed appreciably, and as is well known, the Government withdrew its fifty per cent grant towards the cost of new school buildings and cut teachers' salaries by ten per cent. These cuts remained in force until 1935, and their general effect, coupled with those of the exhortations of the Board of Education, brought about falls in the county's current expenditure on elementary education in 1932 and 1933.[5] Total expenditure on elementary education failed to rise above its 1929 level until 1936, when the worst effects of the economic crisis were abating. However, the general decline of the school-age population reduced the so-called capitation component in the elementary education grant received by local authorities; furthermore, rateable values were rising, so that the rate reduction factor in their education grants was at the same time falling. As a result, the proportion of government grant to the total education expenditure of local authorities was falling itself. The 1936 Education Act represented an attempt to remedy such anomalies and to stimulate Hadow-type reorganisation, for example by restoring the fifty per cent grant on all those new school buildings clearly connected with the former, and creating the 'special agreement' schools to assist the churches in reorganising their elementary schools; local authorities, under the terms of the 1936 Act, were empowered to make grants of up to seventy-five per cent of the cost of building new church senior schools.

By 1939 the County Council had approved in principle, with this assistance, the establishment of thirty-eight new voluntary senior schools of which only one (Huyton St Aloysius) was in operation,[6] and there were fifty-six senior schools in the administrative county altogether. The work of reorganisation was roughly half completed when progress was halted by the war. In this respect Lancashire lagged behind many other local authorities, as is plain from the fact that about two-thirds of all English and Welsh elementary schools had been 'reorganised' by 1939. However, few counties and county boroughs were so patiently punctilious in taking local opinion, however captious, into full account, and few had such a large church voluntary sector in the education field.

In the case of secondary education there was far more cause for a certain self-congratulation, even in 1929, when there were twenty-nine such schools financed or aided by the county accommodating over 13,000 pupils,[7] and when the Education Committee were looking with some pride at the results of a three-year building programme in this sector of their work. The years that followed showed further enterprise in an area that presented fewer diplomatic and religious problems. All but five of the county's secondary schools – and 'secondary', in the language of the thirties, meant 'grammar' – were directly maintained by the Council, with the result that there were fewer independent bodies to provide problems of negotiation. Reflecting the similar provision for the country as a whole, just under one-half of all the secondary school places in Lancashire were free places: in addition, the Council awarded junior scholarships incorporating both fees and a maintenance allowance; 1113 such scholarships, gained by competition in written and oral examinations, were awarded in 1929. However, in September 1932 the Government's crisis measures, already described, were followed by an apparent attack on opportunities for secondary education, and the Board of Education published Circular 1421, which instructed local authorities to raise grammar school fees to a minimum of nine guineas per annum and to make the provision of scholarships and free places dependent on the financial position of pupils' parents. Lancashire County Council, together with other north-western authorities, protested strongly. It was resolved that

> the Lancashire Education Committee deplores the proposed action of the Government in restricting the present limited opportunities for Secondary Education. The Committee has earnestly striven for many years to build up its present Secondary School system, and views with alarm the proposal contained in Circular 1421 which, in the opinion of the Committee will, in the County of Lancaster, in many cases debar children of suitable ability and attainments from receiving Secondary Education.[8]

It is interesting to note that the Education Committee, narrowly based socially as it indeed was, could cherish the notion of widened educational opportunity as much as it did. (There were those who felt even more strongly, like the Lancashire and Cheshire Colliery Deputies' Association, who said that the new proposals 'restore privileges to rich people at the expense of the poor'.[9]) The fact remains that Lancashire's large educated groups cherished the county's grammar schools, and this deeply founded tradition has to be taken into account when assessing its recent educational history. Local authorities, meanwhile, were forced to comply with the controversial circular, although Lancashire managed to negotiate a compromise with the Board of Education whereby the secondary school tuition fees were raised by up to two guineas per annum.[10] A means test was imposed, but the Education Committee retained the right to make special grants to parents of fee-paying pupils who were experiencing hardship and those of free-place pupils who were unable to afford essential school equipment.[11] The government measure was ill devised, and the total fee income of secondary schools in England and Wales actually fell between 1932 and 1935.

By 1933 the number of potential secondary school pupils (of eleven years of age) was falling as the effect of the postwar rise in the birthrate was passing; but, although new admissions to the county's secondary schools were accordingly falling, the total number of pupils nevertheless rose because of increased demand for secondary education and because juvenile unemployment encouraged many pupils to remain at school after fourteen years of age. Expenditure per county secondary pupil fell between 1930 and 1934 but recovered from the following year, remaining relatively steady until the outbreak of war. In September 1939, when all new school-building was suspended in consequence of the outbreak of war, there were fifty-one secondary schools in the county accommodating over 18,000 pupils. Forty-four of these schools were maintained by the Council. A fifty per cent increase in attendance at secondary schools had taken place during the difficult years of the thirties.

Throughout the period, there had been very little change in the curriculum followed by the secondary schools. The latter had remained narrowly academic and non-vocational since 1904, when the Board of Education had insisted on the orthodox grammar school curriculum as a condition of eligibility for grant. After the First World War, the School Certificate was becoming well established, and this examination contributed to the rigidity of the subject patterns followed.

Despite the advances made by the Education Committee, and their enthusiasm in defending what they considered to be an important and successful part of their service, secondary education was still a privilege available only to a minority of abler elementary school pupils, although it is important, in the interest of fairness, to add that, as early as 1927, free-place scholars had dominated the non-academic life of the county's grammar schools.[12] Within the grammar schools, the sixth-formers (sixty per cent of whom passed on to universities or to the study of science and technology in specialist institutions) were a small élite accounting for no more than ten per cent of all secondary pupils at any one time. Secondary education for all, and improved access to sixth forms, was not achieved until after the Second World War.

THE IMPACT OF THE WARTIME YEARS

A child growing up in the wartime years would remember the deviations from the norm: lessons conducted in shelters during air raid alerts, the digging for victory in school plots, and above all the experience of classes crowded with evacuees from 'Bradford, Crosby, London, Manchester, Liverpool, Salford and the Channel Islands', this between 1939 and 1942. After January 1941 there was a decline in the total of evacuees received in this way.[13] Although grammar schools at Stretford and Widnes were emptied of their pupils, much of the movement, especially of elementary children, was short-distance and temporary, so that some 1000 children were moved from Bootle and Liverpool into nearby Huyton,[14] where they were less at risk; and, at the outbreak of war, children from Litherland were evacuated to Blackpool and Thornton Cleveleys.[15] These measures led to much work on the part of Sir George Etherton's staff at County Hall, but evacuation was not pursued consistently, or for very long, as a policy.

Yet, despite such upheavals, the education sector of the county's work proceeded with an air approaching that of 'business as usual'. Edge Hill Training College, it is true, was obliged to transfer its personnel and trainees to Bingley for the duration of the war, but most of the other sections of the Committee's work, overseen by one of the most enlightened chairmen in the Council's history, Sir James Aitken, developed and even flourished. The numbers of secondary school pupils increased steadily, as did those for technical evening classes after a setback in 1939–40, and in 1942 it was remarked that 'the increase of over 2000 evening students is especially gratifying as overtime work and the black-out interfere with evening attendance':[16] meanwhile, the nine junior technical schools continued to operate satisfactorily, and were given considerable stimulus by the feeling that the services of the trainees were required in industry and by the community. Even the overburdened elementary schoolteachers were given aid and succour by a steady inflow of certificated trainees, if also incommoded by the shortage of male teachers at most levels. This inflow did not of course affect the extreme inconvenience of – as could often happen – teaching overcrowded classes in temporary hutments. The County Library played its part in maintaining morale by making books easily available to soldiers and airmen and through a multiplicity of branch library activities,[17] and the county's adult education movement, working with the Universities of Manchester and Liverpool, established regional councils for adult education for HM Forces,[18] while discussion and drama groups in the north Lancashire villages seem to have flourished as never before. It is an interesting sidelight on the social psychology and history of wartime that a rally of men's discussion groups could meet in the little industrial community of Galgate to be addressed by J. B. Priestley on 'Vital Democracy'.[19]

Out of wartime conditions and aspirations grew a remarkable practical scheme of delegation in Lancashire, the great plan for the divisional administration of education, which was an immediate consequence of the Butler Act of 1944. In the July of that year, Sir Percy Meadon put forward proposals for partitioning the county into forty-five divisions plus a single Excepted District. In as much as Lancashire already had twenty-seven Part III authorities of widely varying sizes, thirty-four local committees for elementary education and 106 committees for higher education (which service was also supervised by county Part III bodies), it might have been argued that the newly proposed system represented a tidying-up process. There can be no doubt that delegation to divisional executives, or to local committees after the 1902 Act, was a reaction to pressure from school board members in the earlier case and from the councillors in Part III authorities in the later one. Part III of the first schedule of the 1944 Education Act provided for the setting up of divisional executives in so far as they might be 'conducive to efficient and convenient administration'. Lancashire's scheme, like others, had to be submitted for ministerial approval, and each county of the 109 districts had to be consulted by Sir Percy and his staff.[20] Circular 5, issued by the Ministry of Education in September 1944, recognised the need for flexibility, but suggested that divisions with populations below 60,000 were unlikely to constitute satisfactory administrative units, especially for secondary education, and that the executives themselves should consist of twenty to thirty members, the majority of which should be nominees from district councils within the division.

Lancashire's district councils submitted their observations by 30 November 1944;[21] the county's massive scheme was already on the drawing board by the following January, and may be seen, even after subsequent transmutations, as Sir Percy Meadon's monument. The very large number of divisions reflected a desire at that time to avoid conflict with the former Part III authorities, and it may be noted that eight of the latter (Widnes, Morecambe and Heysham, Lancaster, Accrington, Stretford, Eccles, Ashton and Nelson) applied for Excepted District status under the 1944 Act. Only Widnes and Stretford in fact received such recognition, although the Council, acting diplomatically, delayed making any observations to the Minister until the October of that year.[22] Stretford received Excepted District status largely by virtue of its substantial elementary school population, well in excess of 6000 (although the Ministry preferred 7000 as a minimum).

Another powerful argument for the proposed extreme fragmentation of Lancashire's education system lay in the existence of its district education offices and staffs, all thoroughly tested since the early years of the century; the new scheme in fact grafted easily on to the older administrative system, a point made to the writers by a senior Lancashire official with much experience in the local service.[23] However, a main concern of post-1944 delegation to divisions was that of putting, in each case, primary and secondary education under one controlling body, a matter of principle put forward in the 1943 White Paper, *Educational Reconstruction.* However, the Lancashire scheme proposed too many divisions to be acceptable to the Minister, who finally succeeded in reducing the number of the latter from forty-five to thirty-five, with the two Excepted Districts. Nevertheless, most of the divisions had populations smaller than the 60,000 recommended by the Government. The approved scheme represented a compromise between the use of existing local authority boundaries and efficiency in administration, and there can be little doubt that it had its genesis in diplomatic requirements as well as long previous experience.[24] This was in 1951, after Sir Percy Meadon's successor, A. L. Binns, had been asked by the Ministry of Education in 1948 to cut down the number of divisional executives far more sharply; in consequence, the county and

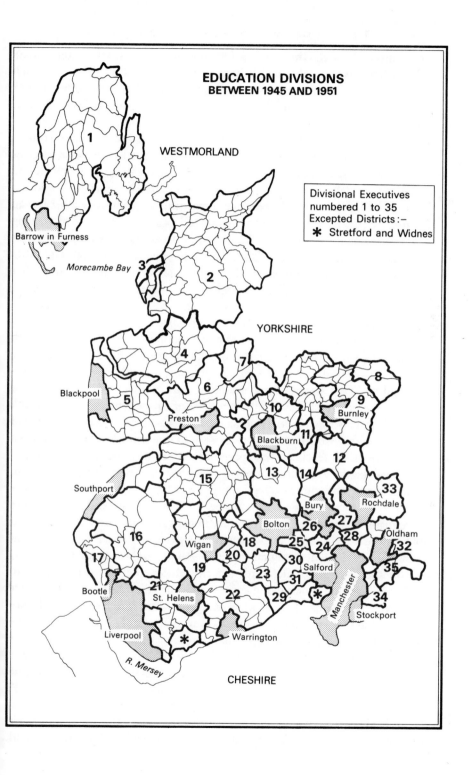

EDUCATION DIVISIONS
BETWEEN 1945 AND 1951

WESTMORLAND

1

Barrow in Furness

Morecambe Bay

3

2

Divisional Executives
numbered 1 to 35
Excepted Districts :—
✱ Stretford and Widnes

YORKSHIRE

Blackpool

4

7

8

5

6

9
Burnley

Preston

10

11

Blackburn

12

13

14

33

Southport

15

Bury

Rochdale

Bolton

26

27

Oldham

16

Wigan

18

25

28

32

20

24

35

17

19

23

30

Salford

31

Bootle

21

22

29

✱

34

St. Helens

Manchester

Stockport

Liverpool

✱

Warrington

R. Mersey

CHESHIRE

the Ministry between them reduced the number of divisions to twenty-four. This scheme was notable for the fact that it brought down the number of executives catering for areas with populations of under 50,000 from nineteen to two. Thereafter there were only minor adjustments in the system, and these are referred to below.

The actual working of a specimen executive of the post-1951 type is examined more closely in a succeeding section, but it will be in place to discuss the functions of such bodies. Circular 5 (1944) had not recommended any delegation of responsibility to executives more revolutionary than existing Lancashire practice regarding district committees (see Chapter 5); further advice came from the Local Government Manpower Committee of 1951, which distinguished between functions unsuitable for delegation (further education, site acquisition, financial control, staff establishments and bulk purchase), those suitable for conditional delegation and those suitable for absolute delegation. Those in the intermediate category, whereby the county authority retained certain controls, included payment of teacher's salaries, school health, special education, school maintenance and repairs, construction of new schools and provision of milk and meals. It is worth noticing that Lancashire's executives exercised most or all of the powers listed in the latter two categories, those unconditionally wielded covering wages of non-teaching staff, nursery schools, the youth service, evening institutes and the purchase of equipment and stores. School attendance had been a local concern since the days following the 1902 Act, and it is also interesting to note that the county's practice in the appointment of teachers was perpetuated from the earlier period; no executive could appoint headmasters or headmistresses without special arrangement with the county authority, although in the case of teachers, applications were received through the divisional officer, and appointments were made by managers or governors 'in consultation with the headmaster or headmistress, subject to confirmation by the divisional executive'. The county LEA alone determined the dismissal of teachers in its own schools, but in the case of ultimate and extreme difference between the county body and the divisional one, disputes could be referred to the Minister.[25]

In several respects, Lancashire's delegatory activities went beyond more general practice, and this was the case in matters of finance and further education. War-induced staff shortages in the Treasurer's Department led to delegation of the power to settle accounts to divisional financial officers (in fact, the chief financial officers of the non-county boroughs, asked to act in that capacity); and when this power was returned to the county treasurer in 1951, considerable residual powers remained with those divisions having a district or borough authority large enough to deal with, for example, the calculation and payment of teachers' salaries. Again,

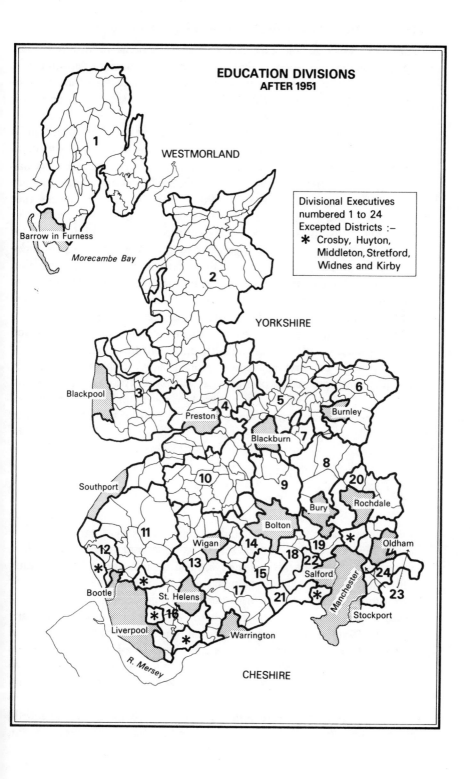

EDUCATION DIVISIONS
AFTER 1951

WESTMORLAND

1

Barrow in Furness

Morecambe Bay

Divisional Executives
numbered 1 to 24
Excepted Districts :-
✱ Crosby, Huyton,
Middleton, Stretford,
Widnes and Kirby

2

YORKSHIRE

Blackpool
3

Preston 4   5   6
Burnley

Blackburn 7

8

Southport

10   9   20
Bury   Rochdale

11   Bolton

12   Wigan   14   19   Oldham

✱   18   22   ✱
Bootle   13   15   Salford   24
St. Helens   17   21   ✱   23

✱ 16   Warrington   Stockport

Liverpool

R. Mersey

CHESHIRE

Lancashire was the first authority to have a scheme approved by the Minister for the delegation of functions relating to further education, and the county was certainly among those most willing to distribute powers to second-tier bodies in a bold (and ultimately successful) manner.[26]

Above all, these bodies, whatever their degree of ultimate authority in the long run, stood for considerable involvement on the part of local communities. Very wisely, the third schedule of the schemes of divisional administration laid down that 'Representatives of the Press shall be admitted to the meetings of a divisional executive.' It should be added that the executives' duties were augmented during the next two decades, a sure sign that they had considerable administrative and other utility, and that at least one of these duties could always be counted upon to rivet the attention of a curious press and of indignant parents. Hence, in 1949–50 the executives took a degree of responsibility for the secondary school selection examination,[27] a task that was retained by them during several phases of experimentation in the fifties and sixties. Their social and geographical nearness to schools and their heads made the executives' offices indispensible to the conduct of choice by assessment and school records. Much later, the executives played a crucial although subordinate part in determining schemes for comprehensive education. Finally, it should be borne in mind that they operated as part of what was basically a three-tier system, in that many councillors were also school managers and governors, with a very real personal involvement in local affairs. More is said on this subject below.

THE POSTWAR UPHEAVAL

The senior schools of the age of Hadow were, for the most part, candidates for the function of the modern school as conceived by the Butler Act; and under the terms of this Act the LEA had the task of providing for each child a suitable primary and secondary education according to age, ability and aptitude. There is more than a touch of wartime idealism in the Council's view of a new 'senior or modern school' which it proposed in February 1945 to build at Garstang to 'provide accommodation for 400 children when the school leaving age is raised to sixteen'. The school 'would be a multilateral school, which would provide, in addition to a good general education, for specialised work or prevocational training in commercial and agricultural occupations....'[28] There was, too, a plan for purchase of a site at Huyton for 'secondary and technical schools'.[29] The linking of the secondary and the technical together was to be, in practice, very largely abortive in the county at large, while the idealism that surrounded the modern school was to be dissipated in the next ten years.

The most important immediate postwar action of the Education Committee was the drafting of a Development Plan in 1946–7, which in turn meant taking stock of needs and educational accommodation on a vast scale, in the face of a shortage of building materials which ordained that new school provision had to proceed in terms of the strictest priorities. The mounting of the plan was a complex operation involving consultation with local planning committees throughout the county, and it rested partially on recommendations from divisional executives as to the siting of new schools; it also embodied the results of consultations with other Lancashire LEAs and with diocesan authorities. The committee commended work in an atmosphere of improvisation, and, sometimes, discouragement: the raising of the school-leaving age to fifteen years on 1 April 1947 necessitated the provision, by the Ministry of Education, of HORSA* huts to give extra classroom accommodation, 140 such huts being provided, some to remain in use until the present decade. For the rest, shortages of materials hindered even the building of essential schools – only one 'extremely urgent' case was at this time recognised in Lancashire, as belonging to the 'operational' category laid down by the Ministry of Education – the Girls' Secondary Modern School at Litherland.[30]

Thereafter much in Lancashire's educational history was determined by a continuous growth of population in new housing areas along its borders, and also, as throughout the country at large, by the postwar 'baby boom' which struck the primary schools in the mid-1950s. This dual problem kept the central education office in Preston, and the divisions, under continual strain; and it should be borne in mind that voluntary school managements, which controlled the majority of primary schools in Lancashire, expressed strong views, sometimes through other bodies, as to the siting of new selective secondary (grammar and technical) schools, and caused the Development Plan to be modified by 1949–50.[31] For the rest, the growing child population was predicted with sound working accuracy during the next period (1950–5), and the Education Committee can be acquitted of any failure to assess a developing situation, especially in the primary sector. In 1952 it was clearly seen that the rate of primary school building was far too slow to meet any actual or likely demand, and 'church halls, Sunday schools, disused schools, huts and a variety of other kinds of premises' were converted for school use.[32] Meanwhile, the raising of the school-leaving age created problems at the other end of the age range, especially in rural areas, where there were still 'unreorganised' or all-age schools, and where the

* Hutted Operation for the Raising of the School Leaving Age.

children staying on had to be transported to the nearest secondary school.[33]

The chief officer who bore the brunt of these problems, Arthur Lennon Binns, succeeded Sir Percy Meadon, a gentlemanly and persuasive administrator, in 1945. Binns had been chief education officer of the West Riding from 1936, and a member of the Fleming Committee on the Public Schools;[34] and, as this had been one of the enquiries leading up to and foreshadowing the 1944 Education Act, Binns was very much *au fait* with the thinking of this period, as was Sir James Aitken, also a member of the Fleming Committee. Aitken was one of the foundation-layers of the post-1944 reorganisation in Lancashire and Binns's first chairman; and it may be that the chance association of the two brought A. L. Binns to Lancashire, where the latter quickly made a reputation as a strong if rather touchy administrator. He was sober, serious, blunt and fair to his immediate subordinates, although he was considered to be 'difficult' by those in other departments with which he dealt, including the Clerk's. His was not a period of innovation or experiment so much as one of massive growth and sheer hard work; possibly, too, one of disappointed hopes, as the modern schools so patently failed to win any parity of esteem with Lancashire's much-cherished grammar schools. Binns himself, in spite of the regard in which both he and his authority were held, did not win appreciable influence with the Ministry of Education, and a number of reasons for this are discernible. At the time of his appointment as minister of education, George Tomlinson had been a Lancashire county councillor, and he was known to be determined to give his native county no favours. Moreover, Tomlinson was much liked by both politicians and civil servants, and his firm attitude to his fellow Lancastrians may have led to quiet amusement and some emulation. Unfortunately, Binns did not easily win allies, nor was there close alliance with a powerful neighbouring authority like the West Riding; and by this quirk of circumstance the two greatest education authorities in the north rarely or never made concerted representations to Curzon Street. It remains true that Lancashire's educational leaders had to work hard to make their cases to the Ministry, and had to do so far beyond George Tomlinson's time. It will be noticed that this contrasts with the record of nearly every other major department in the Lancashire county authority; in this one great field of education, the responsible leaders felt that they were discriminated against by central government.

In fact, Lancashire needed all the assistance and encouragement it could find. Eventually the Ministry's officials began to realise that this north-western county did indeed require rather more than a regular trimming of long lists of school-building and extension projects, although such a realisation dawned only on the eve of what was virtually a population explosion in the secondary schools (1954–7), complicated by vast problems of overspill in areas of new settlement. As the 1953–4 Report of the Education Committee put it, with a dispassionate air that belied the feelings of its leaders:

> ... in framing the Building Programme for 1954–5, your Committee had in mind the great need to increase secondary school accommodation.... At the same time they took into account the demand for additional places in the three areas of Kirkby, Worsley and Middleton.... In these areas houses are being erected at a rate of just over 3000 a year. Your Committee, therefore, sent a deputation to the Ministry of Education and obtained from the Ministry an increase of approximately 33½ per cent in the allocation of money for the Primary and Secondary School Building Programme for 1954–5 over the amount usually allocated....[35]

For the time being the lesson had gone home, and in the 1956–7 building programme the Ministry 'were allowing primary schools to be built to serve new housing areas' and – a real note of triumph – 'secondary schools [are] to be built to cater for expected increases in roll and to effect the reorganisation of rural all-age schools'.[36]

Sir Arthur Binns – knighted in 1954 – was succeeded in 1957 by his deputy Percy Lord, with his reputation assured. During his relatively few years at the helm, a vast administrative machine had grown more vast, and yet had surrendered none of its relative cheapness or efficiency, while the experiment of delegation to the divisions was an almost unqualified success, if one does indeed make the single important qualification that every important decision had to be filtered through those sometimes perverse bodies, the divisional executives. The appointment of a deputy as new chief officer, meanwhile, often thought to be an indicator of administrative conservatism, was becoming, in the cases of Lancashire officers, not so much a temptation as a presumed necessity – only a man brought up in the machinery, and in the tradition, could easily lead it.

SECONDARY MODERN SCHOOLS

A real attempt was made to give these schools a sense of status and purpose. Many a conscientious sociologist of education will now see the incidental means of achieving these things as mere embellishment –

school visits, libraries, commercial courses, the teaching of a second language, training in citizenship, the establishment of dramatic and operatic activities – but they were not then seen as such by dedicated heads and hopeful experimenters. Pupils were even encouraged to study the history and traditions of their own localities, something often denied to the earnestly academic labourers of the grammar schools; and in this connection the work of the Lancashire Record Office should be mentioned, and especially that of the late Miss S. S. Tollit. Parent–teacher associations began to represent a new kind of involvement in local education. Near the end of his term of service, Sir Arthur Binns observed that the schools were 'continuing to develop on the social side, prefects, house systems, school councils, varied school societies and the production of school magazines are pleasing features to be found in many schools'.[37] He did, however, add that it was needful 'to raise the status of the modern school in the eyes of the parent and the general public'; and it is noticeable that this was being done in 1957 through 'an increasing number of schools [which] have entered pupils for the G.C.E.'[38] In other words, the modern school was seeking to emulate its academic partner, the grammar school, and was admitting the need to provide tangible qualifications an an aid to vocational advancement and social opportunity. Yet there was much dedicated or well-meaning experiment aimed at enriching the work of modern schoolchildren, including the backward or totally non-academic.

Under Percy Lord, this general policy of raising the modern schools through academic achievement continued steadily, and was given a new impetus in 1959 when the Education Committee decided that all children in the selective 'border belt' of the eleven-plus examination should be offered places in schools that were undertaking five-year courses leading to the GCE. There were 191 secondary modern schools in the county in 1960, and 61 of them entered GCE candidates in that year, with 705 successful pupils in all. The pressure of external examinations led to small upper-stream classes in these schools, and, since a good many of the latter were also sincerely concerned for their backward pupils,* to the extent of placing them in deliberately small 'C' or 'D' streams, there was overcrowding in the middle streams.[39] It is interesting to note, too, that the emphasis of these modern school GCE subjects was decidedly academic, a discovery that has, and had, worrying implications for a development in county policy which Lord himself had strongly advocated soon after taking office – namely, that of dismissing the secondary tech-

---

* This is clearly indicated in the annual *Bulletin* of the Association of Headmasters and Headmistresses of Lancashire County Secondary Modern Schools (1953–63), for the use of which we are indebted to Mr J. H. Sutton.

nical school as a method of bridging the gap between modern and grammar school education, and instead arguing that there should be some common ground, perhaps of a quasi-technical kind, as between the two established types of school. The headmasters of both types of school were to establish liaison with colleges of further education.

The Lancashire chief officer was, in this way, responding to current thinking as stimulated by the White Paper on Technical Education (1956), while at the same time recognising a *fait accompli*, a general unwillingness to experiment widely with the 'secondary tech'.[40] Regrettably, an examination of the data set out by the chief education officer at this time shows that even this modest policy for bridging the esteem gap was unrealistic, for many of the county's modern schools lacked adequate woodwork, metalwork, science or commercial training facilities.[41] Percy Lord in January 1959 politely challenged the divisional executives to set about pooling or organising their resources in such a way as to overcome these problems; meanwhile, the broaching of such a subject as this tended to give added point to discussion on greater transferability between the secondary modern school and the grammar school, a policy favoured by the Labour Party (in power in the county in 1958–61) as a temporary alternative to comprehensive education, already experimentally established in the Kirkby overspill area. There is no doubt that political cross-pressures in the Council could influence administrative measures marginally in this way, but the purely local variety probably did little to influence the general shape of educational development in the long run.[42]

In the secondary modern schools themselves, heads had insured against the effects of failure in the GCE by encouraging some young people to take the Union of Lancashire and Cheshire Institutes (ULCI) secondary school examination, and in due course (in 1966) the modern schools were able to take advantage of the freedom granted by their power to design CSE work and projects. In that year, for the first time, 190 such schools entered 5294 pupils for the CSE, out of 209 such schools in the administrative county, but a total of 193 hung on grimly to the idea that the GCE represented real respectability, entering 7398 pupils in the same year. A steadily increasing proportion had in fact been submitting candidates, and in this instance 5121 had some kind of success, about half of them in one subject only. A small but increasing proportion of modern school pupils, a total of 190 in all, were actually taking Advanced Level subjects, a remarkable testimony to determined advances on a very narrow front.[43] By this time, ironically, events were in train that would terminate the independent existence of large numbers of county modern schools.

THE SELECTION DEBATE

There had long been, in Lancashire as a whole, a hard-headed appreciation of the social and economic worth of a grammar school education.
Indeed, it was probably the depth of this regard for the career significance
of the grammar school that prompted, paradoxically, a questioning of
the conduct and nature of the secondary school selection examination.
The divisional executives of the county had been, as we have seen,
entrusted with the conduct of the eleven-plus selection tests, and during
Sir Arthur Binns's period of office critical opinion was already filtering
through to the central department at Preston. In 1954–5 'the [Education]
Committee considered several suggestions for modifying the selection procedure',[44] and some two years later, before Sir Arthur's retirement, consideration 'was given to the systems of allocation used by several other
Education Authorities ... and it was decided to set up a special sub-
committee to investigate and report on the possibility of making greater
use of school records supplemented by internal examinations and intelligence tests....'[45] This use of school records became established, and in
1960 the Education Committee decided to dispense with the selection
examination as such, but to use instead a form of assessment based on
three pieces of evidence: namely, the primary school head's own assessment
of the child, the child's performance in a number of objective tests, and
his primary school record as a whole. The work of organising selection
was done by divisional panels composed mainly of the heads of schools,
and these panels found that, while the anxiety element of the eleven-
plus was reduced, primary schools still set too much store on preparation
for the fourth-year objective tests.[46] In other words, a subject not named,
but in effect called 'intelligence', still haunted primary school staffs. The
ultimate act of selection remained.[47]

THE COMPREHENSIVE SCHOOL MOVEMENT

This campaign for comprehensive education commenced life as a
political issue which came to divide the two main parties in the council
chamber, and the contest was at its keenest in the period of Labour rule
between 1958 and 1961. However, this period was not only one of great
population growth in the overspill areas, but also one in which the
original primary age group 'bulge' was entering the county secondary

schools – a fact well illustrated in Table 13.2 below. Accordingly, the then dominant party in the Education Committee, led by Alderman Mrs Katherine Fletcher, was able to argue that very large multi-entry form schools solved adminstrative and population problems, besides introducing the proposed answer to the injustices of eleven-plus selection, comprehensive education. Before its defeat at the polls, therefore, the Labour Group had produced a revised Development Plan for secondary education allowing for '55 schools which were of six, seven or eight forms of entry in size and [which] would house ultimately between 900 and 1350 boys and girls. These schools were of a size hitherto unknown in Lancashire and came midway between the compact and most frequently designed three-form entry school and the large and more dispersed 12-form entry Comprehensive Schools of Kirkby.'[48] The county's education officer and advisers were making a somewhat uneasy study of the problems of the larger-than-average school, together with HMI, and, perhaps because the subject was a politically contentious one, discussion of comprehensive education does not appear, explicitly or at length, in the Annual Reports of the Education Committee until 1965 (although discussion had, of course, taken place in committee). Yet there were four comprehensive schools in the county by 1960, all in the overspill and border areas, and all with an average of well over a thousand pupils apiece; and Lancaster's Our Lady's RC Secondary School, also a comprehensive, was approved in 1960 and opened in 1964.

Labour returned to power, locally and nationally, in 1964, and on 20 July of that year the Education Committee resolved 'that after full consultation with all interests involved, a comprehensive system of education should be introduced into these divisions of the administrative county where it is possible'. The Department of Education and Science (DES), as the Ministry was now called, had issued its famous circular 10/65, calling for the submission by LEAs of plans for reorganisation of secondary education in the long term, and if reorganisation was not to be introduced before 1970 in the short term also. Once again the onus was thrown back to Lancashire's divisions, which had to set up working parties to decide which of three possible schemes might be practicable: the full comprehensive school catering for the age range 11–18, a two-tier system of junior and senior high schools, and the comprehensive with the 11–16 age range combined with a sixth form college. The divisions had to make up their minds by 31 October 1964. Meanwhile, the chief officer was obliged to enter into negotiations with the Anglican and Roman Catholic diocesan authorities, who not only had a direct involvement in many scores of voluntary schools, but who also felt their interests to be much affected by reorganisation. He remarked feelingly that 'for an Authority responsible for an area as complex as Lancashire, to undertake this operation is most difficult and delicate'.[49] The majority of Lancashire primary schools were still voluntary, and so were an increasing number of secondary schools (see Table 13.1). The pullers of the levers of power in central government did not, of course, take such local niceties into full account, and Percy Lord's last few years, terminating in his death in December 1968 just at his retirement and shortly after his knighthood in the January of that year, were ones of great strain.

As the LEA General Purposes Sub-Committee Minutes show for 12 September 1966, there was still a deep feeling of grievance that the County Council were 'not receiving their full allocation of the total national building programme', in view of the probable growth of the Lancashire school population, 'believed to be greater in total then [in] any other local authority area'. It was against this difficult background (a deputation went to the Ministry in August 1966) that the comprehensive schools programme had to develop. The Ministry claimed that Lancashire was more than fairly treated.

By the end of December 1966, all the twenty-nine divisional executives and Excepted Districts had submitted long-term schemes for consideration by the Education Committee, and sixteen of these schemes had been approved by the DES. Of these schemes, the majority (ten) had proposed a system of comprehensives covering the entire 11–18 age range. Meanwhile, a Special Sub-Committee for Reorganisation, under the chairmanship of Alderman M. J. Moore, had to take account not only of the suitability of local schools for becoming parts of a larger whole, but of the possible effects of the raising of the school-leaving age to sixteen. One of its early reports remarked that 'under a system of delegation to Divisional Executives, a delay ... is inevitable, but this is the only way to ensure general agreement to a policy which will determine the shape of secondary education in any area, probably at least for the rest of this century. . . .'[50] Some delay in agreement occurred in otherwise sympathetic localities which feared that building development would not move rapidly enough to accommodate elaborate plans – e.g. in Division 16, covering Kirkby and Prescot areas, where there was already experience of the comprehensive principle in action, and where it was thought that hasty plans 'might do the ideal of comprehensive education grave damage in the eyes of the public'.[51] In other areas there was lack of real enthusiasm, as in the Fylde (Division 3), which stated its opinion that 'the introduction of comprehensive education in the Division is impracticable at present, but, if the county council insist upon a plan of comprehensive education, they favour a plan catering for pupils of the age-range 11–18'.[52] Later

TABLE 13.1
Numbers of Schools in Administrative Lancashire (by types), 1949–70
(as at December of year given)

	1949	1954	1956	1960	1963	1966	1970
Nursery	22	41	42	42	43	43	43
Special	7	19	21	25	33	35	36
Primary							
(Voluntary)							
Aided[1]	n.s.	586	584	574	675	667	651
Controlled[2]	n.s.	105	111	126	141	140	145
Sub-total	697	691	695	700	816	807	796
County	267	298	305	320	439	447	496
Secondary							
(i) Modern							
(Voluntary)							
Aided	n.s.	n.s.	20	18	26	30	32
Controlled	n.s.	n.s.	—	—	—	1	1
Special agreement[3]	n.s.	n.s.	7	25	31	31	25
Sub-total	18	19	27	43	57	62	58
County	110	117	131	148	156	147	117
(ii) Grammar							
(Voluntary)							
Aided	n.s.	3	4	6	6	6	6
Controlled	n.s.	8	8	8	8	8	7
Sub-total	6	11	12	14	14	14	13
Transitionally assisted	7	1	—	—	—	—	—
County	32	35	37	38	39	39	37
(iii) Comprehensive							
Aided	—	—	—	2	2	3	4
Controlled	—	—	—	—	—	—	1
Special agreement	—	—	—	—	—	—	3
County	—	—	1	2	2	2	24
Sub-total	—	—	1	4	4	5	32
(iv) Secondary technical							
County	13	13	13	11	4	2	—
Total schools	1179	1244	1284	1343	1603	1601	1628

[1] In the case of an aided school, the voluntary body running it appointed two-thirds of the managers or governors, who were responsible for the school building itself, towards the repair or extension of which the state made grants of up to four-fifths. The managers appointed teachers.

[2] In the case of a controlled school, two-thirds of the managers or governors were appointed by the local authority, and the managers appointed teachers.

[3] A special agreement was a voluntary controlled secondary school where the local authority had paid between a half and three-quarters of the cost of a new building, or major extension.

evidence makes clear that local direct grant grammar schools were offering resistance.[53]

Yet, interestingly enough, political or educational prejudices did not always play a dominant role, and the first division to be 'reorganised' was the relatively conservative one of North Lonsdale (No. 1), which had numerous young technologists and their families and a fairly high proportion of graduates. This division had its scheme approved by the DES in October 1966, and the former provided for the transformation of the well established and reputable Ulverston Grammar School into an 11–18 comprehensive, with three 11–16 local schools working in close relationship where necessary.[54]

By 1968 the number of comprehensive schools in administrative Lancashire had risen to ten, and by December 1971 to thirty-seven, although not all of the latter were county-owned.[55] Where so many grammar and modern schools remained – 53 of the former and 209 of the latter in 1966 – then the basic problem of selection and transfer remained also. This was done through a system, in operation in that year, whereby the already familiar divisional panels looked at heads' assessments and the primary school records of the individual pupil with the result of a verbal reasoning test. In autumn 1966 6900 children were chosen for grammar schools by these means, as against 21,887 who were sent to 'other' secondary schools.[56]

As we have seen, the modern schools were determinedly catering for their more ambitious or academic pupils. One of the side-effects of re-organisation, as well as of population pressure, was to make modern schools themselves appreciably larger; indeed, according to the county's own statistics for pupils and teachers in such schools, these had grown in size from an average of 432 pupils in 1963 to 538 in 1970, partly the result of amalgamations as schools progressed towards comprehensive status.[57] Their child populations increased, meanwhile, in another up-surge in school numbers in 1968–9, although the numbers of such schools decreased in the late sixties. The primary schools saw a relatively massive boom in numbers, meanwhile (see Table 13.2), and many of them, re-grettably, were still inadequate in the middle and late sixties, this despite a great building drive on the part of the Education Committee which by 1966 had caused 390 new schools to be built. Its Development Plan, however, provided for 1600 of all types, and an occasional revelation shows the startling contrasts between the beautifully planned primary or modern schools set out according to DES specifications,[58] and brought to reality by the skill of the County Architect's Department, and the county infant and junior schools which had to be left aside as other priorities loomed. We read in the Minutes of the Education Committee's

TABLE 13.2
*Lancashire Education Authority Total Pupils and Staff in
Primary and Secondary Schools, all Divisions, 1946–71*

	Primary Pupils	Primary Staff	Approx. Pupil/ Teacher Ratio	Secondary (Modern and tech.) Pupils	Staff	Pupil/ Teacher Ratio	Grammar Pupils	Ratio (samples)
1946	183,208	5,892	31.1	27,725	1,344	20.6	22,252	21·5
1947	189,560	6,111	31.0	36,666	1,653	22.2	20,772	19·7
1948	193,053	6,184	31.2	46,132	1,864	24.7	20,586	
1949	193,450	6,314	30.6	46,271	1,937	23.9	21,581	
1950	196,170	6,454	30.4	47,642	2,019	23.6	21,364	
1951	202,756	6,548	30.9	48,221	2,072	23.3	21,559	
1952	210,266	6,731	31.2	48,807	2,158	22.6	22,080	
1953	214,375	6,873	31.2	52,001	2,267	22.9	22,474	18·7
1954	218,208	7,128	30.6	55,494	2,416	22.9	23,159	18·7
1955	219,072	7,200	30.4	61,889	2,654	23.3	23,968	
1956	221,680	7,333	30.2	66,163	2,869	23.0	24,660	
1957	220,923	7,368	30.0	70,789	3,112	22.7	25,791	
1958	213,073	7,257	29.4	80,573	3,315	24.3	27,955	18·3
1959	207,632	7,174	28.9	85,381	3,577	23.8	29,529	
1960	203,276	7,086	28.7	92,694	4,033	22.9	30,792	19·8
1961	203,636	7,054	28.9	96,096	4,301	22.3	31,855	
1962	205,429	7,053	29.1	92,678	4,264	21.7	32,568	19·3
1963	208,989	7,154	29.2	91,989	4,524	20.3	35,584	
1964	214,060	7,277	29.4	91,405	4,559	20.0	32,951	17.7
1965	220,606	7,421	29.7	92,411			32,840	
1966	230,293	7,681	30.0	92,682			32,978	
1967	240,122	8,039	29.9	93,529	(Comprehensive		32,543	
1968	249,171	8,360	29.8	91,930	schools		31,530	
1969	258,648	8,881	29.1	94,024	introduced during		31,980	
1970	267,049	9,378	28.5	93,879	this period.)		32,035	
1971	273,544	10,034	27.3	93,941			31,518	
1972	n.s.	n.s.	—	79,322			25,373	

Notes
These figures are general totals made available by the Education Department of the Lancashire authority. The teacher–pupil ratios are calculated from them, but differ slightly from 'official' figures. In January 1961, the pupil–teacher ratio, as calculated by the Education Officer's staff, was 29.7 for primary schools and 20.7 for secondary schools. Judging by the data used for these figures, the above totals relate to all teaching staffs, including temporary and unqualified teachers. The Ministry's quota for allocation of teachers for the county was based (1961) on an overall pupil–teacher ratio of 26 (cf. Minutes Primary and Secondary Education Sub-Committee, 13 March 1961, and also Minutes of the same committee, 13 April 1959).

The 1963 primary school ratio was 29.9, which is almost consistent with the figures here given, and the 1964 one was 30.2, which is not, and which was evidently based on slightly different figures for 'the beginning of the Spring Term'. The secondary school overall figures, respectively 19.7 and 19.4, do not differ greatly from the ratios given here (Minutes of the Primary and Secondary Education Sub-Committee, 15 June 1964).

General Purposes Committee (22 May 1967) of Middleton Thornham St John's CE School (Controlled), situated in Samuel Bamford's native countryside and accommodated in 'an early 19th century church', a three-class school for eighty children, and meant to continue as such in the original Development Plan. There was no indoor sanitation, and one classroom had recently been closed as dangerous. Leigh Bedford CE School (Aided) had been erected prior to 1875, but the divisional executive and managers decided in 1967 that 'the school must be retained to serve the surrounding population'.[59] J. S. B. Boyce, the incoming chief education officer in that year and one who was, like his former chief Percy Lord, well experienced in Lancashire ways at the time of his appointment, had plenty of diplomatic problems before him, and had to face anomalies of the kind indicated. But his diplomacy brought the regional Catholic Church into further comprehensive education; they agreed to establish such schools as Maghull (1968) and Skelmersdale (1969).[60]

The Lancashire educational scene, then, exhibited almost as much diversity as the national one, and – statistical matters apart – it is unwise to generalise about it. It contained some schools of much excellence, and some of far lower quality. Its administrators did much to improve the environment in which teaching and education take place, and they would have done far more had national conditions allowed.

COUNCILLORS AND THE THREE-TIER SYSTEM

Administrators kept the machinery of education running from hour to hour, of course, but councillors were responsible for it to the wider world, and their involvements in the work of decision-making and supervision could be extremely arduous. Elected representatives in Lancashire operated at three levels: firstly, on the Education Committee and on several of its ten or more sub-committees; secondly, as members of divisional executives (and often on their sub-committees); and thirdly, as school managers or governors or as council representatives on associated bodies like youth employment committees. So heavy were such commitments likely to be that some county councillors virtually confined their efforts to Education Committee work. On the other hand, a councillor who had undertaken a large number of school manager-ships might not serve on quite as many county Education Committee sub-committees as another who was more lightly loaded at that level, or even as someone who was involved in other county standing committees.

Nevertheless, county councillors might be quite heavily loaded at two or even three levels. In 1967, Councillor R. C. Archibald served on five sub-committees of the Education Committee as well as on the main body, and was also a member of the Public Health and Housing Committee and the Police Committee; in addition, he was an active member of No. 1 Divisional Executive (for the Furness area). Mrs E. W. Muldoon in 1967 served on three central Education Committee sub-committees, and was a manager or governor of at least twelve schools and other educational establishments, principally in the Eccles–Swinton area; she was also a Council representative (for the same area) on the No. 22 Divisional Executive. Another woman member, Mrs E. Jones, representing the Lancaster district, similarly served at three levels. Such examples could be multiplied, although few members did as much committee work at the school and college level as Mrs Muldoon, who had a special interest in Catholic schools.[61]

Most of the prominent members of the Education Committee took some kind of leading part in the divisional executives of their own electoral areas; examples are Mrs W. Kettle at Westhoughton (No. 14 Division), Sir Fred Longworth at Leigh (No. 15), J. Selwyn Jones at Newton-le-Willows (No. 17), H. Nevin at Heywood (No. 20), Mrs K. Lowe at Urmston (No. 21) and J. R. Hull and D. H. Elletson at No. 3. Alderman F. Worsley served on two neighbouring divisional committees, Nos. 5 and 7, for Clitheroe and Accrington respectively.[62] Since each divisional executive had between three and six Council members on it, including at least one prominent leader, the central body was able to exert considerable influence when conditions were favourable. It would, however, be quite wrong to suppose that these bodies were passive recipients of instructions. The following section embodies a brief case study of No. 11 Divisional Executive, that serving the Ormskirk district, and illustrates the independence of mind and attitude that could be encountered in almost any Lancashire district.

It will be in place here to add a little relevant information about the administrative history of the divisions. They were, as has been shown, reduced in number from thirty-five to twenty-four as from April 1951, so that, for example, the outer Fylde was covered by one large division, with a population of some 118,000 people, instead of two as previously. Many divisions remained more compact, and Ormskirk had rather over 66,000 people in 1959. Following the Local Government Act (1958), three additional Excepted Districts, all in 'difficult' border territory, were created at Crosby, Middleton and Huyton-with-Roby,[63] and there was a 'varying scheme' in 1960, and again in 1967, relative to the divisions, but their work and constitutions remained basically unchanged. Kirkby became an Excepted District in 1971.

A DIVISIONAL EXECUTIVE IN ACTION – ORMSKIRK

After the Education Act of 1944, as we have seen, the Lancashire divisional executives were duly shaped, and the Ormskirk area became Division 16. After the reduction of the number of divisional executives in 1951 it became No. 11, but retained its original boundaries, comprising the urban districts of Ormskirk and Skelmersdale and part of the West Lancashire Rural District.[64] The 60,000 acres of the division's territory were primarily agricultural, but in 1951 ninety per cent of its 52,000 population were concentrated in the towns or settlement areas of Ormskirk, Maghull, Burscough and Skelmersdale. The two former areas were by far the largest, having populations of 15,250 and 12,000 respectively; but the subsequent development and rapid growth of population in Skelmersdale not only accounts for a considerable part of the population increase in the division since 1951, but also leads to some interesting examples of the pressures upon the administration that were to be encountered in border and overspill areas of this kind. The problems peculiar to the Ormskirk division, however, will be considered at the end of the section. Up to 1967, part of Skelmersdale was in the neighbouring Division 13 and this part was transferred to No. 11 as part of the 'varying scheme' of that year.

The first meeting of the Divisional Executive for Ormskirk took place in that town on Monday, 10 September 1945, with twenty-four of the twenty-six appointed members attending. Although the Executive increased in size to thirty members in 1965 and thirty-one in 1973, the figures for the Ormskirk division are low when compared with those of other divisional executives in the county, which had an average membership of thirty-nine. The Ormskirk membership was made up in such a way that councillors from authorities within the division consistently formed over half of the body itself; but, further to this, three members were county councillors, each having experience of several of the county authority's standing committees and sub-committees and, as we have indicated, of the Education Committee's sub-committees also. This ensured that some representation was made from many of the committees that might be instrumental in decisions formed at county level and affecting the Divisional Executive's recommendations. Other members of the

Executive were church representatives from Anglican, Catholic and Non-conformist bodies, teacher representatives and a number of co-opted individuals of special qualifications.

At the first meeting, Mr S. H. Hudson was elected to the chair, and a total of thirty-four decisions or resolutions were minuted, six of which were simply concerned with the appointment of committee members or the approval of minutes. A breakdown of the remaining twenty-eight provides a useful insight into the pattern and stress of executive responsibilities: twelve of these decisions related to staff appointments, absences and dismissals; four related to physical exercise and organised games at school; three to facilities for school meals; three to school holidays; two to the repair of school equipment; one each to the letting of school premises, school transfer and the inadequacy of certain school facilities; and, finally, one resolution concerned the accounts of the division. Such matters continued to arise with great frequency in subsequent meetings, which were held monthly, and it is very clear that the primary function of the Executive was to ensure the smooth day-to-day running of the schools under its authority.

In addition, the Executive made use of specially formed sub-committees, and in June 1962[65] eleven sub-committees had been appointed to deal with, respectively, Further Education and Youth Services; the Development Plan and School Accommodation; Staffing Establishments (including those of kitchens and the divisional office); Divisional Estimates of Expenditure; Free Meals and Provision of Clothing for Necessitous Schoolchildren; the Conveyance of Children; School Holidays; the Allocation of Children to Secondary Schools; School Attendance; Discipline; and, finally, Grants to School Camps and Education Visits. These sub-committees met regularly, and ensured that members really were involved in educational administration. They reported regularly to the main executive meeting, which varied its monthly routine only in August, when the chairman, during the holiday period, was charged to deal personally with any outstanding matters that might arise. It should be added that each of the Executive's four chairmen between 1945 and 1974 served for substantial periods; Messrs S. H. Hudson and A. E. Newall acted for five years each until 1955, after which Mr T. A. Farrimond took over for eight years, to be followed by Mr (later Sir) Henry Lumby, who was chairman for eleven years.

Not only did chairmen serve for longer periods as time went on; there was a marked increase in the amount of individual decision-making by the chairman in the absence of colleagues, especially during the last few years of the County Council's existence; and this can be attributed tentatively to at least two factors – a marked increase in the size and number of schools under the executive's purview, especially in Skelmersdale, and deliberate policy, designed to free the rest of the Executive for discussion of matters of principle. Alderman Lumby was chairman of the County Council from 1967, and a trusted member of the Finance Committee, as well as the most experienced member of the Executive itself. Indeed, growing numbers of matters for decision, of a kind that would formerly have been dealt with by the full Executive, were passed increasingly to sub-committees and were only formally ratified by the main body. Prior to March 1968[66] there appear to be no recorded instances (save at holiday times) of the chairman acting on behalf of the Executive. The delegation of certain decisions to chairman or sub-committees actually brought about a reduction in the number of minuted resolutions recorded by the full Executive, as figures from three sample periods show. From April 1951 to March 1954, the minutes show that 1364 resolutions were passed by the whole Executive; between April 1971 and March 1974 the number was 1043. The period in which fewest Executive decisions were made coincides with the years in which the chairman was most active.

The Executive as a whole did in fact regularly focus its attention upon important matters, especially those concerning staffing and staff conditions, which increasingly occupied its time. Of the 1951–4 resolutions, twenty-six per cent were concerned with staffing; while between 1961 and 1964 such resolutions amounted to thirty-four per cent of the total, and between 1971 and 1974 they reached a massive forty-two per cent. The Divisional Executives, it must be remembered, dealt not only with teaching staffs, and their appointments, absences and resignations, but also with such phenomena as they related to kitchen staff, groundsmen, school caretakers and clerical and divisional staff. In addition, the Ormskirk Executive was much concerned with school health and meals, the implementation of the local projects in the Development Plan, school letting and the dates of school holidays. Links with the County Education Committee were maintained through the divisional education officer, to which local post there were two appointments only in the life of the Executive. Mr W. A. Dean held the position from 1945 until 1963, and he was succeeded by Mr W. D. Eade who, like Mr Lumby, combined county-level experience with service in the division. Mr Eade was undoubtedly substantially responsible for the saving of time on purely routine matters in the Executive's discussions, and was backed by his chairman in this respect.

In many of these basic matters, the Ormskirk division undoubtedly resembled its fellows. We now discuss a number of factors and events that gave it its special character.

The salient factor was undoubtedly the new town development within its boundaries. The second-instalment Development Plan[67] of 1951 revealed that there were 6038 pupils attending the division's thirty-five schools. By 1965 the total number of pupils had reached 13,013,[68] and by 1973 it was 26,719. A large part of this increase of over 13,000 pupils between 1965 and 1973 can be attributed to the growth of Skelmersdale. The school population of this new town was 1600 in 1964, shared between the town's one secondary and five primary schools. By 1973 the total number of pupils reached 9175, a figure accounting for fifty-eight per cent of growth in pupil numbers in the entire division from 1964 to 1973. Such development would obviously lead to accommodation problems, and indeed, difficulties had already arisen in the formation of accurate predictions of the numbers, ages and religious composition of the new school population. These predictions were undermined by varying rates of population growth, influenced by national rather than local conditions; expansion was slow in 1966–8, but rapid in 1969–70 and in 1972. Again, whereas early immigrants tended to consist of young families with children of nursery or primary school age, later families moving in, after the housing policy of the new town itself changed during the sixties, brought with them children requiring secondary education. Furthermore, wide variations in the distribution of the Catholic population in south Lancashire and north Merseyside, whence new residents often came, made it impossible to forecast accurately how many Catholic families would move into Skelmersdale, or where in the town they would settle. In September 1973, therefore, the local Executive was obliged to take an unprecedented step in obtaining permission from the county Education Committee (after representations from the governors of St Richard's RC High School) to provide temporary accommodation for a great influx of pupils at this school, despite the Education Committee's policy of not providing such accommodation for aided schools.[69] It will be seen that executives such as this were sensitive to local sentiment, and that they had to develop a self-reliant and flexible policy. Sheer pressure of events and hard realism, notwithstanding any initial political leanings, caused overspill area executives to see the administrative advantages of comprehensive education, which permitted some flexibility in dealing with large numbers; and Skelmersdale itself was one of the pioneers in this respect.[70]

In consequence, comprehensive education, notwithstanding sharp differences in emphasis between the main parties, had become substantially a bipartisan matter by the early seventies; and this trend, together with a failure to appreciate the deep-seated nature of Lancashire local sentiment, led to a considerable misunderstanding on the part of a secretary of state for education. In July 1972 Mrs Margaret Thatcher made an unexpected decision to reject the long-standing plans of the Executive to convert Ormskirk Grammar School into a comprehensive school, thereby threatening the rest of their scheme for introducing such education into the area. The decision was puzzling, because modifications approved by the then Conservative County Council, the Divisional Executive and the school governors, and costing £350,000,[71] had already been carried out at the Wigan Road County Secondary School in Ormskirk in anticipation of its conversion to a comprehensive. Furthermore, £45,000 had been 'wasted' on architects' fees for detailed planning for the conversion of the grammar school.[72] On 17 July the Executive resolved unanimously to 'strongly support the action of the Lancashire Education Committee in seeking an early meeting with the Secretary of State and [to] ask that the Chairman and Vice-Chairman of the Divisional Executive should be included as members of the deputation'.[73]

The eight-man deputation met the Secretary of State on 16 August 1972, but her decision was not altered. A Parent's Association Action Committee, set up eighteen months previously to protect the Grammar School, was jubilant, and was able to feel that it had influenced events,[74] but the sentiment of joy was not shared by the divisional and county education bodies. Alderman Lumby, the (Conservative) chairman of the Executive, remarked that Mrs Thatcher's decision was a result of 'very bad misrepresentation',[75] while his colleague, Alderman J. R. Ashton, chairman of the County Education Committee, expressed some concern that the development of school planning in the area as a whole could be affected.[76] In this instance, an external political decision, affecting detailed local strategy, was clearly resented,[77] and it is interesting to note that regard for the Executive's own work appeared to transcend any party feeling. The defenders of the grammar school were seen, rightly or wrongly, as a violently prejudiced pressure group who had not, in most cases, faced the population and social problems of the division. Our point here, of course, is that the local executives in general were very far from being mere carriers-out of orders, and also that they were part of a pattern of tradition and sentiment that was very typical of the county. Fairly sensitive to responsible communal representation, or informed direction, they refused to be pushed from above or below.

THE 'PERFORMANCE' OF THE COUNTY

We now attempt to review Lancashire's 'performance' as an education authority. We have seen that a given division like No. 11 (Ormskirk) had its own sense of identity and a degree of independence. Moreover, in spite of the reduction in the number of county divisions in 1951, Lancashire still had more of the latter than any other English county,[78] although it may be noted that the West Riding of Yorkshire had a similarly elaborate system. There was in Lancashire a discernible fondness for unusually large local executives, and both before and after 1951 these were considerably larger than ministry expectations suggested. After 1951 their average size was thirty-nine, but the range was from twenty-four members for Division 1 (covering remote Furness) to fifty-two for Division 3 (catering for a large part of the Fylde). Thus, although the Ministry looked for divisional bodies of between twenty and thirty-nine members, only four Lancashire divisions fulfilled this condition; and, indeed, a further five of the Lancashire divisions had between forty-one and fifty members. The county's proposed scheme of February 1945[79] had specified the number of representatives local councils should have on each executive, and as many as six or seven county districts could have several members each, with the addition of teacher representatives, those for voluntary educational bodies, and co-opted persons of special qualification. This tendency to large or elaborate executives was consistent with Lancashire style and sentiment, but it was, of course, much enhanced by the ministry-compelled amalgamations of 1951 and by the refusals of individual county districts to countenance fewer representatives. At the same time, it was becoming clear that local interest was being maintained through these organisations.

It should be stressed that, although there was great consistency, there was nothing pre-ordained about Lancashire's record in this respect; a review of county divisional administration undertaken in 1958 by the Ministry of Education showed that numerous English counties had formal divisional structures not unlike Lancashire's; but, as in the much earlier review of area delegation in 1908, there were wide variations in the degree of success of these schemes of local devolution.[80] Some counties were unduly restrictive in the controls they placed on divisions, and the result was friction and unnecessary delay.[81] Lancashire appears to have avoided the worst pitfalls by accepting the divisional structure as given and attempting to work within it, admittedly assisted by the experience of many years of local devolution.

Nevertheless, it is possible to make strong criticisms of the working and usefulness of divisional administration. It is plainly slow in operation, and the task of the divisional education officer (DEO) is made more arduous by the requirement that he and his officers continually report back to their executive and its sub-committees. Although delegation to sub-committees and the chairman of the Executive may undoubtedly make his job easier, it has been possible to find cases where the DEO has had to approach his chairman for the approval of expenditure on relatively tiny items, and it is certainly the case that much greater freedom of action could have been given to this officer. Again, the loyalties of divisional staff were necessarily divided between their executive and the County Education Department; some officers leaned towards the former, others towards the latter, so that in extreme cases one officer acted as though he was largely the interpreter of county policy to the local members, and another sided almost invariably with his executive. Such aberrations were largely avoided in Lancashire, by virtue of much expenditure of time on discussion with central office staff, with the aim of building up confidence, and through the work of the Lancashire Association of Divisional Executive Officers. Meanwhile, successive reviews by the Ministry have tended to stress the waste of time and the duplication inherent in the three-tier system, whereby executives and school governing bodies exist side by side, and HMIs have argued that the latter more easily represent public sentiment; they have argued, too, that the public have usually been unaware of the structure of local educational administration. In this respect, however, much has depended on the personalities and enthusiasms of the officers concerned, and it is also true that experience of individual schools was valuable in executive discussions. As regards the slow movement of the central–local county dialogue, meetings have been so arranged chronologically as to ensure that proposals have passed through the machinery in the minimum possible time.

The quantitative measurement of education is necessarily difficult, as cost figures for counties measure inputs rather then 'outputs' – and may sometimes conceal wide variations within counties. In 1957–8, for example, at the end of the postwar 'bulge' in primary school pupil numbers, the pupil–teacher ratio for Lancashire's primary schools was thirty-one; but, in fact, roughly one-third of all classes had more than forty pupils in them.[82] Any working teacher knows what this figure indicates, in terms of classroom problems.

Mr MacGregor-Reid has already shown that the relative level of current education expenditure per head of population in Lancashire was low in the thirties but that, since the war, the county has improved its position relative to other authorities.[83] Secondary education expenditure per head of population reflects this, but primary education expenditure has grown virtually in line with that for all counties. However, this information must be used in conjuction with pupil numbers, which, in the case of Lancashire, were considerably affected by overspill. The county started the postwar period with a ratio of primary pupils per thousand

TABLE 13.3
Expenditure per Pupil on Education

Year	Primary education		Secondary education	
	Lancashire	All Counties	Lancashire	All Counties
1951–2	22.92	24.91	42.50	43.97
1952–3	24.04	25.60	45.13	46.55
1953–4	24.45	26.47	45.92	47.64
1954–5	26.72	28.87	48.94	50.26
1955–6	28.52	30.74	51.64	51.91
1956–7	32.74	35.02	59.46	59.45
1957–8	36.14	38.82	64.82	64.32
1958–9	38.67	41.47	62.89	64.30
1959–60	44.73	48.92	76.16	82.93
1960–1	47.31	51.79	81.07	88.15
1961–2	51.34	55.93	91.44	98.70
1962–3	55.95	60.94	101.88	108.32
1963–4	58.98	64.14	106.99	113.83
1964–5	60.60	65.23	113.66	120.46
1965–6	67.36	73.11	129.07	136.21
1966–7	69.06	76.54	137.65	144.64
1967–8	73.25	81.47	145.14	153.18
1968–9	76.53	89.94	150.62	158.63
1969–70	83.29	91.53	161.90	169.47
1970–1	93.23	101.97	174.03	184.42
1972–2	105.51	115.26	200.80	208.02
1972–3	123.67	134.13	231.27	240.20
1973–4	142.82	152.59	249.77	258.12

Source: IMTA Education Statistics.

population that was roughly five per cent above that for All Counties, rising to a peak of nine per cent above in 1957 when it had 110 pupils per thousand population. After this, primary pupil numbers followed national trends but remained roughly seven per cent above the 'All Counties' figure.

These factors are important. If Lancashire had been providing the same level of service per pupil and was as efficient as the average county, we would expect its primary education expenditure per head of population to be *above* that for All Counties. It was approximately the same, and therefore we are left with two possibilities; the county was exceptionally efficient in its use of public money for primary education, *or* the level of service it provided for each pupil was below that generally prevailing. The ratios for secondary education raise the same kind of questions with pupils per thousand population slightly above and expenditure per head of population slightly below that for all counties. This is well illustrated by the relatively low levels of Lancashire's total costs per pupil shown in Table 13.3.

In certain areas, the county education service was highly efficient. This was particularly so in administration, and perhaps in its debt-management policy aimed at keeping interest charges down. Despite evidence suggesting that small administrative units are expensive to operate,[84] Lancashire's divisional administration system was not; its administrative costs per thousand population were around twenty per cent below the average for All Counties. Furthermore, relatively low rent and rates payments per pupil are responsible for slightly lower costs than other counties. Nevertheless, these factors account for only a small part of the gap between Lancashire's cost per pupil and the average for All Counties.

The most important single factor explaining low costs per pupil in primary education is Lancashire's high pupil–teacher ratio, which accounts for about half the gap between it and the average for All Counties.[85] This undoubtedly reflects teacher recruitment problems, as a result of which, until recently, it was difficult to fill ministry quotas of primary schoolteachers.[86] Secondly, it is likely that such a shortage would result in the appointment of relatively large numbers of junior staff, which would further reduce costs per pupil.

Secondly education is less clear-cut. Table 13.4 shows that, in this case, the pupil–teacher ratio was not high relative to other counties. Nevertheless in addition to the factors already mentioned a little more of the gap may be explained by the fact that fewer pupils remained in school after the statutory leaving age than in other counties.

We are left to conclude, therefore, that the figures cited, particularly in the case of primary education, do not necessarily reflect deficiencies in the performance of the County Education Department. We should not forget, however, that in 1971 no less than 22.6 per cent of Lancashire's primary pupils were being educated in schools built before 1903. Yet it is not the job of the historian to condemn; rather it should be made clear that these were problems of a great authority which, in the last analysis, lacked resources to cope with the difficulties created by an ageing industrial environment.

FURTHER EDUCATION

Further education, in the Lancashire context as elsewhere, is a very wide term, embracing technical instruction and vocational study in commercial or other fields, continued liberal education in the adult class and the community centre, and academic study in a university tutorial class. In recent years it has also come to stand for the study and practice of music, drama or folk dancing. The present study, however, will concern itself with the core of further education in Lancashire as represented by its 'technical colleges' or colleges of further education.

TABLE 13.4
Pupil–Teacher Ratios*

Year	Primary education		Secondary education	
	Lancashire	All Counties	Lancashire	All Counties
1951–2	31	30	21	20
1952–3	32	30	20	20
1953–4	32	30	20	20
1954–5	31	30	20	21
1955–6	31	30	21	21
1956–7	31	29	21	21
1957–8	31	29	21	21
1958–9	30	29	21	21
1959–60	30	28	21	21
1960–1	30	28	21	21
1961–2	30	28	20	20
1962–3	29	28	19	19
1963–4	29	28	19	19
1964–5	29.4	27.9	18.6	18.9
1965–6	29.1	—	18.4	—
1966–7	29.0	27.3	18.1	18.4
1967–8	29.0	27.3	17.1	18.4
1968–9	29.3	27.5	18.2	18.4
1969–70	28.6	27.3	18.2	18.3
1970–1	28.1	26.7	18.1	18.1
1971–2	26.9	25.9	17.6	17.7
1972–3	26.4	25.4	16.9	17.2
1973–4	25.8	25.1	17.3	17.6

* Includes full-time equivalent of part-time teachers.
Source IMTA Education Statistics.

In Chapter 5 above there is an outline of the history of the Technical Instruction Committee of the late Victorian years.[87] Technical education in the county did not, of course, cease with the 1902 Act, nor did it greatly burgeon. Evening instruction remained its mainstay, and full-time students were few. The small industrial towns of the administrative county not infrequently contained red-brick, stone-faced buildings of Victorian or Edwardian provenance, containing resounding, rather gloomy corridors and dusty laboratories or lecture rooms; and into these went earnest students after their day's work. One example of such a building – now much transformed – is the former Railway Mechanics' Institute in Horwich, while the Storey Institute in Lancaster is another. Until the mid-thirties, technical education showed no sign of being 'fashionable', and the Annual Reports of the County Education Committee pass over the subject except in the barest outline. The junior technical schools, harboured in the colleges themselves, operated quietly through the years, and four-day continuation schools were in the twenties and thirties the main indication of an interest in technical training on the part of great Lancashire industries.

By 1936–7 the Lancashire Education Committee and its officers were becoming much more clearly aware of new demand in this field. Indeed, in the summer of 1938 there was a massive leap in further education expenditure of £70,000, representing a rise of twenty-five per cent in one year. In the summer of 1936 there had been intensified calling of local conferences on further education, and this was accompanied by the formation of a regional advisory council 'for the purpose of co-ordinating Technical and other forms of Further Education in South-East Lancashire'.[88] This embraced all the south Lancashire county boroughs and representatives of Lancashire County Council and adjoining counties, and it was a forerunner of the type of body recommended in the Percy Report of 1945 and set up in 1947.[89] More practically, the Council was extending or adding to the buildings of its eleven technical colleges. The Council, then and subsequently, pursued a policy, as for example at Wigan, of sharing resources and making them available to county-based students; and it afterwards (in the postwar period) shared the use of the Royal Technical College, Salford, and the Harris College, Preston, in the same way.

This pattern of administration in college-based and other further education was, then, carried over into the post-1944 period, the massive reorganisation of secondary education thereafter absorbing county energies for several years. Other interests and policies, too, spanned the war years, and of these one of the most noteworthy was the county's adult education scheme for North Lancashire, which had taken effect with the appointment of a full-time tutor, working in the rural area round Garstang, from September 1928.[90] Here is a most striking example of local government support for the work of the Workers' Educational Association (WEA) and the university extramural departments, which, of course, received grants from the Council also. This was yet another contribution to the quality of life in county localities which could all too easily go unnoticed. The village adult classes, on literature, local history, drama and music, were supported with books from the County Library; and the work, which had started in some thirteen centres, had reached no fewer than sixty-nine by 1936, having spread through north Lancashire into the Furness district.

Returning to the workaday world of vocational training, further education of that kind did not of course go unconsidered in the intellectual as well as the organisational upheaval of the post-1944 period; and there can be little doubt that the Percy Report of 1945 was, in Mr Michael Argles's words, 'the seminal document of much of the post-war development in technical and scientific education'.[91] This proposed a marked raising of the status of the larger technical colleges, and, *inter alia*, the setting up of regional advisory councils in order to help industrialists and educationalists to bring into focus the facilities that were being made available. As we have seen, Lancashire had already taken action in this way nearly a decade before, and the postwar response in the county and region was to set up no fewer than four such bodies.

The Percy Report, and the policy and advisory bodies that emerged as a result of it from the 'official line' thus set up, undoubtedly played a considerable part in the formation of the further education section of the Education Committee's Development Plan of 1949. The Committee felt that it could spend money far more freely on its still undeveloped and uninspiring further education colleges, and it is significant that it now took up the prewar plans for so doing, making extensions to the Lytham St Annes and Leigh Technical Colleges, and proposing the building of new colleges of further education at Ashton-under-Lyne, Lancaster and Morecambe, and Accrington, where the buildings were 'inadequate' or 'unsatisfactory'.[92] The Further Education Sub-Committee of this period could have had little notion of the vast expansion in buildings, equipment and student attendance that would take effect in the following twenty years. The Development Plan of 1949 originally set out to establish twelve colleges of further education and forty-eight 'county colleges' in the county; and by 1970 there were sixteen colleges of further education or technical colleges (two of them still jointly operated), a school of art, a nautical college and two works schools. During the same period council spending on further education increased, in money terms,

TABLE 13.5

Expenditure on Further Education in Lancashire, 1948–72

	£		£
1948*	752,314	1962	6,748,765
1949	910,624	1964	8,119,646
1952*	1,030,921	1966	11,977,497
1956*	2,653,449	1967	13,968,954
1959	2,935,529	1968	16,184,352
1960*	4,217,911	1970	21,055,813
1961*	6,698,296	1972	27,116,348

* These are selected dates, each one indicating a point of marked increase; otherwise each year can be taken as typical of its immediate period. The annual totals include teacher training and agricultural education.

twenty-fold or more, and the total figures for all types of further education expenditure are given in Table 13.5.[93]

Before going on to describe the more detailed reality that lay beneath these figures, the narrative must here emphasise what has already been mentioned in another chapter,[94] the changing structure of Lancashire industry. The continued decline of the cotton industry, to which much local technical instruction had been directed in earlier years, was counterbalanced by a growing variety and diffusion of new or developing industries and commercial activities, or even developments of retail trade, which had repercussions for the local technical colleges. Light engineering and chemicals, electrical and electronic industries, the motor and motor vehicle component trades, the building craft skills and steel erection, and newer forms of textile production and clothing industry – all called for training, knowledge and expertise, while management arts and catering were to play an important part in the work of the larger colleges of the future. The drastically altered position of the cotton textile industry was reflected in a series of reports from HM Inspectors on textile education provision in Lancashire, made in the spring of 1952. These condemned, on the whole, the smaller training centres and urged the concentration of textile courses in colleges in the larger towns,[95] although the divisional executives, predictably, were unwilling to give up their local classes.

Despite the growing variety and steady postwar development of Lancashire's newer industries, there was at first no automatically and easily exploited market for technical education. However, certain industries were willing to give a lead, and once a fashion had started a momentum and increasing response was to become evident. Hence, it was remarked in

1949 that 'some employers continue to offer day release to enable employees to attend appropriate classes', and among these were the boot and shoe manufacturers of the Rossendale Valley.[96] In fact, day release training was in its infancy, and a growing fashion was to reach its peak in the next dozen years.

The latter was, indeed, the greatest single fact in the technical and further education of the fifties and early sixties. Part-time day release was very largely confined to young persons of seventeen to twenty-one years of age, mainly male, and was given as part of a condition of employment in the great majority of cases, with the engineering industries taking the lead, and large firms especially so. The growth of this form of training in Lancashire was striking if not meteoric, as the county figures in Table 13.6

TABLE 13.6
Technical and Commercial Students on Part-Time Day Release in Lancashire County Administrative Further Education Institutions

1950–1	7,778	1956–7	12,608
1951–2	8,770	1957–8	12,880
1952–3	9,525	1958–9	12,626
1953–4	10,646	1959–60	12,444
1954–5	11,139	1960–1	13,511
1955–6	11,873	1961–2	15,380

show.[97] Some of the increase in day release figures in the mid–fifties was the result of transfer from evening class education, and the number of part-time evening students in 1955–6 at 72,172 showed little increase over previous years. The total number of evening class students in the administrative county was barely more than double that of the immediate prewar years, and more than half of these were students pursuing only one subject; the number of full-time technical and commercial students in the local colleges was still very small – 392 in 1954–5 and 609 in 1957–8.[98] The transformation of the sixties was to make the colleges both more populous and more imposing. It was the plainly developing technology of the USSR, and to a less politically worrying degree that of the United States, that gave a new impetus to the plans for technical education in Britain; and the Soviet challenge received great emphasis by Sir Winston Churchill in his Woodford speech of 1955. The *Times Educational Supplement*, in the January of the following year, was even able to claim that 'there is an anxiety approaching panic in high places'.[99] How far this panic was transmitted downwards is not clear, but the outcome was the White Paper of 1956, *Technical Education*.[100] This was a comprehensive document, promising a major expansion of the technical colleges (which would of course necessitate a large building programme), and urging the promotion of more day release classes and 'sandwich' courses, the latter to be concentrated in colleges of advanced technology (CATs). This had repercussions for Lancashire, for the Royal Salford Technical College which had trained many county students was designated a CAT in 1956, but continued to receive massive aid from the county authority.

The reaction of the County Education Committee to the White Paper was immediate, one of a relief from frustration: this document was welcomed 'because it holds promise of advance in Technical Education which they [the Committee] have been anxious to make. In particular, the Committee are gratified that more building will be allowed and that complete buildings will in future replace "phased" building'.[101] At the meeting following the publication of the White Paper, the Education Committee asked for complete new technical colleges at Horwich and Kirkby, and for substantial phases at Nelson, Widnes, Lancaster and Morecambe, Ashton-under-Lyne and Accrington Colleges. The revolution was under way, in spirit and in some quite striking material terms.[102]

Three years later the Education Committee was able to report that the period had seen 'the infusion of new life and purpose into Technical Education'.[103] It added (as we now know, somewhat simplistically) that 'the retention or acquisition of Great Power status largely stands or falls on a country's technical achievement'. Yet it is too easy to be wise after the event, and there was much satisfaction in the sight of impressive new colleges arising where grimy and gloomy brick had once served. The central office in Preston knew well that these glass and concrete ziggurats were good for the morale of divisional executives – where was the school that could be seen teaching its youngsters eight storeys up? More than this, however, they induced further growth in student numbers; for as the colleges became better equipped, so they were able more effectively to advertise technical education to local industry. Colleges not only 'arranged courses with a view to the needs of industries in the area they serve',[104] but they performed special services of a kind that could easily become irreplaceable, so that Lancaster went to much trouble to organise a novel course in management studies, while Accrington performed research and testing for local industries.[105] By the end of the fifties, these fine buildings provided a strong inducement even to quite small local firms to send their boys on day release, although some case-hardened employers bitterly resisted the idea of the same boys being subjected to improving doses of liberal studies on their days 'off'.[106] By 1958–9 there were, in all colleges owned or used by the county, some 13,000 technical and commercial students on part-time day release, nearly twice the 1950 figure. This was partly the consequence of a powerful drive to bring local managements of industry on to governing bodies, and each college was encouraged to produce shining brochures. 'Training for Industry' conferences represented another important strategem of the time.[107]

Perhaps the most impressive sight of all was the great tower block of the College of Advanced Technology at Salford (now a main building of the university there), the college becoming a direct-grant institution in April 1962.[108] During the late fifties, the county made great investments in this college and in a more striking transformation of the Harris College at Preston (£514,000).[109] In the last-mentioned case, Lancashire was engaged in fostering, unbeknown, a great regional polytechnic of the seventies. To the Salford, Wigan and Harris Colleges the training of technologists and scientists was theoretically entrusted. The White Paper of 1956 had produced, typically of Curzon Street, a neatly conceived, suave and convincing-seeming picture of a graded society of scientists, technologists and 'technicians', set out in medieval-seeming social layers and institutions with each one knowing its place in the educational order. With impassive unrealism, it had apparently overlooked such small considerations as local pride and competition; comparatively small-town colleges would fight fiercely for the privilege of fostering advanced work, especially in this period of unprecedented expansion. By 1962-3, Accrington College of Further Education had launched its own Higher National Diploma (HND) in production engineering – 'a considerable achievement'.[110] By 1965, unhappily for such enterprises, the North-West Regional Advisory Council was considering the concentration of such courses on a regional basis, so that even the fairly large Stretford Technical College was denied its Higher Certificate courses.[111] It is nevertheless pleasing to record that, in 1970, Widnes Technical College was attracting students from local industry to its HND in chemistry.[112]

The experiences of the sixties can be surveyed fairly briefly. They represented further transformation, in that the new colleges contained much greater numbers of full-time students taking GCE courses (the 'second chance' after secondary school became increasingly popular) – catering (in several centres), nursery nursing, business studies and even hairdressing. It will be seen that, in some interesting and subtle ways, these represent social changes of the age, the emphasis being upon the consumer rather than the producer. Indeed, the Further Education Sub-Committee and the leaders of local technical education began to realise that, despite the great advance of day release, there was no break-through in depth to the mass of small and medium firms that made up a great part of Lancashire industry. Engineers and building apprentices still made up the major part of day release students in further education colleges, and

Lancashire day release itself reached a plateau in growth by the mid-sixties.[113] The same leaders could only hope that the Industrial Training Act of 1963, which set out to oblige employers to consent to the systematic training of their juvenile labour force, would 'with the imposition of training levies succeed in engendering a new attitude in those parts of industry and commerce where day release training hardly exists; the position is hardly likely to alter radically. . . .'[114] Day release itself began to undergo structural alterations, as preliminary technical courses were transferred from evening institutes and block release arrangements became more common. On the other hand, 'evening vocational work continued to decline but this was partly offset [1966] by the provision of non-vocational work for adults and of specialist short courses for senior staff in industry.'[115] Day release was, by 1966, once more climbing in popularity, only to reach another plateau in the early seventies,[116] while evening work experienced surges and ebbs throughout the earlier decade.[117]

There is no doubt that the colleges managed to make effective use of much of their capacity; as the opening of phases was awaited, it was no uncommon thing for them to seek temporary accommodation in a multitude of spare buildings, chapels and warehouses in their localities, and in 1965–6 there were serious complaints of 'shortage of accommodation'.[118]

It is, on the whole, true to say that further and technical education offered organisational problems to a supervising authority that primary and secondary education did not. One could forecast the numbers of children likely to attend a group of schools in a given year, but consumer demand in the technical colleges and evening institutes was often unpredictable, and the permanent accommodation was expensive and called for much specialist knowledge. One can ask, therefore, whether administrative costs were correspondingly high. Interestingly, this does not seem to have been the case. In 1962–3, for example, Lancashire's further education costs were well below the average for English counties, at £2521 per 1000 of population as against £2555 for All Counties; while administration and inspection costs were, and had been, generally lower.[119] This interpretation is supported by a report of the Chief Education Officer submitted in September 1959, which stated flatly that: 'As compared with most smaller authorities the County is understaffed, and it is quite impossible for the Organisers to pay sufficient visits to individual schools and Further Education Establishments.' He was at that time making do with only nine further education organisers, of whom three were youth organisers; and it should be borne in mind that there were then twenty-one colleges of further education (FE) in the county, 305 evening institutes, fifty-three maintained youth clubs and 1350 voluntary youth clubs. Not only did these heavily burdened staff members have to visit these colleges and clubs;

they had to grade capitation claims from other authorities, supervise adult education, attend governors' and youth club committees, and *inter alia*, supervise community centre work. In addition (as the Chief Officer somewhat ruefully remarked) his organisers had to represent him 'on the numerous Regional Advisory Committees and Sub-Committees. There is a large amount of this work.'[120] If the field staff were seriously overburdened, there was apparently a similar state of affairs among the FE central clerical staff in 1964: 'Increases in clerical staff had not kept pace with ... developments and in certain aspects of the work the situation had become critical,' largely because of the growing torrent of awards to students.[121]

THE JUNIOR TECHNICAL SCHOOLS AND SECONDARY EDUCATION

These, as we have seen,[122] had roots in the earlier decades of the century. In 1937 there were junior day technical schools at Ashton, Horwich, Lancaster, Leigh, Newton-in-Makerfield, Radcliffe, Stretford and Worsley, with a total of 570 boys 'who intend to enter one of the constructive trades'.[123] They were restricted to the 13-15 age group, and were usually contained within the small colleges of education at the places mentioned. As these expanded in the postwar years, so the junior sections were regarded more and more coolly by principals and staff, as young boys rushed noisily about the corridors. Yet Lancashire seems to have taken this kind of education seriously, and the 1949 Development Plan proposed the establishment of secondary technical schools in twenty-three of the county's educational divisions. By 1957, however, there were (as separate entities) only three secondary technical schools in operation in the administrative county – at Accrington, Nelson and Darwen – each of which was selective, but each of which took students 'below the normal level of admission to grammar school'.[124] In this rather limited provision, Lancashire was much like the country as a whole, and there were then only about 340 (out of 5400 secondary schools) technical schools in Britain.

However, there were several unstated considerations; official opinion still regarded the grammar schools as natural feeders of university science and engineering courses; and, what is more to the point, the gentlemen of the Ministry of Education had been, at best, lukewarm in their efforts to bring about the realisation of the largely missing third partner in secondary education, the technical school. Lancashire's own lack of drive in this direction merely indicated a tame following of current opinion, a policy less thoroughgoing than that pursued by Cheshire (which did not have any secondary technical schools at all). A great industrial county, in a position to bring its own forms of pressure to bear on Curzon Street, could surely have achieved a little more than this. However, the Chief Education Officer had his own carefully formulated justification: 'it would be most undesirable to set a pattern of Secondary Education for the whole country or even for the Administrative County of Lancashire, since tradition, local needs, local views and the existing provision for selective education in a particular area, are all of importance.'[125]

This comment is of course highly significant. Lancashire's administrative network was indeed so sensitive to 'local views' that any heterodox and determined policy in an important sphere of education was unlikely to emerge, still less to be implemented. This particular case also suggests why Lancashire, in educational matters, was not distinguished for dynamism and experiment, as the counties of Hertfordshire and Leicestershire reputedly were. The factors that enabled other Lancashire services – the police, health and welfare, the fire brigade, the County Library – to innovate were evidently not operative in the case of education. On the other hand, the degree of freedom accorded to localities, through their divisional committees, is illustrated in the case study of the Ormskirk Executive in this chapter.[126] It may be that local freedom and originality do not go well together in a service as diverse as education.

ADULT EDUCATION

This survey has by no means adequately covered all the concerns that may fairly be said to come under the heading of the post-secondary services of the county education authority. It had, as we have seen, a flourishing if sometimes sadly understaffed youth service, and also, in the postwar years, an efficient youth employment organisation. There were two reputable schools of art, at Lancaster and Accrington, and the county had a valuable nautical school at Fleetwood.

The Lancashire County Institute of Agriculture was reopened at Hutton after the war, but pressure of student numbers was so great that agricultural courses (as distinct from those in dairying, horticulture and poultry) moved to Winmarleigh Hall in 1949. In 1954 the Ministry of Agriculture gave the Lancashire authority permission to inaugurate a two-year full-time course leading to the National Diploma in Agriculture, and this was based at Winmarleigh. Three years later, HM Inspectors of Education for the Ministry of Agriculture took a logical step in recommending the use of a single centre; and so, with the further agreement of the DES, the county acquired Myerscough Hall and Farm in 1962. It should be stressed, meanwhile, that the County Institute had performed much evening and part-time teaching between 1945 and 1959. It created an extramural department in the latter year, and has since increasingly taught part-time courses on a day release basis. Lancashire's agricultural education, going back to the earliest days of technical instruction, has an outstanding record among the English counties, and the work of two members of the Council, Messrs Windham-Hall and J. W. Fitzherbert-Brockholes, deserves especial mention in this respect.

The county continued to make its contribution to the quality of local life through evening institutes, community centres and adult classes. As we have seen, the evening institutes of the sixties laid greater emphasis on non-vocational classes as more vocational work moved into the FE colleges. One of the county's most important gestures in community service, however, was the provision of adult classes in places far away from centres of population, and this movement, as we have seen, had developed from the late twenties. A report of 1959[127] showed that it continued to burgeon in the most remote communities of north Lancashire, with a very heavy emphasis on drama and music; so that Askam-in-Furness prized its silver band, and Ulverston Choral Society could produce *The Dream of Gerontius*, while the Fylde villages were notable for their passionate adherence to drama competitions.

There were much more serious social challenges and problems in the county, notably those engendered by the creeping growth of 'overspill' and suburban settlements, which lacked any community identity and, apparently, the means of creating any. The 1944 Act had empowered local authorities to aid community centres; and the Council, in a rather halting way, had given aid to both the 'social' type of centre and the committee-guided education-minded type. By 1962 the Education Committee had come to the conclusion that the appointment of a paid warden was 'generally the only way of ensuring success'. He was the only person who could be in a position to 'keep a correct balance between the purely social element of the centre and the more educational activities'. The Committee saw in such an institution 'opportunities for adult education superior to anything that can be accomplished through the more normal and accepted channels'.[128] Accordingly, the Committee agreed to pay fifty per cent of the warden's salary 'if they consider the appointment is justified', and to make a grant to the general expenses of any centre that they felt able to support.

Thereafter there was, in fact, a much more consistent support for these institutions, given in close collaboration with the Lancashire Federation of Community Associations. Meanwhile, from a network of maintained youth centres there grew a significant scattering of permanent establishments, properly housed, served by an increasing team of full-time youth leaders, eight altogether by 1965. In the same year, the Committee was making grants to the Community Council of Lancashire, the Federation of Women's Institutes, the English Folk Dance and Song Society and the National Institute of Adult Education, these accompanying its habitual grants to the Universities of Liverpool and Manchester and the WEA.

THE UNIVERSITY OF LANCASTER

During the development and enrichment of these and many other community activities, the Lancashire County Council became involved in one of the most important and far-reaching matters of policy in its eventful history, the creation of the new University of Lancaster. Here it would be fair to call the Council a midwife rather than the original progenitor; and its role was a characteristic one, in that it acted in response to local sentiment and group pressure, helping to deliver the infant university by, midwife-like, doing the right things at the right time. The City of Lancaster had from 1947 shown a hopeful interest in the possibility of accommodating a university within its bounds, but it was pressure from Blackpool, exerted upon (Sir) Percy Lord and the County Education Committee, that set the crucial events in train just before Christmas 1960. Lancaster itself made an almost immediate representation, and in the first three months of 1961 the Clerk of the Council received further applications from Lytham St Annes, Burtonwood, the Fylde, Southport, Ulverston and Morecambe. The Council thereupon played the role of convenor for an Executive Committee for the Promotion of a University in North-West Lancashire, and this submitted, in May 1961, a case for a university in Lancaster itself. The submission resulted, five months later, in an acceptance of the proposal by the Government. The Council had pledged £50,000 a year for ten years as a support grant for the new university. The chairman of the Education Committee, Alderman Mrs K. M. Fletcher, Sir Patrick McCall, Sir Andrew Smith and Sir Alfred Bates all played substantial parts in the campaign, just as the County Planning and Development Committee cleared the way for the use of the fine Bailrigg site south of the city. This, as we have seen, had been the home and estate of a former chairman of the Education Committee, Sir James Travis-Clegg, a matter of total coincidence; his fine house, for a time the headquarters of the new university, is now its Health Centre. In January 1965 the Council made a gift of £500,000 for the foundation of a new college in the university, and this is today known as the County College.[129]

In the present volume, representatives of the University of Lancaster have been engaged in the, by no means easy, task of assessing the Council's own history. If the writers and researchers succeed in preserving and distilling a little of the basic experience and wisdom gained in the work of more than three-quarters of a century of county government, they will feel that their own labour has been amply justified.

CHAPTER 14

Health

IN surveying, as we shall shortly do, the vast administrative changes embodied in the creation of a comprehensive health service following the National Health Service Act of 1946, it is all too easy to give the impression that what was taking place before the 1939–45 war years was mere prehistory. Even before the great divisional post-1947 devolution was conceived, the county had become responsible, as a result of the Local Government Act of 1929, for fifteen hospitals or similar institutions, acquired from the Poor Law Guardians in the administrative county. This in itself was a vast undertaking. In addition, the county medical officer of health (Dr J. J. Butterworth, from 1917 to 1936) was also the school medical officer, guiding a much more ambitious school service than had been foreseen in the formative Edwardian years.[1] The work of reaching out to a multitude of schoolchildren (128,000 in 1930) involved the division of the county in 1929 into nineteen districts, each in charge of an assistant county medical officer assisted by two or three nurses and health visitors. There were, in addition, school nurses (some of whom were health visitors), responsible for individual children or toddlers and, on occasion, for expectant mothers. There was also a dental staff of fourteen full-time, and one part-time, dental surgeons.[2] The dental clinics in fact served fewer than half the school population,[3] and the school service as a whole was undoubtedly thinly staffed, by the standards of later experience. The Council was also responsible for the creation of child welfare centres, which were also used as school clinics. In 1935 eighty-five such centres were in operation throughout the county districts, but it should be noted that they usually consisted at best of a weekly opening of a room in chapel or church premises.[4] Nevertheless, such centres were the means whereby children suffering from ringworm or ophthalmic or orthodontic defects, or requiring orthopaedic treatment, might have their cases investigated and referred for special treatment; and during the thirties the Maternity and Child Welfare Committee recognised that the next move must be one towards specially designed clinic buildings, the first of which was opened at Bamber Bridge in 1938. There was even a day nursery in one district by 1939.[5]

But, although the visions of the medical staff and council members concerned were generous by the standards of their time, the scale of operations was necessarily limited by staffing and finance. One man, at least, was in a position to measure the development of the school medical service from its inception – Sir William Hodgson, who served continuously on the Public Health (from 1911, the Public Health and Housing) Committee from 1901 to 1945, for twenty-three years of which he was its chairman,[6] and on the School Medical Sub-Committee from 1909 to 1945, during the whole of which time he was its chairman. Nor was Sir William concerned merely with the formalities; he was in the habit of scrutinising every administrative item relevant to the running of the Public Health Department, and the chief clerk had to be prepared to open any and every account book for his information during his regular visits.[7] Nevertheless, it must be said that in this department, as in many similar ones nationally, much of the pressure for experiment and advance came from the members of the medical profession involved.

The thirties, however, represented a watershed in specific matters of administration and outlook; in the Public Health as in other departments, the professionalism of officers had had time to deepen and to take effect. It was almost inevitable, therefore, that the appointment of Dr Frederick Hall as county medical officer of health in September 1936 should bring a bolder and sometimes more imaginative approach on the part of senior medical staff. Drs Sergeant and Butterworth had been meticulous, dedicated and assiduous, and it should not be forgotten that Dr Butterworth had done much for the orthopaedic treatment of children in the county, and for the school health service generally. Dr Hall, however, who had worked in the county service since 1919, brought a well-stored mind to the social problems that confronted his department. With the tacit encouragement of the Ministry of Health, he helped to bring about one of the most significant pieces of health legislation of the period, the Midwives Act of 1936, which required local authorities to provide a domiciliary service of salaried midwives.

There had, it is true, been immense progress since the Midwives Act of 1902, and out of 772 midwives registered in the county in March 1937, 748 held a qualifying certificate – ninety-six per cent of the whole group.[8] The requirements of the new Act, however, led to one of those extensive administrative exercises which were not only enforced by Lancashire conditions, but were to provide invaluable experience for Dr Hall, his colleagues and their surviving committeemen in carrying out the organisational work following the National Health Service Act of 1946. Twenty-one county council midwifery districts were formed, after careful consultation with local welfare councils and district nursing associations together with bodies representing doctors and midwives. Conditions of service were drafted – including, under 'Allowances', an allowance of £5 per annum for 'Bicycle (if deemed necessary)'.[9] Much of this work hitherto had been performed through the largely voluntary effort of local nursing associations, and the Midwives Act Committee had not itself been a large-scale employer on behalf of the county authority. Large areas of the county, however, remained under the direct administration of nursing associations. The numbers of domiciliary births by district, and the acreages of districts, were taken into account when the divisions were formed.[10] Generally speaking, the county-administered midwifery services were in urban areas, and the voluntarily run ones in rural Lancashire.[11] It is worth noticing that, despite the provision for bicycles, almost all midwives were motorised by 1939, and the new Act, as locally applied, represented a noteworthy stride in the fight against deaths or sickness in childbirth. The post-certificate training of midwives was interrupted only by the Second World War.

Enough will have been said to show that the county's special problems naturally pushed its welfare machinery towards a pattern of administration by district, and, at the same time towards the provision of a collaborative system involving doctors, voluntary bodies of several kinds and local authorities. This was especially the case in the working of the Tuberculosis Scheme which covered the administrative county. There were two main units in this scheme, those centring on dispensary treatment, and those on institutions, hospitals or sanatoria. Each type of treatment was represented in each of five dispensary areas, which had both tuberculosis officers and health visitors with main and branch dispensaries. The consultant tuberculosis officer of each area was also its medical superintendent in charge of a sanatorium–hospital; and so, accordingly, he had beds at his disposal like any other consultant colleague, and had the further advantage of knowing the home conditions of patients through his health visitors. The work of dispensary staffs was lightened by fourteen voluntary care committees which assisted needy patients in a variety of ways, and which received council grants of fifty per cent of their actual expenditure. In addition, the scheme brought about close co-operation between the local medical officers, various types of hospital, Guardians' committees and the Unemployment Assistance Board. The scourge of tuberculosis had an effect much like the war which was on the way; it led to memorable feats of communal effort and combined operation. The Lancashire Tuberculosis Scheme, which remained under the direction of Dr Lissant Cox, CBE, until 1946, was the best in England.

It is fascinating to speculate how the health administration of great authorities like Lancashire might have developed if the war had not intervened. Would an inner administrative logic have brought about something simply ready for the imprint of a national health service in the long run? In posing such a question, it is of course necessary to maintain a strict realism; the greater scale of the postwar service was the result of a major social and political upheaval. Yet the health and welfare services of 1939, judged in terms of numbers of full-time county staff, were already two-thirds as strong as those of 1955. The rather surprising figures are shown in Table 14.1.[12]

TABLE 14.1
Health and Welfare Staff, Lancashire County Council

	1939	1947	1955
Full-time			
Health	1064	1682	3052
Health/Welfare	1588	2927	402
Public Health*	46	43	28
Part-time			
Health	21	97	1945
Health/Welfare	501	217	77
Public Health	—	—	—

* i.e. sanitary services and inspection

Nor did greater scale necessarily lead to unmixed advantage; the relatively small central headquarters administrative staff of 1939 could keep in close touch with fieldworkers in its three main areas of school and child welfare services, midwifery and tuberculosis treatment, a point made by a senior officer with experience of prewar and postwar conditions.[13]

The war years, which placed existing and routine services under great strain, saw a direction of energies towards the provision of emergency hospital schemes, and towards the health and welfare of evacuated populations. The extraordinary efforts that were made[14] deserve more than a brief reference; but they are, unfortunately, beyond the major themes touched upon in this book. The immediate postwar years had vast impact, bringing the implementation of the 1944 Education Act, the National Health Service Act of 1946 and the National Assistance Act of 1948.

The historic 1944 Education Act affected the county administration in three ways: the school staffs and school children of twenty-seven Part III authorities, mostly Lancashire municipal boroughs, were transferred to the Lancashire Education Committee together with all other educational functions, adding greatly to the number of children looked after by the school medical service; the Act provided that all medical treatment other than domiciliary should be free of charge for children in local authority schools; and the Act also laid upon the authority the duty of providing schools for handicapped children.

As we have seen, the county's administrators were not without experience of geographically diffused organisational units, as their prewar experience had tended continually in that direction. The devolution of the work of committees into local executives, however, was a new feature, and one that was enforced by the sheer scale of the new services that were being created. Part II of the National Health Service Act (1946) charged county authorities with the work of setting up health centres, supervising maternity and child welfare, midwifery and health visiting, home nursing, ambulance services, vaccination, immunisation and after-care. Several of these services had already been provided with some success, although the acquisition of ambulance, district nursing, and care and after-care services for the mentally handicapped were new developments, as was the provision of health centres as such. At the same time, the County Council lost its responsibilities for hospital care under the terms of Part II of the Act, and its former 'Poor Law' hospitals went to the newly created regional hospital boards. There were two further administrative consequences of note; the old Public Health and Housing Committee was now accompanied by the newly formed Health Committee, a much more comprehensive body, in 1948–9, and the personal health service functions of no fewer than thirty-three autonomous county district health authorities were transferred to the County Council; in consequence, the population for which the Council was responsible in health terms was doubled to a little over two million people.

The shaping of the administrative machine to deal with this great population and its needs occupied the whole of the following five years. Although it was fortunate that Dr Hall and several of his senior staff had the right kind of experience to deal with the problems thus presented, it was less happy that such vast strains had to be incurred immediately after the labours of wartime. When Dr Hall retired in 1950, however, to be succeeded by Dr S. C. Gawne, the foundations (at least) of the new county service were laid on their extensive ground.

The first major move to be related to the reorganisation of the health divisions was the formation of seventeen divisional committees, each

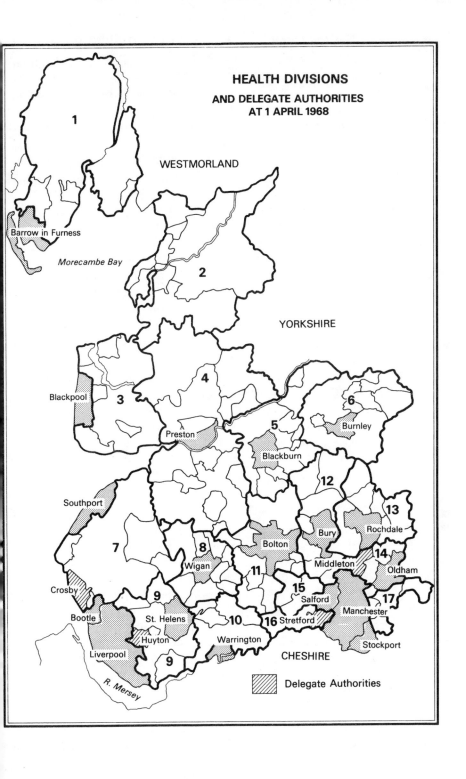

HEALTH DIVISIONS

**AND DELEGATE AUTHORITIES
AT 1 APRIL 1968**

1

WESTMORLAND

Barrow in Furness

Morecambe Bay

2

YORKSHIRE

4

Blackpool

3

Preston

6

Burnley

5

Blackburn

12

Southport

13

Rochdale

Bury

7

8

Bolton

14

Wigan

Middleton

Oldham

11

Crosby

15

9

Salford

17

Bootle

St. Helens

10

16

Stretford

Manchester

Huyton

Warrington

Stockport

Liverpool

9

CHESHIRE

R. Mersey

⬚⬚⬚ Delegate Authorities

charged with the local provision of the services listed above, and covering areas varying in population from 35,559 (No. 1 – the Furness area outside Barrow), to 169,461 (No. 11 – the great conurbation around the county borough of Bolton). The first mentioned was a relatively small committee, with fifteen members, covering a physically large area of 140,000 acres; the second, at the other extreme, covered one-third of the area and had thirty-nine members, mainly from district councils.[15] The mass of urban and rural districts in the populous areas of Lancashire meant that an individual divisional committee had to make room for representatives of up to ten local authorities as well as those of the existing health divisions and hospital management committees. The administrative rationale lying behind the choice of these areas was that of a deliberate coterminousness with 'the catchment areas of the various hospital districts', and was 'within certain limits, decided by administrative convenience [and] based on an average population of 100,000'.[16] However, the geographical position of areas like Furness would make this optimum population difficult to attain, and in thickly settled south Lancashire the figure was more nearly reached in most instances. The general problem of administrative districts is discussed elsewhere.[17]

The work of setting up this basic machinery took the major part of two years (spring 1948 to autumn 1949), and even at that latter date the scheme was 'little more than in its infancy'.[18] The equipment of offices, the interviewing and appointment of new staff (vastly time-consuming to senior officers), the assimilation of the services formerly provided by autonomous authorities or voluntary organisations and 'the preparation of directives and explanatory memoranda for the guidance of divisional staff'[19] all threw heavy strain on the organisers. As has already been pointed out, the new organisation, despite its size and scope, had some very deep tap-roots into the past, and the midwifery service formed under the terms of the 1936 Act was so developed that 'no extensive change'[20] was needed when the postwar health service came into operation after 1947.

This was perhaps fortunate, for the further development of the department after 1947 into personal service organisations now threw increased responsibility on to the Health Committee, which had four sub-committees (Ambulances, Nursing Services, Welfare Services and Mental Health). The old Public Health and Housing Committee remained, much diminished in importance, and dealt with sewerage, water and milk supplies and food and drugs, while the Children's Welfare Committee became, after 1948, the Children's Committee. Sir Thomas Tomlinson remained the chairman of Public Health and Housing. A former colonial judge, he was a most able occupier of this post, highly respected by officers and administrative staff ('you had to be up early in the morning for him' was the remark of a senior officer). Like Sir William Hodgson, Sir Thomas had the keen observation and meticulousness of approach that earned this type of respect; he was, in other words, an administrator's chairman rather than a political leader.

Alderman Harry Lord, who was chairman of the Health Committee from 1948 to 1958 and chairman or vice-chairman for a total of twenty years from the earlier date, was a political leader, being for much of that time the secretary or the chief whip of the Conservative Party on the Council. Political affiliation, however, came to have little relevance in his case, because his identification with the development of the health service in the county became a total one, and he earned respect from opponents as well as political allies – so much so that the leaders of the Labour group were disinclined to interfere with his chairmanship, and did so only by virtue of the demands of general policy. Alderman Lord's deeply felt devotion to the health service had part of its origin in the revelations of conditions in a number of former public assistance institutions which had been allocated to the Council on the transfer of the institutions to the regional hospital boards, so that temporary accommodation could be arranged for the people for whom the County Council was responsible under the National Assistance Act of 1948. The conditions were so bad at the Jericho Institution, Bury, and at Delphside, Whiston, that Alderman Lord confessed in public to have been sickened by them.[21] In the years to come the Committee and its officers were to press steadily for improved accommodation for old or chronically sick people. This tragic episode merely marked the formation of policy.

Indeed, the growing emphasis of the health service of the two postwar decades was on the needs of the aged. This was less obvious in the fifties than it later became, especially in the teething period of the new organisation. In 1950 there were 'difficulties of recruiting sufficient suitable medical, dental, health visiting and nursing staffs', which 'continued seriously to hamper development of the several branches of the health and welfare services'.[22] Nevertheless, progress was made as regards the acquisition and adaptation of hostels for the aged and infirm, the opening of child welfare centres (again something of which Lancashire had previous experience), and the expansion of the home help services, soon established in most of the health divisions. The demand for domiciliary help continued to increase, and the County Medical Officer observed that 'there can be no doubt that nursing and auxiliary personnel of the local health authority will be increasingly called upon to provide assistance in the home to aid the family doctor in his important work there'.[23] Subsequently he pointed out that 'the care and treatment of people in their own homes is more economical than the alternative of providing institutional care'.[24]

However, this patently sensible aim involved a degree of co-ordination and teamwork for which sections of the medical profession were, at best, incompletely prepared. As the County Medical Officer put it at the time, 'There [was] unfortunately great variation in the degree of co-operation between hospital, general practitioner and local authority services', especially with regard to mental illnesses;[25] and general practitioners, despite the fact that health visitors had been a common phenomenon in the county for a generation, were still inclined to resent (in the words of a humorously pungent letter to the *Spectator*) 'smart young women who visit our patients in shining cars'.[26]

However, these were to some extent transitory problems, and the structure of the service tended to bring about co-operation rather than its opposite, the informal meeting often achieving as much as the formal. In the field of maternity treatment or aged sick cases, co-operation between those professional workers involved was seen to come about easily.[27] The difficulties facing workers in the field were, as so often, practical rather than personal, and the reports from divisional officers reflect many of the problems of the early fifties – Division 3, on the Fylde coast, could only with difficulty obtain home helps in the holiday season; Division 13, in central east Lancashire, was short of health visitors, as were several other areas; and still more reported continuing shortages in staffing.[28] The vast extension in this field of local government, as in parallel cases, involved wholesale training and recruitment of those workers who were to be the backbone of the service in the equally great expansion of the sixties. Unfortunately, the shortage of health visitors persisted until the closing years of the decade,[29] considering that shortages are relative; this one arose not simply from difficulties in recruitment, but from a steadily increasing pressure of demand for domiciliary care, especially on the part of old people.

As the County Medical Officer's report for 1958 remarked, 'the number of visits made again showed a substantial increase ... a good deal of time being devoted to the aged and infirm and to problem families'. The home nursing staff, too, tended to be preoccupied with persons 'suffering from senility or other ill-defined conditions'.[30] This was very much the prevailing tendency, and by the sixties the emphasis on geriatric problems concerning both accommodation and treatment, was to be considerable indeed. This in turn brought about further pressure on the personal services provided by the county.

Regarding the other equally important health and environmental matters affecting the Lancashire population at this stage, general environmental improvement can be seen as arising from a multitude of interrelated factors, many of which are difficult to identify individually. It should not,

however, be forgotten that the county's health was at least partially dependent upon environmental change; in this respect, leaving aside intangibles
like general improvement in the quality of life, the work of the county's
sanitary staff played a part. The inspection of drainage, sanitation generally
and housing conditions was one of the county medical officer's statutory
duties, and these inspections were carried out in county districts in rota-
tion, often after long periods. In pursuing this part of his work, the medical
officer was not envied by his colleagues in other departments, highly conscious as always of the need to maintain good relations with county
districts.[31] In fact, the county MOH turned this duty to good account
by engaging in detailed policy discussion with his district colleagues, and
as a result often strengthening their hands in bringing about local sanitary
improvements.[32] The local surveys themselves were carried out meticu-
lously, and make interesting reading; the reports on Brierfield UDC,
Heywood MB and Leyland UDC made in 1949–50 show a careful blend
of praise and criticism, and reflect the progress that had been made in
the interwar years – that of Brierfield was made in the light of the results
of an earlier survey performed in 1922.[33] In these instances, we see the
tutelage function at work; the county, as an information-collecting body,
with the facilities for statistical analysis of the progress of many varied
areas of the county, could convincingly demonstrate the progress of districts
one against the other, and would use local patriotism rather than oppose it.

It is not clear, however, at this stage how far the more tangible aspects
of environmental improvements were affecting the crude death rate of the
county. By 1951 Dr Gawne and his statisticians were taking the view that
the latter had ceased to be a meaningful indicator of general social conditions and that, instead, 'the infant mortality rate ... furnishes the best
single test of the well-being of a community'. This was, at 29 per 1000
live births, the lowest rate ever recorded in Lancashire,[34] viz., the area
outside the county boroughs. There is substantial reason for believing that
the improved training of midwives and the developing co-operation
between the hospital and domiciliary services had produced the remarkable
improvement in maternal mortality rates, reinforced by the introduction
of antibiotics to combat puerperal sepsis. In the maternity service, which
since the prewar days had supplied 'flying squads' to supply blood plasma
and immediate treatment in case of post-partum haemorrhage, there was
genuine and constant co-operation between hospital consultants, county
officers and the midwives and district nurses, who now set new standards
in training and techniques.

By 1957 deaths classified to pregnancy, childbirth and abortion stood
at 0.45 per 1000 total births, a new low record, and in 1968, the year
of Dr Gawne's retirement, the figure was lower still. Developments of

this kind are attributable mainly to the standards of care employed by the medical and nursing teams. On the other hand, tuberculosis, which produced the lowest number of deaths ever recorded in administrative Lancashire by 1957, and which had been the subject of the historic campaign already described, is influenced far more by general social conditions. But there were still other victories of which the doctors (like wartime pilots seeking to claim a shooting-down) could much more reasonably boast; diphtheria and pneumonia, in Lancashire as elsewhere, were effectively conquered and claimed very few victims, largely by virtue of the use of immunisation and antibiotics; and poliomyelitis, that then mystery disease, faded away in the fifties with the use of vaccines, after striking at populous parts of the county in 1947, 1949 and 1950.[35] But cancer of the lung and the uterus, and coronary thrombosis, emerged in the fifties as major scourges. The great Lancashire anti-tuberculosis organisation had been closed down, meanwhile, after the reorganisation of 1944–5.

The period 1951–63 was one of great expansion of the health services, and may well be shown to be that of the greatest growth in welfare services generally in British history. The emphasis in that growth affected elderly people, although by no means entirely so. The county authority could boast of its 'Sunshine Scheme' for the care of old people, its laundry scheme for bedding and night clothing, its chiropody facilities, its special housing schemes for the aged and, associated with the same broad problem, a huge development of the provision of part-time home helps; where some 784 of these workers had been on the county's books in September 1951, there were over 4000 (estimated) by 1963.[36] In this way resources that, two decades previously, would have been deployed against tuberculosis were instead increasingly devoted to the older age groups. BCG vaccination was now defending a largely tuberculosis-free population. In addition to the immunisation schemes mentioned, those for whooping cough, tetanus and (for those travelling abroad) yellow fever should be recorded. In those areas involving large full-time staffs, such as home nursing, midwifery and health visiting, progress was gradual, but in the field of welfare homes and mental welfare staff it was considerable.[37] Progress was especially rapid in the care of the physically handicapped and the mentally disordered; thus, special housing, social visiting and training and occupational activities were together a primary concern of the medical officer's staff, the Health Committee itself and the divisional committees. The Mental Health Act of 1959 had given the Council additional responsibilities for providing residential accommodation and training for adults suffering from mental disorders, and the Health Committee's reaction was decisive. Following the Act, the County 'responded dramatically' as compared with most other authorities, and it was thereby able to economise by employing fewer mental health social workers per 1000 of population.[38]

A significant part of the new welfare accommodation developed as a direct consequence of the special concerns of the school medical service, which had for long felt the need for organised care for 'children suffering from permanent physical disabilities not ordinarily amenable to treatment, for whom there was no suitable provision for their education.'[39] The school medical services were able to provide advice and care in detecting defects in hearing, or dealing with orthopaedic problems, instructing in dental care or dealing with a squint or more complex ophthalmic problems. The preventive and health educational function of the service was immensely important because it applied its resources where its effect was most easily understood, felt or communicated, whether by contact with the parent and child or by utilising the teaching profession as a health educator. The school service, meanwhile, has an interesting feature in that it attracts a high proportion of women doctors.

Athough much remains to be discovered about this subject (as about many others touched upon in this volume), the relationship of the health and welfare services to the general practitioner is and has been an altogether more vexed question. It is very doubtful whether a large number of the profession saw themselves as an integral part of a team, and a good many of the more conservative resented the intrusion of what they saw as 'officialdom'. As late as 1968, the County Medical Officer commented hopefully on 'an awareness of the need for organisation and team work', which was 'gradually pervading medical practice in the community'. He went on:

> General Practitioners are finding they can no longer effectively conduct their practices single-handed.... Already in Lancashire the links between the general practitioner and the local health authority's nurses, midwives and health visitors are being strengthened in many areas by formal arrangements, and in one division a social welfare worker and a mental welfare worker are also 'attached' to two group practices, an arrangement which is working well. In these areas where health centres are being set up these desirable developments will be further promoted. At the time of writing four health centres are in operation and four more are in process of being built.[40]

Seven Lancashire health centres were completed in 1969–71. The advantage of hindsight leads to the view that an extreme slowness in promoting and building health centres (which, after all, had been foreshadowed in the discussions immediately following Section 21 of the National Health Service Act of 1946) had itself prevented demonstration of the tangible benefits of team work in one spot accessible to the general public.

In another important area Lancashire was more successful in making experiments – namely, that concerned with the system of 'sheltered' housing for old people with a warden within easy reach. This sensible and humane idea, which was furthered and developed during the later period of Dr Gawne's term of office, was of course not peculiar to Lancashire, but the county was in a good position to experiment. The provision of such homes also involved serious considerations of teamwork and organisation, in that, because the boundary between infirmity and sickness was so tenuous, and because many elderly people were liable to need medical and nursing attention, both home nursing and hospital beds had to be readily available – if the hospital beds were not ready, then there was a great danger that the homes themselves would sink into the position of 'second-class hospitals'.[41] The cardinal aim of the homes-with-warden scheme, then, was to encourage old people to look after themselves with help within easy call. As Dr Gawne put it on the eve of his own retirement, 'The provision of special housing is of great importance and the further development of projects both by housing authorities and voluntary organisations is something much to be desired. Such is most likely to promote the happiness of those people who by reason of age and personal circumstances can no longer manage unaided in their own homes.'[42]

The Seebohm Committee, meanwhile, was at this stage considering a mass of evidence, and experience, which had accumulated regarding the co-ordination, or the lack of it, in the welfare and health services (which services were now almost inextricably intertwined). Dr C. H. T. Wade, Dr Gawne's successor in 1969, who provides yet another example of a chief officer either formerly experienced in the same county service or taken from another authority within Lancashire, took office in time to deal with the consequences of 'Seebohm', the Local Authority Social Services Act of 1970. This took account of the fact that health committees had had a bewildering range of welfare services to administer, and transferred most of the latter to the social services committees (and departments), which were to be responsible for the formerly separate children's service, maternity and child welfare, home helps and the care of old people and the physically and mentally handicapped, care and after-care of the sick and accommodation for mentally disordered children, adults and the aged. Medical service elements, however, were to remain the province of health committees.[43] It was clearly intended that the welfare and some medical services should work in co-ordination, even in the unlikely event of total non-co-operation by the hospital authorities and the private doctors.

In 1972 Dr Wade summed up his own position in a few words: 'The work of the Medical Officer of Health has changed in character. He is no longer so concerned with the control and treatment of infectious diseases, but more with the provision of services, and non-communicable diseases.'[44] His colleagues on the Health Committee could look back with some pride; since the unhappy revelations of conditions in the public assistance institutions of 1951, they had provided 4000 beds in 100 new county-provided homes, and made further accommodation for 900 other old or handicapped people. In conjunction with district authorities, they had brought about shelter-type housing schemes for nearly 6000 old people – a tiny enough drop in the ocean, indeed, but at least a firm assertion of civilised values. They had taken responsibility for degrees of care (through registration) of roughly 20,000 physically handicapped, blind or partially sighted or deaf persons, a figure that was very far from a mere 'drop', and had built a wide range of facilities for these unfortunate people in the form of residential homes; they had, moreover, provided a wide range of junior and adult training centres for those suffering from problems of mental health. All these institutions and services went to the new Social Services Department.[45]

CHAPTER 15

Planning and Motorways

Planning policies depend more on political than technical objectives; and they are always in a state of evolution. Planning is essentially a service rather than a science in its own right.

Baroness Evelyn Sharp

THE discussion of this chapter is concerned with the work of Lancashire County Council since the Second World War. Road and motorway planning has been a growing activity with the rise in car ownership and motor transport. Likewise, with the passing of the 1947 Town and Country Planning Act new powers and responsibilities were placed on the Council, transforming its approach and role in planning. Faced with the task of surveying the county's work, the writer is conscious of failing to do justice to many individuals, for example, the numerous committee chairmen, vice-chairmen and the staff of the departments. No attempt will be made to deal exhaustively with the statutes,[1] as this would divert us from our main purpose. In the space available it is impossible to deal comprehensively with all the county's work, let alone to discuss national policy exhaustively.

A large literature exists on land use planning in postwar Britain. Many legislative changes have been made in the last thirty years, all tending to increase the degree and scope of planning control. The early postwar years introduced major controls over the citizen's right to build where he pleased, but the initial emphasis of these controls was negative. Over the years, this has changed to a more positive encouragement of particular policies and to direct action by the authorities themselves. Planning is no longer mainly concerned with preventing certain actions, but is now more involved in 'social engineering', an emphasis some find offensive. The discussion of Lancashire's response to these changes provides insights into the impact of national policy at the local level. Discussion of such topics at the county level, showing local adaptation to changing national policy, are as yet rare.[2]

Lancashire's experience, therefore, as formerly one of the country's biggest authorities should be of general interest. Inevitably, much of the discussion will be of a qualitative nature, but it brings out clearly how pervasive has become the local planner's role in our everyday life.

After the discussion of environmental planning there follows a consideration of Lancashire's contribution to the building of the nation's motorways.

PHYSICAL AND ENVIRONMENTAL PLANNING SINCE 1947

The first statutory control of planning came with an Act of 1909. Until the 1947 Town and Country Planning Act, however, the main responsibility for planning rested with the district councils. The transfer of power to the county councils under this Act introduced a new era. Nationally the number of planning authorities was reduced by ninety per cent, from 1441 to 145, and in Lancashire it meant the dispossession of 105 district councils. In the geographical county, following this change, the Council became the planning authority for forty per cent of the population and eighty-six per cent of the land area – the largest single geographical unit of its kind in England – while the seventeen county boroughs took over the responsibilities for the remainder. Changes of this order meant a considerable centralisation and extension of planning powers. The complex relationships between county and county boroughs and the consequent fragmentation of authority in the area were a distinctive feature of Lancashire in our period.

The 1947 Act reflected the established philosophy of a period whose origins could be traced back to the 1930s. In 1940 the report of the Barlow Commission suggested the existence of a megalopolis and urged the need for industrial balance of conurbational growth, and this was followed by the Scott Report in 1942, which emphasised the need to conserve agricultural land, and the Reith Report on New Towns, which advocated positive, paternalistic, planning. Abercrombie's plan for Greater London in 1944 established the style of the grand, end-state, master-plan. These developments provided the basis of the 1947 Act, which apart from nationalising all development rights was based on twin elements: (a) a statutory plan for each authority, and (b) effective powers to control land use without fear that a suit for compensation might be brought.

The Act itself left a good deal of the detail to be settled subsequently by the minister. The form and content of the proposed Development Plan was specified in great detail in 1948,[3] and provided a statement of policy for the following twenty-year period. Each authority was required to Csubmit its plan by July 1951 to the minister for approval. He also reserved the right to 'call in' any planning application for his own decision; and any applicant who had been refused development permission had a right to appeal to him. While scope for local initiative existed within this framework a good deal of reserve power remained with the central authorities.

A good deal has been written regarding the 1947 planning system. One authority[4] has criticised it on technical grounds, arguing that the wrong mapping scale for land use zones was used. The approval procedures were cumbersome and made updating difficult, and by the 1960s the Development Plan system was grinding to a standstill. At the end of 1968 the Ministry had a backlog of over 350 town maps and amendments awaiting approval, and had come to the view that the effort was out of all proportion to their real importance.[5] The professional planner had come to the same conclusion. In 1965 the Planning Advisory Group Report on *The Future of Development Plans* was published and led directly to the 1968 Act and towards a more flexible system in the form of structure and local plans. These changes removed many of the weaknesses of the 1947 plan, but their effect on the former Lancashire authority was marginal, although some internal departmental reorganisations were put in hand to accommodate the new system.

One of the most important responses of the Council to the 1947 Act lay in the selection of its first chief planning officer, and the approach and organisation of the Department still owes something to the style established at the onset. The Planning Committee appointed G. Sutton Brown, the deputy city engineer of Manchester.[6] He had formerly been borough surveyor at Ipswich and had moved to an appointment at Manchester by deliberate choice to work with R. J. Nicholas, the city surveyor, who had a considerable reputation in the planning field.[7] Sutton Brown was, at the time, one of the youngest chief officers in the country. His appointment was not without its critics. The Town Planning Institute wrote and complained that the second largest authority in the country had chosen not to appoint a qualified planner, and when he applied for membership of the Institute it was refused.

Sutton Brown had worked closely with Nicholas on the Manchester Plan; he had been highly praised for his personal contribution, and could draw on this valuable experience in establishing his new department at Lancashire. He is frequently described by his contemporary colleagues as 'brilliant', and was held in high regard. A quiet man, softly spoken, possessing a certain presence, he effortlessly assumed the post of chief officer: meticulous, searching, and a hard task-master. He used pink paper for his personal memoranda: as Mr Bentley, divisional planning officer at Rishton remarked, 'a pink memo from Preston, and everyone jumped!' He was greatly respected and admired by his staff, and is remembered with some affection. He resigned somewhat unexpectedly in 1951–2 to take up a post in Vancouver, and later furthered his career with some success.

While most of the county boroughs at this time incorporated their new planning duties into existing departments, often the Surveyor's Department, Lancashire followed the normal county pattern and established a separate Planning Department in 1948. A tremendous amount of work was waiting, because to submit the county's development plan by 1951 required the simultaneous appointment of staff and organisation of a department. Sutton Brown established at the outset four functional sections covering research, development, architecture and administration. It is noteworthy that this basic organisation remained until 1972, when two further divisions covering reclamation and environment were added. In addition a field organisation was needed to work with the district councils and also to process planning applications. For these purposes the county was divided into six areas, each under a divisional planning officer, with his own office and staff, and these were further subdivided into nineteen divisions based upon district council groupings. In view of the relative shortage of suitably qualified persons, the speedy establishment and appointment of staff for this organisation was itself a noteworthy achievement.

The Development Plan Strategy

The county was greatly aided in the preparation of its own development plan by the existence of four recently published advisory plans for the Liverpool and Manchester conurbations.[8] While these plans were non-statutory, each conveyed the same theme: the immediate regional problem for the postwar years was the concentration of population and the related need to find land for overspill housing. It was estimated that the Manchester area would have an estimated overspill need for 150,000 to 250,000 people, and Merseyside for 258,000. The reports concluded that Manchester, while looking at existing town development in Lancashire, would in the main be looking towards the relatively underdeveloped regions in Cheshire. Merseyside, on the other hand, anticipated the accommodation of two-thirds of its overspill in Lancashire following conurbation growth in the form of spurs and wedges in the adjacent green areas of the county. These policies were of vital significance in the future planning strategy of Lancashire.[9]

Prior to the submission of its statutory development plan, Lancashire's planning officer prepared a consultative plan, published in 1951.[10] The principal theme of this preliminary plan was the problem of postulated overspill pressure on the county up to 1962:

> Throughout the period to be covered by the Development Plan, and particularly during the first five years, house building will be the dominant driving force behind the process of land-use change which it is the planners' job to guide for the benefit of all. Until this land-consuming tide has been safely canalised into reservoirs of adequate capacity, planning to satisfy other potential claims on land can only be an academic exercise. Accordingly the Preliminary County Plan concentrates on these limited objectives: (a) to determine the scale and distribution of imminent demands on land for housing and associated purposes; (b) to determine the scale and distribution of the available resources of land for meeting this demand; and hence (c) to define the bounds within which the urban development can be most advantageously confined.[11]

This choice of overspill as the key issue has been seen as showing great insight on the part of its author, although both the Manchester and Merseyside reports had shown it as the most pressing problem of the period, and it was one already well recognised by both Sutton Brown and Adcock (who had come from Manchester to Lancashire). As Cullingworth cogently put it:

> The County's problem was an acute one.... Salford ... was proposing to extend its boundaries: proposals were also made by Bootle, Liverpool, Manchester, Oldham and several other towns. Indeed, had all these proposals been accepted the Administrative County would have lost 53% of its land, 64% of its population, and 65% of its rateable value: it would have become a small, formless, and predominantly rural area shorn of the major part of its existing wealth and powers. Quite apart from the natural reluctance of the County to agree (in its own words) to 'annihilation', it argued that the need of land for housing alone was not a good reason for boundary extensions...[12]

The achievement of this preliminary plan was substantial: having been produced quickly, it provided the opportunity for consultation with local authorities and other groups affected by its proposals; it provided a definitive and comprehensive statement of the overspill problem; and it did not restrict itself to the administrative county (as the statutory plan would have to) but adopted a regional approach which explicitly incorporated the housing needs of the county boroughs. In short, it viewed problems as they affected Lancashire and not the Council alone.

The method of analysis adopted in the preliminary report was based on a land use survey (to identify the areas of potential building land), data on population change up to 1962, a housing survey (to determine multiple occupancy and unfit property), and data on land required for schools and open spaces. On this basis the additional future land requirements in the county were calculated, to which were added the existing forecasted overspill requirements of the county boroughs and cities. In the county districts a headship rate of 100 per cent was assumed and a similar exercise to the one for the county was carried out, giving a total housing need, converted to land requirements (in acres) using the local densities for the 105 districts. Land need and availability were compared district by district to determine whether population could be imported or exported.

With the aid of hindsight it seems clear now that professional planners were, in those early years, learning their trade, and making serious mistakes and omissions. Later experience has shown population movements to be notoriously difficult to forecast. The assumptions about household formation were crude, and planners failed to anticipate the postwar boom in private sector housing. The structural industrial weakness of the north-west region was inadequately recognised, and while the planning authorities were responsible only for the availability and zoning of land for industry and not its location, physical planners acquiesced too easily in this fragmented approach.[13]

The results of the planning officer's analysis showed that the overspill problem was essentially related to the county boroughs, with ninety-eight per cent of the expected overspill in the Lancashire area coming from them and only two per cent coming from the county districts. Of the estimated total overspill of the region of 639,000 people, the Manchester conurbation provided forty-eight per cent (of which, Manchester provided sixty-five per cent and Salford twenty per cent), a further twenty-nine per cent from Merseyside (of which, Liverpool provided seventy-eight per cent and Bootle fifteen per cent). The figures showed that in the county the 1948 housing stock would need to be increased by forty-seven per cent by 1962. Nineteen per cent of the anticipated extra houses would be to end multiple occupancy, seventeen per cent to house the forecasted increases in population and sixty-four per cent to replace unfit property. The extent of such unfit property showed considerable local variation: in Blackburn and Chorley well over fifty per cent of all property was unfit; in Rochdale, Bolton and Leigh, over forty per cent; in north-east Lancashire overall the figure was nearly forty per cent. To meet the land needs required for these houses and redevelopment, the Plan proposed to increase the total developed in the administrative county by fourteen per cent. Table 15.1 shows the distribution of the extra acreage.

Sutton Brown's policy for dealing with this problem comprehended two parts. First, there would be peripheral and short-distance movement of population close to the conurbations, in schemes not requiring the movement of industry or entailing an intolerable increase in the journey to work. It was estimated that the county overspill could be accommodated in this way, with the exception of the Manchester and Merseyside conurbations, where only twenty-nine per cent and fifty-four per cent respectively of the expected numbers could be so housed. As a consequence, additional long-distance schemes would be required to take up the balance, involving the movement not only of people, but also of industry and employment, which would be self-contained communities of a 'new town' character. The preliminary plan mentioned three sites and firmly proposed one.[14]

TABLE 15.1

Percentage Distribution by Use of the Extra Developed Acreage Proposed in the Preliminary Plan

		%	%
1.	Total housing		59.0
	Sub-tenants	16	
	Redevelopments	25	
	Increased population	18	
2.	Schools		20.0
3.	Open space		18.0
4.	Displaced industry		0.5
5.	Other		2.5
			100

The formal statutory plan of Lancashire was based upon the advisory preliminary plan and was, unlike the latter, conventional, its form and content being closely dictated by government circular. Only twenty-two of the other 145 planning authorities met the ministry deadline of July 1951. Half of the plans, however, had been submitted by the end of that year, and the bulk approved by 1959, while Lancashire submitted in November 1951 and Cheshire in 1952. Both approvals were slow in coming, Lancashire's in 1956 and Cheshire's in 1958. As a result, much local initiative and momentum in local planning was lost.[15]

The development plan for Lancashire extended the time-span of analysis from 1962 to 1971. The total overspill figure was raised slightly, and it was proposed that half should be rehoused by the end of the statutory twenty-year period. The basic approach of the preliminary plan, in terms of the short- and long-distance movement of population, was adopted in the statutory plan. The analysis looked feasible, and provided a reasonable basis for future policy. Estimates had shown that the administrative county could increase its acreage of developed land by up to twenty-two per cent, while its overspill proposals would require a fourteen per cent increase of such land. On the basis of the development plan, Lancashire was committed to providing land sufficient to house two-thirds of the overspill population from the Manchester conurbation and four-fifths from Merseyside: the balance from these conurbations was to go into Cheshire.

Lancashire's assessment of the problem was largely corroborated by Cheshire's submission. Chapman, the planning officer for Cheshire, showed more orthodoxy in his approach, and emphasised the need to disperse industry and to revive agriculture as advocated by Barlow and Scott. The emphasis of Cheshire's proposals lay in expanding existing towns as independent communities, and in a vigorous resistance to Manchester's urban sprawl. The conflict of interest and policy confrontation between Cheshire and Manchester, which arose in the period up to 1970, has been vividly discussed by Lee and Wood.[16] Lancashire, in contrast, appears to have had tolerably amicable relations with Manchester but more strained ones with Liverpool as a result of a long history of territorial disputes.

The principle of urban containment was widely accepted by planners and was implicit in Lancashire's development plan strategy. This strategy reflected local initiative on the part of Lancashire; and, although the principle and practice of designating 'green belt' areas has not gone unchallenged,[17] it was advocated by central government from 1955. Lancashire submitted a green belt proposal to contain the two conurbations on the northern flanks of Merseyside and south-east Lancaster, and two were submitted by Cheshire to cover the equivalent southern approaches. Proposals were approved in sketch plan form in 1956, and formal submissions made in 1960–1. However, although these propositions were accepted in principle by the minister, only one public enquiry was held – that into the Lancashire submission. No statutory decision on any of the proposals was ever given. The effectiveness of Lancashire's containment policy in southeast Lancashire was the subject of a research project on the part of Political and Economic Planning (PEP). In a detailed, technical analysis of two land use surveys covering the south-east Lancashire–north-east Cheshire region, an estimate was made of the growing urbanisation in the area during the 1950–60 period. The authors concluded that with regard to the Manchester conurbation:

> The policy of urban containment has been applied enthusiastically by Lancashire ... and it has had a clear physical impact. During the 1950s and the beginning of the 1960s, these urban areas were increasingly forced to house their surplus populations within their own built up areas.[18]

This evidence suggests that Lancashire's success in promoting the idea of short-distance rehousing schemes, together with the national green belt principle, bore fruit in the prevention of further urban intrusion into the remaining open space in south Lancashire.

New Towns and the 'Worsley Formula'

Lancashire's long-distance overspill proposals were based upon the establishment of new towns, and the county placed great stress on such proposals in their postwar strategy. Great pride is taken in the fact that between 1961 and 1970 two of the three sites earlier proposed by the county have been designated, even though before 1961 pressure of every conceivable sort on the Ministry had drawn a blank. Nothing engenders self-congratulation in a county more than the Ministry capitulating after a protracted struggle! The 'new town' proposal was an integral part of Sutton Brown's policy, and the overspill programme was incomplete without it. Suggestions that the new town idea was itself prophetic cannot be sustained. Abercrombie's wartime London plan contained ten such proposals; the New Town Act was passed in 1946, and between 1947 and 1950 thirteen new towns were designated. Silkin, the then minister, specially requested Lancashire to propose new town sites in 1948, and the preliminary plan duly provided a response. Local initiative, perhaps, was shown in the proposed siting, although areas meeting all requirements were hard to find. Three proposals were put forward by Lancashire: Parbold, Leyland and Garstang. By the time of the publication of the preliminary plan, the last two were considered to be too distant from the conurbations, although Leyland was suggested as suitable for a collaborative expansion by the county and the district council.[19] The choice of Parbold was bitterly opposed locally; and although it represented a superior location, the proposed site included in the development plan was changed to that of Skelmersdale.

When the approval of the plan came through in 1956 the new town proposals were deleted, and it was suggested instead that a local authority town expansion scheme should be substituted. This proposal was not accepted by the county planners, who sustained their belief in the need for a new town in the area to meet the overspill needs of Liverpool, and to stimulate investment and employment. Liverpool probably preferred peripheral development, such as that of Kirkby, in west Lancashire, in order to keep industrial development within the immediate area and to help to provide local employment for the city.

When seen in terms of national policy, the absence of progress on long-distance overspill schemes in the form of a new town during the 1950s was not a failure on the part of the county. With the coming to power of the Conservative Party in 1951, bringing Harold Macmillan as minister, an ideological move was made to reduce the involvement of Whitehall in local matters. A new town via the Development Corporation implied the direct involvement of London, and Conservative policy was to leave the resolution of the overspill problem to local initiatives. In 1957 the Government even announced that no more new towns would be built, but by the end of the 1950s the inadequacies of that approach were acknowledged. Skelmersdale, designated in 1961, just ten years after Lancashire's development plan submission, was the first in England and Wales for eleven years the vanguard of a second generation of new towns in the early 1960s, and a vindication of Lancashire's tenacity and its belief in the need for a new town. Others were to follow: Runcorn in 1964, and Warrington in 1968. In 1970 a central Lancashire new town was designated in the Leyland–Chorley area, a possible site originally discussed in Lancashire's preliminary plan in 1951.

A start on short-distance housing had already been made by the county even before the preparation of the preliminary plan, at Kirkby and in Worsley. The latter was the result of collaboration between the county, the urban district of Worsley, and Salford County Borough. It was a highly successful scheme and became something of an administrative, if not a social, model for the rest of the country. Studies made subsequently of other schemes throughout the country showed that success frequently depended on the presence of a 'champion' who would promote and foster the scheme. Often the individual was the town clerk, but in Worsley's case it was Alderman Edwin Roscoe who was instrumental in persuading the district council (of which he was a member) to accept the scheme, and who also promoted it at the county level. Although the county generally projects a different impression regarding this scheme, its initiation largely resulted from territorial threats from Salford County Borough, which in 1946 submitted a predatory proposal to the Boundary Commission to extend its boundary to take in Worsley, four miles away (as well as the intervening boroughs of Eccles, Swinton and Pendlebury). Worsley did not wish to lost its identity, and Lancashire did not wish to lose a substantial part of its area, population and rateable value.

Against this political background, Lancashire responded firmly. We have already remarked on the county's willingness to face up to the overspill problem, and Salford's case was accepted. The county argued that the need for building land alone was not a good reason for a boundary extension, and that the county and the district council could rehouse the overspill at least as effectively as the exporting authority.[20] The county supported its case with a plan to provide at least 3000 houses. A first phase of 400 houses was commenced in 1948, and the first house was opened by the Minister of Town and Country Planning in October 1949.

Using power under the 1948 Local Government Act, the county guaranteed the district council against financial loss. Later a Joint Management Committee consisting of representatives of the three authorities was set up. Technical assistance[21] was provided by an Estates Development Team staffed by officers of the Council. The county acted as catalyst in this scheme, and the quality of its contribution ensured the successful provision of houses.

However, Worsley had feared for its identity under the original annexation proposal by Salford, and while administratively it maintained its independence, geographically and economically it did not. The overspill scheme achieved its objective from a housing point of view, but it led to a spreading of the conurbation and to unbroken urban development. In terms of employment, much of the expanding population of Worsley was still dependent on the nearby cities. A social survey was conducted on the Worsley estates in 1959 to assess the effect of the changes,[22] based on a ten per cent sample from a cross-section of families. A quarter of the people had come from shared and over-crowded houses and a further third from insanitary accommodation in Salford. A change in life styles (towards a home-centred life) came with the move to Worsley. Contact with relatives had been reduced and the separation from 'mum' was often welcomed, although of course the effect on kinship groups was drastic. Rents had increased up to 300 per cent and there had been an increase in social expenditure resulting in some social and economic strains. The cost of living was higher, but so were standards. Overall, the impression was that the majority of families were thrilled with their new way of life, and an estimated seventy-three per cent did not wish to return to Salford.

The survey also showed that ten per cent of the overspill families had returned to Salford and a further seventeen per cent wished to do so (although, in the main, only if housing of the Worsley standard were available), the usual reason given being the long and expensive journey to work. As part of the development, 3000 jobs had been provided in Worsley but only twenty-five per cent had been taken by the overspill population. Seventy per cent of the latter people worked in the conurbation, involving about one-and-a-quarter hours of travelling per day. Local employment was comparatively poorly paid, and there were few prospects for advancement. Opportunities for female employment, expecially part-time, were scarce. Employment for school-leavers was inadequate – only 12.5 per cent of school-leavers in the four years prior to the survey had obtained work locally. Although many of these phenomena were to be found in other districts during the 1950s, this survey shows that, while living standards might be improved by a rehousing scheme, many social difficulties remained.

These comments provide some contemporary insights into the overspill problem in a project considered on balance a success. It must be remembered, however, that the emphasis of the early postwar years was on sheer size and numbers rather than on quality or social impact. Selection in Salford and Liverpool (for Kirkby) was from the top of the housing list and it was not until perhaps the 1960s that planners began to consider family structure and social balance in its housing communities. However, the importance of Worsley was in the demonstration that co-operation could work in the overspill problem, and that economically it could be worthwhile for the recipient authority. Worsley generated enough increased rateable value within ten years to cover the increased costs associated with the scheme.

In other parts of the county, the achievement of agreement on overspill schemes was a continually difficult problem. Sir Robert Adcock felt it was intractable for Lancashire, and the county failed to reach agreement with districts in ninety per cent of its attempts. Efforts in the 1950s to negotiate schemes, similar to that for Worsley, for 7000 people with Whitefield and 7450 with Heywood came to nothing,[23] west Lancashire persistently took an anti-Merseyside position, and only 300 people were accommodated at Aintree and Maghull. Meanwhile, the Kirkby estate was a source of considerable friction between Liverpool and Lancashire. Building for Liverpool had first been proposed at Kirkby in the 1930s, and in 1946 the Kirkby Trading Estate was taken over by the city. Land in adjacent Kirkby was bought from Lord Sefton for housing. The negotiations with the county were long and difficult, and the estate was the cause of a fierce fight when Liverpool promoted a private parliamentary bill to take it within the city boundaries. Eventually the battle was won by Lancashire after a two-day hearing in the Lords. Originally planned to house 47,500, by 1966 Kirkby housed 55,540 people. At least one prominent leader of the Council has felt that the social planning of Kirkby left much to be desired; for the problems indentified in the social survey of Worsley apply even more strongly to Kirkby and demonstrate the failure of early planners to consider adequately the community aspects of their work. This is a topic that has more recently alerted national attention, and one that deserves fuller examination than is possible here.

Westhoughton too was a place where local agreement could not be secured. Its utilisation was proposed in the county's development plan, and it was mentioned in the Willis Enquiry of 1958 into the siting of Manchester's overspill in Cheshire. Manchester accepted it as an alternative, provided that the original village could be comprehensively redeveloped. After successive negotiations, the orders made excluded ribbons of development that criss-crossed the site. The public enquiry in 1963 into the proposal was opened with the recorded voice of Vera Lynn singing 'Land of Hope and Glory' as 500 objectors slowly marched in procession to the town hall, while prayers were said in local churches against the scheme; 9000 out of 11,000 people on the electoral roll signed a petition; 1400 objections were lodged; and the two local coach proprietors laid on free day-trips to Bolton for the enquiry! Both the city and the county gave up.

By the beginning of 1960 the progress of house-building in the county was flagging, in part as the result of difficulties in reaching agreements, and in part because of the Minister's refusal of a new town. In 1960, with forty per cent of the twenty-year planning period gone, the number of people rehoused in overspill schemes was less than twenty-five per cent, and the number of 'rehousing' dwellings only twenty per cent, of the targets proposed for Manchester's conurbation. Cheshire had by that time achieved only between twelve and thirteen per cent of their target.

The progress made in Worsley, however, was seen as one of outstanding success for Lancashire. The house-building target had been raised to 4505, and 2685 of these were completed by 1959, a rate of building in excess of the original proposal. The scheme was finally completed in 1968, having rehoused 13,554 people. The Worsley project, however, also had national significance. Lancashire had used powers under an Act of 1948 and the scheme devised became known as the 'Worsley formula'. Its success gave rise to a Labour Government proposal, enacted in 1952 by the Conservatives as the Town Development Act. In essence it was an enabling Act and fitted with the Macmillan philosophy of leaving the overspill problem to local authorities; it became the Ministry's approach in the 1950s and the corollary to their negative attitude to any new town proposals. Although the Act was used in some instances with success, it never looked like providing a large-scale solution. In this respect, perhaps, it highlighted a basic weakness in the local government structure, but the Ministry took some time to accept this conclusion. The Ministry, in evidence to the Royal Commission on Local Government in Greater London in 1957, had remarked that experience of working with the Act had shown it most difficult to bring schemes to fruition, Evelyn Sharp remarking[24] that endless conferences took place to persuade exporters and importers of overspill. By the end of the 1950s the weaknesses of the Act were apparent, and recourse was again had to the New Town Act of 1946. Nationally the 1952 Act did not prove to be effective: in the first six years of its operation, only four authorities in the whole country had completed overspill schemes. In the period 1945–69 house-building in 'Expanded Towns' (under the 1952 Act) accounted for only one per cent of all houses built; while in the same period new towns accounted for nearly three per cent.

The county was justifiably proud of the Worsley project; it had made an impact on national and ministerial estimation. Yet over the whole period only four schemes of note were produced in the North-West: two involved Burnley County Borough (in which the county would not be involved), one was the original Worsley project, and another was a Widnes-based scheme for overspill from Liverpool. As described above, this poor showing was not due to a lack of effort by the county; but the Worsley formula was apparently very difficult to repeat.

Economic Planning

In addition to its concern for housing and the overspill problem, the county was keenly interested in industrial development and employment. Since 1934 the basis of the British policy has rested on the designation of special areas in which preferential treatment is afforded towards new industry and special assistance provided for local authorities investing in public capital. This same policy was taken up in the Distribution of Industry Act (1945) and in subsequent planning legislation, the criterion for designation being a high rate of unemployment relative to the national figure.

The discrimination by government policy in favour of specific regions in the period after the Second World War has contained three broad strands: restriction, provision and financial inducement. *Restriction* was exercised via the control of new industrial building by the Board of Trade who, by their use of Development Certificates, would divert industrial building into desirable locations and away from congested regions. *Provision* came in the form of advanced factories built on favourable terms by the Board of Trade. Finally, a variety of *financial inducements* were offered to businesses operating in the favoured areas, including loans, cash grants, tax allowances and, from 1967, a Regional Employment Premium (REP) to subsidise labour. It has been estimated[25] that nationally, in the period 1960-70, expenditure on advanced factories and grants was £48 million, while the average value of investment incentives to a firm located in a development area was seventeen to twenty per cent of capital expenditure; after 1967 the subsidy on labour (REP) was between six and seven per cent of the wage bill.

With regard to Lancashire, four significant periods can be identified. The first period covered 1946-60, during which Merseyside, south Lancashire and (from 1953) north-east Lancashire were designated development areas. The second period covered 1960-6, in which government policy changed to one of designating very precise areas (based on local employment exchanges) as development districts; in Lancashire those designated were Prescot, Merseyside, Widnes and Furness. A third period lasted from 1966 to 1970, when policy again reverted to the designation of broader geographical regions as development areas, and the criterion was was not so rigidly related to percentage unemployment. Merseyside and Furness were given special status during this phase, but designation covering the whole county was refused. After the Hunt Committee Report in 1969 an 'intermediate area' category was introduced, which was given to north-east Lancashire in 1970 and extended to the whole of the county in 1972. This has in some measure supported the case put forward in the 1960s by the county and the other local authorities in the north-west region. The designation of the intermediate area status marked the commencement of the fourth period for Lancashire's policy in 1970.

With the exception of the Merseyside development area, employment in Lancashire has been sluggish and subject to a long-term decline, with a higher proportion of people in the North-West involved in manufacturing, and a lower proportion in the service sector, than elsewhere. There was formerly a concentration in Lancashire on slow-growing, and declining, industries. The textile industry, which in 1921 employed 600,000 people, stood at 200,000 by 1969, having undergone a fall of 200,000 people in the period 1953–69. Mining saw the exhaustion of the easier seams and a concentration of the industry. In 1950 there were seventy pits in Lancashire employing 54,000 people: by 1969 twenty pits and 26,000 people remained. Against this background, the postwar economic policy of the county rested broadly on three approaches: an Industrial Bureau, the promotion of private Acts of Parliament and the ownership of industrial estates.

In 1952 the Industrial Bureau was established in the County Planning Department to act in the field of industrial liaison and to offer guidance to developers on the availability of industrial building sites. While it channelled information concerning all local authority and private sites, the Bureau, in more positive ways, also tried to direct attention to areas of high unemployment or those needing industrial diversification. By all accounts the Lancashire Bureau was a good example of its kind: it was able to help three firms to locate themselves on a private estate at Westhoughton, thereby providing 1650 jobs; in 1956 five out of nine firms moving to Worsley resulted from action by the Bureau; similarly, at a later date, it was instrumental in bringing 400 female jobs to the same area. In terms of the declining employment in the staple industries of Lancashire outlined in the previous paragraph, however, the effect of this sort of approach was feeble when contrasted with the magnitude of the problem.

The second strand of the county's economic policy, the promotion of parliamentary Bills, was one that the county had, of course, often used in the past; but the first attempt to secure special powers for assisting and encouraging local industry lay in the promotion of a Bill in 1960 dealing solely with industrial development in an attempt to offset the adverse consequences for Lancashire resulting from national regional policy. Unemployment had been growing, and there was an increased appreciation by the county that overspill projects needed a more positive policy to promote additional employment.[26] The Parliamentary Committee, therefore, proposed that the county should take increased powers. The county's Industrial Development Act of 1960 gave the county power to purchase land for industrial development, and to construct and maintain industrial buildings. It could also make advances to the developers of sites for up to a maximum of seventy-five per cent of the total outlay.

While the Act gave the county explicit powers, it did not have any significant effects. Nor was the form of the Act a precedent, since the city of Liverpool had been the first in the field with a very similar Act in 1936. Lancashire's own industrial estates pre-dated the Lancashire Act of 1960 and it did not influence their subsequent development: only one loan of significance was made, when £60,000 was provided for a company to set upon an industrial estate in Widnes.[27] The Act, however, may have been a political move, an expression of the county's concern at the deteriorating local employment situation.

An amendment to the Act was incorporated in a General Powers Act for the county in 1968, bringing Lancashire into line with a 1965 Act for Manchester and allowing the county to act as financial guarantor for a developer. Another provision referred to as a 'pioneering' clause allowed loans to be made to a private developer not building on county property. Despite these changes late in the life of the county, no further use was made of the powers taken under the original 1960 Act, or of those added in the 1968 amendment.[28]

A good deal of stress has been placed on both these Acts as evidence of the strong initiatives taken by the county in the industrial development field. There can be little doubt that the 1968 amendment came at a time of great county concern, reflected a reaction to national policy, and indicated how hard the county were fighting for inclusion as a special development area.

The county's case was that, being adjacent to Merseyside, which had the benefit of being a development area, Lancashire was being starved of new development and was suffering from industrial migration into Merseyside. Appeals to the Ministry received no response, as the Hunt Committee was in session (and had been appointed in 1967 to consider the problems of intermediate areas). Its report, in 1969, generally sustained the case argued by local authorities in the North-West. It found that Merseyside's unemployment was generally higher and that, although industrial emigration from the county was not serious, the trend had been rising since 1966. Generally, in terms of the growth in employment, population, migration, industrial growth and the state of the environment, the North-West (and Yorkshire) were considered to be exceptions for the whole country and a special 'intermediate area' status was recommended. The case for full development area status, however, was not accepted.

Industrial Estates

The third and final part of the county's industrial and employment policy was the establishment and ownership of industrial estates. From a total of 200 sites in Lancashire existing in 1974 the county owned only four, the remainder belonging either to county boroughs or district authorities, or else to private development companies. However, although the county's involvement was comparatively small, the provision of industrial estates was considered a significant part of the planners' development strategy. In addition, linked as they were via industrial development to the highly sensitive issue of employment, industrial estates carried an importance in the deliberations of the Council and the politics of the county committee system far in excess of their physical contribution.

The decisions to establish the four county sites fall into two distinct periods, one in the late 1940s and early 1950s, and the second after decisions taken in 1967: the latter were still under development at reorganisation. The first estate, at Haydock in 1954, was in the South Lancashire Development Area, and the second was on land acquired from the Nelson and Colne Borough Council at White Walls. The second phase of activity, in 1967, coincided with the county's campaign on the issue of development area status described above. A report was presented, in November 1967, to the Council's Industrial Development Sub-Committee, suggesting five further sites. On the basis of the chief planning officer's recommendation (by now this was Mr Aylmer Coates), the Committee agreed to reject three – one on grounds of cost, one because of engineering difficulties and one because it was in a development area. Two were accepted – one at Bryn Road, Ashton-in-makerfield, and the other nearby at Wingate, Westhoughton.

A striking feature of these estates is the slowness with which land was taken up on the first two: Haydock was available soon after 1954 but remained unoccupied until 1959 and was only half taken up by 1964, while at White Walls land was first purchased in 1955 but the first plot sale there was not until 1970. The 1970s saw a speed-up in the occupation rate: Wingate was purchased in 1970 and first occupied in 1972, while at Bryn

Road completion of extensive site preparation and the first sale occurred in the same year, 1973. This policy change was no doubt encouraged by the larger size of the last two sites (114 and 138 acres respectively, as against 24 and 42 acres respectively for the first two).

By 1974 the total employment on the four estates was just over 1600 – when compared with the need for additional employment in the areas involved, not numerically significant. The standard criteria used in discussing this topic are the creation of new jobs and the attraction of new firms, and in these respects the county estates had some, if limited, impact. About thirty firms occupied the sites by 1974, of which twelve were companies with their headquarters already in Lancashire and probably, therefore, diverted from other Lancashire locations. This leaves eighteen firms representing the new movement into Lancashire, but while nine of these were from outside the region and therefore provided new employment, the remaining nine were small firms setting up for the first time.

Job density per developed acre was 13.8 for Haydock, 15.4 for White Walls, 29.7 for Wingate and 31.3 for Bryn Road, and the cost to the county per job created was £20 for Haydock and £70 for White Walls. It was by these two figures that local authority planners would assess the success of such schemes, looking for the maximum service to the community and minimum additional loading on the rate burden. Although small in terms of the county's total turnover, the four estates turned out to be remarkably profitable, giving a surplus over cost from the Haydock estate of some £55,000 and from White Walls £38,000.

There can be little doubt that the timing of the decisions to develop industrial estates, and the attention given to attracting firms to them, were directly related to the level of unemployment in the North-West and the political pressure on the county that this generated. Haydock was in a high-unemployment area; the decision to develop White Walls was taken as regional unemployment rose in 1952-3. In 1966-7 a further national and regional decline in employment coincided with the decision to establish two further sites.

Pressure was put on the county by the forty per cent of councillors who were also district councillors, and continuing action on the estates can be identified with the timing of their agitation: in 1962 Councillor Finney (of Haydock UDC) made a sharp attack on the Council for failing to develop the Haydock estate rapidly while local unemployment had risen to four per cent and its subsequent development was much more rapid. Again, the Colne councillors raised the issue of the slowness of development of the White Walls estate in 1967. The County Planning Officer's response to this challenge was that:

> Although the present prospects of obtaining new firms are not good,
> further limited expenditure is logical ... to improve industrial land
> availability in this area which has suffered from outward migration, and
> has a higher than average rate of unemployment and an industrial
> structure likely to provide fewer jobs in the future.[29]

In other words, under pressure from north-east Lancashire, and while
the officials thought little good would come of it, the recommendation
for further development at White Walls was made, and was accepted by
the Committee. It was a political decision, rather than one based on
professional judgement. Even so, it was not until 1969, with regional unemployment again running high and after further district pressure, that
the site was completed.

It would seem, therefore, that the development of the county's industrial
estate policy was a reaction to pressure arising from unemployment. The
scope to show concern and to demonstrate effective action within the
context of local government was limited. The need for such sites in the
North-West had been emphasised by both the Hunt Committee and a
Joint Planning Study in 1972,[30] but the provision made was criticised in
both places. The situation reflected a basic flaw which originated in 1947
when physical planning was divorced from economic planning. The former
was placed under the Department of Economic Affairs. Local authorities,
being responsible for zoning land for industrial use, could do little with
regard to the locational decision of industry. Economic policy was out of
their hands, and location, working through regional policy, was a decision
at the centre. Thus, looking at Lancashire's attempts, the county worked
with the variables at their disposal but followed a not unusual policy on
industry and employment which assumed that simply making land available would itself provide an adequate solution, thus using a physical
planning analysis to solve an essentially economic and political problem.

In the nature of the situation the general initiative, and detailed policy
proposals, had to come from the officers working within their areas of
discretion. The economic policy of the county was developed in terms
of land use, but account needs to be taken of the role of the officer and
the value system of his professional group. The promotion of a private
parliamentary Bill, as for instance in 1960, was an officer's initiative *par
excellence*, for although drafting it would entail a good deal of heavy work,
it also effectively demonstrated to the Ministry the seriousness of the local
council's resolve. Finally, the local campaign on the development area issue,
while in part vindicated by the report of the Hunt Committee, must
inevitably have sprung from and been fostered by the officers; it was also
a means of shifting the campaign away from the county, as well as making
a national issue a focus for local criticism.

Land Reclamation and Environmental Improvement

If the structure of local government and its system made it very difficult for the county to be effective in the reduction of Lancashire's unemployment, the same cannot be said with regard to its policy of land reclamation and environmental improvements. Lancashire readily appreciated the deleterious effect of industrial dereliction, and its record in reclamation is second to none, both in terms of the initiatives taken and of the quality of their achievement. The county planning officers, Coates and Rowbotham, became recognised experts in the field. Mr Rowbotham followed Mr Coates as a member of the Land Reclamation Advisory Group to the Secretary of State, while the former is also chairman of the Local Government Officers' Panel. This expertise is reflected through the department.[31]

Although local government had long been technically responsible for the reclamation of derelict land, it was not until 1966, when grant aid and rate support was made available, that authorities like Lancashire really quickened their reclamation programme – even though there were some experimental schemes at Bickerstaffe and Leigh in 1952–4. This early work, while being mainly cosmetic, provided evidence of technical feasibility, and was among the first of its kind in the country.

TABLE 15.2
Derelict Land Reclamation: Lancashire, 1954–72

Type	Amount (acres)		
	1954–66	1967–72	1972*
Industry	26	140	—
Residential/urban	44	89	6
Open space/recreation	59	114	246
Agriculture	220	84	232
Tree planting	67	5	79
Total	416	432	563

* programme

Lancashire's dereliction problem tends to be concentrated in the mining areas of the south-west. The rate of reclamation is indicated in Table 15.2.[32] The table shows that a high proportion (70 per cent) of the land was earlier devoted to housing and industry, while in the 1972 programme much greater emphasis was placed on recreation.

Analysis of the average costs per acre according to the ultimate land use, and also, with the introduction of government aids in the later 1960s, the increased costliness of the projects undertaken, is illustrated in Table 15.3. A feature of the Lancashire situation was the regional concentration

TABLE 15.3
Derelict Land Reclamation: Lancashire 1954–72

| Type | Average cost per acre (£) | | |
	1954–66	1967–72	1972*
Industry	n.a.	n.a.	n.a.
Residential/urban	454	n.a.	n.a.
Open space/recreational	307	464	1464
Agriculture	292	1011	n.a.
Miscellaneous	301	1743	748
	307	1532	1045

* programme

TABLE 15.4
Derelict Land and Reclamation Projects in Lancashire

| Sub-region | Land justifying treatment in 1967 Area | | Programmed reclamation schemes 1967–71 | | | | Programme as percentage of total area justifying treatment |
	Acres	(%)	Acres	(%)	£	(%)	(%)
Furness	314	(4)	0	(0)	0	(0)	0
Fylde	82	(1)	15	(1)	76,770	(3)	19
Lancaster	37	(0)	0	(0)	0	(0)	0
Mid-Lancashire	346	(4)	15	(1)	1,314	(0)	4
North-East Lancashire	911	(11)	94	(6)	186,656	(6)	10
Merseyside	142	(2)	69	(4)	84,308	(3)	20
South Lancashire	4278	(51)	1094	(64)	1,579,295	(55)	26
Manchester	2277	(27)	415	(24)	970,536	(33)	17
Totals	8387	(100)	1702	(100)	2,898,879	(100)	

of the dereliction, and the preponderance of the county's effort was in the former mining areas. Table 15.4[33] shows the percentage distribution of the derelict land, and the corresponding distribution of the county's programme in the period 1967–71. The disproportionate amount of dereliction in south Lancashire and Merseyside (eighty-eight per cent of total) is exactly matched by the reclamation programme in terms of acres and expenditure. The emphasis on these areas by the county was deliberate policy; later proposals increased the attention devoted to the other areas, particularly the north-east. Fifty-five per cent of the land reclaimed in south Lancashire, and sixty-four per cent in Manchester, consisted of spoil heaps and pits, the former mine workings in the area. In the area east of Wigan, over twenty-five per cent of the land was derelict, and at Ince-in-Makerfield, thirty-three per cent. In 1969 the town map for North Makerfield (after eight reclamation schemes) showed twenty per cent of the land area to be still derelict.

By 1974 the Council had completed twenty-eight reclamation schemes, varying in cost from the smallest at £2769, to the largest, estimated at £660,000, the Bryn Road–Three Sisters scheme in Ashton-in-Makerfield. In analysing five major projects undertaken by the county from the 1960s until reorganisation, one is struck by the long time lapse from the first proposal for a scheme to the completion of the site reclamation, the shortest time taken being of the order of seven years, while fourteen years is not uncommon. The Bryn Road–Three Sisters scheme was first proposed in 1958 and was still in progress in 1974.[34]

TABLE 15.5

Regional Distribution of Reclamation, 1968–71

Region	Area reclaimed (acres)	% of 1968 acreage reclaimed by 1971	Proportion of national total of reclaimed land
		%	%
North-West	1,531	12	12
North Yorks and Humberside	3,596	17	28
Yorkshire and Humberside	1,704	16	13
East Midlands	1,324	17	10
West Midlands	3,117	23	24
South-West	390	2	3
East Anglia	363	12	33
South-East	1,023	19	7
England	13,048	14	100

In 1973 the *Strategic Plan for the North-West* calculated that, even with an increased effort on the part of the local authorities, it would take until 1994 to rid the region of the dereliction believed to be extant in 1974. It is, however, unlikely that the required finance or design staff for such a programme could be made available: it is instructive to look at regional distribution of such schemes in the period 1968–71 (Table 15.5).[35] By acreage reclaimed, by the amount of reclamation relative to dereliction and as a proportion of total reclamation in England, the performance of the North-West is poor. Part of the high acreage for the Northern Region, however, is attributable to its development area status and the consequent high rate of grant-aid in the 1960s – a favour generally denied the North-West. In the West Midlands high land values provided a strong economic incentive for reclamation by private developers who, by the 1970s, accounted for nearly forty per cent of the reclaimed land. In the North-West, on the other hand, approximately ninety-five per cent of all reclamation was undertaken by the local authorities.

It is estimated that, within the North-West region in 1968, seventy per cent of all the dereliction was in the Lancashire administrative county, while the Lancashire county boroughs accounted for ten per cent. In terms of the reclamation completed in the period 1968–71, however, these percentages were reversed, the county undertaking twenty per cent of the total for the region and the county boroughs seventy-four per cent. When the acreage reclaimed in the North-West reached 1000 acres in 1972, with the completion of some major long-term projects, however, the county's share had risen to fifty-six per cent.

If, on the basis of acreage reclaimed or in relation to its impact on the problem, Lancashire performed rather poorly, its high reputation in the field of reclamation, when based on the quality of its schemes, was amply justified, the most spectacular one being in the Ashton-in-Makerfield area. This three-phase project involved the clearance of the former collieries, Bamfurlong and Bryn Hall, which had ceased working in 1930. The first phase included filling thirteen shafts, and clearing old buildings, shale heaps, reservoirs, subsidence and ponding. A second and third phase, at Bryn Road, contained the Long Lane and Garswood Hall Collieries, pit shafts, an expanse of waste over 312 acres, and three 150 ft conical heaps known locally as the 'Three Sisters', two of which were in a state of combustion. This project was one of the biggest undertaken in this country and provided the site, discussed previously, for the Bryn Road industrial estate.

There is considerably more to reclamation than earth-moving and levelling. Each project raises its own technical problems which have to be overcome, not to mention the design work, tree planting and landscaping. One of the most interesting technical exercises undertaken by the county involved a relatively small site of thirty-eight acres at Hall Lane in the Bolton area. The problem, which has recently recurred on other sites, involved toxic sodium chromate waste. The site had been used since 1870 to produce heavy chemicals for the leather industry, and had a residue of spoil heaps containing the chemical waste. The county became aware of the site as a result of a survey in 1960, and in 1967 Aylmer Coates suggested a reclamation project, accompanying plans for a comprehensive school nearby. The land was no longer used for chemical production although toxic seepage from the waste heaps was being treated. The company planned to cease work in 1968, at which time the toxicity of the discharge into the nearby River Croal would double, and thereby become a hazard.

Several initial schemes were tentatively considered, involving some earth movement and tree planting. Alternatively, more far-reaching schemes resulting in clearance and landscaping for recreational uses were preferable as a longer-term solution. The technical problems centred on the potential river pollution from sodium chromate, and the impossibility of bacteriological action, essential in revegetation, because of the chemical sterilisation of the soil. Approaches were made to the soil chemist at the Ministry of Agriculture, Fisheries and Food on the possibility of revegetation. The reply was pessimistic, and the forecast was that the toxicity of the soil was too high to allow revegetation. Representatives of the County Planning Department visited a similar site in Glasgow that had been levelled and where the toxic seepage problem had been successfully overcome by creating a football pitch with an ash surface, but where no attempt had been made at revegetation.

The site was the subject of many meetings and negotiations between the Council and the chemical company during 1969. The County Planning Officer proposed that the company should donate the land; the County Architect suggested it was a liability and should be taken over only with compensation from the company; the company insisted on a sale. The real problem was the uncertain feasibility and cost of the reclamation. By July 1969 the county accepted in principle that it should acquire the site, and possession was obtained in May 1970.

The toxicity rather than the general engineering and site work were the real cause of concern. The county's reclamation team proposed the grading of the tips and a blanket of twelve inches of sub-soil and dried sewerage sludge, and then a planting of trees and shrubs. Professor Bradshaw of Liverpool University suggested that a green sward could not survive, and wanted a covering of at least twelve inches of soil to be laid and seeded, with field experiments to monitor the percolation of the chromate toxicity. The site work was held in abeyance until the experimental work was completed.

In the meantime experimental tests were conducted on the problem at the county's Hutton College of Agriculture, where it was shown that a nine-inch covering was insufficient to prevent the death of vegetation: the addition of between three and ten tons per acre of iron sulphate, followed by thirty to forty tons of dried sewerage, however, would overcome the problem. The dried sewerage was available locally for the cost of transport, and the county was able to buy iron sulphate at £4 per ton from a firm for whom it was an unwanted by-product, instead of at the normal price of £30 to £40. On this basis the work went forward in 1972, and the solution appears to have met the difficulty. The total cost of the scheme was £96,470: land purchase £20,000, engineering and site work £69,053, and the cost of the chemical analysis £7417. The scheme qualified for a seventy-five per cent grant, and of the balance, Bolton County Borough agreed to cover ten per cent. The gross cost per acre of the reclaimed land amounted to £2539, which compares favourably with the average for England at £3200. Thus was concluded one of the most technically difficult projects of the time, showing a creditable degree of tenacity on the part of those involved. In 1973 the Men of the Trees Society donated 150 trees for planting at Hall Lane, and civic planting took place in March 1974.

From the discussion above it is clear that from the 1950s this work was undertaken in spite of poor ministerial financial support. A major incentive to the local authority did come after 1966, when increased and easier grants were made available. With reclamation the county had to wait on finance, but in the case of recreational provision, despite joint local authority interest in a Croal-Irwell Valley improvement scheme and the county's surveys of the Forest of Bowland in 1966, serious county activity had to follow government legislation. Undoubtedly the major stimulus came from the Ministry with the translation of the National Park Commission into the Countryside Commission, and the passing of the Countryside Act in 1968, emphasising public access to the countryside and holding out the possibility of seventy-five per cent grant aid for approved schemes.

Naturally the county responded and created a new sub-committee, which met from 1969 until its function was taken into the new County Estates Department in 1972. The sub-committee adopted a four-point strategy: to give access to the countryside near centres of population; to develop parks in coastal districts; to develop recreational facilities in the Forest of Bowland; and to give priority to the use of derelict land in the provision of recreational sites. On this basis seven priority areas in the county were designated for action over a five-year period, four involving land reclamation.

From its establishment in 1969, the sub-committee put in a great deal of work. County parks were opened at Beacon Fell and at Bardsea. Proposals covering Anglezarke were planned by the old authority and commended to the new at reorganisation in 1974. The detailing of schemes ould go on to include access agreements, co-operation with county boroughs and encouragement to the district councils to develop minor schemes of their own, not to mention a major study in 1974 of rivers and canals. By 1971 the county owned and managed 189 acres; by 1974 this had been expected to rise to 853 acres but the target was not achieved. Up to the time of reorganisation it was a growing activity, however, very much complementary to the tradition the authority had developed in land reclamation. National policy after 1968 provided the push to which the county was beginning to respond by 1974.

Development Control

The discussion thus far has been concerned with development *planning*, the prime concern of the headquarters staff in Preston. Another major activity working under divisional planning officers was development *control*. The development plan laid down land use policy, but in addition each individual application for a change in existing land use required consideration and positive decision, handled by the county through the divisional organisation, established by Sutton Brown in 1948-50 and described above. While, originally, each of the nineteen divisions had its planning committee on which were representatives from the constituent county districts and the Council, from the beginning the county adopted a policy of maximum delegation of decisions to the district councils. This system identified three types of planning application: a first category raised no issues of principle and the district was free to determine the matter; a second raised such issues, and the district was subject to the recommendation of the county's divisional planning officer; and a third category was reserved for decision by the county's Development Control Sub-Committee. The allocation of applications into these categories was decided by the county's divisional planning officers. Throughout the period 1948-74, the proportion of cases determined at county level remained virtually constant at seven to eight per cent, leaving ninety-two to ninety-three per cent to be determined in the districts. In general, the system appears to have worked well. In the case of smaller councils, the districts relied heavily on the professional guidance of the county divisional officers.

The management and co-ordination of the county planning divisions illustrated the personal styles of the three chief officers of the old county. Their approaches differed quite sharply, particularly in the case of Sutton Brown and Aylmer Coates. The former assumed an open style, visited the divisional offices frequently, knew the names of the staff and talked to people at all levels. He fostered the initiative of his divisional colleagues, as instanced in a number of small ways, such as providing the divisional officer with his own headed note paper, and permitting him to attach his personal signature to correspondence rather than that of the county's chief officer; and he organised, and attended, their regular meetings. The organisational structure was taken over by his successor, Aylmer Coates, and not changed significantly. However, the latter's personality was quite different. As a public advocate of the county's case he was formidable, and actively promoted its interests through a number of bodies, such as the Sports Council, the Town Planning Institute and the North West Economic Planning Council, where a former chairman still remembers his strong voice on such matters as new town development in the North-West. These demands on the chief officer's time had their price, and he was compelled to concentrate his leadership on the department at Preston. Contemporaries in Preston acknowledged his extraordinary memory for detail and, at times, his impatience with subordinates who were not able to match his mental agility. In consequence, he conveyed the impression to some people of being authoritarian and egocentric. He would often prefer direct contact at all levels to delegation, obtaining information and acceptance of his ideas through informal chats. The divisional staff saw less of Coates than they did of his predecessor, and they assumed he attached less significance to their work. The divisional officers' meetings instituted by Sutton Brown proved unfruitful and were in regular form abandoned.

An illustration of the human relationships involved in maintaining an administrative balance between the headquarters in Preston and the divisional offices concerned the preparation of town maps. Where these were prepared, they became part of the statutory development plan for the county, but the initative for their preparation lay with the planning authority, relying heavily, however, on the local, detailed knowledge of the divisional staff. Although by the mid-1960s the whole 1947 development plan system was showing strain, the town maps symbolised for the divisional staff the divisions' place in the determination of the planning policy; and at the practical level they provided authoritative backing to the local staff's evidence at any subsequent enquiry into their committee's refusal of planning permission. Because of the long time scale involved in preparing and approving such town maps, Aylmer Coates thought them to be a 'waste of time', gave them little encouragement: as one divisional officer remarked ruefully in contrasting the styles of the county's chief officers, 'Sutton Brown would have seen the work was done!'

Jeffrey Rowbotham had been with the department since its inception in 1948, and was appointed successor to Coates, having been his deputy: he was also appointed chief officer to the successor authority. He was popular with his committee, and was highly regarded professionally. His style was much closer to that of Sutton Brown, and emphasised the need for good personal relationships. He encouraged, for example, the meetings of the divisional officers again and generally raised the status of their work.

While these sorts of changes were a matter of degree, none would deny that the development control work was profoundly important. For the public it was, as such, often their only direct contact with planning. Many people, of course, believed that the job was all done by the district councils, and thus the county's work and responsibility could go unacknowledged. The experience of staff work in the divisions was, for some, an essential part of senior officers' training, as it was for Rowbotham in Wigan and his successor as deputy in the old authority, Mr Richard Turner.

A particularly relevant question concerns the test that can be applied in judging the quality of the work done in controlling development, work that often lies hidden in files, unknown to the public, who see only the outcome, and hear something of appeals but cannot observe the prevention of bad planning and design. One way of judging, however, is to consider the planning application statistics.

The number of planning applications considered in the administrative county in 1950 was 10,387. By 1957 this had risen by fifty per cent, and it had doubled by 1965. In 1973 24,059 planning applications were processed, each of them the subject of an individual committee minute, the ultimate responsibility of the county. The county's own Development Control Sub-Committee took, in 1973, decisions on 1925 applications (averaging 175 per meeting), each involving matters of principle which therefore could not be decided by the division or the district council concerned. Table 15.6[36] gives data for refusals, appeals and appeals upheld

TABLE 15.6

Lancashire Administrative County: Percentage of Planning Applications Refused, Percentage Appealing and Percentage of Appeals Upheld by Ministry

| | 1950-9 | | 1960-9 | | 1970-3 | |
	Range of percentages	Average annual percentage	Range of percentages	Average annual percentage	Range of percentages	Average annual percentage
	%	%	%	%	%	%
Percentage of applications refused	6-12	9	12-24	12	14-17	16
Percentage appealing	8-27	23	12-28	16	9-14	11
Percentage of appeals upheld	n.a.	20	n.a.	12	n.a.	17

by the Ministry. It shows that there was a rising trend for the percentage of applications within the county that were refused, implying either an increased toughness, or an increasing number of more dubious applications. However, the table also shows a falling trend in the percentage of people who, having been refused permission, went on to exercise their right of appeal. This fact, together with a tendency for the Ministry to uphold a smaller proportion of any such appeals, suggests that, as the planning authority's policies were being upheld, fewer dubious applications were passed.

A comparison of the Lancashire figures with the national figures for appeals upheld shows the Lancashire percentage to be about fifty to sixty per cent of the national average throughout the period 1950–73: in 1950 Lancashire was twenty-seven per cent and the national figure forty-four per cent; the 1964 figures were twelve and twenty-two per cent respectively, meaning that there was a greater probability of the inspector agreeing with Lancashire's decision than there was on a national basis.

In the public's eye nothing within the local authority system highlights the question of decision-making more than that of planning permission for development. The issues have been put succinctly[37] in terms of the policy formation and executive functions and their distribution between the officers and members. The formal position, one doggedly publicised by the officers, urges that the objectives and priorities are set by the members, the officers being solely concerned with execution. The minuted passing of each application by the Committee reinforces this position. An alternative model (in an extreme form) puts the officers as setting the planning objectives and the Planning Committee as executing the policy by its detailed decisions. The reality, no doubt, lies somewhere between these two. The truth is difficult for an outsider to ascertain: officers tend publicly to take shelter behind their committee, and the committee firmly believes they are in control. When this issue was raised with Alderman Roscoe, for many years chairman of the Development Control Sub-Committee, he stood by the supremacy of the Committee by pointing to the close consultations between him and the chief officer, with the latter occasionally calling at his home to discuss planning matters. In another example, Alderman Roscoe proposed the motion on a particularly controversial planning application.[38] One cannot be sure, in fact, that this constitutes reliable evidence. Observation of chief officers with their chairmen suggests that a good and close relationship is a matter of high priority for a county department, essential for its smooth working. When the relationship is so close, with each party in a dependent relationship with the other, it is difficult to see who is responsible for a particular decision.[39] In another context one administrator put the point by saying that he was scarcely required to speak at meetings; after all, he continued, if the chairman has been briefed about what you want him to say, you should not need to speak!

In the planning field this issue, made sharper by its technical subject matter, is raised more than in most others. One study team on development control in 1967 estimated that sixty to seventy per cent of all planning decisions are effectively delegated: technical questions and policy become interwound; a whole series of administrative decisions establish policy. Prior discussions with developers, contact with Whitehall at short notice, representation at appeals and enquiries – all strengthen the role of the officials. One commentator has remarked that, if the Planning Committee had concentrated entirely on policy, it might have found it necessary to meet twice a year and in the meantime delegate the detail to its officers.[40] Before reorganisation, the legal framework would have prevented this. However, no committee or councillors would see this happen, and so they reacted by immersing themselves in the most extreme detail. The danger for the elected representative is that he becomes buried in paper work and fails to notice the key policy decisions, which are often contained in plans and reports formally adopted by his committee.

One of the most controversial cases considered by the county in recent years was that of Samlesbury Brewery in 1969–70. The case arose from a planning application to construct a major plant in a rural area (where refusal would normally be anticipated) submitted on behalf of Whitbread's Brewery. After study and advice from consultants, the choice in the Lancashire area had narrowed to two localities: Skelmersdale New Town, or a site in the Blackburn/Preston area. From the company's point of view, the economic factors in the decision centred on the availability of a suitably skilled labour force, the willingness of the Board of Trade to grant an Industrial Development Certificate, the possibility of government investment grants and financial incentives and the technical ability of the local sewerage and water authorities to meet Whitbread's demands at a low cost. Skelmersdale, to a degree, could meet all these requirements; and more to the point, the Development Corporation was anxious to have the new plant and was being most persuasive. The company, however, preferred the Blackburn/Preston area, partly to use its existing skilled labour at Blackburn, partly to have access to the good transport of the M6, and partly because in terms of company operations this location had a slight advantage. The company's consultants searched for a site in the area and twenty-six were evaluated. The majority could not meet the technical requirements, and while the Samlesbury site met all criteria immediately the remaining alternatives either were not immediately available or else required the expensive capital construction of additional sewerage, water and roads.

An application was submitted for a fifty-five acre site at Samlesbury, about half a mile from the M6, for a development that offered early employment to 700 and ultimately to 6950, two-thirds of which represented new jobs. In economic terms, the prospective employment from this development would be seen as good news to a locality with high unemployment, in need of an injection of vitality. Unfortunately Samlesbury was a small rural community with a voting population of 880 people. The site lay one-and-a-half miles from the built-up edge of Preston and four miles from Blackburn. This five-mile stretch of land between the motorway and Blackburn was a pleasant stretch of open countryside. It had Intermediate Area Status, and while not in a green belt was not an area in which one would consider the development of a £7 million complex as a matter of routine. A controversy quickly gained heat and centred on the issue of employment versus environmental protection. The local residents reacted sharply, as did the local branch of the Council for the Protection of Rural England (CPRE).

The application appeared as the third item on the agenda at the meeting of 20 January 1970. The Ministry of Agriculture had no views; the River Authority commented, technically, on the water aspects, but passed no opinion. Blackburn County Borough had initially raised objections in terms of the general development and sewerage, but then subsequently 'indicated' that they raised no objection in principle. Preston County Borough, the Central Lancashire New Town (CLNT) consultants, the district council and Samlesbury and Cuerdale parish Councils all objected. The same was true of the CPRE, various landowners, the vicar (whose vicarage was directly affected), the local NFU and the Country Landowners Association. There was also a local petition against the scheme from 373 objectors, organised by the parish council.

These were reported to the Committee by Mr Coates, who went on to summarise the technical questions of site suitability in terms of services. Turning to the general appropriateness, the environmentalists' argument was countered by pointing out that the area was 'white land', on which no prohibition to development had been placed in the county development plan, and that on this point the Committee could exercise discretion. Two further points were raised; the first concerned the employment needs of the area, while the second was that Skelmersdale would be delighted if the development went there: the plant would either be located at Samlesbury or be lost to the area. Mr Coates recommended the Committee to approve the application, subject to certain modifications of landscape architecture that would soften the environmental impact. The Committee accepted the recommendation and the application was passed.

Correspondence with the Ministry followed, plus publicity and lobbying. In March the county was informed that the Minister was 'calling the application in' for the Minister to determine, and a public enquiry was held on June 1970, where evidence was taken from the company, the local authorities in the area, the parish council, the Action Group and the CPRE. Among a large number of other documents submitted were sixty-nine letters of objection received by the Action Group, plus 536 signatures on a petition against the scheme, plus those from a further 109 residents in favour!

The Inspector's report submitted to the Minister was heavily influenced by the environmental intrusion and, in suggesting other possible areas such as the CLNT, recommended that the application be refused. In August 1970 the Minister, Mr Peter Walker, rejected the opinion of his inspector and approved the company's application, which he felt was warranted by the local employment situation. Given the administrative decision procedures, that settled the matter – or it should have done. But if the matter had raised passion beforehand, the furies were now let loose.

As a planning decision, the matter centred upon two key issues, the protection of open countryside and, in direct opposition, the economic welfare of the urban population. Taking the choice at its face value, it rested heavily on a judgement concerning these two prime considerations: environment versus employment. The problem became further exacerbated because of the social split such choices often involve. The environmental lobby is powerful and well organised, generally drawing its support from the professional and middle-class groups. The urban dweller, exposed to the realities of unemployment and poor prospects, no doubt weighed the economic aspects more heavily. The brewery case raised the political and philosophical issues of how society is to reach a decision where, no matter which course of action is taken, one section of the community will be aggrieved. However, whether the administrative procedures of the British planning system adequately incorporate the essentials of the democracy its society supports is something the parties to the Samlesbury dispute would have seen as violently controversial. In the 1970s we have become accustomed to action groups and protests. A difference in this case, however, was that it openly split the local authorities as well as other official bodies, and internally caused open dissension between officers and also between officers and members. The then clerk to the County Council, Sir Patrick McCall, felt in retrospect that it was a bad decision made by London; Alderman Roscoe, chairman of the Sub-Committee, felt it was right. The County Planning Officer, despite general misgivings on the part of other authorities and the local objectors, felt that, as the matter stood, it was better to support the application and recommend approval.

The controversy escalated to the national level, and, inevitably, the focus of attention shifted. Allegations of local corruption were made; an offer by Whitbreads to rehouse the vicar was publicised as an attempt to buy him off; notice for a farmer to quit (legal and anticipated) became eviction, and the Samlesbury lobby was joined by the anti-big business, anti-Government movement. *Private Eye* turned up a political contribution from the company to the Conservative Party of £20,000 two years previously, and questioned the Conservative Minister's integrity. By this time Mr Walker had become secretary of state for the environment, and the new minister for local government was Mr Graham Page. Questioned about the decision in the Commons in 1970 by a local MP, the Minister launched into a vitriolic attack on the campaigners, the press and all and sundry, in defence of his ministerial colleagues and officials. The village of Samlesbury was accused of stirring a foul campaign against ministers. The site of the brewery, far from spoiling a beautiful area, would be next to 'Blackburn's sewage works, and close to a very ugly paper mill, whilst close by was a garish modern pub'.[41] A fortnight later Lord Molson, chairman of the Council for the Protection of Rural England, raised the matter in the Lords as an issue involving environmental protection. But by now things were going too far. While many deplored the decision (Lord Greenwood, a former housing minister, was one example), the attack was now seen not essentially as a planning decision, but as an attack on the integrity of ministers, and all sides were at pains to dissociate themselves from that. A backlash had built up in defence of public life, the CPRE gracefully capitulated, the campaign had run its course. The brewery has been built.

The Samlesbury brewery case highlights more than any other the nature of the planning process. Inevitably, the rights and liberties of individuals are subject to control and limitation. Whether it should have been allowed or not is still the subject of argument, and in the nature of things must remain so. The author, being abroad at the time of the controversy and later hearing reference to it, took the opportunity on passing through Samlesbury on the A59 to seek it out. Unable to find it without assistance, he asked to be directed to it. A mental note was made that it was not easy to find, and certainly not easily spotted. Upon approaching the site, which was indeed well hidden, the impact of the building on the visitor was surprisingly pleasant. But, then, the author is an economist; and besides, one more opinion is scarcely sufficient to settle a contentious planning decision.

THE ROAD PROGRAMME AND THE BUILDING OF MOTORWAYS

The discussion of the Samlesbury brewery illustrates the difficulty of making an objective assessment in the field of environmental planning. Alderman Barber-Lomax has commented that he found 'Planning an Eleusinian Mystery, with the Delphic Oracle as the chief exponent'.[42] It is a view with which many would sympathise. Road-building appears more tangible. As a major item of expenditure, the financial data for road construction, together with road mileage figures, provide an index of performance. Policy formation is essentially a political process. Not all the circumstances are reflected in the figures, but these at least provide a firm foundation for a discussion.

Any discussion of roads in postwar Lancashire or in Britain as a whole must take note of James Drake (later Sir James), whose appointment as County Surveyor and Bridgemaster covering the years 1945-72 virtually spans the whole postwar period of the authority. In 1967-8 J. H. Dean, his deputy, acted as county surveyor during Drake's temporary absence as first director of the North Western Road Construction unit. On Drake's retirement he was succeeded by J. R. Ingram, who held office from 1972 until reorganisation. Drake served as an engineering assistant in Bootle in the 1930s, and had been appointed borough surveyor of Blackpool in 1938, at the extraordinarily youthful age of thirty-one. It is interesting to note that the county made two youthful appointments in their surveyor and their planning officer in the early postwar years.

Drake was a Lancastrian, proud of his birth in Accrington, and of his county. An outstanding chief officer, he could have been equally successful in private industry, as his full-time working directorship with Leonard Fairclough's (which he took up on his retirement from county service) demonstrates. He was not a good bureaucrat. Anyone wishing to see Mr P. Schofield (county surveyor, 1920-45) would be required to make an appointment with his chief clerk. One could approach Drake, however, by a knock on his door, and, in the reverse situation, he was likely to shout a name down the corridor for somebody to step into his office. Drake, as county surveyor, was a blunt person and perfectly at home in the hard-headed negotiations of a construction site. Despite this, he was considerably more understanding of other people than might have appeared. He had a flair for selling his schemes to those who would be affected by a new road. In this he was a man of the people, who could carry the public with him. He was introduced to one meeting of objectors in Bolton as 'The Bureaucratic Bull-dozer from Preston': by the end of the evening, however, those present were satisfied and the differences were settled without a public enquiry. Drake believed in facing the public; thus he could see their point of view, and could win their confidence.

Engineers tend to be task-orientated individuals, good at finding satisfactory solutions to identifiable problems. They are not good at setting social priorities and goals or at policy formation. In the 1950s and 1960s the approach to road-building was 'predict traffic growth and build'.[43] Lancashire's policy in this period followed this national philosophy. Drake was essentially a civil engineer, with a reputation in inter-urban transport, not in transport policy. Although his department made a considerable contribution to traffic analysis and engineering, Drake was a road-builder much more than he was County Surveyor and Bridgemaster.

The 1949 Road Plan[44]

In November 1947, with prompting from the County Surveyor, and in anticipation of the transport and roads survey that was to be required for the county's development plan, the Highways and Bridges Committee asked that a road plan for the county be prepared within twelve months. The final report was the first of its kind to be published in this country.

This report contained twelve chapters and ran for 141 pages. It is interesting to note that twenty-three years later one expert[45] urged road planning to be based on what he calls a 'transportation study'. While the elements of this approach are necessarily more sophisticated than Lancashire's in 1949, the basic framework is very similar. Lancashire's road plan commenced by surveying the existing road network, which at that time followed routes established over the centuries as dictated by the physical features of the land. Data obtained in a 1938 traffic survey and updated for the postwar period demonstrated the inadequate capacity of the main arterial routes. Accident figures showed the designs to be hazardous, a characteristic made worse by the ribbon development of the 1930s. Lancashire's roads were congested and severely restricted by traffic regulations: sixty-four per cent of the main routes in the southern half of the county were subject to 30 mph speed limits. The plan concluded that industrial recovery and private amenity needed an improved road system.

From this analysis, it was concluded that improvement schemes for existing roads would prove costly and inadequate. Lancashire needed a *new* system of roads. In the period 1930–5, as a result of the Depression, expenditure on roads throughout the country had been low. The building of the East Lancashire Road in this period, as recounted by Dr Marshall in Chapter 10 above, was exceptional. In 1935–9 a heavy national road programme was undertaken. The grant system had been amended by the Trunk Roads Act in 1946, and much thought was given to new roads and motorways from 1938 onwards. This culminated in the Special Roads Act of 1949, which provided the legislative authority for the provision of new restricted-access roads. These trends were all conducive to the hope that, after the war, a new and major assault on the road problem would be undertaken. Lancashire's proposals in 1949 were consistent with this national approach.

The programme proposed in the Plan divided the problem into two parts. Firstly, there were new roads to be built, and certain existing ones were to be improved. Secondly, there was a statement of policy on the maintenance and general improvement of all county roads. The Plan was to be considered as a programme for action, and it made three explicit assumptions: (1) the cost of the road programme must imply a feasible level of expenditure; (2) proposals were to be based on a thirty-year planning horizon; (3) traffic volumes were expected to peak twenty years from 1949, at twice the 1938 levels.

The new road programme identified a road system based on three groups. Group 1 routes, twelve in all, would provide main express routes to carry long-distance through traffic, and included a main north-south route (originally proposed in 1936 and later to become the M6); an east-west route from Liverpool to Hull (later to become the M62); and routes from Preston and Manchester into north-east Lancashire. 67.5 per cent in this group were to be new roads, and 32.5 per cent improvements. In Group 2 there were seventy-eight routes, connecting town with each other and inter-connecting the express routes, of which 32 per cent were new roads and 68 per cent improvements; and Group 3 routes, numbering eighty-three, linked smaller towns and completed the system, and were divided into 34 per cent new roads and 68 per cent improvements (see Table 15.7).

TABLE 15.7
Milages Proposed to the Three Groups in 1949 Road Plan Programme

Group	Motorways	Dual carriageway	Ordinary	Total
1	94	123	—	217
2	17.2	190.7	200.7	408.6
3	—	18.2	263.7	281.9
				907.5

The mileage of new roads to be built would represent an increase of 25 per cent in the total mileage existing within the county in 1949. A total of 275 new bridges and the alteration of 345 others would be required. There was also a maintenance programme. The county were responsible for maintaining 2232 miles of roadway, and the arrears in 1948 were estimated at £10 million. The policy of the road plan was based on the dual needs of safety and traffic flow improvement. Two major problems existed, one relating to the sett pavings, which affected 7.5 per cent of the existing trunk roads and 22 per cent of the Class 1 category, and the second that of bumpy surfaces. Data on the unevenness of roads were collected in terms of 'bumps per mile'. The county's maintenance policy was to be directed towards the elimination of sett paving and the removal of the worst bumpy surfaces.

The proposals were costed to assess the financial feasibility of the Plan, and at 1949 prices were put at £145 million (excluding £24 million for two national routes, one of which was the ultimate M6; both of these could well have been included). Over the thirty-year period of the Plan this represented proposed annual expenditure by the committee (at 1949 prices and inclusive of grants) of around £4.9 million per annum, compared with an actual expenditure of £3.1 million in 1938 (at 1949 prices). However, the question of feasibility was to be based not on actual prewar expenditure levels, but on Lancashire's road expenditure capacity as calculated in the road plan by the county surveyor, which showed, in the opinion of Drake, what the county could be expected to achieve. The calculation took the national average expenditure per mile in 1938, adjusted the figure for wartime inflation to 1949, and then increased this figure by eighty-eight per cent to allow for a higher population per mile in Lancashire, giving a figure of £4.6 million per annum, or £136.5 million over thirty years.

Although the Plan concluded the programme to be financially feasible, in those same terms it was an ambitious one. While the Committee accepted the proposals with enthusiasm, they could not fully have appreciated the increased commitment of county resources that was implied. Using national norms adjusted upwards for Lancashire's higher population density per mile of road, the calculations showed that in 1938 Lancashire should have been spending £1440 per mile, whereas actual spending came nearer to £1050. On the programme proposed in the plan and budgeted at £147 million, the anticipated warranted expenditure fell short by seven per cent, and after adjusting the 1938 levels for inflation the shortfall would have amounted to twenty-four per cent. After allowing for grants the Highways Committee took 9.3p per pound of rateable value in 1938, and 8p in 1949. Drake calculated that the warranted amount was 14.2p in the pound in 1949, and that the road programme would require 15.4p in the pound (at 1949 prices) over a thirty-year period.

How far did the subsequent spending measure up to the target of the 1949 Plan? Figure 15.1 shows the annual rate of spending by the county at constant 1949 prices, indicating that the 1938 rate in real terms was not achieved until 1957. The target rate of the Road Plan was not attained until 1961, largely as a result of the M6 (which had been excluded, in any case, from the plan's financial calculations). While the first decade of the programme fell considerably short of the target, the 1960s did something to remedy this. Figure 15.2 shows the cumulative expenditure of the Committee in the years up to 1972: not until 1968 does total expenditure exceed the 1949 programme.

Despite the failure of the Plan to anticipate the general shortfall of public expenditure by the Government on which Lancashire was entirely dependent for grant aid, the Road Plan proved to be of tremendous significance. For example, it analysed the interaction of road design environment and accidents. In this field it provided basic research (ahead of the Ministry of Transport, which formally adopted its work on design speed standards in 1961) and was a seed-bed for Lancashire's subsequent high reputation in this area. On traffic analysis it introduced the notion of 'natural attraction', despite ministry scepticism. Today this concept, in the guise of 'generated traffic', is a fundamental aspect of transport analysis.[46]

Apart from these technical illustrations, the Plan did much to establish Drake with his committee. The relationship of the officer to his committee was discussed above: in the case of the Highways Committee the leadership was to come unquestionably from Drake, who managed his committee with great skill. Notwithstanding this, however, the committee chairman, vice-chairman and Drake made a formidable trio who became nicknamed the 'three musketeers' because of their constant campaigning on Lancashire's behalf. While others within the county were pessimistic about the possible achievement of the road programme, these three maintained their optimism, and used every opportunity of speaking at conferences to promote their cause. In working with his committee, Drake as the professional man was able to present the Plan, a long, complex and visionary document, to members who were, in reality, in no position to question its detail. When the bulk of the money would come from ministry grants, they would not seriously question the financial detail of a thirty-year plan, going so far ahead in time; and besides, finance was dealt with in another committee. While Drake remained in office, of the forty-one members of the 1948 Highways Committee, only eight remained on the Committee during the twenty years to 1969.

The Plan also did much to establish the leadership of the county among

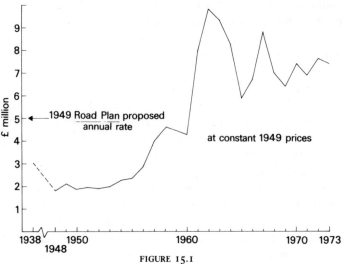

FIGURE 15.1
Highways Committee Annual Expenditure 1938–73

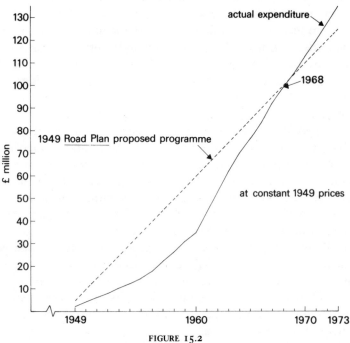

FIGURE 15.2
Highways Committee Cumulative Expenditure 1949–73

local authorities in the North-West. No priorities for schemes were set in 1949, for these were to be determined later. At the beginning of the 1950s, tremendous public pressure was being exerted by the Lancashire and Merseyside Industrial Development Association, the Eccles Town Council and the Committee of Lancashire MPs for first priority to be afforded by the Ministry to the Stretford–Eccles bypass (an existing swing bridge over the canal being a cause of serious congestion). Lancashire rightly saw that, in the scramble for inclusion in the ministry programme, the scheme might displace the Preston bypass (later part of the M6 and in 1958 the first motorway in Britain). This was a testing time, crucial for Lancashire's leadership in the planning of roads in the North-West. The county came out of this successfully and within a short space of each other, both schemes were included in the official programme.[47] In the 1950s Lancashire became the unchallenged leader. By the later 1960s nobody planned road schemes in the North-West without co-operating with Lancashire. Until 1974 not one objection was raised by a local authority to a Lancashire road proposal – a record of which the county administration is proud.

In the early period of the Plan, too much progress was expected as the planners began to believe their own forecasts. By 1960 Drake was publicly showing his frustration.[48] Very much an individualist among county surveyors, he was being held back by lack of agreement from the Ministry. Drake never criticised anybody in Lancashire, although the financial backing of the county was not tested until 1968. The blockage was always provided by the Ministry, which would not programme Lancashire's schemes (or, for that matter, those of other counties). While his relationships with individual officers was very good, Drake did not refrain from venting his anger generally at the Ministry's tardiness. After 1960, no doubt sweetened by some success, Council documents urging particular road proposals become more persuasive and aimed at rallying public support, while in addition they provide the hard technical argument necessary for the official acceptance of such schemes. The road plan itself stood the test of time, but the county matured and became less pushing in making its demands.

The Plan was an early exercise in corporate planning by a local authority; indeed, Drake has argued that the department was a business organisation. The document established physical planning targets, and any subsequent scheme established its pedigree by showing its place in the 1949 Road Plan. Many schemes became upgraded, from dual carriageways to motorways. Some schemes were additions, like the M62 south Lancashire motorway, which was said to have been conceived by Drake while he was lying awake in a Chicago hotel in 1959.

Drake was later the co-author of a book on motorways,[49] and became known among his friends as 'Mr Motorway'. However, while 111 miles of motorway were proposed in the Plan, in no way could Lancashire or Drake be credited with the concept. The *autobahn* of the early 1930s established the design principles and much international interest was aroused: Drake himself was part of a delegation from Britain in 1938. As Dr Marshall shows in Chapter 10, Schofield had developed a proposal for a north–south route, incorporated in a 1938 national motorway plan of the County Surveyors' Society. Drake had proposed a motorway ring road for Blackpool when he was the town's engineer. By 1944 the Ministry of Transport was preparing design standards, and the Act of 1949 made motorways legally possible.

The incorporation of motorways in the plan of 1949 showed the county to be in the national vanguard, and Drake to be a man of his time. As a traffic engineer he was already convinced of their superior efficiency in promoting vehicular movement and greater safety. In 1949 motorways were warranted by forecasted traffic growth. But as national policy moved in its favour, and as traffic growth outstripped the earlier forecasts, the need for planning in terms of motorways grew. Drake, the designer and civil engineer, embraced the new philosophy, and motorways were shrewdly seen as prestigious: nothing less would do for Lancashire and his authority. Growing national concern with accidents in the 1950s[50] led Drake to give greater emphasis in his campaign to the issue of safety. This was to appeal readily to the public conscience. The history of speed limits[51] had shown the political difficulty of cutting road accidents by legislation. Road-building was a popular solution, accepted by Parliament and public opinion in the 1950s, and Lancashire was only too willing to seize the opportunity. By 1968 the county's road programme had increased its motorway target from the previous 111 miles to 238.[52]

County Priorities and Lancashire's Share

In terms of the mileage of new roads completed in Lancashire during the period 1957–72, motorways were by far the most significant. In that fifteen years, 144 miles of motorway were laid down, while trunk roads added only seven miles to the total. The 'principal road' classification was introduced in 1967 and in the following five years, when motorway construction had slowed considerably, Lancashire added only a further six miles of new principal road.

The map shows the motorway network that existed at reorganisation and indicates the further projects in the course of planning or under

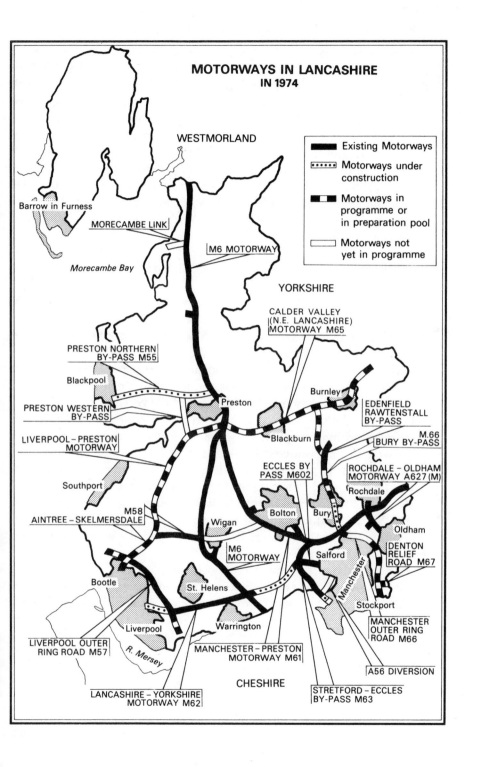

MOTORWAYS IN LANCASHIRE
IN 1974

WESTMORLAND

Legend:
- Existing Motorways
- Motorways under construction
- Motorways in programme or in preparation pool
- Motorways not yet in programme

Barrow in Furness

MORECAMBE LINK

Morecambe Bay

M6 MOTORWAY

YORKSHIRE

CALDER VALLEY (N.E. LANCASHIRE) MOTORWAY M65

PRESTON NORTHERN BY-PASS M55

Blackpool

Preston

Burnley

EDENFIELD RAWTENSTALL BY-PASS

PRESTON WESTERN BY-PASS

Blackburn

M.66 BURY BY-PASS

LIVERPOOL – PRESTON MOTORWAY

ECCLES BY PASS M602

ROCHDALE – OLDHAM MOTORWAY A627 (M)

Southport

Rochdale

M58 AINTREE – SKELMERSDALE

Wigan

Bolton

Bury

Oldham

DENTON RELIEF ROAD M67

M6 MOTORWAY

Salford

Manchester

Bootle

St. Helens

Stockport

MANCHESTER OUTER RING ROAD M66

Liverpool

R. Mersey

Warrington

MANCHESTER – PRESTON MOTORWAY M61

A56 DIVERSION

LIVERPOOL OUTER RING ROAD M57

CHESHIRE

STRETFORD – ECCLES BY-PASS M63

LANCASHIRE – YORKSHIRE MOTORWAY M62

construction at that time. The M6, as part of the national motorway system, forms the keystone of the Lancashire motorway structure. The work on the seventy-one miles of the M6 in Lancashire commenced in 1956 with an eight-and-a-quarter-mile section bypassing Preston, and was completed in December 1958. A second twelve mile section bypassed Lancaster and was completed in 1960. Together these sections involved the construction of forty-nine bridges and proved to have one of the lowest construction costs per mile of any motorway in Britain, at approximately £300,000. A third section from Thelwall to Preston covered thirty-six miles, included eighty-four bridges and viaducts, and was completed in 1963. One such bridge on this section was the Thelwall Viaduct crossing the Ship Canal, measuring 460 feet in length – at that time the longest and biggest construction in the country. The fourth and final section connected Preston to Lancaster, a distance of sixteen miles, containing forty-four bridges, which was opened in January 1965.[53]

An earlier scheme referred to above was a relatively short six-mile stretch of principal road motorway which was contemporary with the Preston and Lancaster sections of the M6. This was the Stretford–Eccles bypass, opened in 1960, and including the Barton High-Level Bridge over the Ship Canal, a massive feat of engineering rising 100 feet above the water and 2425 feet long. This was the first urban motorway, and as it was a principal road twenty-five per cent of the cost was covered by the county itself. Although by 1975 there existed only fifty-five miles of such principal road motorways in the country, forty-seven per cent of those miles were in Lancashire. It is worth noting that not one mile remained with the authority after reorganisation. Following the completion of the M6 in Lancashire, the most significant addition came with the twenty-nine miles of the M61, opened in 1970, which linked the East Lancashire Road to the M6 at Preston, followed in 1970–1 by a section of twenty-three miles from the East Lancashire Road to the Yorkshire boundary, forming part of the M62.

The map shows that these routes compose a series of main arteries, and it is noteworthy that these correspond in concept and pattern (excepting the as yet incomplete south Lancashire section of the M62) to the 'express routes' designated in the 1949 Road Plan, including virtually all the alignments that correspond with proposals made in the plan. Progressive roadbuilding in Lancashire has largely been the conversion of road plan proposals to actual roads in the twenty-five years since the plan was published. Further work in progress or under consideration represent the completion of the network or the interconnection of the main routes. It has been pointed out how Preston, the county headquarters, appears as a central node of the system; there is no evidence to suggest that this results from anything but traffic plan analysis and the consequent need for such roads.

A number of questions have been put forward in connection with Lancashire's road policy priorities. For example, was the building of motorways in Lancashire done at the expense of other roads, for reasons of prestige? Or did the system of reimbursing the authority 100 per cent for motorway schemes, cause other roads to suffer neglect? Figure 15.3

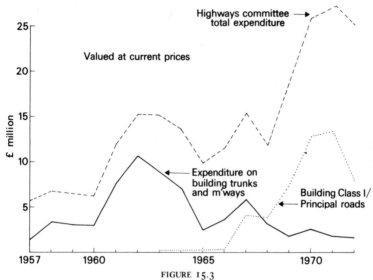

FIGURE 15.3
Highways Committee Total Expenditure and Road Building Expenditure 1957-72

analyses the financial evidence on this point. It shows that, up to 1967, motorway spending was an extremely significant item in the total county highways expenditure. Its influence led to sharp yearly fluctuations. After 1967, however, the significance of motorways diminishes. In terms of county spending, Class I and principal road improvements in the earlier years were negligible. After 1963 they grew in importance, until after 1967 they outstrip motorway spending. These schemes, as with motorways, were proposed by the county but were programmed by the Ministry as part of the national road-building budget. The phenomenal growth of principal roads schemes reflects a change in ministerial priorities.[54] The figures for the West Riding and Cheshire and the total for all the English and Welsh counties exhibit, in perhaps a lesser form, the same change in emphasis as in Lancashire. Lancashire, therefore, could be said to be reacting in part to national priorities. It is conceivable that, prior to 1966, the county could have pressed for more Class I schemes. These, however, carried only a seventy-five per cent grant, and lack of acceptance by the

Ministry in the early years explains, in great measure, the low level of spending on this type of road. In so far as it had discretion, clearly the county wanted motorways.

The county, and James Drake, placed great stress on environmental impression and motorway maintenance.[55] In practical terms this took the form of painting motorway bridges (including the concrete retaining walls) in different colours and cutting the grass verges, as well as maintaining the road surfaces.[56] The county were constantly under attack for exceeding ministry norms on 'non-essential' expenditure. Figure 15.4(a)[57] shows that,

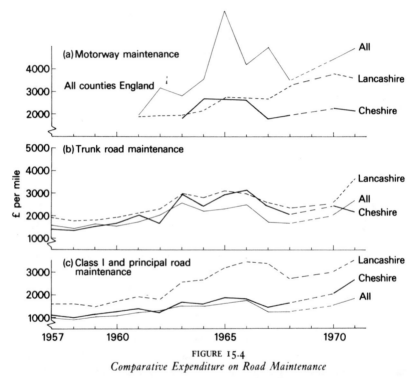

FIGURE 15.4
Comparative Expenditure on Road Maintenance

in expenditure per mile on motorways, Lancashire is considerably below the figure for All English Counties. In part this results from good standards of construction in Lancashire and in part also from good housekeeping, but Lancashire tends to be above its neighbouring county, Cheshire.

Figures 15.4(b) and (c) relate to the maintenance of other classes of roads. Lancashire generally spent more per mile on maintaining trunk roads, although it should be said that none of these figures makes allowances for inflation. In real terms, standards of maintenance declined throughout the country, and Lancashire was no exception. At constant 1970 prices Lancashire in 1957 spent £3740 per mile, grouping motorways and trunk roads together: by 1972 it had dropped to £2910 – the lowest rate of spending since 1957. As Lancashire constantly reminded London, if regard is had to the large increases in traffic in these years, the real standard of maintenance is even lower. The county acted as agent for the Ministry on motorway and trunk roads and was reimbursed for its work: in the case of Class I and principal roads, however, maintenance was entirely the county's financial responsibility. In Figure 15.4(c) the data show Lancashire to be considerably above Cheshire, and at times twice the All Counties figure on these roads. Lancashire was also generally higher than the West Riding and other northern counties. Thus, on maintenance there is little support for the argument that Lancashire overspent on motorways: trunk road maintenance costs followed other counties fairly closely or somewhat above, and on Class I and principal roads, Lancashire's record was much better than elsewhere.

Finally there is the question of whether Lancashire secured its share of the national road programme relative to other authorities. Inevitably, in the 1960s, the question of shares would be judged in terms of the motorway programme, and for Lancashire this represented a main priority. Figure 15.5 shows the share of Lancashire, Cheshire and the West Riding

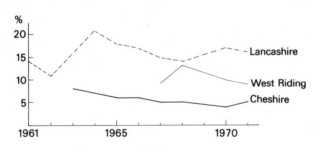

FIGURE 15.5
Motorway Mileage in Three Counties as a Proportion of Total Mileage in All Counties in England

in the mileage of motorways opened in All English Counties, in a period of a six-fold increase in total motorway mileage. Lancashire is shown to have had around fifteen per cent of the mileage, although containing only about ten per cent of the population; Cheshire's mileage comes close to its share of the population at four per cent, while the West Riding had ten per cent of the mileage and about seven per cent of the population. The figures show that Lancashire maintained its place in the 1960s motorway league.

A second way of looking at Lancashire's share is to consider the extent to which the county funded its highway expenditure from government grants. This factor can work in two directions: it permits high levels of spending, but it also makes the consequent large organisation very dependent on ministerial approval. Figure 15.6 shows the proportion covered

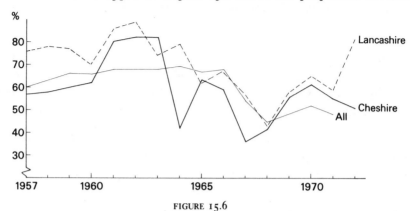

FIGURE 15.6
Government Grant Aid as Proportion of Total County Expenditure

by grants, a volatile figure as motorway projects are brought to fruition. Up to 1966 Lancashire secured a much higher proportion than both that of other counties taken together, and (most of the time) of Cheshire. Indeed, in 1962 the proportion of Lancashire's total highways budget covered by government grant went as high as eighty-nine per cent. Not only did Lancashire do relatively well, but the high level of spending meant the employment of a large and highly skilled team within the department. It was good for the ratepayers, too, in that, for example in 1963, Lancashire ratepayers contributed only 2.5p in the pound for highway purposes, while in Cheshire ratepayers contributed 3.23p, in the West Riding 3.08p and in Westmorland and Cumberland (neither of which benefited much from the grant system), 8.0p and 8.36p respectively. In the latter half of the decade, with the rundown in motorway expenditure, and despite the increased building of other roads, Lancashire's grant proportion moved

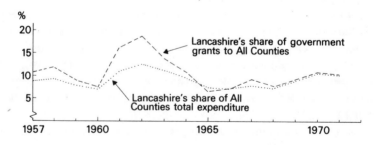

FIGURE 15.7
Lancashire's Share of Government Grants Compared with Share of Total Expenditure

much closer to that of other counties. The burden on the Lancashire ratepayers rose too, reaching 9.0p in 1971.

The data contained in Figure 15.7 provide further insight into Lancashire's share of national resources and her changing fortunes in later years, showing that, until 1965, the county's share of government grants distributed specifically for highway purposes was much higher than its share of All Counties total highway expenditure. In the last six years, however, the two shares correspond remarkably closely, and from being exceptional Lancashire became on a par with the English county average.

Could Lancashire maintain the pace: was Drake's drum beginning to falter?

What was Lancashire's strategy, and could it be sustained? At the local level the successful promotion and completion of schemes depended on the basic approach by the county to motorway building. This stemmed largely from the personality of Drake himself, who emphasised the need for good public relations with those affected. The county maintained its own land section, which did much to help public relations and speed up that side of the work. In the case of the Preston bypass section of the M6 the records show that in one instance work was held up by a farmer whose private lane had been used as a site access for contractors' works vehicles, disrupting the farm work and involving negotiations with solicitors, land agents and allied persons until a deadlock situation was reached. At this point, the County Surveyor personally intervened. In a brief meeting with the determined farmer, a demand for £100 compensation was quickly settled for £75 and work restarted.

Drake took a great deal of interest himself in the construction side of these early schemes, generating a tremendous sense of teamwork among all his staff and providing a strong managerial and entrepreneurial leadership for these projects he considered to be *his*. He would regularly visit the site, bringing his sandwiches with him. On site, because of the mud, he used a stick. If anything displeased him, he would throw his stick into the air and shout. He was unpopular with contractors because of such demonstrations, and also because of his toughness in dealing with claims for supplementary payment: his attitude to the latter was largely one of policy. The county's credibility with the Ministry depended very much on an ability to keep costs down and to complete projects on schedule. Unforeseen difficulties with the first schemes marred Lancashire's record somewhat on both scores, and subsequently tended to leave the county on the defensive, although they were proud that no scheme was ever delayed by a labour strike.

Success in securing schemes for Lancashire depended entirely on an ability to persuade the Ministry of Transport to include proposals in the national road programme. The Ministry, in the early postwar years, was professionally weak, in terms of both its experience and its staffing of the road section.[58] Drake personally badgered and bullied, never taking 'no' for an answer. He visited the Ministry regularly and chased the progress of the Lancashire schemes through its offices. It is said that the officials installed a bell which was rung whenever he entered the building, to forewarn staff! Drake discovered this and occasionally took another route through buildings to take people by surprise. Confronted by such a strong-minded Lancastrian, who knew exactly what he wanted, the men at the Ministry were forced to make concessions. The mass media and publicity were used to the full. Any agreement, promise or expression of sympathy from a public official or figure was immediately headlined in the local press. This strengthened the campaign and increased the pressure, making it very difficult for a promise to be retracted. Every opportunity to enlist support was taken. The publication by the British Road Federation of the county's proposals in 1966 was one example, the lobbying of MPs and the generation of questions in Parliament are others.

Lancashire's campaign on roads, developed from the early road plan, followed a characteristic strategy. One principle was always to press for particular schemes, rather than to campaign on a broad front. The county maintained a rolling portfolio of four or five specific proposals, which could be identified, in one form or another, in the original 1949 Plan. As schemes passed from proposal to firm acceptance, new projects were brought into the campaign.[59]

The earlier schemes, for example that for the M6, were in the county plan and in the 1938 proposals of the County Surveyors' Society. Lancashire's achievement was in pulling forward their timing and securing this rural motorway in Lancashire ahead of schedule. The Ministry agreed to build the M6 by starting in Lancashire and working south to Birmingham.

A second principle of the strategy can be identified in other schemes which were primarily an extension and development of the network. These were by no means certain of official acceptance; they were fragmented and promoted sequentially. For example, the 1966 British Road Federation report, *Lancashire Needs*, pressed four schemes, one of which was for a seven-mile section from north Liverpool to the Skelmersdale–M6 section of the motorway, which the Ministry had recently put out to tender. The report foresaw a future possibility of continuing the route to connect the M6 with the M61. In 1972, when the 1966 proposal was already included in the firm ministry programme and designated as the M58, a major campaign was in progress for this additional section. This sequential planning strategy did not involve a massive programme and a large share of national resources: each was a manageable section, viable in itself and financially feasible.

Such an approach required a great deal of foresight. Once, however, existing schemes incorporated design features to enable a stitching-on of future schemes, these features were then used *ex post hoc* in the campaign to secure the next section. For example, the Broughton interchange, built in the early 1960s, was designed by Lancashire to accommodate the Preston northerly bypass. At the time, this motorway to Blackpool, not built until 1975, had the status of being a county proposal not, as yet, accepted by the Ministry. A more striking case is that of the *Mid-Lancashire Motorway* report published jointly by Lancashire, Wigan and Bolton County Boroughs in 1972, in support of the M6–M61 link mentioned above. This report pointed out that the M61 (opened in 1970) incorporated a major motorway bridge at Bolton in anticipation of the link now being campaigned for in 1972, and carried a full plate picture of the M61 bridge on its back cover, while on the front was a picture of a major interchange already built on the M6 to accommodate its western junction.[60] The Ministry was aware of what was happening. In 1970, however, in answer to a parliamentary question, Mr Michael Heseltine, on behalf of his Minister, said in connection with the proposal that: 'The criteria for including a road as a strategy route were that it would justify improvement to dual carriageway standard.... This proposed extension ... on present forecasts ... could not be expected to meet these criteria.'[61] At the time of this statement, the junctions for the scheme that was in process of rejection by the Minister had already been built, and land had been reserved for its future route.

In support of its longer-term strategy, the county was also prepared to engineer some short-run traffic congestion. The Broughton interchange again provides an illustration. The ultimate linkage of the Preston and Lancaster sections of the M6 were assured. The northerly exit of the Preston section terminated south of Broughton village on the A6, the pre-motorway main north–south trunk route. The terminal for the Preston section could easily have been north of the village, but the south was deliberately chosen, thus channelling two lanes of northbound motorway traffic onto the congested A6, a constricted road involving a junction controlled by traffic lights. The case for proceeding as quickly as possible with the next section of motorway became unanswerable. The junction of the A683 and the M6 at Lancaster provides another instance. Morecambe traffic from the south is channelled into Lancaster before crossing the River Lune. This supports the county's case for a direct motorway link between the M6 and Morecambe, but so far this scheme has not been accepted. It has also been suggested that the A583 from Preston to Blackpool could have benefited from improvement schemes, which would have eased congestion. Such expenditure was not undertaken because it would have weakened the case for the preferred M55 motorway.

Through the 1960s, however, the situation was changing. Greater control by the Ministry was one factor making it more difficult for the road-builders. A high density of population, together with industrial importance as well as government regional policy, helped the county in promoting its schemes – but the trend was nevertheless for greater control from the centre. Apart from the planning strategy just outlined, the county in earlier schemes had anticipated formal ministry approval and had prematurely commenced work. For example, in the case of the Barton High-Level Bridge, on a county Class I road where the county had to find twenty-five per cent of the cost, prior to the letting of contracts and the commencement of construction scheduled by the Minister to take place in 1956, the county went ahead and used 400,000 tons of waste slag from a local steel works in 1953 in preparation for the embankments, giving an estimated saving of £100,000. In another scheme Drake personally negotiated, with the support of his chairman, a land deal with a golf club in anticipation of a road proposal, two or three years before the project was under serious consideration. In the case of the Lancaster bypass, work was started on the site six months before the compulsory purchase order. In these early days, the county surveyor was doing the sensible thing; this was what local initiative was taken to mean. The Ministry turned a blind eye, but as time passed control tightened, and civil servants saw to it that procedures were followed.

In the sixties, too, the Ministry became more insistent on the application of design standards. Bridges are an example. Lancashire's work in this field was outstanding. The open spandrel bridge over the Lune at Lancaster is a fine example of technical design and aesthetic sensitivity. Each bridge is individually designed and blended to its environment: Lancashire's bridges are attractive both to the motorist and the inhabitants. The county insisted, in spite of the Ministry, in painting these bridges different colours, and making extensive use of facing material for purely cosmetic purposes. Thus, Lancashire's roads have pioneered good design; but, as the Lofthouse report[62] illustrates, this approach was more expensive and it lessened ministry control over design standards.

Many lessons were learnt from the first schemes. For example, the use of cut-and-fill methods, utilising inadequate local material, which proved unsatisfactory on the Preston bypass, were never repeated. This first scheme was opened with a temporary top surface, usual at that time. The county was, however, determined to open the first motorway and set an example for the rest of the country. As is well known, the eight-mile Preston stretch was opened by Harold Macmillan in December 1958 and closed by Jack Frost in January 1959. The use of local shale in the sub-base, which became waterlogged through bad weather, was a professional risk which proved to be a false economy. The risk was known and the county was unlucky when the temperature rose from 8° to 43°F in thirty-six hours and damaged the surface. The fanfare and glory of six weeks earlier turned to a challenge to the county's reputation, and a further £8000 was spent on improved drainage. Lancashire's experience of problems surmounted, however, helped other projects throughout the country and provided a central pool of experience in London, inevitably leading to greater control in the future.

After the 1964 election, the Labour administration pushed ahead with its policies of central economic planning. Economic crises tended to enforce greater scrutiny of public expenditure proposals. The development of cost–benefit analysis led to the evaluation of transport projects in terms of their financial returns. The Ministry introduced a computer-based system requiring a scheme to justify itself on the basis· of its first-year rate of return, and a later development of this system scrutinises a thirty-year period.[63] Some have doubted the worth of these techniques because of the great effort they involve, and because of the masking of large elements of judgement still being exercised.[64] Lancashire's early approach was based on traffic appraisal, and also on explicit judgement, based on local knowledge; these new techniques represent a trend away from this and from the previous style adopted by Lancashire, in common with many other counties. The course was getting stiffer in the 1960s and more hurdles were set up.

A major organisational change was brought about by the establishment in 1967 of six road construction units covering the whole country. Barbara Castle had become Minister in January 1966 and in March her ministry sent a confidential memorandum to the County Councils Association and County Surveyors' Society, proposing a new system for handling the road programme.[65] The ultimate proposal required all motorway and trunk road design and construction costing over £1 million to be channelled through the new road construction units. Counties would still handle principal roads, and the Ministry would continue to co-ordinate this work through the divisional road engineer. A civil servant would direct each unit's headquarters staff. Sub-units were also established – two in the North-Western Road Construction Unit (NWRCU), one for Lancashire based in Preston and one for Cheshire in Chester. (Westmorland and Cumberland were covered by the NWRCU, but being smaller authorities did not have separate sub-units.) The sub-units were to be staffed by their counties, with employees on secondment, and the head of each was the county surveyor acting on a part-time basis. It was intended that the counties might still campaign and propose schemes. Road planning and programming would remain under the control of London, but all design work and construction would be the responsibility of the unit's director who, as a civil servant, would be a ministry official.

In November 1966, the Ministry wrote to Lancashire, suggesting that county as the best area for the first unit. By December 1966 Drake had agreed to be the Unit's first director, on secondment, but with a possibility of permanency. This was a flattering and shrewd move by the Ministry and enlisted the support of a strong critic. It could have been predicted that Drake, temperamentally, would be cramped in the civil service environment. He returned to the county in December 1968, although as county surveyor he maintained his contact as head of the Lancashire sub-unit.

Nationally, county councils feared a loss of status under the new arrangements. Events have since shown the system to be a source of stress. The Ministry promoted the idea as a partnership, but under the organisational structure the county surveyor is responsible to the unit director, and thereby a master-and-servant relationship has tended to arise, despite earlier intentions. Problems have arisen in the gradings and pay differentials between local authority and civil service staff. Civil service procedures are standardised, while local government tends to work on an *ad hoc* basis. In 1968 the Ministry proposed a civil service type of inspection of local government staff in the sub-units, to check the quality of their work; at a national level this was vigorously resisted and the idea in that form lapsed. Central purchasing has been another source of local frustration.

The original changes were presented as an updating of procedures, to improve efficiency, and to herald a new era in road-building. In part, they were a counter-proposal by the Ministry to a BRF campaign, then current, for a National Road Board. Basically, however, the Ministry was not happy with the agency system, and wanted a more direct say in the work done at the local level. The county surveyors saw the difficulties as residing in the Ministry. One can sympathise with their case. For purposes of national economic planning, the Ministry requested the submission of a five-year programme of proposals, asking for more information and more data, and then appeared to give no decisions.

By 1970 the county councils were quite open in their criticisms of the new system, having lost a direct line to London in their campaigns on road schemes. As will be clear from the earlier discussion of Lancashire policy, motorway and trunk proposals had been directly promoted at the Ministry, providing direct access to the heart of the decision-making process. Under the new arrangements more advice was channelled through the Ministry's regional organisation, which had no delegated powers and had to pass matters upwards. Conversely, the work of the local authority staff in the sub-unit was now subjected to more rigorous checking than previously. Whitehall had begun effectively to insulate itself from dynamic influences such as James Drake.

What has been the impact of this change on Lancashire? Even by 1974 the state of road-building was still transitional. At its formation, the NWRCU took over a number of Lancashire schemes in progress, and with them the county's programme of proposals. By 1974 all the schemes completed or still in progress were taken over and no totally new schemes or initiatives had been developed. By 1974 sixty per cent of all construction in progress by the unit, and seventy-three per cent of projects in the firm programme, were in Lancashire. However, only thirty-eight per cent of projects in the preparation pool, i.e. in the early design stages,

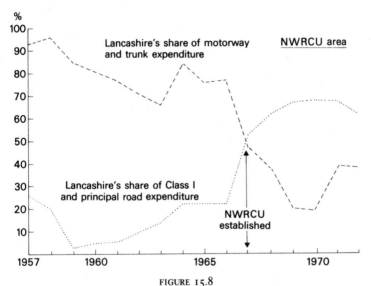

FIGURE 15.8
Lancashire's Share of Road Improvement Expenditure in the NWRCU Area

were in the county. Cheshire, in particular, had increased its share. Comparison of NWRCU and national figures suggest that the Ministry, from 1972–3, had begun actively to discriminate against the region in accepting schemes into its firm road programme. Indeed, by 1975, the Ministry had concluded: 'compared to many other areas of the country, the North West has benefited from a more dynamic road construction programme in previous years and as a result is now relatively well provided with motorways and high quality trunk roads.'[66]

The change inaugurated by the road construction units left the old system intact as far as principal roads were concerned. Figure 15.3 above shows a marked switching by Lancashire after 1966 from motorways to principal roads. This same phenomenon is exhibited in Figure 15.8, which shows Lancashire's road-building as a proportion of the four counties that make up the NWRCU area. The enormous reduction in Lancashire's share of motorways is offset by her principal road expenditure, suggesting a response on the part of the county to the tighter control system of the Ministry. The latter must have accepted Lancashire's proposals, but the direction of the county's initiatives had most certainly changed.

Conclusion

In the 1970s there has arisen a new phenomenon in the form of the anti-motorway lobby, which brings the whole of national policy in motorway-building into question. Traffic is regulated by congestion; the demand for cars and road space is not self-regulating and likely to decline at some fixed date; new roads provide no solution and severely threaten the environment and our quality of life – thus runs a contemporary line of thought. Furthermore, the political and bureaucratic process is a massive juggernaut which only protest and direct action can halt. It is certainly true that Lancashire road schemes of the mid-seventies are not essentially traffic schemes, but are far more instruments of regional rejuvenation promoted under the influence of political factors like marginal consti-tuencies. Fortunately for Lancashire, it has been able to promote its rural motorways in a different climate of opinion. In their time, these were new, and the marvels of the moment. How rapidly they are taken for granted! The early 1960s will go down in history as the era of new universities and motorways.

In 1949 Lancashire was presented with a vision. It is convenient to end with a quotation from one man who dedicated his life to its cause:

> The building of a motorway is sculpture on an exciting and grand scale, carving, moulding, forging and adapting materials provided by nature – earth, rock and minerals – into a finished product, which must be functional and pleasing to the eye, as well as economical and durable. But in trying to accomplish this, one must be humanitarian and remember that all this affects people. The civil engineer on motorway projects, as on other public works, is the servant of the people, using his specialist knowledge on their behalf for the good of the whole community and, at the same time, mindful of their views and the rights of the minority who are affected. *Drake* [67]

PART IV
General Conclusion

CHAPTER 16

The County Council
in Retrospect

IN looking back over the work and achievements of the Lancashire county authority during the greater part of this century, it is not difficult to be overcome by awe in face of its sheer scale of operation. Such temptations must be firmly resisted by the historian. It is not difficult to show that this great organisation, or complex of organisations, functioned with considerable efficiency, managing to satisfy many members of the public who were at least aware of its operations and, just as important, managing not to antagonise large numbers of them. Its interactions with the mass of the electorate were often superficial, if only because its doings were poorly reported in the newspaper press; and it is to be doubted how far the person helped by its health visitors or librarians looked beyond them to the county councillors nominally responsible for the employment of the officials concerned. Apart from this very great problem, its relative efficiency was not in itself an argument for its continuation; nor was its range of achievements, *in spite of* its size, an argument for very large local government units, covering county or larger areas. Lancashire's county councillors and officers were keenly aware of this problem of sheer size of area, and to their great credit they had themselves proposed a tripartite division of the county into 'ridings' long before the dismemberment in fact took place in 1974. They were, in any case, far more interested in defending a two-tier system of local government, which, more than any other in England, they had worked to make operate successfully and agreeably in face of huge and complex problems of administration. In a variety of differing guises, the county authority was the great co-ordinator and the great diplomat, exercising sway over county districts and divisions occupying widely various localities as much as forty or fifty miles from County Hall. Its real triumph lay in its diplomacy and in its interrelationships with district councils and their representatives.

363

Its leaders and rulers, county gentry or 'public persons', had always understood the importance of local sentiment. It is, of course, easy to see them as mere token or lay figures, going through the motions of public representation while the real work – on behalf of an all-seeing central government – was carried out by highly skilled officers. The truth is more complex, and perhaps more instructive. Central government relied upon the localities to give substance to its legislation, and was often dependent upon local experiment in order that it could gain a greater degree of wisdom, just as it was dependent upon local co-operation for the spirit as well as the substance of what was on the statute book. This is easily appreciated. A great authority like Lancashire did not, however, merely take orders; it could set its own terms in innumerable details, whether in the siting of towns or the building of major roads; and it could organise powerful lobbies in pursuit of such aims. Evelyn Sharp, at the Ministry of Housing, is known to have treated Lancashire's clerk and its delegations with rather more than her customary courtesy; and, *per contra*, Sir James Drake's forceful incursions in face of Whitehall procrastination were at one period a source of much discomfort to officials there. Given, then, a strong intermediary authority, interreacting powerfully and often constructively with London and at the same time showing sensitivity to the feelings of district councils, we have here a consideration of much importance to the accumulated experience of government in England. The tragedy is, of course, that a large part of industrial Lancashire, isolated in separate county borough 'pockets', did not always gain from this arrangement. The county councillors, as we have seen, often represented both district and county in a dual capacity, and were not likely to permit local interests to be overlooked; at the same time, County Hall could be a great educator away from the parochial or the sectarian, and the increasing turnover of membership of the Council, a feature of the middle twentieth century, and one that did indeed have the unfortunate consequence of permitting an elderly leadership to remain unchallenged, can also be seen as equivalent to an enhanced education in government for many scores of individuals. County Hall was a college of unique character.

The officers, heading powerful departments, were only too willing to act as tutors and guides. Had their committees – or seminars – been full of the brightness, as well as the recalcitrance, of youth, much might have been gained that would have been of value to the future government of the region. But, as we have seen, the average age of the really dedicated students of local government was high, their prejudices were often set; the knowledge of procedure and technology required was enormous, and the occasional application of party whips in the postwar period limited the amount of independent judgement that could be applied. It should be said in fairness that the technical nature of many decisions limited that judgement, or choice, even further. Moreover, only chairmen or vice-chairmen of committees saw their respective officers frequently enough to have an opportunity to learn a great deal about the fields in which they operated; information might be freely given on request, but journeys to Preston were often lengthy, and in any case there is now plenty of evidence, especially that set out by Mr Hands and Mr Denver in Chapter 12, that the power to influence events was limited to comparatively few.

This power was, for much of the life of the Council, seen as a reward for long service, and of course (a point that should not be overlooked) for the judgement and knowledge that go with such service. But the corollary of this was that a council member had to have leisure – or professionally available time – at his disposal, with the result that membership of the chamber was self-limiting. In the days when county leadership had in any case come from gentry or the affluent, this hardly mattered, and in any case the early functions and work of the Council simply did not provide the 'issues' or the challenges that could have called forth working-class contenders. No member of the Independent Labour Party (ILP) or the Social Democratic Federation (SDF) would have spent his time calling for better roads or more policemen or more lunatic asylums; and a not very well organised Labour Party only began to react to the public assistance problem long after the Party nationally had begun to form governments. Before that time, much of the work of county government had been of a kind that might have been congenial to a man steeped in the duties of the magistracy, but which certainly offered few charms to any other person. *Demos*, in the form of the self-educated artisan, had been willing to fight for a place on a School Board, or sometimes on a Board of Guardians; but we find few people complaining about their virtual exclusion from a county authority before 1930.

The post-1944 period, as we have shown, brought massive transformations at several levels. The social composition of the body of councillors had already been steadily changing to the point that it somewhat more nearly reflected that of the electorate. There was a memorable swing towards politicisation of the conduct of the Council itself. Yet, as is shown in Chapter 4, the earliest signs of this were manifested in the twenties and thirties. It should not be forgotten, too, that this development had been preceded by a slow humanisation of Council involvements. But during this pre-1939 period a concern for the problems of some deprived human beings was scarcely reflected in a growth of interest on the part of the electorate. A distant paternalism, marked by occasional angry demonstrations in the council chamber, had widespread apathy as its companion. And, after all, why should the Lancastrian, who for the most part was not directly affected, have taken much interest? The Council's debates were hardly ever reported in detail in his local newspapers, and they rarely bore significantly on the locality that most concerned him, that centred on his own parish or main street.

The relative upsurge of public response in the Council's elections after 1946 is to be seen largely in terms of national political trends and behaviour, although it should be noted that personal-service involvements on the part of the Council, growing on an unprecedented scale, may have increased the awareness of a postwar generation in some small degree. The return, after nearly two generations, of a large number of contested elections from the 1930s did something for political education of a limited kind. It should be remembered, too, that not only did the personal and other services of the Council spread vastly; they also became more *visible*, as new schools, fire stations, ambulances and divisional offices began to display the Council's title at many a gateway or on hundreds of vehicles. We do not claim much for this fairly obvious form of advertisement; for, as appears later (and in Appendix 1), members of the public could remain quite extraordinarily resistant to this information. But, at a level of much keener awareness, the spread of delegated services and of divisionalisation did have the effect of involving many hundreds of councillors and 'public persons', and here the work of Lancashire County Council must be seen as memorable, and possibly beyond praise in the circumstances of the time. Here, at least, was a very English, as well as a Lancastrian, organisation which succeeded in being something more than an efficient bureaucracy, permitting an outraged citizen to feel that he could protest, or even hurl abuse, at something or somebody tangible. (Nor is this a sentimentality; more than one Lancashire private citizen has had occasion to make himself a nuisance at the expense of planning and other officials and committees, and readers are invited to try to do the same in the case of a regional statutory body, with a similar effect.)

The vast growth of the county machine, then, did not cause it to become any more remote from the citizen's standpoint, although divisional administrators, and more especially field officers, found that the middle and senior ranks of the central administration were more distant or unapproachable, and that unrealistic demands could result. It should be stressed that all such propositions really call for the most meticulous research, and much detailed evidence. The personal services, by a paradox, appeared to become more impersonally run, and the chief officer of a department might often reach a point, usually in the middle or late 1950s, where he did not know all his own staff; gone were the days when a Sir George Etherton could give avuncular advice on how to order his life to a youthful worker in County Hall. As departments became steadily larger, they became more inward-looking and somewhat less prone to co-operate, a division of identities that could be made much more acute when there was a vast difference in technical specialisms. With the growth of powerful departments, and with them of equally powerful specialist chief officers, the clerk tended to lose something of his dominant position among officials. The beginning of this process was signified when the most determined and influential of postwar chief education officers (CEOs), (Sir) Arthur Binns, insisted that the Clerk's Department should cease to determine any main item that went into the Education Committee agenda. When chief officers' regular meetings were set up, from the early fifties, it became noticeable that differences between the CEO and the Clerk, and their respective departments, were somewhat more likely to arise than in the case of any other pair of officials, although it should be stressed that there is not the slightest evidence that this affected the general efficiency of either organisation. (Sir Patrick McCall confessed ruefully that 'You could get nothing tougher than Sir Arthur Binns', and the Clerk had a difficult time as chairman of this meeting.) The point here is that the enormous pressures of the period were forcing officers into ever more departmental preoccupation; and attempts, especially by the Labour Party, to bring them together in bulk buying and similar collectivist schemes tended to cause difficulty at this high interdepartmental level. Individualist officers like the road engineer Sir James Drake, who were in any case specialists with a professional ethos of their own, found – as Sir James's own comments confirm – that such meetings could be tedious or irritating.

Within departments there was, of course, a marked *esprit de corps*, just as there were often strong bonds of friendship between senior officers, some of whom, like the medical officer of health, could offer advice and help of a valued kind. Nor did the Clerk of the Council's department lose all its predominance; for it had long tended to nurture the highest quality administrators, who then moved into other departments, just as, in the postwar period, it trained future clerks of the Lancashire County Council. As a common service department of high stature, it continued to play a leading role by virtue of its very function of providing committee clerks. But if it was *primus inter pares*, first among equals, then the latter were becoming more equal. Yet the process was gradual, and some departments felt themselves to be very much out of the status race until their own heads were eventually given membership of the chief officers' meeting – the children's officer and chief fire officer in the early sixties and the county librarian somewhat later.

Not all departments were in the fortunate position of joining in the general expansion as a matter of course; and the staff of the county tuberculosis service was fragmented, after the reorganisation of 1946–7, 'among four or five or more public bodies', although the central departmental staff moved under the Manchester Regional Hospital Board in highly unpleasant circumstances, 'amid an unforgiveable invasion of their emptying suite of rooms by decorators and anxious combating searchers for rooms', to save their position by finding new accommodation in the Park Hotel, Preston.[1] All in all, this was a sad end to a remarkable campaign, even though much of the experience of the scheme was disseminated in space and time. The *esprit de corps* of a department shows most clearly in a situation of crisis, as it undoubtedly did in this instance. For the rest, sheer growth in size and fragmentation of functions made for impersonality rather than team spirit, and when every allowance is made for nostalgia, it remains true that veteran council administrators are firmly of the opinion that devotion to duty and professional and social fellowship were at a higher level in the days of smaller staffs and more modest functions.

This brings us to the history of the county's administrative staffs and their organisations, an important subject which could hardly fit into the series of case studies so far given. The first association of Lancashire county officers owed its origin, very aptly, to the tireless J. E. Gee of the Health Department, who, as we have seen, ran that organisation for the medical officer on a salary that to later eyes seems insulting when compared with that of his chief. Gee appears to have conceived the idea of a County Officers' Association simultaneously with the inauguration of NALGO in 1905, and the County Association received formal local approval in 1908, and acceptance into NALGO in 1911. It had, however, been meeting for recreational and other purposes for some years before that date. At this period, and until the Second World War, the Council fixed its own salary scales, albeit with some reference to prevailing scales elsewhere. The County Association was at first unable to deal frontally with service conditions, and there was for many years no satisfactory system of consultation with staff representatives; nor, indeed, was there any council superannuation scheme until 1922, although both this scheme, and security of tenure, were strenuously canvassed in the First World War.[2] Although Whitley Councils were born in this war, they were soon afterwards rejected by the respective associations of local authorities, and so local associations of officers such as that of Lancashire tended to evolve their own methods of negotiation and consultation which accordingly followed an individual pattern in later history. Meanwhile, the addition of Poor Law officers to the county strength in 1929–30 led to the reorganisation of the county branch of NALGO, stimulated by the fact that the new members were scattered round the county, often far from the Preston offices; hence followed the formation of twenty sub-branches based on the former Guardians' (or public assistance) districts.

The rise in professional status of local government officers was, of course, influenced by a variety of factors; among these, the 1929 Local Government Act itself, and the 1934 Hadow Committee, which recommended staff gradings of a generally acceptable kind. But, once again, wartime conditions and aspirations played a vital part in the history of local government staff, in that those who were 'left behind', with increasingly heavy responsibility, were determined to improve affairs for their brethren in the armed services. Thus the war years, despite Sir George Etherton's paternalism and the appeals to patriotism of Sir William Hodgson, brought a period of unprecedented abrasiveness in staff–employer relationships; and ultimately a Joint Consultative Committee was formed in June 1943, with Sir James Aitken acting as a mollifying influence on behalf of the Council itself. This body began seriously to tackle grading appeals, recommendations for promotion and mileage allowances 'without seeking much help from the District Officer in Manchester', and succeeded, before the end of the war, in reaching agreement on conditions of employment which were superior to those set out in the national charter (1946) for local government officers. Simultaneously, the Whitley Council principle was recognised in Lancashire in 1944. Thereafter the county branch ceased to operate as a force in isolation and used the advice of NALGO district officers more consistently, although the branch's Conditions of Service Committee was still enabled to deal with anomalies caused by transfer, and with grading claims, holiday entitlements and educational qualifications, without recourse to the Whitley Council or the district officers.[3]

The National Joint Council of 1944 eventually produced, in 1946, the 'Scheme of Conditions of Service' more generally known as the Local Government Charter; and, although no local authority was at first compelled to fall into line, the Industrial Disputes Tribunal of 1952 laid down that every authority must observe recognised terms and conditions of employment. The view of the National Joint Council was that recruitment, qualification, training and promotion of officers should be dealt with by an establishment committee in each local authority.[4]

However, Lancashire County Council had an establishment officer as early as 1947; the decision to form an establishment committee was taken within two years, and the committee itself was in operation by 1950. (It should be added that in earlier years the Committee of Chairmen (1918–31) had dealt with the salaries of senior officers, followed by the Co-ordination Committee,[5] while the Finance Committee, with the respective departments, had covered superannuation and employment matters.) Initially chaired by Robert Guymer, the new committee contained numerous representatives of the Finance Committee and the Co-ordination Committee. Its scope of reference was so vast that it is difficult to imagine that any member of it succeeded in mastering the hundreds of individual cases referred to in its minutes over the years. It dealt with recruitment, promotion through examination, assisted study; it had a disciplinary function (although an officer who felt his case had been misjudged could appeal to the Provincial Council of the National Joint Committee); and its area of competence ranged from the employment of departmental officers right through to clerical staffs and cleaners in schools. It dealt with the application of (literally) many hundreds of salary scales and a multitude of joint negotiating bodies, from the Nurses' and Midwives' Council to the North-Western Whitley Council for Manual Workers and the Joint Negotiating Committee for Engineering Craftsmen, or the Standing Joint Advisory Committee for the Staffs of Children's Homes.[6]

To the Committee, then, fell the mind-blowing job of reviewing the cost of manpower used in the Council's service. The mere fact of established scales at every level served to make its work barely possible. The Council was, by the mid-fifties, employing labour on a scale and of a range and variety that dwarfed that of almost any local employing body in England; and for the most part all its officers and committee members could do was to ascertain national or specifically arranged practice and give approval. Selwyn Jones perhaps summed up its earlier efforts fairly enough: 'the Council has little direct control over the rising cost of its wages bill, but this Committee can legitimately claim to have contributed, by its detailed investigation of staffing proposals, to the very necessary task of keeping the use of manpower to the minimum compatible with efficiency'.[7] The minute books of the Committee became, increasingly, masses of pasted-in agenda items (often representing decisions taken long in advance of any meeting), interesting mainly for occasional reports on manpower and its use. The fifties saw a massive increase in the use of part-time employment, especially in education, and up to 1970 the number of part-timers steadily caught up with the full-time. By that year there were 43,317 full-time employees of the county and 31,635 part-time employees, a total of 74,952. Of these, a high proportion were teachers, and many of this vast mass saw the Council only as a distant employer. Only at the Preston offices, perhaps, was there any distinct sense of community, strengthened by the work of the common service departments, by the social activities of NALGO and by the deliberate actions of departmental chiefs in calling their field officers together.

As Mr Hands and Mr Denver show, the rate of turnover of councillors was fairly high throughout the existence of the County Council, and this inevitably left much power in the hands of a small handful of enduring and dedicated figures. However, as we have stressed the work of representation as members of the county authority could be highly educative, and the limited freedom of action and judgement accorded to most councillors could nevertheless have a rather more than token significance. It is of the utmost importance that any action taken by the Council's officers could be scrutinised, even though such scrutiny was simply impracticable for by far the greater part of the time, and even though chairmen and vice-chairmen were often the only people who could discuss the inner workings of departments – and that briefly. Despite this fact, the central staffs of departments regarded the senior Council members on their particular committees with considerable deference, although it is also possible that senior or chief officers built up this form of respect as additional control over their own office teams. This, like many matters touched upon in this volume, suggests an interesting topic for further investigation. The chief officers, as we have seen, could wield much personal power, and a few, like Sir Arthur Binns, Sir James Drake, Chief Constable Palfrey and the planning officer Aylmer Coates, probably attracted more publicity, at times, than did any elected representative.

Nevertheless, this power was derived power, produced by a given and limiting set of circumstances, and publicity itself created safeguards. Sir James Drake had to work in association with great contracting firms, and so special precautions were adopted when tenders were opened and examined in his department.[8] Scrupulousness was not only there, but had to be seen to be there; and it is perhaps significant that the county's most forceful and in some ways individualistic officer could react in this way by making such an arrangement.

The general ethos of the county authority remained one of consciousness of a public trust, expressed in concern over economy as well as efficiency, and it is striking that both of the main political parties of the postwar era came close to the traditional concerns of earlier chairmen and county leaders. The Conservatives might be rather more economy-minded over the social services than their opponents, and the Labour Group tended to have a deeper distrust of senior officers and their requirements, but by and large the attitudes of both groups tended to converge, especially in the late fifties and sixties. Consequently, it was difficult for a senior officer to make an application for considerable or expensive increases in staff without a carefully prepared case, and of course extra staff requirements were often implicitly or explicitly related to new legislation or local government practice. The members of the Establishment Committee were well aware of the difficulties of their position, but staff requirements were carefully discussed in other committees, or in private conferences with officers, and the result was that staffing increases in this great county were certainly not more marked, and may at certain stages have been relatively less, than the norm for English counties in general.

There is no indication that sheer size led to excessive recruitment of new officials, and there are clear indications that the great 'divisionalised' services, education and health, were run comparatively cheaply. As has been shown, the chief education officer could only apply for new advisers, or for more clerical workers, in his further education section if it was demonstrated that these members of his department were grossly overloaded or likely to be so.[9] A comparative return issued by the Institute of Municipal Treasurers and Accountants jointly with the Society of County Treasurers, showed that in 1962–3 the cost of education in Lancashire was *below* the average for all English counties, being £18,440 per 1000 population as against the national average of £18,844. In that particular period the greatest economy in the Lancashire educational structure was in the field of secondary education, expenditure on which was well below the national average, while further education was appreciably if not greatly below this level.[10] However, primary education in Lancashire cost considerably more than the national average, and this cost would, a year or two later, have been transferred to secondary education. This disparity arose not from administrative circumstances, but demographic ones; Lancashire had ninety-seven primary pupils per 1000 population, as against eighty-eight nationally, while the secondary population was much closer to the national norm.[11] Our point must remain, then, that there is not, in sample cases like the one cited, the slightest evidence that Lancashire created heavy administrative costs, and net educational expenditure on administration and inspection chargeable to rates and grants stood at £500 per 1000 of population, as against £590 nationally.[12]

Several years later, the Lancashire County Council health service was subjected to a somewhat similar scrutiny, and the drift of the resultant findings – made, once more, by the Institute of Municipal Treasurers – was much the same. In costs per annum in 1967–8 of day nurseries, child welfare, health visiting, home nursing and welfare homes, it was argued that those for Lancashire were 'below the average costs for the 45 English counties. The single exception is in relation to the Home Help service.'[13] Just as important, the actual cost of administering the Lancashire health service was relatively less than the average for All English Counties; the percentage here (10.7 per cent for Lancashire) represents the ratio of administrative staff salaries as against all other running costs, the average percentage for all forty-five English counties being 13.9.[14]

Cheapness of administration combined with delegation, democracy and local involvement; this makes, and made, an attractive formula. Our purpose here, however, is simply to dispel the notion that such a vast organisation necessarily resulted in the creation of a welfare-dispensing juggernaut. Lancashire's health service was efficient, and in the light of these figures it was administratively cheap. As Mr MacGregor-Reid's researches indicate, Lancashire *per capita* spendings on health over the postwar years were higher than that for the UK local government service in general. This was a reflection of need, as Mr Reid's figures suggest, but also of deep inadequacy in other types of provision.[15] The private medicine sector of Lancashire and the North-West was but indifferently staffed, and the needs of the region, judged in terms of the relatively high incidence of disease and ill health, were high. General mortality rates were above the national average, as were infant mortality rates and sickness benefits paid out; and the response of the region and its local authorities to a general shortage of doctors and dentists was to employ more staff in health service *per capita* of population. The taxpayer as well as the local rate-payer had to bear the burden of Lancashire ill health, and also to carry that caused by the unwillingness of the private practitioner to work in an industrial environment. The region, which had seen the end of a triumphant campaign against tuberculosis, nevertheless continued to be a geographical black area as regards a growing incidence of cardiac and cerebrovascular diseases and respiratory afflictions like bronchitis, although it should be stressed that the administrative county usually lay in the penumbra of the worst localities, which were nearly always in the great urban centres.[16] Against this unfortunate background, the Council acquitted itself honourably and efficiently with the resources placed at its disposal; and, as is shown in Chapter 14, it undoubtedly contributed to the reduction of infant mortality and tuberculosis, although precise effects and contributions are impossible to assess.

We do not even know how far a greater concentration of resources would have made people more healthy, other things being equal, and the results of certain kinds of medical care and of education are notoriously difficult to measure. On the other hand, economy in some public services and campaigns is not necessarily a virtue, and this is demonstrated in the case of the County Library, which (unlike most of Lancashire's services) cost considerably more to run in 1951–2 than did many English county library services, and which, at £206 1s per 1000 of population, was far above the English counties average of £147 9s. But the Lancashire County Library, in the same period, stocked more books per 1000 of population than the average (1123 as against 939) and issued more books (6953 as against 6402 per 1000 for All English Counties).[17] Since the whole purpose of a library system is to provide wide choice and reading experience, the high cost element is, in this instance, far more likely to be an index to civilized attitudes than of spendthrift behaviour by the Education Committee.

This vast and often cumbersome county machine, then, worked with effect. Its adult classes and drama groups reached into the remotest hamlets, and its community enlivened or enriched the existence of people in numerous otherwise dreary suburban tracts, while its youth leaders and youth clubs did at least something for those who could be helped to find worthwhile company. The only criticism that could be made was the obvious one that there were never enough resources to bring real community sense and enrichment to Lancashire's subtopian overspill, never enough to bring adequate care and after-care to Lancashire's sick and elderly, never enough to bring about the shining health centres that Dr Gawne and his colleagues had hoped to see in every Lancashire community of any size. What the county authority did undoubtedly achieve, however, was to show that these things were worth having, that they could be provided, and that they could be sacrificed for. Perhaps a new generation will have to rediscover the need for this sacrifice, and will have to find that the hard effort expended by an unsung generation of public figures and officials is rarely rewarded in its own time.

It can be said that administrative Lancashire should never have existed in the rambling, untidy form of the period 1889–1974. That its county government operated at all, let alone with considerable efficiency, is a remarkable phenomenon, and there are many lessons to be learned, not so much from its failures as from its successes. Lancastrian councillors and officials knew well enough that a journey from Dalton-in-Furness to County Hall, or the reverse, was a tiresome experience in winter, and that overspill from Liverpool, the reception of which earned one little thanks and much hatred, should not really have been inflicted on a local authority, however large and accommodating. At least one clerk of the County was virtually haunted by the word 'overspill', just as his predecessors had been continually worried by the claims of Lancashire county boroughs to county territory. Lancashire was never a community, but a great congeries of communities, and what geographers choose to see as Lancastria has never been, in most senses, a social or an economic unity. This reality was seized upon in the deliberations of the Redcliffe-Maud Commission (1969) which remarked that 'the social and economic pattern of central Lancashire is not yet so interwoven that either a single or a first-tier authority is needed for the whole of it.'[18] If this is true of central Lancashire, what can be said of the rest?

Yet there was little hostility to the county administration at the district level, and it was mainly in border territory, on the part of authorities like Stretford or Crosby, that deep-felt antagonisms smouldered. Interestingly, some kind of day-to-day *modus vivendi* was established between the county and the county boroughs (whereby relations, as Sir Patrick McCall put it, were 'never bad'), and sharp and apparently irreconcilable viewpoints appear mainly in official inquiries. The county body, too, early appreciated that the administrative patchwork caused by the existence of the county boroughs could be overcome only by the creation of sub-regional upper-tier authorities, carved out of the greater body of administrative Lancashire, and able to provide large-area services like those of police, fire and ambulance without bedevilment by great-town boundaries. The story of the early discussions around the theme of the so-called 'Three Ridings Scheme' has been traced,[19] and the idea of the possible division of Lancashire lay in abeyance during the fifties, when, as we have seen, extraordinary effort produced workable delegation and divisional systems for complex services.

Possibly this somewhat unwieldy system would have operated more or less indefinitely had it not been for a series of governmental enquiries in the sixties. In no case was there anything approaching adequate scientific and comparative investigation into the costing, grass-roots operation and detailed administrative procedure of major local government bodies, either in the enquiries following the Local Government Act of 1929 or in the Commission of 1966-9. There were, indeed, some research studies in the course of the latter, notably a survey of community attitudes which found what had long been a commonplace in industrial and rural Lancashire, namely that 'the community area ... is not geographically extensive. In urban areas approximately three quarters of electors define their "home" area as being of a size no larger than the equivalent of a "ward".'[20] Elsewhere it was noted with equal ceremony that 'People live in neighbourhoods ... not in administrative counties.'[21] By the time that this discovery was made, it had already become clear that the administrative mould of Lancashire was to be broken completely, and it is worthwhile briefly to trace the steps by which this happened.

The Local Government Commission of the early sixties,[22] then, produced three reports with relevance to Lancashire, in particular a North-West Review Area Statement (1965), which focused much attention on south-east Lancashire and the Manchester area and argued for a Manchester-based 'county' with a second tier of strong multi-purpose authorities, whereby the 'county' would be responsible for police, fire and ambulance services but other powers (planning, highways, housing) would be held concurrently with the second-tier authorities. The Statement otherwise suggested extensions to a series of Lancashire county boroughs.[23] Not surprisingly, both Lancashire and Cheshire, supported by the great majority of their county districts, argued for the existing two-tier system, and Lancashire expressed its belief that the powers of the Commission were not wide enough 'to establish a satisfactory system of local government over Lancashire as a whole'.[24] The genesis of the Lancashire disappointment is not difficult to trace, too, in that the Commission displayed some pusillanimity regarding a continuous Merseyside 'county', because it would be 'difficult to devise good second-tier areas' in a large part of it, and most of the districts were too small and their amalgamation would be 'artificial'.[25] Lancashire's attitude to the Merseyside border areas, although certainly never stated in such unequivocal terms, was conditioned by experiences, with roots back into the 1920s, which suggested that the trouble-making potential of that group of county districts was unlimited; indeed, there is little doubt that a somewhat unedifying book could be written about it. Overspill, town planning problems, housing problems, inflated school populations, mutual jealousies – with luck, one could be rid of them at a stroke, and here was a Royal Commission that would not even face up to the proposition.

But political change was in the air; the swing of the political pendulum brought Labour narrowly into power, and by December 1965 Mr Crossman was already hinting, in a speech to the Association of Municipal Corporations, that there was to be a drastically new approach to local government reorganisation. The appointment of the Redcliffe-Maud Commission followed, in February 1966.[26] The emphasis, as was soon understood, was to be on the interdependence of town and country, now accentuated by population shift and the motor vehicle. The chief Lancashire spokesmen (tutored, it would seem, principally by Sir Patrick McCall) appeared to recognise the trend in government thinking, and decided that the time was ripe for re-submission of what was substantially its 1947 Three Ridings Scheme. This was duly put forward in 1966,[27] but, of course, the Lancashire viewpoint was widely known before that year, and the county's alliance with Cheshire came temporarily to grief because of it. Both Lancashire and Cheshire had worked together in the early sixties to defend their respective territories against major reorganisation, but the former's tripartite scheme alarmed the southern county – with some reason, for the Redcliffe-Maud Commission in 1969 proposed to dismember it into three – two metropolitan counties based on Liverpool and Manchester, and a large unitary authority to the south.[28]

Lancashire, however, was to have fared even worse; besides the two metropolitan areas mentioned, 'Redcliffe-Maud' recommended the splitting of administrative Lancashire into five other areas, of which four were based on major county boroughs, Blackburn, Burnley, Preston and Blackpool. These were to have been all-purpose authorities, combining town and country in the way that had been foreshadowed in 1966, and of course their adoption would have meant the end of the two-tier system supported by county and district authorities. In the south-east, the massive SELNEC territory was to have been based on the Manchester conurbation and to have taken in parts of the West Riding, Derbyshire and Cheshire.

It must be said in retrospect that the Commission's attempts to find economically and socially balanced or homogeneous areas in Lancashire, with a view to the imposition of unitary authorities upon them now carry a faintly ludicrous air. It expressed uncertainty as to the interrelationships of the area chosen for the Central Lancashire New Town, and was unsure whether it ought to recommend the unitary authorities that in fact were recommended, 'or one large unitary authority comprising the whole of the territory occupied by the four just mentioned; or a two-tier unit with a planning, transportation and development authority for the whole area and four second-tier authorities for education, the personal social services, housing and other functions'.[29] Mr Derek Senior, in his famous Memorandum of Dissent, showed no such uncertainty: 'The North and Central Lancashire districts based on the centres of Barrow, Lancaster, Blackpool, Preston, Blackburn, and Burnley are as sharply distinguished in character and in personal-service need as any in England.'[30] The same, no doubt, could have been said of a dozen districts in between.

The reaction of the Council's leading spokesman to the Redcliffe-Maud proposals was in outline predictable, but in detail interesting. On 31 July 1969, the Parliamentary and Co-ordination Committees presented a report that stated that they were 'totally opposed to the setting up of unitary authorities in Lancashire',[31] and a special meeting of the Council on 25 September confirmed this attitude. The Chairman, Henry Lumby, reflected a widely held view when he commented that:

> Perhaps the Commission's great task would have been considerably eased, and their deliberations a little more informed, if they, like their predecessors, had taken time off now and again to see something of local government at work in various parts of the country and to talk with people engaged and experienced in local government....

In general, the Council thought that unitary areas would be 'neither effective in terms of functions nor responsive to local needs and opinions'.[32]

Again, a national political swing affected the progress of local government reform, this time in the Conservative direction, and in July 1970 the Parliamentary Committee reported to the Council that following the general election the Labour Government's proposals were 'a dead letter'. Meanwhile, the upper-tier or county lobby had been hard at work in the region, and Lancashire and Cheshire joined in discussions to explore the possibility of a five-counties scheme for the North-West, with Cumberland participating willingly and Westmorland less willingly and less happily. (The Big Five were to be the two metropolitan 'counties', with Lancashire, Cheshire and Cumbria.)

The Conservative Government, meanwhile, showed sympathy for some of the Redcliffe-Maud concepts if not for unitary authorities, and its own White Paper on Local Government Reform (1971) agreed that 'The division between counties and county boroughs had prolonged an artificial separation of big towns from their surrounding hinterlands for functions whose planning and administration need to embrace both town and country.'[33] By then, however, it was known that the prevailing mode of thinking was again set towards the two-tier system, and on 29 April 1971 the Parliamentary Committee of the County Council welcomed the government's decision to implement 'an exclusive two-tier system throughout the County as a whole, thus ending the present County/County Borough anomaly'.[34] Naturally enough, it recognised the need for the two metropolitan counties in south Lancashire, and accepted that 'three Counties should be created in the remainder of the North-West, namely for the Counties of Lancashire, Cheshire and Cumberland and Westmorland'.[35] It is consoling, too, to have to record that, against the more general background of conflicting opinion, political shifts, assertions and counter-assertions, the transfer of Furness to the new county of Cumbria at least had a certain uncharacteristic and un-English rationality about it, in that the roots of Furness, if not of Barrow as such, were in Cumbrian life and tradition. Unhappily, the traditionalist could have claimed that Furness had been associated with the infant county of Lancaster since Norman times, and with a fitting sadness the Parliamentary Committee prepared to say farewell to it. Many of the councillors and citizens of Barrow, spurning any commitment to their 'hinterland', would have preferred to keep the town's autonomy. The same could have been said for the other Lancashire county boroughs, which (shorn of their status) now looked forward to extending their areas of influence in some activities if not in others.

The Local Government Act of 1972 finally reorganised the governmental structure of Lancashire, eighty-four years after the Lancashire County Council had come into being. The new system, formally established on 1 April 1974, still has to prove its worth, and has entered its lifetime against a background of economic stagnation, monetary inflation and considerable prejudice. The local government reformer, having discovered that primarily local interests motivate the common man, would do well to reflect on the words of Sir Robert Adcock, who in the course of a career in Lancashire formed the following opinion:

> The first loyalty [of councillors] is to Lancaster or Morecambe or West-houghton or Tyldesley. They will support Lancashire cricket teams, but when it comes to local government, their first loyalty is to their county district. It is difficult to get them to look at the problems of *Lancashire*: this is irrespective of political complexion.[36]

This insight leads on to the question – will the same councillors, now

serving considerably larger districts, find themselves any closer in spirit
to the new county authority? Contrariwise, will the new county authority
command the same degree of support from county districts as the old one?
This question, too, is worth posing, for the outstanding achievement of
the old Lancashire authority lay in the degree of involvement and *rapport*
it brought about *vis-à-vis* many county district officers and seasoned
councillors. This identification of viewpoint, at the representative or professional level, was only partially a product of dual or two-tier representation, and it occurred too noticeably to be a negligible or accidental
factor. The 1965 report on south-east Lancashire remarked that:

> Most district councils praised the excellent services provided by the
> county councils. Many authorities in Lancashire specially mentioned
> the willingness of the County Council to delegate responsibility, though
> some of the larger authorities in both counties [Lancashire and Cheshire]
> were obviously restive under county control. . . .[37] Many authorities gave
> the impression that administrative difficulties with their County Council
> were unheard of. This shows that the two-tier system can win
> friends. . . .[38]

Had there been lurking or smouldering resentments, the latter would
surely have emerged, even in veiled form, in the evidence given to the
Redcliffe-Maud Commision in 1966–8, for the districts and municipal
boroughs of Lancashire, which supplied a mass of commentary, had
plenty of opportunity to express criticism, and sometimes did so. Even
if full allowance is made for the two-tier commitment of the local
authority associations concerned, and for their suspicion of county
boroughs, the paeans of praise are often remarkable. Horwich Urban
District Council was unequivocal: '. . . it is maintained that the past record
of the Lancashire County Council is one of outstanding success in the
field of local government administration and that the benefit of the
experience of such a progressive authority . . . should be applied. . . .'[39]
The Ince-in-Makerfield UDC held that the County Council had carried
out 'all the major functions most effectively and economically',[40] while
Little Lever, which admitted to 'an intense community interest' probably
typical of many parts of the county, 'had no observations to make on or
complaints about the two-tier government in the Administrative County
of Lancashire'.[41] Newton-le-Willows reported in similar vein,[42] and
Oswaldtwistle wrote that 'a successful partnership has been established
over the years between county and county district councils'.[43] Poulton-le-
Fylde stood firm 'in its desire to remain as part of a two tier system of
local government within Lancashire County',[44] and Turton Urban District
referred to another supposed variety of local patriotism, that of county

rather than neighbourhood: 'This pride in a geographical county should be maintained for the sake of fostering the identification by people of themselves with local government.'[45] Nor does this claim seem wholly fanciful in view of an unequivocal statement by Ulverston Urban District Council, one of the most remotely situated, far away across Morecambe Bay: 'the area is well served by the County Council and ... County services are well administered'.[46] The Ulverston council offices were some fifty miles by road or rail from County Hall.

A comparable tribute came from Mossley Municipal Borough, far away in a roughly opposite direction: 'The Council consider that a very high standard of service has been received in the Borough from the Lancashire County Council, that despite the distance from the County Council's offices ... little difficulty has been experienced in this regard....'[47] Colne wished to state its 'satisfaction with the major services provided by the Lancashire County Council',[48] and Heywood, another industrial borough, spoke of its own 'direct and happy experience of co-operation and harmony between the Lancashire County Council and the County Districts....'[49]

However, a number of municipal boroughs refused to comment in this vein, and instead argued for extensive reorganisation of local government. Nelson disliked 'the *ad hoc* committees appointed by county councils', and Prestwich objected strongly to a proposal to amalgamate it with Salford, while Stretford simply wished for county borough status.[50] It is very noticeable that few of the district council comments of 1968 dealt specifically with the Three Ridings Scheme, perhaps because only a minority of those actually submitting views were affected by it; but Whiston Rural District, in a long and careful statement,[51] put the case for a Merseyside Metropolitan County, and drawing attention to the new problems created by suburban growth and sprawl remarked that 'informal arrangements' had 'worked tolerably well' in Lancashire, and that the county had become adept at dealing with such problems 'due to the existence of seventeen County Boroughs'.[52] This slightly grudging compliment, coming from a small border authority, was in reality the most weighty and memorable of all.

Lancashire's tactical and delegatory skill, the results and lessons of which then seemed to weigh so little with government or commission, had undoubtedly served the county well. These compliments, designed or otherwise, came from officers and councillors who were plainly used to working in the county's administrative ethos, and who were probably not anxious to consider working on any other terms. It would be foolish to pretend that they were objective representations of the views of the consumer, the man and woman in the street or lane; and if the chairman of the

Lancashire County Council was able to complain that he and his colleagues had not been adequately consulted, or were not given sufficient time to consider the Royal Commission's findings, then it must be said that the receiver of the Council's services attracted little or no attention at all.

It was with this depressing proposition in mind that the research team responsible for the present volume decided to arrange for an investigator to approach members of the public and to find out their degree of interest in county councils and their sense of involvement with such organisations. It should be borne in mind that this enquiry was pursued in the later summer months of 1975, after local government reorganisation, and that any conclusions to be drawn from this exercise must relate to the present county regime quite as much as the deceased one. One of the fruits of reorganisation was that of 'greatly enhanced information services', and our first comment (see Appendix 1) must be that such services appear to be desperately necessary, and that they were plainly lacking previously.

A total of 102 citizens, taken at random from all over north, central and east Lancashire, were asked a series of basic questions relating to bare knowledge of county government and electoral representation. It should be said at once that the indications are that this sample was not totally representative of the county council electorate as a whole, the voting turnout of which, in 1970, was rather over thirty per cent. This sample yielded under twenty per cent of voters, and it is therefore not entirely surprising to find that a similarly small proportion of the group knew the names of their Lancashire County Council representatives. Nevertheless, it is alarming to find that, out of a total of over 100 persons, only fourteen could name their county councillor. What is equally disturbing is that roughly half of all those questioned could not distinguish between the work of the county authority and that of the district in which they lived. On the other hand, only a small minority (nearly thirteen per cent) had had direct dealings with the county authority, while a much larger sample were either favourably disposed to it or spoke well of it. People in rural or small communities, interestingly enough, were more clearly aware of the Council's existence than those in a more urbanised setting – an interesting footnote to the Royal Commission Research Project 9 Report on the mental horizons of voters. The matter of involvement by direct experience has been stressed at an earlier point in this book, with relevance to the Children's Department (and, of course, with equal relevance to the work of welfare and personal services in general). The truth of the matter seems to be that the traditional county emphasis on some *non*-personal services has tended to underpin the inherent remoteness of county government, and that, in the absence of any profound social or political stimulus to greater awareness, such as happened in the fifties, the outlook for public or democratic participation is not especially encouraging.

This is a sober note on which to end a commemorative history. We have attempted to pay tribute to a number of those whose work would undoubtedly have been more appreciated had the level of public participation and awareness been higher, and we have attempted to look judicially and fairly at the work of a great organisation. There have been sins of omission or commission; nevertheless, we have tried to do what many of the most experienced former aldermen, councillors and officers would unquestionably have wished us to do, namely to seek at least a few of the lessons that have lain waiting to be revealed within the texture of over eighty years of county government.

Appendix 1: Attitudes to the Lancashire County Council

THE following piece of research, undertaken by Mr W. T. Koc and consisting of interviews, was designed to show attitudes to, and information about, the past and present County Council. It was supported and organised via the University of Lancaster. These interviews took place on twelve days during the three-week period in July and August 1975. The standard questions put to those who agreed to answer were as follows:

1. What do you see as the main differences between your local council (in your locality) and the County Council in Preston?
2. Do you know what are the responsibilities of the County Council as distinct from the responsibilities of the local council in your locality?
3. Have you voted (within the last five years) to choose a representative of your area to become a *county* councillor (as distinct from voting for local bodies)?
4. Do you know the name of the person who is the current representative of your area or locality on the *County* Council?
5. Are you satisfied or not satisfied with the performance of the County Council within their proper concerns?
6. Have you ever had any experience of personal dealings or contact with the County Council's work or its representatives?

It was fully realised that these questions were blunt and to the point, and that some difficulties might arise. The respondents were also asked to comment freely on any aspect of the County Council's operations, work or standing they pleased.

The selection of places to visit was dictated by three circuit treks planned along minor roads after street interviews at Lancaster. The aim was to stop and talk to people away from extensive traffic. Interviewing casual passers-by in Preston was deliberately excluded, as it was not possible there to use *location* as the readily understood criterion of distinctiveness between the county and the *local* authority.

Altogether, 121 persons who looked approachable were asked, and of these 102 produced answers and some comments (Table A1). The age and occupation of the respondents were not tabulated since the resulting groupings would have been far too small to warrant any comment. The age distribution appears to have been approaching normal, with twenty-four persons (or 19.8 per cent) below thirty and seventeen persons (or 14 per cent) over sixty, the youngest being eighteen and the oldest eighty-one. Similarly occupations, though varied, seemed on the whole to be characteristic of the region (excluding middle-class suburbs and solidly industrial working-class streets), with a good many farmers and their wives, and several shopkeepers.

TABLE A1
Response

| | Those approached | | | Those responding | | |
	Men	Women	Total	Men	Women	Total
Lancaster etc.	17	14	31	14	14	28
Lune Valley	13	15	28	10	13	23
North of Ribble	17	13	30	14	10	24
South of Ribble*	15 .	17	32	12	15	27
Totals	62	59	121	50	52	102

*8 persons on the South of Ribble circuit were approached *after* damage to the tape recorder.

Table A2 shows the breakdown of answers to standard questions by area of the respondent. It may be noticed that the awareness of distinction between the local and central council appears to be more pronounced among smaller communities than in larger towns (e.g. Lancaster) or in their proximity (e.g. near Blackpool, Preston and Blackburn).

As one might have expected, a slightly larger proportion of respondents were aware in general terms of the distinction between their local body and the county authority than were sure about their respective spheres of competence. The percentage of those who voted for Council represent-atives was also predictably small, but even smaller was the proportion of those who could even guess at the name of whoever was eventually elected. Nevertheless, the public appeared to have been quite satisfied with the

County Council's work (whatever it was) and in many cases expressed pleasure at not being bothered or involved in any of it and in being left alone. Very few had any personal experience of the county authority or had ever met anyone working for it. Yet the comments were, in a great majority, either favourable or very favourable.

There were, inevitably, several vocal critics, using a variety of expressions to voice their displeasure; they reproached the County Council with

TABLE A2
Answers to Questions

(a) *Questions 1 and 2*

	Aware of differences				Aware of responsibilities			
	Yes	%	No	%	Yes	%	No	%
Lancaster etc.	12	(42.9)	16	(57.1)	12	(42.9)	16	(57.1)
Lune Valley	15	(65.2)	8	(34.8)	14	(60.9)	9	(39.1)
North of Ribble	9	(37.5)	15	(62.5)	9	(37.5)	15	(62.5)
South of Ribble	18	(66.7)	9	(33.3)	8	(29.6)	19	(70.4)
Totals	54	(52.9)	48	(47.1)	43	(42.2)	59	(57.8)

(b) *Questions 3 and 4*

	Voted in CC elections				Knew name of own representative to CC			
	Yes	%	No	%	Yes	%	No	%
Lancaster etc.	5	(17.9)	23	(82.1)	3	(10.7)	25	(89.3)
Lune Valley	5	(21.7)	18	(78.3)	6	(26.1)	17	(73.9)
North of Ribble	3	(12.5)	21	(87.5)	3	(12.5)	21	(87.5)
South of Ribble	6	(22.2)	21	(77.8)	2	(7.4)	25	(92.6)
Totals	19	(18.6)	83	(81.4)	14	(13.7)	88	(86.3)

(c) *Questions 5 and 6*

	Satisfied with the work of CC					Ever had any personal dealings with CC			
	Yes	%	No	%	(n.c.)*	Yes	%	No	%
Lancaster etc.	22	(78.6)	5	(17.8)	(1)	3	(10.7)	25	(89.3)
Lune Valley	18	(78.3)	5	(21.7)		3	(13.0)	20	(87.0)
North of Ribble	15	(62.5)	5	(20.8)	(4)	5	(20.1)	19	(79.1)
South of Ribble	20	(74.1)	7	(25.9)		2	(7.4)	25	(92.6)
Totals	75	(73.5)	22	(21.6)		13	(12.7)	89	(87.3)

*No definite comment was offered on 5 occasions on the issue of satisfaction: Column n.c.

being too big (4), too bureaucratic (2), careless of money, costly (4), too hierarchical, inhuman, impersonal, given to intrigues and infighting at their huge Preston headquarters, self-centred and office-oriented, misinformed, parasitic, remote (6), restrictive over planning decisions, secretive, small-minded, self-important, tight-fisted and wasteful. Mention was also made of lazy council workers and confused officials, over-generous councillors' expenses, wrong priorities, especially far too much spent on education (5) and too little on the police or roads. There were also complaints (in general terms) of unnecessary activities and personnel, but without any specific examples of these being given. Other comments referred to lack of control over spending, 'jobs for the boys', and lack of understanding regarding the problems (unspecified) of the working or the common man.

It may be noted, however, that of the twenty-two persons who were dissatisfied only one had ever had any dealings with the authority. Many of the adverse comments appear or reflect either the stereotyped attitudes that could be, and often are, assumed towards any authority or institution, or very generalised criticisms not backed by any specific cases or occurrences or persons involved. In view of the widespread ignorance of the county authority's work evident within the sample, it is likely that a great deal of the criticisms expressed arose from misinformation.

The favourable comments were expressed in no less varied terms; the County Council was seen good at administration (4), approachable, businesslike (3), clever, conscientious, 'cunning at getting their way with Whitehall' (!), decent, decisive, efficient (10), good employers, experienced, fair (3), friendly (2), helpful (3), honest (4), well informed (3), knowledgeable, Lancashire-oriented, well versed in local needs and problems, mindful of local heritage and traditions, good to old people, progressive, professional, good planners (2), quiet (reticent), reasonable (3), rational, oriented to rural questions, sensible, straight, understanding (4), and good value for money. Efficiency and friendliness of the police, good roads, sensible leadership and direction given to smaller local bodies, etc., were also mentioned on several occasions, as well as specific examples of personal experience, like, e.g. great help given during the Wray flood emergency, or efficient and fair dealing over a highway access in Kirkham.

Several respondents stated simply that they saw no reason or occasion to complain when things run smoothly and they were prepared to leave it all to the experts. The county was praised for not wasting time or money on unnecessary publicity or self-promotion and for not making too much fuss over their work. Even those with little to say were inclined to see the County Council here as no worse and probably better than elsewhere, occasionally even as the best in the country. It was appreciated for not interfering too much with individuals or smaller authorities, for not committing obvious or shocking blunders and – pointedly, and on more than one occasion – for not shaming Lancashire with any Poulson-like scandals and corruption, which appeared to be very much in people's consciousness.

Appendix 2: Chairmen of Lancashire County Council: Biographical Notes

1. HIBBERT, (Sir) John T. B. (5 January 1824–7 November 1908). The most distinguished national figure connected with the Lancashire County Council, of which he became chairman on 14 February 1889. He was MP for Oldham 1832–74, 1877–86 and 1892–5; secretary of the Poor Law Board 1871–4 and 1880–3, under-secretary of the Home Department 1883–4, financial secretary to the Treasury 1884–5, 1892–5; secretary to the Admiralty 1885–6. He was instrumental in passing the Execution Within Gaols Act (1868), the Married Women's Property Act and General Disabilities Bill (1879). The Municipal Corporations Council was a 'retirement' activity, and he retained the chairmanship until 14 March 1908, while representing the Cartmel division, where he lived (at Grange-over-Sands). He was a Gladstonian Liberal in politics, a barrister by training. He was especially well equipped to steer the new County Council, having served on several parliamentary commissions concerned with local government, and was the first chairman of the County Councils Association. In addition to *ex officio* chairmanship of council committees, he was chairman of Lancashire Inebriates Board, chairman of the Mersey and Irwell and Ribble Joint River Boards, chairman of the Royal Albert Asylum, Lancaster, a former governor of Owen's College, Manchester, and a member of the court of the University of Liverpool and of the Victoria University, Manchester.

2. SCOTT-BARRETT (Sir) William (28 November 1843–5 June 1921). Chairman from 14 March 1908 to 3 February 1921. A colliery owner with a Liverpool background, and a Liberal in politics, he was one of the pioneer county councillors. He was sixty-five years of age, like Sir John Hibbert (*supra*) when he took the chairmanship. He was a member of the

Standing Joint Committee and the Lancashire Asylums Board during the whole of his county service, and chairman of the former from 1889 to 1921 and of the Asylums Board from 1900 to 1908; and as vice-chairman of the Council from 1906 to 1908, he was *ex officio* a member of all council committees. He lacked the national stature of his predecessor, but was a diligent and respected leader.

3. HIBBERT, (Sir) Henry Fleming (4 April 1850–November 1927). Chairman from 10 March 1921 to 10 March 1927. He was educated at Chorley Grammar School, but obliged to give up his formal education at fourteen years of age. He became a farina merchant, and in 1890 a director of Blackburn Chamber of Commerce, having pursued his education in evening classes. In 1883 he became a Conservative councillor in the newly incorporated borough of Chorley, and was mayor of the town in 1889. During this period he was constantly involved in public work in the town, and was thereby the first County Council chairman with previous 'district' experience. He joined the County Council in June 1891 as a representative for his own borough and became chairman of the Technical Instruction Committee (having helped to found a technical college in his own town). After the 1902 Education Act, he was chairman of the Lancashire Education Committee until March 1921, when he became chairman of the Council. He was appointed a member of the Consultative Committee of the Board of Education and of the Science in Education Committee. From 1913 to 1918 he represented Chorley as Conservative MP and latterly as a Coalition Unionist. He was no relative of Sir John Hibbert (*supra*), although there is a passing similarity to the career of the first chairman in that Sir Henry had wider political commitments than was common in county council leadership. The only baronet (1919) to take the chairmanship, he died in 1927, a few months after retirement.

4. WADE DEACON, (Sir) Henry (18 October 1852–29 July 1932). Chairman from March 1927 to January 1931. The son of Henry Deacon, alkali manufacturer of Widnes, he was educated at King's College, London, and went into legal practice. Subsequently he became chairman of the Quarter Sessions for the West Derby Hundred of Lancashire. In 1891 he retired to 'devote himself to public and philanthropic activities'. Became county councillor for Widnes South in March 1892, and in March 1898 a county alderman. Became especially expert in county finance; was chairman of the Finance Committee from 1904 to 1927; a member of the Standing Joint, Parliamentary and Education Committees; vice-chairman of the Council from 1921 to 1927. A chairman of the British Hospitals Association and the Liverpool Gas company; director of the London and

Lancashire Insurance Company. Pro-chancellor of the University of Liverpool, honorary LLD of that University. Knighted 1931.

5. TRAVIS-CLEGG, (Sir) James (13 June 1875–13 October 1942). Chairman from March 1931 to March 1937. The son of John Travis-Clegg, JP, of High Crompton, he was educated at Lytham, later at Eton College, and 'took up public work after leaving school'. Elected to the Council in March 1898 for the division of Crompton; in 1911 became county alderman. Interested in education, and chairman of the Education Committee from 1921 to 1937; also a member of the Standing Joint Committee for eleven years, the Ribble Joint Committee, the Lancashire Agricultural Committee, and a chairman of the County Councils Association; in 1935 he was vice-chairman of Lancashire Quarter Sessions. Had also been a chairman of Crompton Urban District Council, of Crompton Conservative Association and the Oldham Conservative Party; stood as Conservative candidate for the Stalybridge constituency in the 1905 and 1906 by-elections. Later he resided near Lancaster in Bailrigg, and was a member of the South Lonsdale Bench. His main council achievement was in overseeing the implementation of the 1929 Local Government Act.

6. HODGSON, (Sir) William (? 1858–26 February 1945). Chairman from March 1937 to February 1945. Became county councillor for Fleetwood in March 1901, and was described as 'Gentleman'. Was a member of the Fylde Board of Guardians in 1881, chairman of same in 1900. Also first chairman of Poulton-le-Fylde UDC. Became a county magistrate in 1896; was a strong Conservative and active in Poulton Conservative Club (chairman 1938). Member of no fewer than twelve county council committees, some of them for over forty years; e.g. the Public Health (and Public Health and Housing) Committee from 1901 to 1945), chairman of the same committee from 1916 to 1937. Served on the County Rate Committee (chairman from 1924 to 1930), the Highways and Bridges, Education, Finance and County Rate Joint Committees; also Local Pension, Tuberculosis, Public Assistance, Standing Joint and Lancashire Agricultural Committee. Vice-chairman of the Council from 1931 to 1937, he became chairman at the age of seventy-nine. Was knighted in 1935. Sir William was the last chairman to serve for two consecutive periods of office until Sir Henry Lumby (*infra*) did so.

7. MACDONALD, (Sir) Percy (? 1879–23 July 1957). Chairman of the Council from March 1945 to February 1946. First elected to the Council in 1915 as a councillor for Stretford. After a modest apprenticeship on the Smallholdings and Allotments, Diseases of Animals and Highways and Bridges Committees, he became an alderman in 1926, and greatly widened

his administrative experience, especially on the Standing Joint Committee, of which he became a member in 1925, and of which he was chairman from 1939 to 1952. He was also a member of the Parliamentary Committee from 1928 to 1946, but his most memorable contribution was on the Highways and Bridges Committee, 1916–52, of which he was chairman from 1935 to 1941. During his service on this committee, several important Lancashire road schemes were realised, including the East Lancashire Road; also the north–south route (the present M6 motorway) was planned. After his short chairmanship of the Council he continued as alderman until 1952, and then retired to Anglesey, where he died in 1957. He was knighted in 1941.

8. AITKEN, (Sir) James (? 1880–5 March 1948). Chairman from March 1946 to March 1948. Born in Barrowford, E. Lancashire, he became a solicitor in his home town, and was elected to the Nelson Town Council in 1913, remaining a member for nineteen years, and becoming mayor of Nelson in 1925–7. Like many other district or borough councillors, he joined the County Council in 1921, and became a county alderman in 1937. Meanwhile, like Sir James Travis-Clegg, he tried to enter Parliament, in his case as a Liberal, and in 1924 came within a modest distance of defeating Arthur Greenwood in the Nelson and Colne constituency. In 1946, however, he became chairman of the Council at the relatively youthful age of sixty-six. He was especially interested in the work of the Education Committee and was a member from 1921 to 1948, and from 1932 to 1948 was the chairman of the Co-ordination Committee, as well as chairman of the Education Committee from 1937 to 1948. He was president of the Association of Education Committees of Great Britain and Ireland for a period of four years, and, amid a mass of other commitments, was a member of the Burnham Committee for teachers' salaries from 1938 to 1948. He nevertheless contrived to hold office in a variety of public posts in the Nelson area, and was a county court registrar there from 1935, a president of the Nelson Football Club and a senior circuit steward of the Nelson Methodist Circuit. He died in 1948 at the end of two years in office in the County Council chairmanship. He was knighted in 1941.

9. HYDE, (Sir) Harry (? 1879–2 January 1957). Chairman from March 1948 to April 1949. A wholesale druggist and merchant, he was elected to the Council in 1923 for Ashton-under-Lyne, and reached the aldermanic bench in 1937. His most significant experience was as a member of the Finance Committee, 1931–57; he was also chairman of the Co-ordination Committee from 1947 to 1952. He became vice-chairman of the Council

in 1946, and chairman as a result of the untimely death of Sir James Aitken (*supra*); his service of one year, like that of Sir Percy Macdonald, reflected the social and political currents in the Council itself, which was searching for younger chairmen. Hyde was knighted in 1953, after he had withdrawn from the chairmanship, and he continued to work actively in county affairs and those of his own district, Ashton.

10. BATES, (Sir) Alfred (3 July 1897–   ). Three times chairman; 1949–1952, 1955–8 and 1961–4. The youngest chairman in the history of the Council. The son of a Morecambe solicitor, he was educated at Lancaster Royal Grammar School; served with the East Lancashire Regiment in France and Flanders, 1914–18, and received the MC. Clerk and solicitor to the old Heysham UDC from 1921 to 1928, and entered county council politics on 6 March 1931, when he became Conservative member for Lonsdale South; he became a county alderman on 3 February 1949, only two months before he became chairman of the Council. Although he had had experience of eight committees in his eighteen years of service, his most significant contribution was as a member of two important ones, the Standing Joint and the Parliamentary. He was also a valued member of the Co-ordination Committee and the Education Committee, and, at the time of his elevation to the council chairmanship, was also a member of the Selection and Finance Committees. Both his relative youth and his legal experience were of great importance to the Council at a time of administrative change and upheaval. He alternated the chairmanship with (Sir) Andrew Smith, the Labour leader on the Council, during the fifties, and was himself the leading figure in the Conservative Party on the Council. In 1948, meanwhile, he became chairman of the Planning Committee of the County Councils Association, a post which he retained until 1968, and was a vice-president of the Association in 1969. He was a member of the Lake District Planning Board from 1953 to 1955, and of the Merseyside Industrial Development Association from 1955 to 1958. He was also a key figure in the setting up of the new University of Lancaster, and a deputy pro-chancellor of the University, which conferred on him the degree of Doctor of Law in 1964. In 1965 he gave up the leadership of the Conservative group on the Council, but continued as an alderman until the reorganisation of 1974.

11. SMITH, (Sir) Andrew (11 March 1880–22 August 1967). Twice chairman, 1952–5 and 1958–61. Born in Keighley, Yorkshire and, after coming to Nelson at the age of nine, was largely self-educated. After commencing as a newspaper boy, he became editor of the *Nelson Gazette* and an effective political journalist. Was elected to the Nelson Town

Council in 1911, and served nearly continuously on that body until 1958; was mayor of Nelson, 1927–9. He was elected to the County Council for Nelson North on 2 March 1934, his division adjoining that which elected (Sir) James Aitken (*supra*). After his election he was primarily interested in three committees, Public Assistance, Education and Finance. Meanwhile, he had become a major figure in the Nelson and Colne Divisional Labour Party, and continued in that role for more than fifty years. He was a determined leader of the Labour Party in the County Council, and, with his colleagues, campaigned for more generous relief policies through the public assistance organisation in the thirties. He was also a member of the Lancashire Education Committee for thirty-two years (1935–67), and became chairman of this body in 1964. In addition he was, at different times, a member of the Children's, Parliamentary, Welfare, Planning, Selection, Health and Public Health Committees. His ultimate elevation to the council chairmanship (1952) came at the age of seventy-two, after sixteen years of council membership. He was a strong personality, firm in the leadership of his party group, and uninterested in the trappings of office. Nevertheless, he was knighted during his second term of office as chairman, in 1960. His last few years as a member (1961–7) were marked by failing health, and he died in 1967.

12. LONGWORTH, (Sir) Fred (15 February 1890–29 August 1973). Sir Andrew Smith's successor in the county chairmanship, 1964–7. A former miner and later a county official of the National Union of Mineworkers; a prominent Methodist in his home district of Tyldesley. He was already a member of Tyldesley Urban District Council in 1940 when he was elected to the County Council on 4 March 1946. He became chairman of his district council in 1948, and thus had the indispensable background in local administration that benefited so many county council leaders. Nevertheless, his selection for the chairmanship was unexpected, as his experience was limited, although he had a deep and abiding interest in education. He was sometime chairman of Leigh Divisional Education Committee, and held numerous governorships of colleges and schools. A popular chairman and Labour group leader, he was knighted in 1966. He was a member of the Fire Brigade Committee, 1948–73, and of the Finance Committee from 1953; he had a special interest in road safety, of which committee he was chairman from 1958. He was vice-chairman of the Council from 1967 to 1973.

13. LUMBY, (Sir) Henry (9 January 1909–). The last chairman of the old Lancashire County Council, from 1967 to 1974. Educated at Merchant Taylors' School, Crosby, and subsequently a stockbroker, he became a

member of the Northern Stock Exchange. Served in France and the Middle East in the Second World War; three years as prisoner of war. Elected to the County Council on 4 March 1946, representing the Ormskirk division. In 1948 he became chairman of the Fire Brigade Committee age of fifty-eight, after twenty-one years of council membership. He was also, early in his career, a member of the Parliamentary Committee. He became a county alderman in April 1956, and was created a CBE in 1957. In 1961 he attained the important position of chairman of the Finance Committee, and four years later he succeeded Sir Alfred Bates as the leader of the Conservative Group on the County Council, and became the vice-chairman of the County Council. In 1967, at the triennial election, the Conservative Party obtained a majority of the council seats, and Henry Lumby became the last chairman at the comparatively low age of fifty-eight, after twenty-one years of council membership. He was in fact the first chairman to serve two successive terms of office since Sir William Hodgson (*supra*). He was knighted in 1973, and retired from county politics on the dissolution of the old Lancashire authority on 1 April 1974.

CLERKS OF THE LANCASHIRE COUNTY COUNCIL, 1889–1974

1. HULTON, Frederick Campbell. Clerk from 1889 to 1899. Born in 1842, the son of William Adam Hulton of Penwortham, an old county family. His father was called to the bar, and was also a county treasurer, as was his grandfather. F. C. Hulton, with a strong legal tradition behind him, was already Clerk of the Peace for Lancashire when the County Council was formed, and he combined the two offices. He was registrar to the Preston County Court, clerk to the Lancashire Asylums Board and to the Sea Fisheries Joint Committee. He took a major part in the boundary reorganisation following the 1894 Local Government Act. He died on 27 May 1899, at the relatively early age of fifty-seven years.

2. CLARE, (Sir) Harcourt Everard. Clerk from 1899 to 1922. Born in 1854. Educated at Repton, he became a solicitor in 1875; assistant solicitor to the Liverpool Corporation in 1880, deputy city clerk, 1883, chief clerk, 1885–9. Responsible for the purchase of electric lighting and tramway undertakings in the City, and conducted Liverpool's opposition to the Manchester Ship Canal. When he joined Lancashire, he set about improving relations with district councils, under strain through educational reorganisation; later (1911) he played an important part in implementing local arrangements under the National Insurance Act. Held the clerkship of the Lancashire Asylums Board, Lancashire Inebriates Board, Lancashire Education Committee and the Lancashire Insurance Committee. A prominent member of the County Councils Association.

Member of Royal Commission on Bovine Tuberculosis, 1901, and Royal Commission on Taxation, 1920; a noted consultant on local government problems generally. Knighted in 1916. Was responsible for Lancashire Drainage Act (1922), designed to strengthen the work of the County Agricultural Committee. Died when still in office, 1 March 1922.

3. ETHERTON, (Sir) George Hammond. Clerk from 1922 to 1944. Born in 1876, educated at Horsham College. Followed his father in the legal profession; became deputy town clerk of Woolwich, 1902; deputy town clerk of Portsmouth, 1903–08, then town clerk of Portsmouth, 1908–20. In 1920 became town clerk of Liverpool, where he remained for two years before joining Lancashire; was then Clerk of the Peace for Lancashire, county solicitor, clerk of the Lancashire Mental Hospital Board, clerk of the Lancashire Rivers Board. In 1921 was a member of Lord Newton's Departmental Committee on the Lea and Thames Rivers; in 1931 was on Viscount Chelmsford's Committee on Regional Development; in 1936, on Lord Finlay's Committee on Assize Towns. Member of Land Drainage Commission, 1927, War Damage Commission, 1944–8, Requisitioned Land and Works Commission, 1947–8, Local Government Boundary Commission, 1945–8. County civil defence controller, 1939–44. Knighted in 1927. Died in retirement, 3 December 1949.

4. ADCOCK, (Sir) Robert Henry. Clerk from 1944 to 1960. Born in 1899. Assistant solicitor to Manchester County Borough, 1923–6; assistant solicitor and assistant Clerk of the Peace, Nottinghamshire County Council, 1926–9; senior assistant solicitor of Manchester County Borough, 1929–31; deputy town clerk, Manchester County Borough, 1931–8; town clerk of Manchester, 1938–44. Represented Manchester in the Association of Municipal Corporations; gave evidence on local government reorganisation in Lancashire to the Trustram Eve Boundary Commission. Instrumental in the establishment of Lancashire's first overspill area at Worsley, and in subsequent schemes (Skelmersdale, Kirkby). Played major part in co-ordinating the work of county departments in the great administrative expansion of 1944–8 and subsequent years, and was a strong believer in delegation; also played major legal–administrative role, with Sir James Drake, in the development of motorways in Lancashire. Especially concerned with the furtherance of good relations with district councils. Retired through ill health, 1960. CBE, 1941; knighted, 1950.

5. McCALL, (Sir) Patrick. Clerk from 1960 to 1972. Born in 1910. Junior solicitor with Hackney Metropolitan Borough 1935–6; junior solicitor with Dorset County Council, 1936–9; war service with RAF 1939–46;

senior solicitor with Hampshire County Council, 1946–9; subsequently deputy clerk of the Lancashire County Council; succeeded Sir R. Adcock in 1960. Gave evidence to the Trustram Eve Boundary Commission. Was responsible for furthering New Town development after 1960, and took important part in reclamation of derelict land in the county. Major legal supervisory role over motorway and other road schemes, and in development of schemes for comprehensive education. MBE 1944; knighted, 1971. Important role in preliminary discussions leading to the 1974 local government reorganisation. Left local government service to work for Economic and Social Committee of EEC.

6. INMAN, Peter Donald. Clerk from January 1973 to 1974, and clerk of the reorganised County Council. Born in 1916. Admitted as solicitor, 1946; served with County Borough of Dewsbury, 1943–8; assistant solicitor, Lancashire County Council, 1948–9; chief assistant solicitor to Lancashire County Council, 1949–51; second deputy clerk, 1951–60; first deputy clerk, 1960–72; appointed clerk of the Lancashire County Council in January 1973.

CHIEF EDUCATION OFFICERS OF THE LANCASHIRE EDUCATION AUTHORITY

1. SNAPE, Henry Lloyd. Director of education, 1901–19. Born in Liverpool in 1861, the son of Alderman Thomas Snape, chairman of the Lancashire Technical Instruction Committee. Educated Liverpool Institute; University College, Liverpool; Owens College, Manchester; University College, London; Universities of Berlin and Goettingen. DSc (London) and PhD (Goettingen). Became professor of chemistry, University College, Aberystwyth, and extramural lecturer to Edinburgh University, 1888–1901; secretary and chairman of the Faculty of Science and member of the Executive of the Court and Senate of the University of Wales; subsequently chairman of the Association of Directors and Secretaries of Education, of the Union of Lancashire and Cheshire Institutes and of the Sub-Committee of the Lancashire and Westmorland Pensions Committee to provide training for disabled sailors and soldiers; member of the departmental committee to consider salaries of teachers in higher educational institutions, and of the Secondary School Examinations Council; member of the Court of the University College of the South-West of England. An original scientist who contributed frequently to the *Journal of the Chemical Society* and other learned journals. Died 2 March 1933.

2. GATER, (Sir) George Henry. Director of education, 1919–24. Born in Southampton in 1886. Educated Winchester; New College, Oxford. Assistant director of education for Nottinghamshire, 1912–14. Came to Lancashire after distinguished war service (despatches four times, twice wounded, CMG, DSO and bar, Commander Legion of Honour, Croix de Guerre). Left Lancashire in 1924 to become education officer of London County Council, 1923–33, and then the clerk of that authority, 1933–9. Then moved into the service of central government to become permanent under-secretary of state for the colonies, 1939–47; KCB, 1941, GCMG, 1944. Served in various capacities in wartime government. Died 14 January 1963.

3. MEADON, (Sir) Percival Edward. Director of education, 1924–45. Born in Stoke-on-Trent in 1878. Educated at St Mark's College, Chelsea; St John's College, Oxford. Assistant educational secretary, Oxfordshire County Council, 1908–15, after experience as assistant teacher and head-master; director of education, Essex County Council, 1915–24. Created CBE, 1930, and knighted in 1937. President of the Association of Directors and Secretaries of Education, 1932. Sir Percival helped to organise the first elaborate scheme for (1944) the 'divisionalisation' of Lancashire education, but retired soon afterwards to Oxfordshire, and later to Surrey. Died 17 November 1959.

4. BINNS, (Sir) Arthur Lennon. Director of education, 1945–57. Born in Grimsby in 1891. Educated at Wintringham Grammar School and St John's College, Cambridge. Military service (Lincolnshire Regiment and general staff), 1914–19. Chief education officer to the West Riding of Yorkshire, 1936–45. Member of Flemming Committee on Public Schools, 1944, and of the Colonial Office Advisory Committee, 1945–53; member of the Beveridge Committee on the BBC, 1940; special commissioner in Sierra Leone, 1949; chairman, Colonial Office Mission to East and Central Africa, 1951–2. CBE, 1945; knighted, 1954. Chairman of Standing Conference of Regional Examining Unions, 1957–60. Visiting lecturer, University of British Columbia, 1958. President, North of England Education Conference, 1962.

5. LORD, (Sir) Percy. Chief education officer, 1957–68. Born in Spring-head near Oldham in 1903. Educated at Oldham High School; University of Manchester, MEd 1936. Teacher at Clitheroe Royal Grammar School, Oldham High School and High Storrs Grammar School, Sheffield, 1926–1942; organiser, Bradford Education Committee, 1942–4; assistant education

officer, Nottingham, 1944–7; Lancashire, 1950–7. Sir Percy was knighted in 1968, but died on 31 December of that year.

6. BOYCE, J. S. B., TD, MA. Chief education officer, 1968–74. Born in Buckinghamshire. Educated at St John's College, Oxford, MA in modern languages. Taught modern languages in schools for seven years, and served in Second World War (infantry and combined operations). Divisional education officer, East Hertfordshire, 1946–7; assistant education officer, Hertfordshire, 1947–51, under Sir John Newson; deputy chief education officer, West Sussex, 1951–7, and Lancashire, 1957–69; chief education officer, Lancashire, 1969 to 1974.

Appendix 4: Chairmen and Vice-Chairmen of the Standing Committees of the Lancashire County Council

Lancashire County Council

Chairman		Vice-Chairman	
Sir J. T. Hibbert	1889–1908	C. R. Jacson	1889–1892
Sir W. Scott Barrett	1908–1921	Sir W. H. Houldsworth	1892–1906
Sir H. F. Hibbert	1921–1927	W. S. Barrett	1906–1908
Sir H. Wade Deacon	1927–1931	V. K. Armitage	1908–1912
Sir J. Travis-Clegg	1931–1937	H. F. Hibbert	1912–1921
Sir W. Hodgson	1937–1945	H. Wade Deacon	1921–1927
Sir P. Macdonald	1945–1946	J. T. Travis-Clegg	1927–1931
Sir J. H. S. Aitken	1946–1948	W. Hodgson	1931–1937
Sir H. Hyde	1948–1949	P. Macdonald	1937–1945
Sir A. Bates	1949–1952	J. H. S. Aitken	1945–1946
Sir A. Smith	1952–1955	H. Hyde	1946–1948
Sir A. Bates	1955–1958	A. Smith	1948–1952
Sir A. Smith	1958–1961	A. Bates	1952–1955
Sir A. Bates	1961–1964	A. Smith	1955–1958
Sir F. Longworth	1964–1967	A. Bates	1958–1961
Sir H. Lumby	1967–1974	A. Smith	1961–1964
		A. Bates	1964–1965
		H. Lumby	1965–1967
		F. Longworth	1967–1973
		T. Hourigan	1973–1974

Standing Joint Committee, 1889–1964

Chairman		Vice-Chairman	
J. T. Hibbert	1889–1893	L. G. N. Starkie	1889–1894
C. R. Jacson	1893–1894	W. S. Barrett	1894–1899
L. G. N. Starkie	1894–1899	*—	1899–1922
W. S. Barrett	1899–1922	J. T. Travis-Clegg	1922–1927
*—	1922–1927	*—	1927–1937
J. T. Travis-Clegg	1927–1937	P. Macdonald	1937–1939
*—	1937–1939	*—	1939–1952
P. Macdonald	1940–1952	J. Eastham	1952–1957
A. Bates	1952–1964	J. Selwyn Jones	1957–1964

Police Committee, 1964–9

Chairman		Vice-Chairman	
A. Bates	1964–1969	J. Selwyn Jones	1964–1969

Finance Committee, 1889–1974

Chairman		Vice-Chairman	
E. Guthrie	1889–1904	A. Greg	1889–1904
H. Wade Deacon	1904–1927	W. L. McClure	1904–1918
J. Whittaker	1927–1931	W. T. Bourne	1918–1922
J. H. Smith	1931–1942	R. C. Assheton	1922–1939
T. Atkinson	1942–1952	W. J. Garnett	1939–1952
A. Smith	1952–1955	J. Selwyn Jones	1952–1955
R. Guymer	1955–1958	A. L. Williams	1955–1958
J. Selwyn Jones	1958–1961	R. Guymer	1958–1961
H. Lumby	1961–1964	J. Selwyn Jones	1961–1964
J. Selwyn Jones	1964–1967	J. G. Barber-Lomax	1964–1967
J. G. Barber-Lomax	1967–1974	J. Selwyn Jones	1967–1970
		J. Selwyn Jones	1970–1973
		R. Foulkes	1973–1974

Parliamentary Committee, 1889–1974

Chairman		Vice-Chairman	
M. W. Peace	1889–1892	V. K. Armitage	1889–1892
V. K. Armitage	1892–1913	C. G. Jackson	1892–1907
S. Taylor	1913–1933	T. O. Clinning	1907–1916
G. H. Ashworth	1933–1944	J. Lawrence	1916–1922
A. Bates	1944–1958	R. Foulds	1922–1926
A. Smith	1958–1961	G. H. Ashworth	1926–1933
A. Bates	1961–1964	J. H. S. Aitken	1933–1946
F. Longworth	1964–1967	R. L. Hughes	1946–1958

* Not a member of the council.

H. Lumby	1967–1974	R. Guymer	1958–1960
		A. Bates	1960–1961
		A. Smith	1961–1964
		H. Lumby	1964–1967
		F. Longworth	1967–1973
		F. Longworth	1973–1974

Main Roads and Bridges (*Highways and Bridges*) *Committee, 1889–1974*

Chairman		*Vice-Chairman*	
W. W. B. Hulton	1889–1907	W. Macfie	1889–1892
J. Shuttleworth	1907–1916	J. T. Wood	1892–1898
J. Aspell	1916–1935	J. E. Sheppard	1898–1903
P. Macdonald	1935–1941	W. Sagar	1903–1905
F. Hindle	1941–1952	J. Shuttleworth	1905–1907
C. W. Doodson	1952–1955	J. Aspell	1907–1916
T. Hargreaves	1955–1958	J. Walker	1916–1931
C. W. Doodson	1958–1961	P. Macdonald	1931–1935
T. Hargreaves	1961–1964	M. S. N. Kennedy	1935–1936
C. W. Doodson	1964–1967	W. J. Bridge	1936–1937
W. D. Cooper	1967–1974	M. S. N. Kennedy	1937–1939
		F. Hindle	1939–1941
		W. J. Bridge	1941–1952
		T. Hargeaves	1952–1955
		C. W. Doodson	1955–1958
		T. Hargreaves	1958–1961
		C. W. Doodson	1961–1964
		T. Hargreaves	1964–1966
		W. D. Cooper	1966–1967
		C. W. Doodson	1967–1970
		Ellis Wood	1971–1974

Public Health and Housing Committee, 1889–1970

Chairman		*Vice-chairman*	
G. A. Pilkington	1889–1890	A. Forrest	1889–1890
A. Forrest	1890–1892	T. Fair	1890–1894
G. A. Pilkington	1892–1894	G. A. Pilkington	1894–1895
T. Fair	1894–1896	J. C. Clark	1895–1896
J. C. Clark	1896–1898	R. C. Fletcher	1896–1898
R. C. Fletcher	1898–1901	R. Sephton	1898–1901
R. Sephton	1901–1916	J. Fletcher	1901–1907

W. Hodgson	1916–1937	C. J. Trimble	1907–1937
Sir T. S. Tomlinson	1937–1958	E. Boothman	1937–1938
J. W. Thorley	1958–1961	W. J. Lucas	1938–1949
F. L. Neep	1961–1970	W. J. Throup	1949–1952
		R. H. Rowlands	1952–1958
		F. L. Neep	1958–1961
		J. W. Thorley	1961–1964
		T. G. Harrison	1964–1970

Education Committee, 1889–1974 (1889–1903 – Technical Instruction Committee)

Chairman		Vice-Chairman	
T. Snape	1889–1901	L. C. Wood	1892–1901
H. F. Hibbert	1901–1921	R. C. Fletcher	1901–1919
J. T. Travis-Clegg	1921–1937	J. T. Travis-Clegg	1919–1921
J. H. S. Aitken	1937–1948	W. Hodgson	1921–1945
Sir H. Hancock	1948–1952	O. Gillett	1945–1947
Mrs K. M. Fletcher	1952–1955	Sir H. Hancock	1947–1948
J. Welch	1955–1958	A. Smith	1948–1952
Mrs K. M. Fletcher	1958–1961	Sir H. Hancock	1952–1955
J. R. Hull	1961–1964	A. Smith	1955–1958
A. Smith	1964–1966	J. R. Hull	1958–1961
H. Nevin	1966–1967	Mrs K. M. Fletcher	1961–1964
J. R. Hull	1967–1971	J. R. Hull	1964–1967
J. R. Ashton	1971–1974	H. Nevin	1967–1970
		H. Nevin	1970–1974

Executive Cattle Plague–Diseases of Animals–Agriculture Committees

Chairman		Vice-Chairman	
A. E. Egerton	1889–1891	L. C. Wood	1889–1891
L. C. Wood	1891–1912	G. W. Rawlins	1891–1892
W. F. Fitzherbert-Brockholes	1912–1924	R. Assheton	1892–1895
		R. C. Assheton	1895–1905
W. B. Hale	1924–1948	W. F. Fitzherbert-Brockholes	1905–1912
		W. F. Egerton	1912–1919
		W. B. Hale	1919–1924
		S. T. Rosbotham	1924–1937
		J. B. Hodgkins	1937–1946
		J. W. Fitzherbert-Brockholes	1946–1948

Smallholdings and Allotments Committee, 1948–70

Chairman*

T. Hargreaves	1948–1952
H. Gorton	1952–1955
J. Mawdesley	1955–1963
W. D. Cooper	1963–1966
J. P. Ennis	1966–1970

Diseases of Animals Committee, 1948–70

Chairman*

J. W. Fitzherbert-Brockholes	1948–1964
L. Ball	1964–1966
J. P. Ennis	1966–1970

Allotments Committee, 1893–1907

Chairman	Vice-Chairman	
C. H. Giles	J. Unwin	1893–1897
J. Whittaker	J. Hatch	1897–1901
J. Whittaker	J. Hatch	1901–1907
J. Whittaker	R. J. Clegg	1907

Smallholdings Committee, 1892–1907

Chairman	Vice-Chairman	
H. P. Hornby	L. C. Wood	1892
A. Greg	A. Burrows	1893
C. E. Beazer	T. Snape	1907

Smallholdings and Allotments Committee, 1908–1919

Chairman	Vice-Chairman	
J. Whittaker	W. Garnett	1908–1910
J. Mercer	W. S. Kinch	1910–1919
	P. J. Hibbert	1919

Committee for the Adjustment of Financial Arrangements between the County and County Boroughs, 1889–1905

Chairman		Vice-Chairman	
J. Fell	1889–1892	H. Maden	1889–1890
W. L. McClure	1892–1905	W. L. McClure	1890–1892
		W. S. Barrett	1892–1894
		A. Burrows	1894–1905

*For some of the time, the chairman of the Smallholdings Committee served as vice-chairmen of Diseases of Animals Committee and vice versa. The two committees were re-combined after 1966.

County Rate Committee

Chairman

C. T. Royds	1889–?
W. S. Barrett	(at least from December 1901 to March 1907, but met very intermittently; no vice-chairman given)
W. L. McClure	1907
W. T. Bourne	1920–1922
G. H. Ashworth	1922–1929

Midwives Act Committee, 1904–48

Chairman		Vice-Chairman	
J. Chadwick	1904–1926	(apparently no vice-chairman)	
G. Scarr	1926–1929	A. Kershaw }	1905–1926
H. Winstanley	1929–1930	G. Scarr }	
J. C. Beckitt	1930–1936	H. Winstanley	1926–1929
H. F. Jeffrey	1936–1938	J. C. Beckitt	1929–1930
Lady Worsley-Taylor	1938–1948	H. F. Jeffrey	1930–1936
		Lady Worsley-Taylor	1936–1938
		Lady Openshaw	1938–1947
		Mrs A. Bottomley	1947–1948

Tuberculosis Committee, 1914–47

Chairman		Vice-Chairman	
J. T. Travis-Clegg	1914–1921	P. J. Hibbert	1914–1921
P. J. Hibbert	1921–1927	C. J. Trimble	1921–1927
C. J. Trimble	1927–1935	E. Boothman	1927–1935
E. Boothman	1935–1938	Sir T. S. Tomlinson	1935–1938
Canon A. Kershaw	1938–1943	E. Clegg	1938–1944
P. F. Mannix	1943–1947	G. E. Hardman	1944–1947

Public Assistance Committee, 1930–48

Chairman		Vice-Chairman	
W. Hodgson	1930–1945	B. Boothman	1930–1937
W. J. Garnett	1945–1948	W. J. Garnett	1937–1945
		R. Newton	1945–1946
		P. Barron	1946–1948

Health Committee, 1947–74

Chairman		Vice-Chairman	
Sir T. S. Tomlinson	1947–1948	E. Smethurst	1947–1949
H. Lord	1948–1958	J. Eastham	1949–1955
T. Hourigan	1958–1961	W. J. Throup	1955–1958
H. Lord	1961–1964	H. Lord	1958–1961
T. Hourigan	1964–1966	T. Hourigan	1961–1964
J. W. Geere	1966–1967	H. Lord	1964–1967
H. Lord	1967–1969	J. W. Geere	1967–1971
Mrs M. M. C. Kemball	1969–1971	J. W. Geere	1971–1974
Mrs C. M. Pickard	1971–1974		

Co-ordination Committee, 1932–53

Chairman		Vice-Chairman	
W. A. Spofforth	1932–1934	G. E. Slack	1932–1934
J. Aitken	1934–1947	?	1934–1935
H. Hyde	1947–1952	R. Barrow	1935–1949
J. Eastham	1952–1953	F. Hindle	1949–1952
		A. Hewitt	1952–1953

Planning Committee, 1947–74

Chairman		Vice-Chairman	
A. B. Higham	1947–1952	B. Tynan	1947–1950
W. Bannister	1952–1961	W. Bannister	1950–1952
H. Carrington	1961–1964	W. Alderson	1952–1958
R. Foulkes	1964–1967	H. Carrington	1958–1961
Travis Carter	1967–1974	W. Bannister	1961–1964
		H. Carrington	1964–1967
		R. Foulkes	1967–1974

Planning and Development Committee, 1944–5

Chairman	Vice-Chairman
C. R. Ingham	J. C. Robertson

Children's Committee, 1946–1974

Chairman		Vice-Chairman	
Mrs K. M. Fletcher	1946–1952	J. Eastham	1946–1952
W. J. Throup	1952–1955	Mrs W. Kettle	1952–1955

Mrs E. A. Fell	1955–1958	Mrs M. Kemball	1955–1958
Mrs W. Kettle	1958–1961	Mrs E. A. Fell	1958–1961
Dr M. K. Hall	1961–1964	Mrs W. Kettle	1961–1964
Mrs W. Kettle	1964–1967	Dr M. K. Hall	1964–1967
Mrs C. M. Pickard	1967–1970	Mrs W. Kettle	1967–1970

(Functions taken over by Social Services Committee: last meeting held on 17 December 1970.)

Establishment Committee, 1948–74

Chairman		Vice-Chairman	
R. Guymer	1948–1952	W. J. Lucas	1948–1952
B. Wood	1952–1955	R. Guymer	1952–1955
R. F. Mottershead	1955–1958	E. Wood	1955–1958
E. Wood	1958–1961	R. F. Mottershead	1958–1961
R. F. Mottershead	1961–1964	E. Wood	1961–1964
E. Wood	1964–1967	R. F. Mottershead	1964–1967
R. F. Mottershead	1967–1970	E. Wood	1967–1974
L. Bell	1970–1974		

Fire Brigade Committee, 1948–74

Chairman		Vice-Chairman	
H. Lumby	1948–1952	T. Hourigan	1948–1952
T. Hourigan	1952–1955	H. Lumby	1952–1955
H. Lumby	1955–1961	T. Hourigan	1955–1958
J. Martin	1961–1967	J. Martin	1958–1961
B. Greenwood	1967–1974	B. Greenwood	1961–1967
		J. Martin	1967–1974

Civil Defence Committee, 1950–68

Chairman		Vice-Chairman	
L. Green	1950–1963	R. H. Jackson	1950–1952
B. Wood	1963–1967	A. L. Cheall	1952–1958
A. F. Williamson	1967–1968	E. Wood	1958–1963
		A. F. Williamson	1963–1967
		G. E. Pailin	1967–1968

Road Safety Committee

Chairman		Vice-Chairman	
F. Longworth	1958–1964	T. Halsall	1958–1964
T. G. Harrison	1964–1967	G. Annett	1964–1967
G. L. Annett	1967–1971	T. G. Harrison	1967–1970?

Transport Committee, 1964–74

Chairman		Vice-Chairman	
F. Ainsworth	1964–1967	A. R. Holden	1964–1967
A. R. Holden	1967–1974	F. Longworth	1967–1974

Library Committee, 1965–74

Chairman		Vice-Chairman	
L. Ball	1966–1967	F. Worsley	1966–1967
A. L. Cheall	1967–1971	L. Ball	1967–1970
D. H. Elletson	1971–1974		

Estates and Industrial Development Committee, 1970–4

Chairman	
M. A. H. Bates	1970–1974

Social Services Committee, 1971–4

Chairman		Vice-Chairman	
T. Jackson	1971–1974	Mrs W. Kettle	1971–1974

Notes

1 See A. F. Davie, 'The Administration of Lancashire, 1838–1889', in S. P. Bell (ed.), *Victorian Lancashire* (Newton Abbot, 1974), p. 14 and *passim*.
2 Davie, *op. cit.*, p. 34.
3 See J. P. Dunbabin, 'The Politics of the Establishment of County Councils', *Historical Journal*, vi, 2 (1963), especially pp 251–2.
4 See *Jubilee History of County Councils: Lancashire* (London, 1939), pp 15–20; and Mr Hands and Mr Denver in Chapter 12 below, pp 193–4.
5 J. P. D. Dunbabin, 'Expectations of the New County Councils', *Historical Journal*, viii, 3 (1965), pp 378–9.
6 See pp 55–6 below.
7 See *Lancaster Guardian* (13 October 1894), for Sir John's Oldham speech on the new (1894) dispensation.
8 *Lancaster Guardian* (16 June, 23 June, 16 November and 8 December 1894).
9 See *Proceedings* of the Meetings of the Lancashire County Council (1894–5), p. 312 and *passim* for examples; cf. also *Proceedings* (February 1895) for Report of the Parliamentary Committee, pp 67–8.
10 Dunbabin, *op. cit.*, p. 375.
11 *Report of the Finance Committee to the County Council* (February 1913), which gives a list of boundary adjustments from 1889.
12 British Parliamentary Papers, xxxvii (1892), pp 221ff.
13 Cf. obituary reports in *Preston Herald* (24 May 1899); and *Preston Guardian* (27 May 1899). See also Appendix 3 to this volume. Hulton died at the early age of fifty-seven.
14 *Proceedings of a Meeting of the Lancashire County Council* (7 February 1895), p. 3.
15 See Table 2.2 below. An estimate of staffing can be made from the county *Abstract of Accounts*, published annually.
16 See pp 60–5 below.
17 For his estate, see *Royal Commission on Agriculture* (1894), Report by Asst Commissioner Wilson Fox on the Garstang District, p. 53, Appendix B5.
18 Details of his career through successive committees were extracted by Mr Terence Karran; for a late tribute to him, see *Proceedings* (1924–5), p. 143 (Report of the Education Committee).

19 R. O. Knapp, 'The Making of a Landed Elite: Social Mobility in Lancashire Society' (Ph.D. thesis, University of Lancaster, 1970), especially pp 338–9; 349–52.

20 Some sixty of the original members of the Council were also justices of the peace. The (successful) battle to establish industrialists on the Lancashire bench had been won by the middle of the nineteenth century; see D. Foster, 'The Changing Social and Political Composition of the Lancashire County Magistracy, 1821–51' (Ph.D. thesis, University of Lancaster, 1971), especially p. 272 and ff; and D. Foster, 'Class and County Government in Early 19th Century Lancashire', *Northern History*, vol. ix (1974), pp 48–61, especially pp 52 and ff.

21 Biographical details in W. T. Pike, *Lancashire at the Opening of the 20th Century* (Brighton, 1903), p. 158; for other leaders of the Council, see pp 158–92, 350, 359, 367, 391.

22 *Lancashire Daily Post* (3 February 1921).

23 *Lancashire Daily Post* (10 March 1927).

24 Electoral lists in *Proceedings, passim*.

25 *Preston Guardian* (17 October 1942).

26 *Ibid*.

27 *Lancashire Daily Post* (15 March 1945).

28 *Ibid*.

29 Vide *County Council Yearbook* (1891), pp 488–9, which shows that the West Riding was ahead of Lancashire in appointing its medical officer, Dr Whitelegge, and that it was also ahead in appointing a county sanitary inspector.

30 *County Council Yearbook* (1892), pp 34–8 and *passim*.

31 *Preston Herald* (4 March 1922).

32 *Ibid*.

33 See Chapter 2, p. 27.

34 Information by courtesy of Mr Harold Counsell.

35 References to salaries in the newly formed county councils are scattered through the *County and Local Government Magazine* – see, e.g., vol. xix (August 1890), p. 13, for salaries paid to the chief officers of Hertfordshire, which were well under half the Lancashire salaries in several instances.

36 Clare was, for example, in receipt of a basic salary as clerk of some £5000 p.a., and was receiving a further £300 p.a. as clerk to the Lancashire Asylums Board, with £109 war bonus; as clerk under the Mental Deficiency Act he received a further £200. These were only main items, it would appear, in a Poo-Bah-like list. See, e.g., *Preston Herald* (25 March 1922).

37 Vide *Preston Guardian* (4 March 1922); *The Times* (2 March 1922).

38 *Royal Commission on Local Government in England*, Cmnd 4040, 3 vols, 1969.

39 See the list of outline biographies of chief officers in Appendix 3 to this volume.

40 Jeffrey Stanyer, *County Government in England and Wales* (London, 1967), pp 10–11.

CHAPTER 2

1 See, for comparable data, *County Council Yearbook* (1891), *passim*.

2 See Chapter 3 below, pp 34–5.

3 *County Council Yearbook* (1891).

4 *Proceedings of the Meetings of the Lancashire County Council* (hereafter *Proceedings*) (1931–2), p. 430.

5 Printed *Accounts of the County Treasurer* (1896–7), p. 7; *County and Local Government Magazine*, xix (August 1890), p. 13.

6   *Accounts* (1896–7), p. 1 and *County and Local Government Magazine, loc. cit.*
7   *Ibid.*
8   *Ibid.*
9   Mr Gee, one of the most distinguished servants of the county administration in terms of service and devotion, entered local government at Bolton in 1885 and transferred to the County Health Department in 1891, remaining there until superannuated in 1936; he subsequently became mayor of Preston, 1944–5. See the commemorative publication, *Jubilee of the Lancashire Branch of NALGO,1911–1961* (Preston, 1961), pp 8–10.
10 Data from *Proceedings* (1931–2), p. 461.
11 See p. 89 below.
12 As Dr Davie shows on p. 103 below, the police before 1889 operated through twenty-one police divisions, an organisation that was maintained afterwards. Hundred boundaries were, and continued to be, used.
13 *Proceedings* (1931–2), p. 467.
14 *Ibid.*, p. 468.
15 *Proceedings* (1901–02), p. 69.
16 See p. 96.
17 *Proceedings* (1931–2), p. 460.
18 *Ibid.*, p. 450.
19 *Ibid.*, p. 448; also *Accounts of the County Treasurer* (1904), 'Tabular Statement of Gross Expenditure of the County'.
20 See, in this connection, *The Jubilee of County Councils: Lancashire* (London, 1939), p. 98, for an interesting observation.
21 See p. 41.
22 *Proceedings* (1931–2), p. 436.

CHAPTER 3

1   Except the Clerk of the Peace (who was also always clerk of the County Council), who was appointed by the Standing Joint Committee for the Police until 1933.
2   In 1904, the Finance Committee ceased to exercise their industrial school powers, which were then delegated to the Education Committee: *Proceedings* (4 August 1904).
3   *Proceedings* (12 March 1906).
4   For numbers of members of all county council committees see Table 2.2 in Chapter 2.
5   Barrister-at-law of Park Hall, Chorley; county treasurer, 1860–1915.
6   As a result the local authorities in Lancashire were now 19 non-county boroughs, 100 urban districts and 27 rural districts = 146: Technical Instruction Committee *Minutes* (7 November 1895).
7   Another main committee formed in 1889 was the Main Roads and Bridges Committee.
8   *Proceedings* (4 February 1894).
9   The Board of Agriculture and Fisheries from 1903 and the Ministry of Agriculture and Fisheries from 1919.
10 *Proceedings* (1 February 1894).
11 Few samples were submitted for analysis up to 1914.
12 *Proceedings* (2 February 1908).
13 John Broughton from the Gartside estate near Leeds, county land agent, 1912–48.
14 The Committee took over the powers of the following drainage authorities: the Alt Commissioners; the Croston Commissioners; the Glaze Brook, Overton; Spen Dyke; and Slyne Drainage Boards.

15   The Small Holdings Colonies Acts of 1916 and 1918.
16   *Proceedings* (31 July 1930): 'Report on Small Holdings as at 31 December 1929'.
17   *Proceedings* (7 February 1924).
18   *Proceedings* (3 February 1910).
19   The term 'county district' was now used to cover all local authorities in the admini-
     strative county–non-county boroughs, urban districts and rural districts.
20   *Proceedings* (3 November 1921).
21   *Proceedings* (8 May 1919).
22   Elswick, High Carley, Peel Hall, Heath Charnock, Chadderton, Rufford, Wrighting-
     ton and Withnell.
23   Lancashire County Council also formed a Midwives Act Committee in 1904.
24   *Proceedings* (5 August 1920).
25   The Standing Joint Committee is dealt with separately in Chapter 8.
26   *Proceedings* (7 August 1902).
27   Excluding Oldham, which refused to join.
28   Under the Salmon Fishery Act of 1865 – *28 and 29 Vict. C.121 s.4.*
29   The names are the names of the rivers in the districts of the boards.
30   *Proceedings* (3 May 1900).
31   Membership consisted of: Lancashire 8, Cheshire 2, six Welsh counties 10, eleven
     fishery boards 11, twenty-one Lancashire and Cheshire county boroughs 21, the Board
     of Trade (Board of Agriculture and Fisheries from 1903) 30.
32   Island fortress in Walney Channel near Barrow-in-Furness.
33   *Proceedings* (7 May 1891).
34   *Proceedings* (14 March 1889).
35   *Proceedings* (11 March 1920).
36   Numbers of committees of which members of the Council were members in 1929:

Number of committees	1	2	3	4	5	6	7	8
County aldermen	1	8	8	8	5	4	–	1
County councillors	11	36	34	12	6	3	1	–
Totals	12	44	42	20	11	7	1	1

37   Except the Standing Joint Committee. The vice-chairman of the Council also
     was not an *ex officio* member of the Education Committee.
38   All financial figures have been taken from the booklets published each year by the
     County Council entitled County of Lancaster – County Accounts.
39   See Chapter 5.
40   For a discussion of rate income see Chapter 11.
41   These figures are taken from local taxation returns published yearly by the Ministry
     of Health.
42   The government took over the prisons in 1877, but the justices and then the County
     Council remained responsible for pensions of prison officers.

CHAPTER 4

1   *Hansard*, 3rd series, vol. cccxxix, col. 907.
2   *Hansard*, 3rd series, vol. cccxxiii, col. 1643.

3 See, for example, Edmund Knowles Muspratt, *My Life and Work* (London, 1917), which makes no mention of Muspratt's service on Lancashire County Council from 1889 to 1904.

4 Referred to hereafter simply as '*Proceedings*'.

5 *The Jubilee of County Councils 1889 to 1939* (London 1939).

6 *Lancaster Gazette* (19 January 1889).

7 *Manchester Guardian* (5 January 1889).

8 *Lancaster Gazette* (23 January 1889).

9 *Manchester Guardian* (8 March 1913).

10 At first the decision of 1889 to select aldermen only from among councillors was taken to mean that aldermen themselves could not be re-elected as aldermen for a further term. As a result, in 1892 and 1895 a number of aldermen whose term of office was ending resigned before the triennial election in order to stand as candidates. In February 1895 the following resolution was passed by 41 votes to 32: 'That, having regard to services rendered by retiring Aldermen, the next meeting of the Council be respectfully urged to consider these services in selecting the new Alderman, by allowing them to be eligible for re-election for a further term of office' (*Proceedings*, 7 February 1895, p. 23). After this, re-election of sitting aldermen became virtually automatic, and selection of new aldermen was made on the basis of seniority within the Hundreds. It seems likely that there was a point of some importance at issue here, for in the debates on the 1888 Act some Liberals had expressed strong opposition to aldermen on the grounds that they would not be subject to regular popular re-election. The matter had already been raised at the annual meeting in March 1892 where an attempt to get a similar resolution through was unsuccessful.

11 It is interesting to note that the rate of replacement in Lancashire seems to have been considerably greater than that in Cheshire at this time. See J. M. Lee, *Social Leaders and Public Persons* (Oxford, 1963), Appendix A.

12 Information about the occupation of council members has been derived from the return of election results printed in the *Proceedings* after each triennial election. The descriptions given there are those used by councillors themselves on their nomination papers. As with all attempts to group occupations, problems of classification arise. These are made worse here by the fact that we have had to rely on self-descriptions. For instance, terms like 'gentlemen' and 'esquire' were often used very loosely; some women gave an occupation, others simply described themselves as housewives; and similarly, some retired people gave their former occupation, others simply said 'retired'. Because of these problems we have used rather broad categories and restricted our comments to the main trends that appear.

13 *Manchester Guardian* (6 March 1931).

14 The number of committees varied from time to time, but see list in Table 2.1. In a few cases our information about chairmen and in particular vice-chairmen is incomplete. For the purposes of the analysis that follows we have excluded the Smallholding and Allotments Committees up to 1908, when they were combined, and also the County Rate Committee, because it met only intermittently and seems to have been of little importance.

15 *Manchester Guardian* (6 March 1931).

16 *Proceedings* (1904–05), p. 730.

17 *Manchester Evening News* (3 March 1922).

18 W. S. Barrett, *Lancashire County Council 1889–1910* (small privately printed booklet in the Lancashire Record Office, dated 24 January 1910).

19 *Hansard*, 3rd series, vol. cccxxix, col. 917.

20 J. M. Lee, *Social Leaders and Public Persons* (Oxford, 1963), p. 61.

21 *Manchester Guardian* (11 March 1898).

22 W. S. Barrett, *op. cit.*
23 *Nelson Gazette* (14 February 1928).
24 *Nelson Gazette* (28 February 1928).
25 *Lancaster Observer* (6 March 1925).
26 *Manchester Guardian* (6 March 1931).

CHAPTER 5

1 See MS Minutes of the Technical Instruction Committee, at the Lancashire Record Office, TIM.
2 So galvanic was the promise of whisky money that a special committee of the Council met to consider its use on ten occasions between October 1890 and August 1891.
3 Cf. *Yearbook of the Lancashire County Council* (1892), pp 34–8, and individual county reports, which frequently refer to enterprise in technical instruction.
4 *Proceedings, passim*; occupations of members are given in lists of those elected triennially. For biographical details of Thomas Snape, see W. T. Pike (ed.), *Lancashire at the Opening of the Twentieth Century* (Brighton, 1903), p. 192.
5 J. A. Bennion, *Report of the Director of Technical Instruction* (Preston, 1895), at the Lancashire Record Office, TIR/L.
6 *Ibid.*, 'Report from the Borough of Chorley' in Appendix, and *passim*.
7 *Ibid.*, xx.
8 *Proceedings* (1898–9), p. 330 (Report of the Technical Instruction Committee, August 1898).
9 *Proceedings* (1898–9), p. 343.
10 *Proceedings* (1899–1900), p. 376 (table of entries).
11 Cf. in this connection the useful short study of the early days of Lancashire education by A. H. Miles, I. Sellers and A. Woodward, 'Lancashire and the Education Act of 1902', in *Lancashire Education, 1870–1970* (centenary pamphlet, Lancashire Education Committee, 1970).
12 *Report of the Director of Education for 1901–2*, Lancashire County Council (University of Lancaster Library), pp 19–20.
13 *Ibid.*, pp 31–2.
14 For his biographical details, see Appendix 2.
15 Cited above – notes 12 and 13.
16 *Report of Lancashire Education Committee: Scheme for the Constitution of Local Education Areas* (1903), Lancashire Record Office, EKR 1b.
17 E. W. Cohen, *Autonomy and Delegation in County Government* (London, 1953), p. 14.
18 *Proceedings* (1902–03), pp 644–5. The Technical Instruction Committee had included people who were plainly unqualified for their task.
19 Cf. report of the Elementary Education Sub-Committee (27 March 1905), with the printed Minutes of the Lancashire Education Committee, Lancashire Record Office, EM.
20 Each of these sets of minutes, which in most cases run up to 1974, is at the Lancashire Record Office, references EAM to EYM.
21 Cf. Appendix I to the Minutes of the Lancashire Education Committee (17 October 1904), which sets out in full the 'Regulations for Local Area Education Sub-Committees', and also Appendix II, 'Duties of Clerks to Local District Committees'. Cf. *Report of the Consultative Committee of the Board of Education Upon the Question of Devolution of County Education Authorities* (BPP, 1908), p. 10 and *passim*. Sir Henry Hibbert was a member of this committee.

22 Cf. printed *Proceedings of the Elementary Education Sub-Committee* (8 May 1905), minute 113.

23 See below, p. 146.

24 Attendance reports, published in statistical form in the Annual Reports of the Education Committee, *Proceedings, passim.*

25 Reports of the Accommodation, Attendance and Staff Sub-Committee (Monthly Returns of School Attendance), with the printed Education Committee Minutes, *passim.*

26 Oral history research undertaken at the Centre for North-West Regional Studies, University of Lancaster, in 1974–5. This is a controversial subject, and other researchers contradict the suggestion that people enjoyed their schooldays, which experience the censoring effect of memory tends to obliterate.

27 Minutes of the Elementary Education Sub-Committee (16 January 1905), Minute 1134.

28 *Proceedings* (1918–19), p. 256.

29 Data from *Proceedings* (1913–14), pp 87–8; *Proceedings* (1920–1), pp 88–9, 94, 97; and *passim* in succeeding Annual Reports of the Education Committee.

30 *Proceedings* (1920–1), pp 76–7.

31 *Ibid.*

32 Minutes of the Lancashire Education Committee, 21 November 1904, 17 April 1905.

33 *Proceedings* (1913–14), pp 112–15.

34 *Proceedings* (1913–14), p. 87.

35 *Proceedings* (1920–1), pp 67–8.

36 *Proceedings* (1927–8), p. 126.

37 *Proceedings* (1920–1), p. 78.

38 *Proceedings* (1927–8), pp 132–3.

39 *Proceedings* (1918–19), pp 254–5.

40 See Appendix 2.

41 *Proceedings* (1924–5), p. 144.

42 *Proceedings* (1927–8), p. 122.

43 Cf. *Proceedings* (1920–1), p. 88.

44 *Proceedings* (1927–8), p. 143. It should be added that this was not the result of neglect, but rather of policy, in that the Council preferred to concentrate its resources in building new schools. Much work was in fact done by the education staff and the Architect's Department, in drawing up improvement plans, and considerable negotiation took place with the managers of non-provided schools. As has been pointed out, these church schools remained an encumbrance through much of the century.

CHAPTER 6

1 MS Minutes of the Public Health Committee, Lancashire Record Office (CCS/1, Misc. Vol.), entry for date.

2 H. Finer, *English Local Government* (London, 1933), p. 94.

3 Lancashire County Council, *Report of the Medical Officer of Health for 1889* (filed at the Lancashire County Record Office), p. 4.

4 *Ibid.*, p. 7.

5 Statistics in Lancashire County Council publication, *Report of the Medical Officer for 1972* (Preston, 1973).

6 *Ibid.*

7   R. Lawton, 'Population Trends in Lancashire and Cheshire', *Transactions of the Historical Society for Lancashire and Cheshire*, vol. 114 (1962), p. 212.
8   Medical Officer's *Report* for 1889, p. 16.
9   *Proceedings* (1904–05) (Report by MOH), pp 345ff.
10   Minutes of the Public Health Committee (3 July 1891), and *passim*.
11   *Royal Commission on Agriculture: Report by Asst Commr Wilson Fox on Garstang District, 1894*, p. 10 (comment by Dr Day).
12   Cf. *Proceedings* (1889–90), pp 146–9; for an excellent detailed account of the medical officer of his own official duties, see *Proceedings* (1900–01), pp 699–701.
13   *Proceedings* (1900–01), pp 696–8.
14   *Proceedings* (1904–05), p. 467.
15   See Chapter 5.
16   There is an admirable summary of the early years of this service by Dr R. W. Eldridge in *Fiftieth Annual Report of the School Medical Officer* (Lancashire Education Committee, 1958), pp 22–31.
17   *Ibid.*, p. 23.
18   *Ibid.*, p. 24.
19   *Ibid.*, p. 27.
20   Report of the Public Health Committee in *Proceedings* (1904–05), pp 467–8.
21   *Proceedings* (1904–05), pp 494ff.
22   Report of the Midwives Act Committee (20 October 1904) in *Proceedings* (1904–05), p. 621.
23   *Proceedings* (1904–05), p. 868.
24   Printed pamphlet, *The Jubilee of the Lancashire County Branch of NALGO, 1911 to 1961* (Preston, 1961), p. 20.
25   *Report of the Special Committee on the Housing, Town Planning and C.Act, 1909* (Lancashire County Council, 4 March 1912).
26   MS and other file material, Series G139, Inspections of County Districts, Health Departments, especially 1–113.
27   We are grateful for some valuable notes from the County Health Department, which give items on this topic.
28   *Proceedings* (1917–18), p. 15.
29   *Proceedings* (1927–8), p. 618.
30   *Proceedings* (1927–8), pp 467ff.
31   Tabulation material by courtesy of the Health Department of the County.

CHAPTER 7

1   With the consent of the Local Government Board.
2   Amounderness, Blackburn, Leyland, Salford and West Derby.
3   Because George Holme, surveyor of roads and bridgemaster for West Derby Hundred, refused to resign.
4   PEP 61 and 62 Vict. C.1.
5   1913: main roads, 650 miles, 5 furlongs, 58 yards; under direct control, 315 miles, 7 furlongs, 202 yards.
6   On balance main roads increased by only 63 miles from 1889 to 1913.
7   1909: secondary roads, 1144½ miles; district roads, 3012½ miles; total, 4157 miles.
8   John Loudon McAdam made roads with layers of river stones, broken small so as to have sharp points which under pressure from rolling fitted together.
9   Termed in Lancashire 'lonkey' setts.

10   Subject to approval by the Local Government Board.
11   Lancashire C.C. *Proceedings* (6 August 1914), report by county surveyor.
12   Lancashire C.C. *Proceedings* (6 May 1915).
13   Sheeting – covering with a layer.
14   Proportions in Lancashire: 1912 – motor 2, horsedrawn 5; 1920 – motor 11, horse-drawn 1 (census taken by county survey in these years).
15   County surveyor of roads, 1898–1921; county surveyor and bridgemaster, 1921–30.
16   Lancashire C.C. *Proceedings* (1 February 1923).
17   The Hundred of Lonsdale was more lightly rated for roads than the other Hundreds.
18   Lancashire C.C. *Proceedings* (2 May 1922).
19   Originally called 'motor danger signals'.
20   The principal part of the information in this chapter is drawn from Lancashire County Council's *Proceedings* and from the Minutes of the Highways and Bridges Committee (MBM) at the Lancashire Record Office.

CHAPTER 8

1   Lancashire County Council and the justices were required to agree as to the numbers for the membership of the Standing Joint Committee. If unable to agree, the home secretary fixed the number.
2   The appointment was, however, subject to the approval of the home secretary.
3   Lancaster (for the Hundred of Lonsdale), 2; Preston (for the Hundreds of Amounderness, Blackburn and Leyland), 4; Salford (Hundred of Salford), 6; Liverpool (Hundred of West Derby), 6.
4   The Standing Joint Committee gradually made 'standing agreements' for mutual aid in times of emergency with the counties of Cumberland, Westmorland and the West Riding of Yorkshire and eleven county boroughs and four municipal boroughs having their own police, all in Lancashire.
5   The 'quarters' were 1 March to 31 May; 1 June to 31 August; 1 September to 30 November; 1 December to 28 February.
6   In 1889, 33; in 1920, 31.
7   In 1889, 21; in 1895, 20.
8   In number, fourteen in 1889, to which were added Warrington (1900), Blackpool (1904) and Southport (1905).
9   Accrington, Ashton-under-Lyne, Bacup, Clitheroe and Lancaster.
10   Chorley, Colne, Darwen, Eccles, Haslington, Heywood, Leigh, Middleton, Morecambe, Mossley, Nelson, Rawtenstall and Widnes.
11   Fonteth Park, Walton-on-the-Hill, Wavertree and West Derby added to Liverpool.
12   1890: police apprehensions, 13,396; summoned, 21,471. 1913: police apprehensions, 7560; summoned, 11,972.
13   1983 in 1919; increased to 2014 in 1920.
14   Special constables were first appointed under the Special Constables Act of 1831, being appointed by the justice of the peace to supplement the services of the police.
15   Standing Joint Committee Minutes (15 July 1926).
16   Usually situated in or near police stations.
17   As percentages of county revenue expenditure:

	1890–91	1904–05	1917–18	1928–29
Police	39.9	17.4	19.6	16.3
Education	–	39	54.1	47.6

18 In 1928–9, under the 1896 Act, £4424. Under the 1923 Act, £7523.
19 The Standing Joint Committee was an independent statutory committee and therefore had no obligation to report on its work to the Council.

CHAPTER 9

1   See especially R. Robson, *The Cotton Industry in Britain* (London, 1957). We are also grateful for the comments of an industrialist who has also been a member of the County Council, J. G. Barber-Lomax.
2   Wilfred Smith, 'Trends in the Geographical Distribution of the Lancashire Cotton Industry', *Geography*, 26 (1941), pp 11–12.
3   *Ibid.*, p. 13.
4   *Ibid.*, pp 14–15.
5   T. W. Freeman, H. B. Rodgers and R. H. Kinvig, *Lancashire, Cheshire and the Isle of Man* (London, 1966), p. 209.
6   W. Beveridge, *Full Employment in a Free Society* (London, 1944), pp 344–5.
7   Freeman, Rodgers and Kinvig, *op. cit.*, p. 215.
8   Beveridge, *loc. cit.*
9   *Proceedings, passim* (date given in Annual Budgets for the 1930s) and *Jubilee History of County Councils: Lancashire* (London, 1939), p. 93.
10 *Ibid.*
11 Hands and Denver, Chapter 12 below, pp 198–9.
12 See Chapter 11, pp 179–80.
13 *Annual Reports of the Medical Officer of Health for Lancashire, passim.*
14 See Chapter 14 below, pp 301–3.
15 P. D'Arcy Hart and G. Payling Wright, *Tuberculosis and Social Conditions in England* (London, 1939), *passim.*
16 Dr Bradbury had joined the Lancashire Tuberculosis Department in 1927 (see *Proceedings* (1927–8, pp 812–13), and was the author of *Causal Factors in Tuberculosis* (London, 1933); see also *Proceedings, passim*, for Reports of the Tuberculosis Committee, and *Reports of the Tuberculosis Officer* for 1924 and 1930, Lancashire Record Office, TR.
17 K. W. Wallwork, 'The Cotton Industry in North-West England, 1941–61', *Geography*, 47 (1962), p. 251.
18 Freeman *et al.*, *op. cit.*, p. 145.
19 R. W. Daniels on industrial estates, Chapter 15, pp 322–4.
20 Freeman *et al.*, *op cit.*, p. 137, cf. also R. C. Estall, 'Industrial Change in Lancashire and Merseyside', *Geography*, 46 (1961), p. 56.
21 For a general survey see Freeman *et al.*, *op. cit.*, p. 137 *et seq.*
22 *Ibid.*
23 Estall, *op. cit.*, p. 56.
24 Freeman, *et al.*, *op. cit.*, p. 149.
25 *Ibid.*, p. 151.
26 *Ibid.*, p. 121.
27 *Ibid.*, p. 151.
28 Wallwork, *op. cit.*, p. 250.

29 Freeman *et al.*, *op. cit.*, p. 153.
30 Census of 1971, England and Wales, County Report for Lancashire, Part 1, pp 2–3.
31 *Ibid.*
32 T. W. Freeman, *The Conurbations of Great Britain* (Manchester, 1959), p. 239.
33 Freeman, *et al.*, *op cit.*, p. 245.
34 Freeman, *Conurbations, loc. cit.*: and Lancashire and Merseyside Industrial Development Association, *The Lancashire Coast Area* (Manchester, 1951), p. 13.
35 *Report of the Medical Officer of Health for Lancashire* (1961), pp 17–18.
36 Census of 1971, *loc. cit.*
37 J. R. James, 'Regions and Regional Planning', *Geography*, *54* (1969), p. 135.
38 See pp 137–8 below (on the Three Ridings Scheme).

CHAPTER 10

1 See comments in Chapter 5.
2 See Chapter 12, pp 198–9.
3 *Proceedings* (1929–30), pp 585–7.
4 Schedule of Guardians' Committees, *Proceedings* (1929–30), pp 592ff.
5 Cf. *Proceedings* (1947–8), First Schedule of Health Divisions, pp 684ff.
6 Sir Robert Adcock, CBE, kindly giving oral information to the writer (1974).
7 A phrase used by Professor Peter G. Richards in *The Reformed Local Government System* (London, 1973), p. 30.
8 This claim is made in the *Jubilee History of County Councils: Lancashire* (London, 1939), pp 92–3, and is borne out by, e.g., the Minutes of the Central Relief Sub-Committee (Lancashire Record Office, PRM) between 1930 and 1938. Substantiation for comments in this paragraph is in the same Minutes (14 April 1930, 23 January 1933, 20 November 1933 and 17 December 1934) (an especially troublesome removal case).
9 *Proceedings* (1928–9), p. 589.
10 *Proceedings* (1937–8), p. 233.
11 See Chapter 13, especially pp 256–78.
12 We should like to record our thanks for the help afforded by a departmental history, or notes thereto, made available by the County Librarian, Mr A. Longworth.
13 Personnel lists, kindly provided by the Treasurer's Department.
14 *Proceedings* (1937–8), p. 215 (part of the *Annual Report of the Education Committee* for 1936–7).
15 See Chapter 7.
16 For financial details of the Liverpool–East Lancashire Road, see Lancashire County Council *Abstract of Accounts* (1931–2), Appendix 11; for opening, see *Proceedings* (1937–8), p. 473.
17 *Proceedings* (1937–8), p. 477 (para. 33 of *Special Report of the Highways and Bridges Committee*, presented July 1937).
18 *Proceedings* (1937–8), p. 469.
19 Plans in *Proceedings* (1937–8), pp 482–3.
20 Notably to the *Jubilee* volume, and to most useful historical notes kindly provided by the Chief Constable and the Council, with incidental information from senior officers.
21 *Preston Guardian* (21 March 1931).
22 *Ibid.*, and also 17 October 1942.

23 See, e.g., *Proceedings* (1932–3), pp 226–33.
24 *Lancashire Daily Post* (18 March 1837; 15 March 1945); *Preston Guardian* (17 February, 3 March 1945).
25 *Proceedings* (1937–8), p. 266.
26 Oral information by Mr Frank Young, CBE.
27 Information by courtesy of Sir Robert Adcock, CBE, who gave us the outline details of his career; the adjectives are our own, and those of colleagues who worked with him.
28 Information from the County Surveyor's Department.
29 *Lancashire Daily Post* (5 February 1931, 5 March 1948).
30 *Manchester Guardian* (3 January 1957); *Lancashire Daily Post* (11 March 1948).
31 See *Lancashire Evening Post* (28 April 1949) for biographical details of Sir Alfred Bates; information by courtesy of H. T. G. Hands and D. Denver.
32 Details from an eye-witness who was present at the banquet.
33 An example of prejudice as an enlivener of an Education Committee meeting was observed by the writer. The Education Department had invited councillors to see a film on sex education. This film caused much misgiving, notably on the part of the religious right wing, and the apparent threat to innocence and the family was much emphasised (1970).
34 Personnel Budgets, by courtesy of the County Treasurer.
35 *Proceedings* (1947–8), p. 502.
36 *Ibid.*, pp 504ff.
37 *Ibid.*, p. 507.
38 See pp 379–80.
39 *Proceedings* (1947–8), p. 523.
40 Compiled from the annual 'Summaries of Net Expenditure' in Lancashire County Council *Abstracts of Accounts, passim.*
41 Departmental historical notes, by courtesy of the County Treasurer.
42 *Ibid.*
43 Information from a senior officer concerned with the appointments.
44 *Proceedings* (1947–8), p. 762; historical pamphlet, *Lancashire County Fire Brigade, 1948 to 1974* (Lancashire Brigade, 1974), p. 4.
45 *Lancashire County Fire Brigade, op. cit.*, p. 1.
46 *Ibid.*, p. 8.
47 *Ibid.*, p. 3.
48 Calculation by courtesy of Mr G. MacGregor-Reid.
49 *Proceedings* (1967–8), pp 128–9.
50 *Ibid.*, p. 130.
51 *Lancashire County Fire Brigade, op. cit.*, p. 31.
52 See p. 103 above.
53 *Annual Report of the Chief Constable for Lancashire for 1966* (Lancashire Record Office, PLA 1/3), p. 6.
54 *Ibid.*, and historical notes provided by the Constabulary.
55 *Ibid.*
56 *Annual Report of the Chief Constable for Lancashire for 1964*, p. 3.
57 *Annual Report of the Chief Constable for Lancashire for 1969*, pp 1ff.
58 Historical notes provided by the Constabulary.
59 *Ibid.*
60 Details by courtesy of Mr G. MacGregor-Reid.
61 See pp 32, 146–7 and 233.
62 Minutes of the Children's Committee (17 April 1946), Lancashire Record Office, CWM 1.
63 Minutes of the Children's Committee (17 April, 14 May 1946).

54 We are indebted to Miss Marion Jay and Miss Ruth White, former children's officers in north Lancashire, for detailed explanations of the day-to-day work within areas.

55 Minutes of the Children's Committee (1 September 1948).

56 *Proceedings* (1955–6) (Report of the Children's Committee), p. 138.

57 We are here indebted to the compiler of some very valuable historical notes from the Children's Department, based partly on material provided from field officers.

58 Minutes of the Children's Committee (20 January 1955).

59 See, for example, the use of council houses for these purposes at Failsworth, Swinton, Hindley and Radcliffe: *Proceedings* (1967–8) (Report of the Children's Committee, July 1967), p. 392.

70 *Proceedings* (1967–8), pp 624–8.

71 See *Annual Report of the Medical Officer of Health for 1953*, p. 41.

72 *Proceedings, passim*; we are also indebted to some valuable historical notes provided by the County Librarian.

73 Treasurer's Department, Personnel Budgets.

74 *Abstracts of Accounts* (1968–9), pp 264–7.

75 See Reports of the Selection Committee, *Proceedings, passim*.

76 *Abstracts of Accounts* (1968–9), p. 364.

77 Specified in Section III of the Local Government Act (1888); see also *British Parliamentary Papers, xxxvii* (1892), *passim*. The moneys thus raised went to the Exchequer Contribution Account of each county, and was used by its administration.

78 Cf. *Proceedings* (1955–6), p. 620 (Report of the Contracts Committee).

79 *Proceedings* (1955–6), p. 114.

80 *Ibid.*

81 A comment based upon the reports of the Contract and Finance Committees, in *Proceedings, passim*. This is a subject worthy of considerable detailed research.

82 See pp 223–4.

83 See J. M. Lee *et al., The Scope of Local Initiative* (London, 1974).

84 See Hands and Denver in Chapter 12.

CHAPTER 11

1 Valuable background material was gained from the following texts: H. V. Wiseman (ed.) *Local Government in England and Wales 1958–69* (London, 1970), Ch. 6; A. T. Peacock and J. Wiseman, *The Growth of Public Expenditures in the U.K.* (London, 1967), Ch. 6; N. P. Hepworth, *The Finance of Local Government* (London, 1970); J. A. G. Griffiths, *Central Departments and Local Authorities* (London, 1966); H. Finer, *English Local Government* (London, 1950), Part V. Information on Lancashire County Council was gained variously from the annually published *Proceedings, Budgets, Abstracts of Accounts, Lancashire County Finance, Budget Speeches* and *Treasurer's Notes*. Statistical sources are fully described in the Appendix to this chapter and are not, in general, referred to in the text.

2 *Budget Speech* (1951), p. 7. See also *Budget Speech* (1946), pp 10, 11; *Budget Speech* (1948), p. 5; *Budget Speech* (1949), p. 4.

3 All the trends referred to in this chapter are ones of exponential growth. The trend growth rates were derived by the regression of the logarithm of the variables in question on time.

4 Trends are best estimated over a long span of years. The pre- and postwar periods are treated separately because reliable war year expenditures for the UKLGS are not available.

5 *Proceedings* (1932–3).

6   *Budget Speech* (1954), p. 7; *Budget Speech* (1960), p. 8.
7   *Budget Speech* (1940), p. 13.
8   *Budget Speech* (1949), p. 13.
9   *Budget Speech* (1954), p. 2; *Budget Speech* (1958), p. 4; *Budget Speech* (1965), p. 13; *Budget Speech* (1971), pp 5, 6.
10 *Budget Speech* (1947), p. 9; *Budget Speech* (1949), p. 4; *Budget Speech* (1951), p. 5; *Budget Speech* (1952), p. 6.
11 Lancashire County Council's rate poundage was generally low by county council standards too. See, for example, *Budget Speech* (1952), p. 8; *Budget Speech* (1955), p. 7; *Budget Speech* (1960), p. 10; *Budget Speech* (1966), p. 11.
12 Hepworth, *op. cit.*, pp 27–33.
13 *Budget Speech* (1945), pp 4, 5, 7, 14–16, 28–30.
14 *Budget Speech* (1945), p. 6; *Budget Speech* (1946), p. 7.
15 *Budget Speech* (1958), p. 12.
16 *Budget Speech* (1939), p. 15.
17 Wiseman, *op. cit.*, pp 159–62.
18 *Budget Speech* (1956), p. 9.
19 *Budget Speech* (1963), pp 14, 20.
20 The structures of finance for the spending categories are based on time series derived from the *Abstracts of Accounts*.
21 Wiseman, *op. cit.*, pp 162–8.
22 *Budget Speech* (1954), p. 5.
23 *Budget Speech* (1944), p. 8; *Budget Speech* (1952), p. 5.
24 For example, the Council gave high priority to heavily rate-financed welfare expenditure. It also encouraged overspill schemes (see Chapter 15 below, pp 309–22).
25 *Budget Speech* (1950), p. 6. See also *Budget Speech* (1956), p. 4.
26 *Budget Speech* (1939), p. 19.
27 *Ibid.*
28 *Budget Speech* (1957), p. 4.
29 Hepworth, *op. cit.*, p. 137.
30 *Budget Speech* (1966), p. 7.
31 Hepworth, *op. cit.*, pp 137, 138.
32 *Building Programmes and Forecasts of Capital Payments, 1972–3 to 1975–6* (Preston, 1973), *passim.*
33 *Budget Speech* (1957), p. 4; *Budget Speech* (1962), p. 3; *Budget Speech* (1966), p. 2; *Budget Speech* (1968), pp 2, 5.
34 *Budget Speech* (1966), p. 2.
35 *Budget Speech* (1957), p. 4.
36 *Budget Speech* (1956), p. 3.
37 Over 1953–4 UKLGS capital expenditure fell by fourteen per cent. Spending on categories for which Lancashire County Council had responsibility was cut by nearly fifty per cent.
38 Revenue contributions were recorded in both the revenue and capital accounts of the Council. Their use to cushion the effects of loan sanctions is exampled in *Budget Speech* (1955), p. 24.
39 *Budget Speech* (1950), p. 2.
40 *Budget Speech* (1956), p. 4; *Budget Speech* (1957), p. 22.
41 *Proceedings* (1931–2), p. 432.
42 *Budget Speech* (1972), p. 5.
43 See, for example, *Budget Speech* (1963), p. 8.
44 This growth rate pertains to UKLGS capital formation gross of housing and trading enterprise expenditure.

45 *Budget Speech* (1973), pp 2, 12. *Treasurer's Notes* (1973), p. 5.
46 *Abstract of Accounts* (1974), pp 8, 9.

CHAPTER 12

1   So far as we know, the only existing complete run of the *Nelson Gazette* is in the possession of the Nelson and Colne Constituency Labour Party. We are grateful to Mr L. Dole for allowing us to consult it.
2   For a discussion of the provisions of the 1929 Act with respect to poor relief see B. B. Gilbert, *British Social Policy 1914–1939* (London, 1970).
3   See pp 65–70 above.
4   *Nelson Gazette* (14 February 1928).
5   *Nelson Gazette* (30 January 1931).
6   *Ashton Reporter* (10 March 1934).
7   *Nelson Gazette* (2 March 1934).
8   *Nelson Gazette* (2 March 1937).
9   After the Second World War, some Liberals began to call themselves 'Progressives', but we have generally continued to refer to them as 'Liberals'.
10 *Nelson Gazette* (3 March 1937).
11 *Proceedings* (1931–2), p. 719.
12 *Proceedings* (1933–4), p. 589.
13 *Proceedings* (1934–5), p. 28.
14 *Nelson Gazette* (27 March 1934).
15 Conservative Group Minutes (7 March 1946). We are very grateful to Sir Henry Lumby and Mr T. Jackson for allowing us to consult and quote from these minutes.
16 *The Nelson Gazette*'s explanation of this is not entirely convincing; 'There was only one unexpected happening ... the defeat of the two sitting Labour aldermen, and it was just as surprising to the Anti-Labour people. It was caused by a clerical mistake in some voting papers – quite accidental, but it had the effect of electing two new Labour aldermen in place of two retiring ones.' *Nelson Gazette* (26 March 1946).
17 Conservative Group Minutes (5 February 1948).
18 Copies of the 1948 Agreement and of the 1957 revision were kindly made available to us by the present clerk to the County Council.
19 *Nelson Gazette* (16 March 1948).
20 Paradoxically, Labour's share of the total vote increased in 1949. This was due to the fact that in 1949 many more Labour candidates were opposed than had been the case in 1946.
21 Conservative Group Minutes (11 and 13 April 1949).
22 Conservative Group Minutes (8 April 1946).
23 The data for county boroughs and all county councils are derived from the appropriate volumes of the *Registrar General's Statstical Review of England and Wales* (London, HMSO).
24 The figures for county boroughs and all county councils are again based upon the *Registrar General's Statistical Review of England and Wales*. The fact that the number of seats contested varied from year to year creates problems for analysis because turnout varied from one kind of seat to another. This makes it difficult to distinguish genuine trends from fluctuations arising simply from variations in the number of seats contested. However, we calculated turnout figures for the divisions that were contested regularly between 1952 and 1970 and compared them with the figures for Lancashire shown in Table 12.9 and in fact the trends in both cases are very similar.

25 As before, variations in the number of seats contested might have given rise to distortions. However, using a similar procedure to that described in note 24 above, we found once again that any distortion was not significant.

26 We are grateful to Gallup Polls Ltd for making these data available.

27 R. T. McKenzie, *British Political Parties* (London, 1955), p. 532.

28 Financial compensation for council members had been introduced in stages. From 1930, under the 1929 Local Government Act, travelling expenses could be claimed; from 1946 subsistence allowances for attendance at authorised conferences were included; and finally the 1948 Local Government Act provided for the reimbursing of members' losses of earnings.

29 J. M. Lee, *Social Leaders and Public Persons* (Oxford, 1963).

30 The figures are based on information in the County Council *Yearbooks*, and may not be complete. This information is first given in the 1931–2 *Yearbook* and for that reason we have taken 1931 and not 1928 as the starting point.

31 The election of 1937 was the first after a major revision of divisional boundaries in which fifteen new seats were created. The election of 1946 was the first for nine years.

32 *Nelson Gazette* (18 March 1941).

33 *Nelson Gazette* (4 March 1952).

34 *Proceedings* (1952–3), p. 593.

35 *Proceedings* (1953–4), p. 201.

36 *Proceedings* (1952–3), p. 621.

37 For an example of the kind of analysis that would be necessary see J. E. Alt, 'Some Social and Political Correlates of County Borough Expenditures', *British Journal of Political Science*, 1 (1971), pp 49–62.

38 *Preston Guardian* (23 July 1910).

39 *Budget Speech* (1951). The speeches of chairmen of the Finance Committee introducing the annual budgets together with brief explanatory notes on the budgets were printed in pamphlet form by the County Council.

CHAPTER 13

1 See Chapter 11, pp 179–80.

2 See p. 81 above.

3 P. E. Meadon, 'The Administration of Education in Lancashire', Section (h) of Education in Lancashire (National Assn of Head Teachers, 1932), p. 14.

4 *28th Annual Report of the Lancashire Education Committee* (1930–1), p. 1.

5 We refer to money expenditure here and take no account of price changes; the prices of goods and services purchased by the public sector remained almost constant in the 1930s.

6 *36th Annual Report of the Lancashire Education Committee* (1938–9), p. 13.

7 *27th Annual Report of the Lancashire Education Committee* (1929–30), p. 3.

8 *30th Annual Report of the Lancashire Education Committee* (1932–3), p. 2.

9 B. Simon, *The Politics of Educational Reform* (London, 1974), Appendix I.

10 *31st Annual Report of the Lancashire Education Committee* (1933–4), p. 1.

11 *31st Annual Report of the Lancashire Education Committee* (1933–4), p. 2.

12 *25th Annual Report of the Lancashire Education Committee* (1927–8), p. 5.

13 A vivid account of wartime conditions is contained in *38th Annual Report of the Lancashire Education Committee* (1940–1) in *Proceedings* (1941–2), pp 162–6. Details of evacuation, etc. are given *Proceedings* (1942–3), pp 162–3.

14 *Proceedings* (1942–3), pp 162–3.
15 *Ibid.*
16 Wartime *Annual Reports, passim,* as given in *Proceedings.*
17 *Proceedings* (1943–4), p. 146.
18 *Proceedings* (1942–3), p. 140.
19 *Ibid.*
20 Cf. Education Act, Public and General Act (1944), c.31, First Schedule, p. 310; and cf. *Proceedings* (1944–5), pp 407, 485–90. Vide also pp 80–1 (*supra*) for Lancashire's work with area committees after 1902, and Lancashire Education Committee, *Memorandum of the Director of Education on Administrative Functions* ... (5 July 1944), p. 12.
21 *Proceedings* (1944–5), p. 490; Ministry of Education, *Circular 5; Local Administration of Education, Schemes of Divisional Administration,* paras 24 and 29.
22 Lancashire Education Committee, Minutes of the Full Committee (16 October 1944).
23 The writers are here glad to acknowledge the helpful advice of Mr William Whalley, senior administrator in the Lancashire education service, who was present through the events described.
24 *Educational Reconstruction,* Cmnd 6458 (London, 1943), especially p. 29; E. W. Cohen, *Autonomy and Delegation in Local Government* (London, 1953), especially p. 18, which has an interesting comment on the problem of boundaries versus functional efficiency.
25 *Proceedings* (1944–5), p. 528; *Second Report of the Local Government Manpower Committee,* Cmnd 8421 (London, 1951), *passim.*
26 Vide especially J. R. Sampson, *Delegation of Services within Counties* (IMTA, London, 1952) Chapter 4 and *passim.*
27 *47th Annual Report of the Lancashire Education Committee* (1949–50), p. 20.
28 *Proceedings* (1944–5), p. 457.
29 *Proceedings* (1944–5), pp 458–9.
30 *44th Annual Report of the Lancashire Education Committee* (1946–7), in *Proceedings* (1947–8), pp 238ff.
31 *47th Annual Report of the Lancashire Education Committee* (1949–50), p. 1.
32 *49th Annual Report of the Lancashire Education Committee* (1951–2), pp 6–7.
33 *Ibid.*
34 *Report of the Committee on Public Schools Appointed by the President of the Board of Education* (1944).
35 *51st Annual Report of the Lancashire Education Committee* (1953–4), p. 6.
36 *54th Annual Report of the Lancashire Education Committee* (1956–7), p. 5.
37 *47th Annual Report of the Lancashire Education Committee* (1949–50), pp 26–8.
38 *54th Annual Report of the Lancashire Education Committee* (1956–7), p. 15.
39 Cf. *58th Annual Report of the Lancashire Education Committee* (1960–1), p. 18.
40 Minutes of the Lancashire Education Committee (9 September 1957), Appendix A.
41 Minutes of the Primary and Secondary Education Sub-Committee (12 January 1959), Appendix; see also *50th Annual Report of the Lancashire Education Committee, loc. cit.*
42 We are grateful to Mr G. MacGregor-Reid and Mr T. Karran for tracing the general trends of local and national educational expenditure as related to changes of national party government.
43 *64th Annual Report of the Lancashire Education Committee* (1966–7), pp 16–19.
44 *52nd Annual Report of the Lancashire Education Committee* (1954–5), p. 14.
45 *54th Annual Report of the Lancashire Education Committee* (1956–7), p. 16.
46 *60th Annual Report of the Lancashire Education Committee* (1962–3), p. 19.
47 Lancashire Education Committee, Minutes of the Primary and Secondary Education Sub-Committee (9 October 1961) (Report of Consultative Committee).

48 Minutes of the Primary and Secondary Sub-Committee (13 February 1961).
49 *62nd Annual Report of the Lancashire Education Committee* (1964–5), p. 23.
50 Education Committee Minutes, General Purposes Sub-Committee (16 May 1966), Appendix.
51 *Ibid.*
52 Education Committee Minutes, General Purposes Sub-Committee (11 July 1966), Appendix A.
53 Education Committee Minutes, General Purposes Sub-Committee (19 June 1967), Appendix (Report of Special Sub-Committee).
54 *64th Annual Report of the Lancashire Education Committee* (1966–7), p. 21.
55 *65th Annual Report of the Lancashire Education Committee* (1967–8), p. 26; *69th Annual Report of the Lancashire Education Committee* (1971-2), p. 24, tabulation material from *Reports, passim.*
56 *64th Annual Report of the Lancashire Education Committee* (1966–7), p. 20.
57 Cf. *68th Report of the Lancashire Education Committee* (1970–1) and *67th Report of the Lancashire Education Committee* (1969–70), p. 21.
58 For an insight into the development of ministry policy regarding school plans, cf. Ministry of Education Pamphlet No. 33, *The Story of Post-War School Building* (London, 1957), *passim.*
59 Lancashire Education Committee, Minutes of the Architectural Sub-Committee (4 September 1967).
60 *66th Report of the Lancashire Education Committee* (1968–9), p. 25.
61 Cf. Report of the Selection Sub-Committee in Minutes of the Lancashire Education Committee (5 June 1967).
62 *Ibid.*
63 *Proceedings* (1960–1), pp 158–9.
64 Lancashire Education Committee, 'Schemes of Divisional Administration' (August 1971), p. 12.
65 Lancashire Education Committee, Minutes of Divisional Executive No. 16 (10 September 1945); Minutes of Divisional Executive No. 11 (18 June 1962), Resolution No. 11.
66 Minutes of Divisional Executive No. 11 (18 March 1968), Resolution No. 321.
67 Lancashire Education Committee, 'Development Plan for Primary and Secondary Education', 2nd Instalment (February 1951), Division 16, p. 5.
68 Minutes of Divisional Executive No. 11 (17 December 1973).
69 Minutes of Divisional Executives No. 11 (September 1973), Resolution No. 284.
70 Cf. *64th Annual Report of the Lancashire Education Committee* (1966–7), p. 20.
71 *Lancashire Evening Post* (18 July 1972).
72 *Ibid.*
73 Minutes of Divisional Executive No. 11 (17 July 1972), Resolution No. 65.
74 *Lancashire Evening Post* (12 July 1972).
75 *Lancashire Evening Post* (18 July 1972).
76 *Lancashire Evening Post* (17 July 1972).
77 We should like to thank Sir Henry Lumby for his help and guidance in this field. He is not responsible for any comments made here.
78 Cohen, *op. cit.*, Appendix 1, p. 80.
79 The entire scheme is set out *in extenso* in *Proceedings* (1944–5).
80 Ministry of Education, Circular 344, *Divisional Administration in Excepted Districts, Report of a Review of the Working of Divisonal Administration* (1958), para. 3.
81 *Ibid.*, paras 10 and 11.
82 Minutes of the Primary and Secondary Education Sub-Committee (16 June 1958).
83 See Table 11.2 for Mr MacGregor-Reid on the cost of education.

84 J. Sleaman, 'Educational Costs and Local Government Structure in Scotland', *Scottish Journal of Political Economy*, vol. 12 (1965), pp 281–92.

85 Calculations from IMTA and other sources by P. Regan.

86 Minutes of the Primary and Secondary Education Sub-Committee (13 April 1959).

87 See pp 76 and 79.

88 *Proceedings* (1937–8), p. 208.

89 O. M. V. Argles, *South Kensington to Robbins* (London, 1964), pp 86–8.

90 *Proceedings* (1929–30), p. 142.

91 Argles, *op. cit.*, p. 85.

92 Education Committee, 'Report on the Development Plan' (March 1949) (in Lancashire Record Office, EKR 46).

93 Figures extracted from Education Department records by Mr Terence Karran.

94 See Chapter 9, pp 114–5.

95 Lancashire Education Committee, Further Education Sub-Committee Minutes (19 May 1952).

96 *Development Plan, op. cit.* (see n. 67 above), p. 29.

97 Figures extracted from Annual Reports of the Lancashire Education Committee.

98 For figures, see Minutes of the Education Committee, Further Education Sub-Committee (7 January 1957 and 8 December 1958).

99 *Times Education Supplement* (27 January 1956), quoted in S. F. Cotgrove, *Technical Education and Social Change* (London, 1958), p. 176.

100 *Technical Education*, Cmd 9703 (London, February 1956).

101 *53rd Annual Report of the Lancashire Education Committee* (1955–6), p. 47.

102 *Ibid.*

103 *56th Annual Report of the Lancashire Education Committee* (1958–9), p. 40.

104 This basic principle of compaign was already noticed in the *52nd Report of the Lancashire Education Committee* (1954–5), p. 25.

105 *Ibid.*

106 An observation by one of the authors (J. D. Marshall), who was working in Lancashire technical teacher training during these events.

107 *56th Annual Report, op. cit.*, p. 42; Proceedings of the Education Committee, Further Education Sub-Committee Minutes (13 April 1959).

108 *60th Annual Report of the Lancashire Education Committee* (1962–3), p. 30.

109 *55th Annual Report of the Lancashire Education Committee* (1957–8), p. 31.

110 *60th Annual Report of the Lancashire Education Committee* (1962–3), p. 31.

111 *63rd Annual Report of the Lancashire Education Committee* (1965–6), p. 37.

112 *67th Annual Report of the Lancashire Education Committee* (1969–70), p. 42.

113 *62nd Annual Report of the Lancashire Education Committee* (1964–5), pp 31–2.

114 *Ibid.*

115 *63rd Annual Report of the Lancashire Education Committee* (1965–6), p. 36.

116 *70th Annual Report of the Lancashire Education Committee* (1972–3), p. 39, for graphical representation of trends.

117 *Ibid.*

118 *63rd Annual Report of the Lancashire Education Committee* (1965–6), p. 37.

119 Data based on a return published jointly by the Institute of Municipal Treasurers and Accountants and the Society of County Treasurers; cf. Minutes of the General Purposes Sub-Committee of the County Education Committee (9 March 1964).

120 Appendix to Minutes of the General Purposes Sub-Committee of the County Education Sub-Committee (14 September 1959).

121 General Purposes Sub-Committee of the Education Committee Minutes (9 March 1964).

122 See pp 77–8.

123   *Proceedings* (1937–8), p. 206.
124   Minutes of the Lancashire Education Committee, Primary and Secondary Education Sub-Committee (9 September 1957), Appendix A.
125   *Ibid.*
126   See pp 270–4.
127   Minutes of the Education Committee, Further Education Sub-Committee (13 July 1959), Appendix.
128   Minutes of the Education Committee, Further Education Sub-Committee (9 July 1962), Appendix.
129   Marion E. McClintock, *The University of Lancaster: Quest for Innovation* (Lancaster, 1974), esp. pp 6–17, 75–9.

CHAPTER 14

1   See pp 89–90 above.
2   For a comprehensive account of the school medical service at this period, see R. W. Eldridge, *Fifty Years of the School Medical Service in Lancashire*, contained in *Fiftieth Annual Report of the School Medical Officer* (1958). See especially pp 17–19.
3   *Ibid.*
4   Vide Report of the County Medical Officer of Health for 1935, pp 205–06.
5   *The Jubilee of County Councils, 1889–1939: Lancashire; Fifty Years of Local Government ment* (London, 1939), p. 72. The district concerned has not been identified.
6   Eldridge, *op. cit.*, p. 43; cf. also Sir William's obituary in *Lancashire Daily Post* (15 March and 18 March 1945).
7   Oral information by courtesy of Mr Harold Counsell, a former senior administrative officer in the department, and Mr Fred Robinson.
8   *Proceedings* (1937–8), p. 302.
9   *Ibid.*, p. 306.
10   *Ibid.*, pp 309–25.
11   *Ibid.*; vide attached map.
12   File of personnel employed, 1939 and 1947, by courtesy of the County Treasurer; 1955 figures from the *Annual Personnel Budget*, pamphlet prepared by the Treasurer as from 1952–3.
13   Dr S. C. Gawne, who gave as an instance the work of Mr Charles Appleby, administrative officer for nursing services, who was well known for the instant attention he would give to an organisational problem. This would be sorted out even during Mr Appleby's own lunch hour. 'Divisionalisation' probably made this type of service impossible by making the central office more remote.
14   There is a vivid account of these in Eldridge, *op. cit.*, pp 43–4.
15   *Interim Report of the Medical Officer of Health for 1947* (April 1949), pp 37–41.
16   *Ibid.*, p. 36.
17   See pp 135–7.
18   *Annual Report of the Medical Officer of Health* (1948), p. 30. (These reports are at the Lancashire Record Office under PHR.)
19   *Ibid.*
20   *Ibid.*, p. 42.
21   Cf. the unprecedentedly forcible language in the normally staid *Proceedings* (1951–2), pp 507–16.
22   *Annual Report of the MOH* (1950), County Medical Officer's personal report, p. 10.

23 *Ibid.*
24 *Annual Report of the MOH* (1951), p. 10.
25 S. C. Gawne, 'The Public Health Services under the National Health Service' (cyclostyled copy of speech to the British Medical Association, Toronto, 1955), p. 8.
26 S. C. Gawne, 'Some Reflections on Co-ordination in the Health Service', *Public Health* (December 1953).
27 *Annual Report of the MOH* (1953), p. 32.
28 *Ibid.*, pp 30–1.
29 *Annual Report of the MOH* (1958), p. 47, with special reference to east Lancashire.
30 *Ibid.*, p. 17.
31 Personal information.
32 Personal information.
33 *Annual Report of the MOH* (1950), pp 85–6.
34 *Annual Report of the MOH* (1951), p. 9.
35 *Annual Report of the MOH* (1950), p. 9.
36 Cf. *Proceedings* (1962–3), pp 631ff.
37 *Ibid.*
38 Cf. David M. Boswell in H. P. Ferrer (ed.), *The Health Services, Administration, Research and Management* (London, 1972), pp 341–6.
39 Eldridge, *op. cit.*, p. 54. There is a detailed account of these institutions in Eldridge.
40 Cf. Dr Gawne's review of the first twenty years of the Health Service in *Annual Report of the MOH* (1968), p. 13.
41 S. C. Gawne, 'Community Service for the Elderly' in a pamphlet published by the Manchester Regional Hospital Board, *Regional Conference on the Hospital Geriatric Services* (Manchester, 1967), pp 9–10.
42 Personal information.
43 Information kindly supplied by the former Health Department.
44 *Annual Report of the MOH* (1972), p. 13.
45 Historical notes provided by the former Health Department.

CHAPTER 15

1 A complete discussion can be found in J. B. Cullingworth, *Town and Country Planning in England and Wales* (London, 3rd edn 1970).
2 See, for example, *ibid.*
3 See *ibid.*, p. 83, for some details.
4 Lewis Keeble, *Town Planning at the Crossroads* (published by *Estates Gazette*, 1961), p. 44.
5 Evelyn Sharp, *Ministry of Housing and Local Government* (London, 1969), p. 145.
6 Sir Robert Adcock also joined the County from Manchester, and Sutton Brown would have been known to him.
7 See, for example R. J. Nicholas, *City of Manchester Plan* (Manchester, 1945).
8 *Ibid.*; R. J. Nicholas, *Report on Tentative Regional Planning Proposals* (Manchester and District Regional Planning Committee, 1945); R. J. Nicholas and M. J. Hellier, *An Advisory Plan* (for South Lancashire and North Cheshire Advisory Planning Committee, 1947); F. Longstreth Thompson, *Merseyside Plan, 1944* (London, 1945).
9 For a fuller account see Peter Hall *et al.*, *The Containment of Urban England* (London, 1973), vol. ii, pp 570–80.
10 Cf. G. Sutton Brown, *A Preliminary Plan for Lancashire* (Preston, 1951).
11 *Ibid.*, p. 3.

12   J. B. Cullingworth, *Housing Needs and Planning Policy* (London, 1960), pp 147–8.
13   G. Sutton Brown, *op. cit.*, pp 15–16.
14   Discussed below, pp 314–5.
15   The Lancashire Statutory Plan Review was formally submitted in 1962, and, for the reasons concerning the Ministry and noted earlier, approval was never granted. Development plans were phased out under the 1968 Act.
16   J. M. Lee and B. Wood, *The Scope of Local Initiative* (London, 1974).
17   Keeble, *op. cit.*, pp 67–9.
18   Peter Hall *et al.*, *op. cit.*, vol. i, pp 369–84.
19   By 1959 the county's attitude had changed.
20   Cullingworth, *Housing Needs*, *op. cit.*, p. 148.
21   Vital for the success of the scheme. For some scathing comments on the general quality of district council expertise, see Keeble, *op. cit.*
22   J. B. Cullingworth, 'Overspill in South-east Lancashire: The Salford–Worsley Scheme,' *Town Planning Review*, 3 (October 1959).
23   Some of these negotiations by Lancashire in the 1950s did break ground for other fruitful schemes of the 1960s. Manchester was able to reach agreement to house 5000 people in Whitefield, and Heywood for 6300 people. At a later date, Salford housed 20,000 people at Middleton, 4000 at Denton and 2600 at Irlam. These negotiations, between city and districts, came later. The County was not directly involved.
24   Sharp, *op. cit.*, p. 184.
25   B. Moore and J. Rhodes, 'Evaluating the Effects of British Regional Policy', *Economic Journal* (March 1973), p. 87.
26   The Willis enquiry into Manchester's overspill at Lymm in addition to Westhoughton mentioned Leyland as a possible Town Development Act scheme that could be developed with Lancashire county. The latter itself had proposed such a project in its Development Plan. Manchester approached the county with a proposal that was turned down on the grounds that no likelihood existed of industrial development. This was in 1959, at a time when Lancashire was pressing for a new town at Skelmersdale.
27   An explanation for only one loan being made was the insistence of the Board of Trade that local authorities lend at commercial rates and not at the PWLB rate plus ¼ per cent. The former gave the county no financial advantage.
28   One commentator on the old authority felt that the pre-1974 county's attitude to industrial development was largely political, not taken seriously or achieving very much.
29   County Council Industrial Development Sub-Committee Agenda (6 November 1967).
30   North-East Lancashire Planning Unit, *North East Lancashire Plan* (London, 1972).
31   See, for example, J. Casson and L. A. King, 'Afforestation of Derelict Land in Lancashire', *Surveyor* (1960); U. A. Coates in Civic Trust, *Derelict Land* (1964); J. Rowbotham, 'Lancashire Reclamation', *Journal of Town Planning Institute* (1973); D. Tattersall, 'Reclamation of Lancashire', *Manchester Statistical Society* (1970).
32   The data in Tables 15.2 and 15.3 originate from Lancashire County Council and are quoted in K. W. Wallwork, *Derelict Land* (Newton Abbot, 1974), p. 265.
33   Based on data in North-West Economic Planning Council, *Derelict Land in the North West* (London, 1969).
34   For the political scientist interested in the democratic process, it would be instructive to consider the implications of these projects. The outline proposal must inevitably originate with officers, and the subject matter is highly technical and requires multidisciplinary skills. Endless consultations with landowners and the Ministry must take place over prices, costs, grants, loan sanctions etc. – all this over a ten-year period. What influence therefore could be exerted by an elected representative?
35   Data from the Department of the Environment quoted in Wallwork, *Derelict Land*, p. 223.

36 Data from Lancashire County Planning Department.
37 Lord Radcliffe-Maud and B. Wood, *English Local Government Reformed* (Oxford, 1974), Ch. 6.
38 Samlesbury brewery, discussed below.
39 See, for example, D. McGregor, *The Human Side of Enterprise* (New York 1960); and *The Professional Manager* (New York, 1967).
40 P. Buxton, *Local Government* (Harmondsworth, 1973), Ch. 7.
41 *Lancashire Evening Telegraph* (4 November 1970).
42 Private note, March 1976.
43 Stephen Plowden, *Towns Against Traffic* (London, 1972), Ch. 1, pp 11–22.
44 See Lancashire County Council, *Road Plan for Lancashire* (Preston, 1949).
45 Stephen Plowden, *op. cit.*, Ch. 1.
46 J. H. Dean and J. Drake, 'The Lancashire Road Plan: twenty years after', *Proceedings of the Institute of Civil Engineers, 44* (November 1969); G. R. Wells, *Highway Planning Techniques* (London, 1971), p. 82.
47 Evidence from Lancashire County Council File, 1952–61.
48 Lancashire County Council, *Lancashire Roads, Situation Report* (Preston, 1960).
49 J. Drake, H. L. Yeadon, D. I. Evans, *Motorways* (London, 1969).
50 William Plowden, *The Motorcar and Politics 1896–1970* (London, 1971), pp 330–335.
51 W. Plowden, *op. cit.*, p. 390.
52 Dean and Drake, *op. cit.*, p. 234.
53 These brief facts scarcely do justice to the design, engineering, and effort represented in Lancashire's motorways. Full accounts, graphically illustrated, can be found however in Drake, Yeadon, and Evans, *op. cit.*; see also Lancashire County Council, *M6 in Lancashire, An Illustrated Brochure* (Preston, 1966).
54 Government White Paper, *Transport Policy*, Cmnd 3057 (London, 1966), p. 8; *Roads in England* (House of Commons 238, 1970–1 session), p. 14.
55 Drake, Yeadon, and Evans, *op. cit.*, p. 185.
56 It has been alleged that Drake would order all motorway maintenance to stop on days when an official government car was passing through the county to ensure that Lancashire would be shown at its best.
57 All the data used in these figures were taken from the *Highways Expenditure*, Society of County Treasurers and County Surveyors Society *Annual* (1957–72). Figure for 1969 not available.
58 W. Plowden, *op. cit.*, p. 348. From 1947 to 1959 the Ministry had a permanent secretary who had spent his career in shipping.
59 Compare for example, *Lancashire's Roads* (Preston, 1960) and *Lancashire's Needs* (Preston, 1966).
60 The report cited utilises the existence of the bridge and junction in making its case on p. 36.
61 Quoted in same report, p. 9.
62 National Economic Development Office, *Efficiency in Road Construction* (London, 1966), pp 11–13.
63 For a fuller discussion see G. R. Wells, *Highway Planning Techniques: the Balance of Cost and Benefit* (London, 1971); and *Traffic Engineering: an Introduction* (London, 1970).
64 J. M. Thompson, *Motorways in London* (London, 1969), especially p. 49.
65 Drake's rank among county surveyors can be gauged from the fact that Lovell as president of the Society and Drake both received prior copies for comment before wider distribution. The memorandum was introduced to the first meeting of the Society as 'a breath-taking document'.

66 Secretary of State for the Environment, *Roads in England 1974–5* (London, 1975), p. 3; see also p. 5.
67 Drake, Yeadon, and Evans, *op. cit.*, p. 209.

CHAPTER 16

1   H. F. Hughes (ed.), *The Jubilee of the Lancashire County Branch of NALGO* (Preston, 1961), p. 22.
2   *Ibid.*, pp 6–8. We were also greatly assisted by Mr William Whalley, former chairman of the Lancashire County Branch of NALGO.
3   *Ibid.*, pp 34–5.
4   Norman Wilson, 'The Local Government Service Since the War', *Public Administration*, xxx (1952), pp 132–3.
5   For examples, *Proceedings* (1929–30), p. 16; *Proceedings* (1949–50), *passim*; Minutes of the Co-ordination Committee at the Lancashire Record Office (GM) (1931–49).
6   Vide Quarterly Reports of the Establishment Committee in *Proceedings* (from 1950), *passim*.
7   Minutes of the Establishment Committee (14 February 1951) (under XM at the Lancashire Record Office).
8   Eye-witness information kindly supplied by Mr T. Barton.
9   See pp 286–7 above.
10 Minutes of the Lancashire Education Committee, General Purposes Sub-Committee (9 March 1964).
11 *Ibid.*
12 *Ibid.*
13 Minutes of the Lancashire Establishment Committee (27 October 1969) (Lancashire Record Office, XM 30).
14 *Ibid.*
15 *Strategic Plan for the North-West* (Manchester, 1974), pp 48–9, Figs 3.1a and b.
16 Cf. the Presidential Address to the Geography Section of the British Association by Professor G. M. Howe, at the University of Lancaster, 7 September 1976 ('Where the Bell Tolls Loudest').
17 Minutes of the Lancashire Education Committee, Libraries Sub-Committee (1 June 1953).
18 *Report of the Royal Commission on Local Government* (Recliffe-Maud) (London, 1966–9), vol. 1, Ch. VII, p. 79 (1969). The work for this section of the chapter was greatly assisted by Mr Terence Karran.
19 See pp 137–8 above.
20 *Royal Commission on Local Government, Research Studies, 9: Community Attitudes Survey* (London, 1969), p. 3.
21 P. J. Madgwick with N. Griffiths and V. Walker, *The Politics of Rural Wales* (London, 1973), p. 227.
22 *Reports and Final Proposals of the Local Government Commission for England and for Wales* (1958–66).
23 *Reports of the Local Government Commission for England* (December 1965), North Western General Review Area Statement of Draft Proposals, p. 5, para. 23; p. 16, para. 68.
24 *Ibid.*, p. 27, paras 1, 2; *Royal Commission on Local Government* (Redcliffe-Maud);

'Written evidence of County Councils' (1968), p. 149, para. 1; J. M. Lee *et al.*, *The Scope of Local Initiative* (London, 1974), p. 56.

25   North-West Review Area Statement (1965), p. 13, para. 54.

26   For an interesting insight into regional politics at this time, see Lee *et al.*, *op. cit.*, pp 60–4.

27   The Lancashire 'Three Ridings Scheme' is described in the *Royal Commission on Local Government*, 'Written Evidence of County Councils' (1968), p. 163, para. 45; but, as the Council Chairman later pointed out in his speech on the Royal Commission proposals on 25 September 1969, it had been submitted to the Trustam Eve Commission in 1947, 'and again to the Hancock Commission in 1959'.

28   Cf. Lee *et al.*, *op. cit.*, p. 64.

29   *Royal Commission on Local Government, Report*, vol. 1 (1969), p. 79, para. 303.

30   *Royal Commission on Local Government, Report*, vol. 2, Memorandum of Dissent by Mr D. Senior (1969), p. 9, para. 34.

31   *Proceedings* (1969–70), p. 200.

32   *Ibid.*, p. 392.

33   White Paper, *Local Government in England: Government Proposals for Reorganisation* Cmnd 4584 (London, 1971), p. 6.

34   *Proceedings* (1971–2), p. 53.

35   *Ibid.*

36   Interview with Sir Robert Adcock, CBE, 26 October 1974.

37   S.E. Lancs Report, etc., p. 55.

38   *Ibid.*, p. 56.

39   *Royal Commission on Local Government*, 'Evidence of Urban District Councils', p. 300.

40   *Ibid.*, p. 322.

41   *Ibid.*, p. 362.

42   *Ibid.*, p. 405.

43   *Ibid.*, p. 430.

44   *Ibid.*, p. 444.

45   *Ibid.*, p. 607.

46   *Ibid.*, p. 615.

47   *Royal Commission on Local Government*, 'Evidence of Non-County Borough Councils', pp 210–11.

48   *Ibid.*, p. 65.

49   *Ibid.*, p. 166.

50   *Ibid.*, pp 212, 265, 264.

51   *Royal Commission on Local Government*, 'Evidence of Rural District Councils'.

52   *Ibid.*

Select Bibliography

I. The Newspaper Press

Ashton Reporter
Lancashire Daily Post (1893–4, 1907–48), at the Harris Library, Preston
Lancashire Evening Post (1886–   ), by courtesy of the LEP Office, Preston
Lancaster Gazette (1801–93), at the Lancaster Central Library
Lancaster Guardian and Observer (*Lancaster Guardian*) (1870–   ), at the Lancaster Central
   Library
Manchester Evening News
Manchester Guardian (*The Guardian*) (1821–   ) at the Manchester Central Reference
   Library
Nelson Gazette, at the offices of Nelson Constituency Labour Party
Preston Guardian
Preston Herald (1875–   ), at the Harris Library, Preston

II. Periodicals

Administrative Science Quarterly
The County Councils' Gazette
The Historical Journal
The Local Government Chronicle and Magisterial Reporter
Municipal Review
Political Quarterly
Public Administration
Rural District Review
Town Planning Review

III. Publications by HM Government

Report of Select Committee on Local Government Acts. 1886 and 1894, etc. Minutes of Evi-
   dence, BPP vii (1911)
Report from the Commissioners Under the Local Government Act 1889. Cmd 6839, 1892.
   (BPP xxxvii, 1892)

435

Royal Commission on Secondary Education, 1894–5 (Bryce Commission). HMSO, 1895

Report of Consultative Committee on Devolution by County Education Authorities. Cmd 3952, 1908. (BPP lxxxii, 1908)

Proposals for Reform in Local Government and in the Financial Relations between the Exchequer and the Local Authorities. Cmd 3134, 1928

Royal Commission on Local Government in England. 1st Report, Cmd 2506, L925; *Second Report*, Cmd 3213, 1929; *Final Report*, Cmd 3436, 1929

Ministry of Education, *Higher Technological Education* (Percy Report). HMSO, 1945

Local Government Manpower Committee. First Report, Cmd 6579, 1950; *Second Report*, Cmd 8421, 1951

(White Paper) *The Areas and Status of Local Authorities in England and Wales.* Cmd 9831, 1956

(White Paper) *The Function of County Councils and County District Councils in England and Wales.* Cmnd 161, 1957

Local Government Finance. Cmnd 209, 1957. (BPP xxvi, 1956–7)

Report of the Committee on Administrative Tribunals and Enquiries (Franks Committee). Cmnd 218, 1957

Report of the Committee on Further Education for Agriculture provided by the Local Education Authorities (De la Warr Report). Ministry of Agriculture and Fisheries and the Ministry of Education, 1958

Local Authority Borrowing. Cmnd 2162, 1963. (BPP xxxi, 1962–3)

The Management of Local Government (Report of the Maud Committee). HMSO 1967

Report of the Committee on Staffing of Local Government (Mallaby Committee). Ministry of Housing and Local Government, 1967

Report of the Committee on the Civil Service, 1966–8 (Fulton Committee). Cmnd 3638, 5 vols, 1968

Report of the Royal Commission on Local Government (Redcliffe-Maud). Cmnd 4040, 3 vols, 1969

Registrar General's Statistical Review of England and Wales (issued annually)

Hansard

IV.   Publications by Lancashire County Council, and by Lancashire and North-Western Public Bodies

Annual Reports of the Lancashire Education Committee
Annual Reports of the Medical Officer of Health for Lancashire
Annual Reports of the School Medical Officer
Annual Reports of the Chief Constable for Lancashire (1964–   )
Yearbook of the Lancashire County Council (1891–   )
Proceedings of the Meetings of the Lancashire County Council

Lancashire Education Committee, *A Scheme for the Constitution of Local Education Areas* (Preston, 1903)

Lancashire Industrial Development Association, *Weaving Area* (1948)

Lancashire Industrial Development Association, *The Furness Area* (1948)

Lancashire County Council, *Road Plan for Lancashire* (Preston, 1949)

Lancashire Industrial Development Association, *The Coal–Chemical Area* (1950)

Lancashire Industrial Development Association, *The Lancashire Coast Area* (Manchester, 1951)

G. Sutton Brown, *A Preliminary Plan for Lancashire* (Preston, 1951)

Lancashire County Council (Surveyors' Department), *Preston By-Pass* (official opening booklet) (Preston, 1958)

Lancashire County Council, *Lancashire Roads, Situation Report* (Preston, 1960)

Lancashire County Council, *The Worsley Project – 3000th House Opening* (pamphlet of the County Council Information Centre) (Preston, 1961)

Lancashire County Council, *Worsley, Social Survey of Mount Ship Housing Estate* (County Council Information Report No. 17) (Preston, 1962)

Lancashire County Council, *The Worsley Project; 4500th House Opening* (County Council Information Centre pamphlet) (Preston, 1966)

Lancashire County Council, *Overspill in Lancashire* (County Council Information Centre Report No. 40) (Preston, 1966)

Lancashire County Council, *M6 in Lancashire, An Illustrated Brochure* (Preston, 1966)

North-West Economic Planning Council, *Derelict Land in the North-West* (London, 1969)

Lancashire Education Committee, *Lancashire Education, 1870–1970* (centenary pamphlet) Preston, 1970)

Lancashire County Council (Surveyors' Department), *The Construction of the Motorway in Lancashire* (County Council Information Centre pamphlet) (Preston, 1970)

North-Western Economic Planning Council, *Housing in the North-West Region* (Manchester, 1970)

North-East Lancashire Planning Unit, *North-East Lancashire Plan* (HMSO, London, 1972)

Lancashire County Council (Surveyors' Department), *Lancashire Needs* (County Council Information Centre pamphlet) (Preston, n.d.)

Lancashire County Council (Surveyors' Department), *Mid-Lancashire Motorway: Report* (County Council Information Centre pamphlet) (Preston, 1973)

Lancashire Fire Brigade Committee, *Lancashire County Fire Brigade, 1948 to 1974* (Preston, 1974)

North-West Joint Planning Team, *Strategic Plan for the North-West* (Manchester, 1974)

V. General and Specialist Books, Pamphlets and Articles Relative
to County and Local Government

General

Alt, J. E. 'Some social and political correlates of county borough expenditures', *British Journal of Political Science, 1*, (1971), pp 47–62.

Arnold-Baker, C. *The New Law and Practice of Parish Administration* (London, 1966)

Bachrach, D. *The Theory of Democratic Elitism* (London, 1967)

Bauer, R. 'The study of policy formation: an introduction', in R. Bauer and K. Gergen (eds), *The Study of Policy Formation* (New York, 1968)

Beveridge, W. *Full Employment in a Free Society* (London, 1944)

Birch, A. H. (ed.), *Small Town Politics* (Oxford, 1959)

Birch, A. H. *Representative and Responsible Government* (London, 1964)

Blackburn, F. *George Tomlinson: A Biography* (London, 1955)

Blau, P. *The Dynamics of Bureaucracy* (Chicago, 1955)

Budge, I. 'Electors' attitudes towards local government', *Political Studies, 13* (1965), pp 386–92

Bulpitt, J. G. 'Party Systems in Local Government', *Political Studies, 11* (1963), pp 11–35

Bulpitt, J. G. *Party Politics in English Local Government* (London, 1967)

Butler, D. and Stoker, D. *Political Change in Britain* (London, 1969)

Chester, D. N. *Central and Local Government* (London, 1951)
Clarke, J. J. *A History of the Local Government of the United Kingdom* (London, 1955)
Clarke, J. J. *Outlines of Local Government of the United Kingdom* (London, 1969)
Cohen, E. W. *Autonomy and Delegation in County Government* (Royal Institute of Public Administration pamphlet) (London, 1953)
Cole, M. *Servant of the County* (London, 1956)
Crozier, M. *The Bureaucratic Phenomena* (London, 1964)
Dunbabin, J. P. D. 'The Politics of the Establishment of County Councils', *Historical Journal, 6,* 2 (1963), pp 22–25
Dunbabin, J. P. D. 'Expectations of the New County Councils and their Realisation', *Historical Journal, 8,* 3 (1965), pp 353–69
Eckstein, H. *Pressure Group Politics* (London, 1960)
Etzioni, A. *A Comparative Analysis of Complex Organisations* (New York, 1961)
Finer, H. *The Theory and Practice of Local Government* (London, 1950)
Finer, H. *English Local Government* (London, 1930; 1950 edn)
Frankenberg, R. *Communities in Britain* (London, 1966)
Frazer, W. M. *A History of English Public Health, 1834–1939* (1950)
Freeman, T. W. *The Conurbations of Great Britain* (Manchester, 1959)
Freeman, T. W., Rodgers, H. B., and Kinvig, R. H. *Lancashire, Cheshire and the Isle of Man* (London, 1966)
Gowan, I. 'Role and Power of Political Parties in Local Government' in D. Lofts (ed.), *Local Government Today and Tomorrow* (London, 1963)
Gilbert, B. B. *British Social Policy 1914–1939* (London, 1970)
Green, L. P. *Provincial Metropolis* (London, 1959)
Griffith, J. A. G. *Central Departments and Local Authorities* (London, 1966)
Grove, W. J. and Dyson, J. W. (eds), *The Making of Decisions; a Reader in Administrative Behaviour* (New York, 1964)
Grove, W. J. *Administrative Decision-Making; a Heuristic Model* (Chichester, 1964)
Hampton, W. *Democracy and Community* (Oxford, 1970)
Hampton, W. 'The County as a Political Unit', *Parliamentary Affairs, 19,* 4 (1966), pp 462–74
Hart, J. *The British Police* (London, 1951)
Hart, W. O. *Introduction to the Law of Local Government and Administration* (London, 1962)
Headrick, T. E. *The Town Clerk in English Local Government* (London, 1962)
Hill, D. *Participating in Local Affairs* (Harmondsworth, 1970)
Hollander, E. P. *Leaders, Groups and Influence* (Oxford, 1964)
Jackson, R. M. *The Machinery of Local Government* (London, 1965)
Jackson, W. E. *Local Government in England and Wales* (Harmondsworth, 1963)
Jones, G. W. *Borough Politics* (London, 1969)
Jones, R. E. *The Functional Analysis of Politics* (London, 1967)
The Jubilee of County Councils 1889–1939 (London, 1939)
Keith-Lucas, B. *The Local Government Franchise* (Oxford, 1952)
Keith-Lucas, B. 'The Government of the County in England', *Western Political Quarterly, 9,* 1 (1956), pp 449–55.
Kingsbury, J. E. *Telephones and Telephone Exchanges; their Invention and Development* (London, 1915)
Layton, E. *Building by Local Authorities* (London, 1961)
Lee, J. M. *Social Leaders and Public Persons* (London, 1963)
Lee, J. M. et al. *The Scope of Local Initiative* (London, 1974)
Lindblom, C. E. *The Policy-Making Process* (Prentice Hall, New Jersey, 1968)
Lipman, V. D. *Local Government Areas, 1834–1945* (Oxford, 1949)

MacColl, J. E. 'The Party System in English Local Government', *Public Administration, 27* (1949), pp 69–75.

McKenzie, R. T. *British Political Parties* (London, 1955)

Mackenzie, W. J. M. 'The Conventions of Local Government', *Public Administration, 29* (1951), pp 345–56.

Mackenzie, W. J. M. *Theories of Local Government* (Greater London Paper, No. 2, London School of Economics) (London, 1961)

Martin, E. W. *The Shearers and the Shorn* (London, 1965)

Muspratt, E. K. *My Life and Work* (London, 1917)

Redlich, J. and Hirst, F. W. *The History of Local Government in England*, 2 vols (London, 1958)

Reynolds, J. 'The South Lancashire Project', *Town Planning Review* (July 1966), pp 102–12

Richards, P. G. 'Delegation in Local Government – Recent Developments', *Public Administration, 36* (Autumn 1958), pp 271–7

Richards, P. G. *The New Local Government System* (London, 1968)

Richards, P. G. *The Reformed Local Government System* (London, 1973)

Ripley, B. J. *Administration in Local Government* (London 1970)

Robson, R. *The Cotton Industry in Britain* (London, 1957)

Robson, W. A. 'The Central Domination of Local Government', *Political Quarterly, 4* (1933), pp 85–104

Robson, W. A. *Local Government in Crisis* (London, 1966)

Sampson, J. R. *Delegation of Services within Counties* (London, 1952)

Schofield, A. N. *Local Government Elections* (London, 1962)

Sharp, Evelyn *The Ministry of Housing and Local Government* (London, 1969)

Simon, H. A. *Administrative Behaviour*, 2nd edn (New York, 1957)

Slack, K. M. *Social Administration and the Citizen* (London, 1966)

Smellie, K. B. *A History of Local Government*, 4th edn (London, 1968)

Webb, H. L. *The Development of the Telephone in Europe* (London, 1910)

West Midland Study Group, *Local Government and Central Control* (London, 1956)

Education

Adamson, J. W. *English Education, 1789–1902* (Cambridge, 1930)

Argles, O. M. V. *South Kensington to Robbins* (London, 1964)

Banks, Olive *Parity and Prestige in English Secondary Education* (London, 1955)

Barnard, H. C. *A History of English Education from 1760* (London, 1961)

Cotgrove, S. F. *Technical Education and Social Change* (London, 1958)

Dent, H. C. *Growth in English Education, 1946–1952* (London, 1954)

Eaglesham, Eric *From School Board to Local Authority* (London, 1956)

Edwards, H. J. *The Evening Institute* (London, 1961)

Harrison, J. F. C. *Learning and Living, 1790–1960* (London, 1961)

Kelly, Thomas *A History of Adult Education in Great Britain* (Liverpool, 1962)

Silberston, Dorothy *Youth in a Technical Age: A Study of Day Release* (London, 1959)

Venables, P. F. R. *Technical Education* (London, 1955)

Finance

Doodson, N. *Local Authority Borrowing* (London, 1962)

Hepworth, N. P. *The Finance of Local Government* (London, 1970)

Marshall, A. H. *Financial Administration in Local Government* (London, 1960)

Planning

Cullingworth, J. B. *Housing and Local Government* (London, 1966)
Cullingworth, J. B. *Town and Country Planning*, 3rd edn (London, 1970)
Crossman, R. H. A. *The Diaries of a Cabinet Minister, Vol. I, Minister of Housing 1964–66*
    (London, 1975)
Hall, Peter *Theory and Practice of Regional Planning* (London, 1970)

Health

Bradbury, F. C. S. *Causal Factors in Tuberculosis* (London, 1933)
D'Arcy Hart, P. and Payling Wright, G. *Tuberculosis and Social Conditions in England*
    (London, 1939)
Farrer, H. P. (ed.) *The Health Services, Administration, Research and Management*
    (London, 1972)
Parker, Julia *Local Health and Welfare Services* (London, 1965)

Index

LCC = *Lancashire County Council*

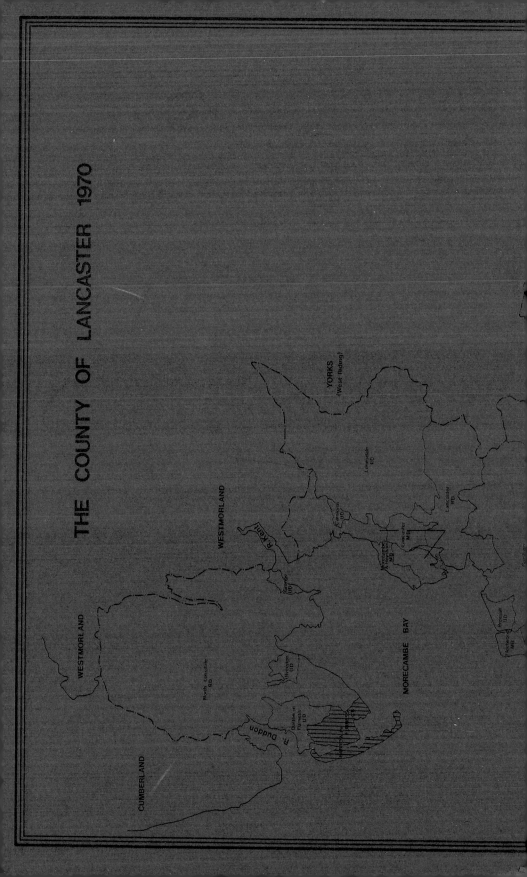

THE COUNTY OF LANCASTER 1970

CUMBERLAND

WESTMORLAND

WESTMORLAND

MORECAMBE BAY

R. Duddon

R. Kent

North Lonsdale
RD

Millom
UD

Dalton in
Furness
UD

YORKS
(West Riding)

Lonsdale
RD

Lancaster
RD

Lancaster
MB

Morecambe
& Heysham
MB